T0276946

Security Strategies in Windows Platforms and Applications

Robert Shimonski

Michael G. Solomon

JONES & BARTLETT
LEARNING

World Headquarters
Jones & Bartlett Learning
25 Mall Road
Burlington, MA 01803
978-443-5000
info@jblearning.com
www.jblearning.com

Jones & Bartlett Learning books and products are available through most bookstores and online booksellers. To contact Jones & Bartlett Learning directly, call 800-832-0034, fax 978-443-8000, or visit our website, www.jblearning.com.

Substantial discounts on bulk quantities of Jones & Bartlett Learning publications are available to corporations, professional associations, and other qualified organizations. For details and specific discount information, contact the special sales department at Jones & Bartlett Learning via the above contact information or send an email to specialsales@jblearning.com.

28201-6

Production Credits

Vice President, Product Management: Marisa R. Urbano
Vice President, Content Strategy and Implementation: Christine Emerton
Sr. Product Manager, Cybersecurity: Ray Chew
Director, Content Management: Donna Gridley
Manager, Content Strategy: Orsolya Gall
Content Strategist: Sara Holloway
Content Coordinator: Samantha Gillespie
Technical Editor: John Shovic
Director, Project Management and Content Services: Karen Scott
Manager, Program Management: Kristen Rogers
Project Manager: Belinda Thresher
Senior Digital Project Specialist: Angela Dooley

Marketing Manager: Mark Adamiak
Content Services Manager: Colleen Lamy
Manufacturing Buyer: Bob Valentine
Composition: Straive
Project Management: Straive
Cover Design: Briana Yates
Text Design: Briana Yates
Media Development Editor: Faith Brosnan
Rights & Permissions Manager: John Rusk
Rights Specialist: Liz Kincaid
Cover Image (Title Page, Part Opener, Chapter Opener): © Ruslan Gi/Shutterstock
Printing and Binding: Sheridan–Michigan

Library of Congress Cataloging-in-Publication Data

Names: Shimonski, Robert, author. | Solomon, Michael (Michael G.), 1963- author.
Title: Security strategies in windows platforms and applications / Rob Shimonski, MS, Capella University, Michael G. Solomon, Emory University.
Identifiers: LCCN 2023035247 | ISBN 9781284281958 (paperback)
Subjects: LCSH: Microsoft Windows (Computer file) | Computer security.
Classification: LCC QA76.9.A25 S658 2025 | DDC 005.8–dc23/eng/20230823
LC record available at https://lccn.loc.gov/2023035247

6048

Printed in the United States of America
27 26 25 24 23   10 9 8 7 6 5 4 3 2 1

Contents

iii

CHAPTER 7

PART III   Microsoft Windows Operating System and Application Security Trends and Directions   257

CHAPTER 11   Hardening the Microsoft Windows Operating System   259

CHAPTER 12   Microsoft Application Security   291

Contents

Preface

This book is part of the Information Systems Security & Assurance Series from Jones & Bartlett Learning (www.jblearning.com). Designed for courses and curriculums in IT Security, Cybersecurity, Information Assurance, and Information Systems Security, this series features a comprehensive, consistent treatment of the most current thinking and trends in this critical subject area. These titles deliver fundamental information-security principles packed with real-world applications and examples. Authored by Certified Information Systems Security Professionals (CISSPs), they deliver comprehensive information on all aspects of information security. Reviewed word for word by leading technical experts in the field, these books are not just current, but forward-thinking—putting you in the position to solve the cybersecurity challenges not just of today, but of tomorrow, as well.

Part I of this book focuses on new risks, threats, and vulnerabilities associated with the Microsoft Windows operating system. Particular emphasis is placed on Windows 11 on the desktop, and Windows Server 2012, 2016, 2019, and 2022 versions. More than 90% of individuals, students, educators, businesses, organizations, and governments use Microsoft Windows, which has experienced frequent attacks against its well-publicized vulnerabilities. Part II emphasizes how to use tools and techniques to decrease risks arising from vulnerabilities in Microsoft Windows operating systems and applications. Part III provides a resource for readers and students desiring more information on Microsoft Windows OS hardening, application security, and incident management, among other issues.

Learning Features

The writing style of this book is practical and conversational. Step-by-step examples of information security concepts and procedures are presented throughout the text. Each chapter begins with a statement of learning objectives. Illustrations are used both to clarify the material and to vary the presentation. The text is sprinkled with Notes, Tips, FYIs, Warnings, and sidebars to alert the reader to additional and helpful information related to the subject under discussion. Chapter Assessments appear at the end of each chapter, with solutions provided in the back of the book. Chapter Summaries are included in the text to provide a rapid review or preview of the material and to help students understand the relative importance of the concepts presented.

Audience

The material is suitable for undergraduate or graduate computer science majors or information science majors, students at a 2-year technical college or community college who have a basic technical background, or readers who have a basic understanding of IT security and want to expand their knowledge.

New to this Edition

This new edition covers the latest versions of the Microsoft Windows operating system, Windows 11, and Windows Server 2022. It also includes updated coverage of industry best practices and tools used to manage Microsoft Windows environments. The *Fourth Edition* further expands on previous discussions to include more coverage of cloud computing topics, IPv6, and the Internet of Things (IoT). Malware and encryption sections have been completely updated as well to include the latest threats, mitigation techniques, and tools available. In all, the *Fourth Edition* includes the latest information needed to implement and manage Windows platforms in today's dynamic environments.

Cloud Labs

This text is accompanied by Cybersecurity Cloud Labs. These hands-on virtual labs provide immersive mock IT infrastructures where students can learn and practice foundational cybersecurity skills as an extension of the lessons in this textbook. For more information or to purchase access to the labs, visit go.jblearning.com/solomon4e.

Acknowledgments

The authors would like to thank Jones & Bartlett Learning for the opportunity to write this book and be a part of the Information Systems Security & Assurance Series. I would also like to thank the editorial staff who helped me bring this book to its current state with all new and current information to address current technology trends.

About the Authors

Robert Shimonski, CASP+, CySA+, PenTest+, is a technology executive specializing in healthcare IT for one of the largest health systems in America. In his current role, Rob is responsible for bringing operational support into the future with the help of new technologies such as cloud and artificial intelligence. His current focus is on deploying to Cloud (Azure, AWS, and Google), DevOps, DevSecOps, AIOps, digital transformation, machine learning, IoT, and the development of new technologies in healthcare. Over the past 10 years, Rob has focused on producing new technology advancements in healthcare technology to include AI/ML, Big Data, Cloud, and analytics. Rob spent many years in the technology "trenches" doing networking and security architecture, design, engineering, testing, and development. A go-to person for all things security related, Rob has been a major force in deploying security-related systems for 25+ years. Rob also worked for various companies reviewing and developing curriculum as well as other security-related books, technical articles, and publications based on technology deployment, testing, hacking, pen testing, and many other aspects of security. Rob holds dozens of technology certifications, including SANS.org GIAC, GSEC, and GCIH as well as many vendor-based cloud specialized certifications from Google, Microsoft Azure, and Amazon AWS.

Michael G. Solomon, PhD, CISSP, PMP, CISM, PenTest+, is a security, privacy, blockchain, and data science author, consultant, and speaker who specializes in leading teams in achieving and maintaining secure and effective IT environments. As an IT professional and consultant since 1987, Dr. Solomon has led project teams for many Fortune 500 companies and has authored and contributed to more than 20 books and numerous training courses. Dr. Solomon is professor of cyber security and global business with blockchain technology at the University of the Cumberlands and holds a PhD in computer science and informatics from Emory University.

The Microsoft Windows Security Situation

Microsoft Windows and the Threat Landscape

MICROSOFT WINDOWS is the most common operating system used on computers today. Nearly 76% of desktop and laptop computers and 33% of servers use a Window operating system. Microsoft provides operating system software for a wide variety of solutions, including client computers, servers, and cloud computing services. The latest Window releases for all environments provide the most advanced features of the Windows product line.

Each new Windows release contains new and updated usability and security features. Each year brings new and unique threats that could compromise a system's security. Whether the goal is to crash a system, access information without authorization, or disrupt normal system operations, **attackers** are always finding new vulnerabilities to exploit.

It is important to understand the threats to Windows system security and the steps to protect it from attackers. The first step to creating and maintaining a secure environment is learning how to find and mitigate vulnerabilities and how to protect your systems.

Chapter 1 Topics

This chapter covers the following topics and concepts:

- What information systems security is
- What the tenets of information security are: the confidentiality-integrity-availability (C-I-A) triad
- What mapping Microsoft Windows and applications into a typical IT infrastructure is
- What Microsoft's End-User License Agreement (EULA) and limitations of liability are
- What common Windows threats and vulnerabilities are
- What the discovery-analysis-remediation cycle is
- What common forms of attack on Windows environments are

Chapter 1 Goals

When you complete this chapter, you will be able to:

- Review key concepts and terms associated with information systems security
- Discuss the tenets of information security: C-I-A triad
- Explain how Microsoft Windows and applications map to a typical IT infrastructure
- List the main objectives of the Microsoft EULA
- Describe the limitations of liability in the Microsoft EULA
- Categorize Windows threats and vulnerabilities
- Recognize the anatomy of common Microsoft Windows vulnerabilities
- Summarize the discovery-analysis-remediation cycle
- Analyze common methods of attack
- Discuss emerging methods of attack

Information Systems Security

As computers become more complex, we see attackers increasing in sophistication. Attackers are continually crafting new methods to compromise even the most secure environments. The job of the security professional is becoming more difficult because of the complexity of systems and the sophistication of attacks. No single action, rule, or device can protect an information system from all attacks. It takes a collection of strategies to make a **computer environment** safe. This approach to using a collection of strategies and controls is often called **defense in depth**. To maintain secure systems, it is important to understand how environments are attacked and how computer systems and networks can be protected. The focus here is specifically on securing the family of Microsoft Windows operating systems and applications.

The main goal in information security is to prevent information loss and unauthorized disclosure. Today's information is most commonly stored in electronic form on computers, also referred to as information systems. Although printed information, or hard copy, needs to be protected, this text only addresses issues related to protecting electronic information stored on information systems.

The two goals of protecting information from unauthorized use and making the information available for authorized use are completely divergent and often require different strategies. Ensuring information is readily available and accessible for authorized use makes restricting the data from unauthorized use more difficult. Most information security decisions require careful thought to ensure balance between security and availability. Information that is secure is simply serving the purpose for which it is intended. It is not being used for unintended purposes.

Mechanisms used to protect information are called **security controls**. Security controls can be part of the operating system or application software setup, part of a written policy, or a physical device that limits access to a resource. There are two methods for categorizing controls. These are not the only methods used to classify controls, and a single control may fit into more than one category. The first method looks at what the control is. Security controls belong to at least one of the following types:

- **Administrative controls** are written policies, procedures, guidelines, regulations, laws, and rules of any kind.
- **Technical controls** are devices or processes that limit logical access to resources. Examples include user authentication, antivirus software, and firewalls. Technical controls are also called **logical controls**.
- **Physical controls** are devices that limit physical access to or otherwise protect a resource, such as fences, doors, locks, and fire extinguishers.

Security controls can also be categorized by the type of function they perform—also referred to as what they do. Here are the most common types of security control function types:

- **Preventive controls** prevent an action. They include locked doors, firewall rules, and user passwords.
- **Detective controls** detect that an action has occurred. They include smoke detectors, log monitors, and system audits.
- **Corrective controls** repair the effects of damage from an attack. They include virus removal procedures, firewall table updates, and user authorization database updates.

Tenets of Information Security: The C-I-A Triad

The practice of securing information involves ensuring three main attributes of information. These three attributes are often called the tenets of information security, or the **C-I-A triad**. Some security professionals may refer to it as the A-I-C triad, but the concept is the same. The three tenets of information security are as follows:

- **Confidentiality**—The assurance that the information cannot be accessed or viewed by **unauthorized users** is confidentiality.
- **Integrity** The assurance that the information cannot be changed by unauthorized users is integrity.
- **Availability**—The assurance that the information is available to **authorized users** in an acceptable time frame when the information is requested is availability.

Each of the tenets interacts with the other two and, in some cases, may cause conflict with other tenets (**FIGURE 1-1**). In this section, you will look at each tenet in more detail and observe how each one may cause conflicts with the others.

Confidentiality

In some cases, it is not enough to ensure information is protected from changes. Some information is private, privileged, business confidential, or classified and must be protected

FIGURE 1-1

The C-I-A triad.

© Jones & Bartlett Learning.

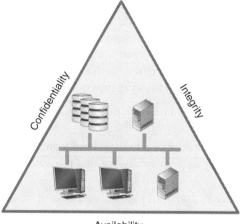

from unauthorized access of any type. Part of the value of confidential information is that it is available only to a limited number of authorized users. Some examples of confidential information include financial information, either personal or corporate; personal medical information; and secret military plans.

Confidentiality also introduces a need for an additional layer of protection. Sometimes, it is necessary to limit users with access to many resources by only allowing them to access specific resources on a need-to-know (NTK) basis. For example, a manager may have access to project documents that contain sensitive information. To limit the damage that could occur from accidents or errors, it is common to limit access to documents that directly relate to the manager's projects only. Documents that do not directly relate to the manager's projects are not accessible. This means that although a user possesses sufficient access for a resource, if the user does not have a specific need to know what a resource stores, the user still cannot access it.

A successful attack against confidential information enables the attacker to use the information to gain an inappropriate advantage or to extort compensation through threats to divulge the information.

Confidentiality has long been the subject of many types of legislation. Legislative bodies in many countries have enacted laws and regulations to protect the confidentiality of personal medical and financial information. Attorneys and physicians have long enjoyed the privilege of confidentiality when conversing with clients and patients. This assurance of confidentiality is crucial to the free flow of necessary information.

Integrity

Information is valid only when it is correct and can be trusted. The second tenet of information security ensures that information can be modified only by authorized users. Ensuring integrity means applying controls that prohibit unauthorized changes to information. Controls that ensure information integrity can be based on the user's role. Other examples of integrity controls are security classification and user clearance.

Since information may change as a result of application software instructions, it is important that controls ensuring integrity extend to the application software development process. Regardless of the specific controls in use, the goal of integrity is to protect information from unauthorized changes.

Availability

Secure information is serving the purpose for which it was created. This means that secure information must be available when the information is requested by authorized users.

Many attacks focus on denying the availability of information. One common type of attack that denies the availability of information is the denial of service (DoS) attack. This type of attack does not need to actually access or modify information, but it prevents authorized users from accessing it. For example, an attack that denies access to Amazon's web-based information would have a negative impact on sales. Amazon can't afford to allow its information to be inaccessible for any length of time. Since so many businesses rely on available information to function properly, unavailable information poses a risk to their primary business functions.

Over the last decade, a different type of adversary has joined the ranks of cyber attackers. These attackers use their skills to make social statements. These activists with hacking abilities, called **hacktivists**, often target victims with the goal of making some sort of social impact. Hacktivists are behind more and more large-scale attacks, the intent of which is generally to bring attention to some political or social issue. For example, Charles Tucker, also known as the "Bitcoin Baron," was recently sentenced to 20 months in prison for carrying out a series of hacktivist attacks in 2015. One of the attacks for which Tucker was convicted was a distributed denial of service (DDoS) attack against the 911 service of Madison, Wisconsin. This attack severely degraded the ability of Madison 911 Emergency Services from responding to critical requests for help. Tucker stated that his activities were in response to the shooting of a suspect by a Madison police officer. Hacktivists are increasingly disrupting critical services with the hope of bringing attention to a specific issue.

Mapping Microsoft Windows and Applications into a Typical IT Infrastructure

Satisfying the C-I-A triad requires more than just implementing controls on a single system. Today's IT environments consist of a collection of computers and network devices connected to one or more networks and, in many cases, the internet. In fact, many of today's IT infrastructure components may exist in other organizations' environments. Today's IT environments are increasingly made up of components from remote networks that are connected through the internet. These remote, or cloud-based, components are routinely integral parts of today's IT infrastructure. The collection of all computers, devices, and network components that make up an

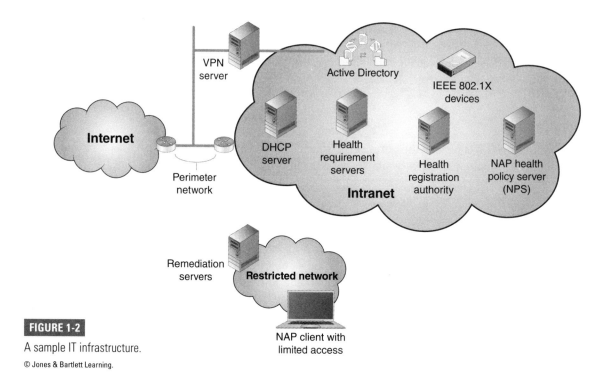

FIGURE 1-2

A sample IT infrastructure.

© Jones & Bartlett Learning.

IT environment is called an IT infrastructure. An IT infrastructure diagram depicts the various components that work together to satisfy the organization's information processing requirements (**FIGURE 1-2**). Some common infrastructure components include the following:

- Client platforms
- Network segments
- Network devices
- Server instances (often listed by function)

   In most environments, the Microsoft Windows family of operating systems fills both the roles of client and server. In fact, many organizations currently use cloud-based Microsoft offerings as well, such as Office 365 and Azure. Windows systems can also operate as network devices, such as gateways or routers. However, it is more common to see either purpose-built devices or Windows servers providing device services. This text will focus on the client and server roles of Windows.

Windows Clients

Client systems exist to provide functionality to end users. These systems are often called customer-facing systems and increasingly include mobile devices as well as desktop and laptop computers. Each specific application can be deployed on client systems as either a thin or a thick client.

Thin clients collect information from end users or other data sources, send it to a server for processing, and display the returned results back to the end user. Most of the actual processing of the data occurs on a server. This is the most common model for applications running on mobile devices such as smartphones or tablets. Some of the most common examples of a thin client application include web browsers and mobile apps.

Thick clients collect information from the end user and process some, or all, of the information locally. Commonly, the information is stored in a database running on a server. The client handles a large amount of the information processing work. Examples of thick client applications are legacy enterprise applications that provide accounting and manufacturing control.

The following are the most common Windows operating systems in use on client computers:

- Windows 11 (the newest and most popular Windows client operating system)
- Windows 10
- Windows 8.1

Windows client computers are often general-purpose computers that provide end-user applications for various purposes. It is common for a single Windows client computer to have a web browser, an email client, and an office productivity suite, as well as proprietary application software installed. Client computers are rarely single-purpose devices. This multirole functionality often makes securing these computers more difficult.

The newest version of Windows, Windows 11, recognizes that all clients are not just typical computers. Windows 11 introduces an updated and cleaner user interface that works well on desktops, laptops, and mobile devices. Windows 11 may look different from earlier versions, but the strategies to keep it secure are very similar to those of other legacy Windows clients. Due to advancements in the operating system (OS), there are also new features and functionality as well.

Windows Servers

Server computers exist in the IT infrastructure to provide specific types of services to client applications, either directly or indirectly. Common server applications may include web servers, application servers, and database servers. Microsoft provides several different server products to satisfy various needs. In each version, it is common to tailor the specific applications installed on the server to customize the services provided. Microsoft markets several server packages, all based on the following supported Windows server products:

- **Windows Server 2012 R2**—Currently the next server ready for End of Life (EOL) in the Windows operating system for the server's family and end of extended life support is October 10, 2023, unless there is a Software Assurance (SA) subscription in place or workloads are migrated to the cloud in Azure. While still deployed in many enterprises, it is starting to be replaced by newer versions of the OS. This Windows product is available in four different editions.
  - **Foundation**—Cost-effective, entry-level server for small businesses
  - **Essentials**—More features than the Foundation edition for most small- to medium-sized businesses

- **Standard**—Suitable for most server functions, along with limited virtualization ability
- **Datacenter**—Designed for large-scale deployment on servers that support extensive virtualization
- **Windows Server 2016**—This server product contains many updates to the prior version and is available in three different editions:
  - **Essentials**—Packaged for small businesses with basic IT requirements and a limited number of IT administration and support personnel
  - **Standard**—Suitable for most server functions, along with limited virtualization ability
  - **Datacenter**—Designed for large-scale deployment on servers that support extensive virtualization
- **Windows Server 2019**—This server product is available in three different editions:
  - **Essentials**—Packaged for small businesses with basic IT requirements and a limited number of IT administration and support personnel
  - **Standard**—Suitable for most server functions, along with limited virtualization ability
  - **Datacenter**—Designed for large-scale deployment on servers that support extensive virtualization
- **Windows Server 2022**—This server product is the latest and is available in three different editions:
  - **Standard**—Suitable for most server functions, along with limited virtualization ability
  - **Datacenter**— Designed for large-scale deployment on servers on premise that support extensive virtualization
  - **Datacenter: Azure Edition**—Designed for large-scale deployment on servers in the Azure cloud that support extensive virtualization

Microsoft's End-User License Agreement

A software license agreement must be accepted prior to the installation of any Microsoft Windows product. The software license agreement contains the Microsoft Software License Terms and is also referred to as the **End-User License Agreement (EULA)**. It is important to read the EULA before accepting it—don't just blindly choose the "I accept" option. Each edition of Windows ships with a specific version of the EULA, so it is important to know the contents of the EULA for each edition of Windows present in your environment.

The Windows install folder or the Microsoft website contains the EULA. Do the following to find the EULA on a computer with Windows currently installed:

1. Click the Start button, and then, in the Start menu, click My Computer.
2. Under Hard Disk Drives, double-click the drive where Windows is installed. This is often the drive labeled (C:).
3. Double-click the Windows folder, double-click the System32 folder, double-click the en-US folder, double-click the Licenses folder, and then double-click the Default folder.
4. Double-click the folder that corresponds to the edition of Windows that's installed on your computer, and then double-click License.

To find the EULA for any edition of Windows, do the following:

1. Open a web browser, such as Internet Explorer or Microsoft Edge.
2. Enter the following address: https://www.microsoft.com/en-us/useterms/.
3. Enter the requested information for
   a. How the software was acquired
   b. Product name
   c. Version
   d. Language
4. Select the link for the desired EULA document.

A few sections of the Windows EULA are of interest to security personnel. Make sure you read the following sections fully and are prepared to agree with Microsoft's statements before accepting the agreement. **TABLE 1-1** highlights the sections of the EULA that are of most interest to security personnel.

In summary, the EULA states that it is your responsibility to secure all Windows platforms.

TABLE 1-1 Security-Related Sections of the Microsoft EULA

EULA SECTION	DESCRIPTION
Updates	Windows periodically checks for updates to installed operating system and application components. When found, these updates may be downloaded and installed automatically. By accepting this agreement, you permit these updates to be applied without further notice.
Additional Notices—Networks, Data, and Internet Usage	Microsoft provides internet-based services with Windows and may transmit information. This section of the EULA provides details of services and potential information that may be transmitted, i.e., details about system information resulting from a crashed program. Windows will optionally send information to Microsoft in an effort to find a resolution for the problem that caused the program to crash.
Limited Warranty	Only the purchase price of Windows can be recovered, regardless of any damages incurred as a result of a Windows fault or incident. This clause alone provides an excellent reason for security personnel to protect organizations by securing all Windows environments.
Exclusions from Limited Warranty	The cost of a Windows license cannot be recovered if an organization suffers damages caused by its personnel.

Windows Threats and Vulnerabilities

Securing any platform requires an understanding of its capability and the most likely ways the platform can be compromised. Simply understanding everything about Windows will not make your systems secure. The main goal in securing an operating system and application environment is recognizing risks and implementing controls to mitigate the risks. In this section, you will look at risks and observe how to handle them.

A **risk** is defined as any exposure to a threat. A **threat** is any action that could lead to damage, disruption, or loss. A threat by itself is not necessarily dangerous. For example, lighting a fire could be considered a threat. In the right environment, such as on a camping trip or in a fireplace, lighting a fire is desirable. However, lighting a fire in an operational datacenter is not desirable at all. Such an action will likely result in business process disruption and possibly even damage.

For damage to occur, there has to be a threat, such as lighting a fire, in a vulnerable environment, such as in a datacenter. Attackers look for vulnerabilities, or weaknesses, in the operating system and application software. Once vulnerabilities are discovered, the next step is to devise an attack that will exploit the weakness. A successful attack is defined as one that realizes, or carries out, a threat against vulnerabilities.

It is important to understand the most common methods of attack in a Windows environment. This understanding allows you to devise controls that limit an attacker's ability to realize threats. The controls you implement can directly address vulnerabilities or restrict an attacker's ability to get into a position to realize a threat. Either way, by breaking the attacker's ability to carry out a threat against a vulnerability, you make your environment more secure.

Anatomy of Microsoft Windows Vulnerabilities

Let's take a look at a grouping of well-known Windows attacks and the vulnerabilities that make such attacks possible. It is instructive to examine how real vulnerabilities have been exploited by attackers and helps to drive home key security concepts learned throughout the book. Such analysis helps to understand the nature of vulnerabilities and methods of protecting systems from attackers.

The next three attacks listed in this section are ransomware. In recent years, this has become the most publicized of malicious attacks, largely because of attacks on critical infrastructure and other largely important entities. **Ransomware** is a type of **malicious software** that renders files or volumes inaccessible, demanding a ransom payment in exchange for access to the captured resources. Most ransomware encrypts data and demands a payment using cryptocurrency in exchange for the decryption key. But ransomware alone isn't destructive to computers. All malware needs an opening, or a **vulnerability**, to succeed. In many cases, users provide common vulnerabilities that malware can exploit. In two of the following attacks, users gave the malware the opening it needed by opening a document or following a link.

CryptoLocker

Although ransomware has been around since about 1989, most attacks were small and targeted. CryptoLocker signaled a change in tactics when it was released to the world in late 2013. This ransomware attack infected more than 250,000 Microsoft Windows computers. The attackers were paid an estimated $3 million by victims before an international effort took down the botnet and servers. CryptoLocker used a combination of operating system filename obfuscation and social engineering to take over victims' computers. Here is how the CryptoLocker attack unfolded:

- The victim received a legitimate-looking email message with an attached ZIP file that contained the disguised executable file payload.
- Since Windows hides file extensions by default, the malicious executable file appeared to be a PDF file, and many users opened the file, executing the payload.
- The payload added a key to the Windows Registry that caused it to run at boot time and then attempted to connect to the ransomware server.
- Once a connection was established with the server, the ransomware created a public and private key pair and sent the private key to the ransomware server.
- Then, CryptoLocker found all files with common extensions and encrypted them with the generated public key.
- Finally, CryptoLocker displayed a message to the victim and demanded a payment in bitcoin within a short window of time, generally 72 hours.

CryptoLocker's success depended on authorized users executing the malicious payload. The ransomware only had to convince victims to click on the attachment and the encryption process began. As soon as victim reports surfaced, anti-malware software signature databases were updated to better detect CryptoLocker's attachments before users ever saw them. But by that time, many victims had already been successfully attacked.

Locky

Locky was another form of ransomware that was released in 2016. The Locky attack, like CryptoLocker, was delivered as an email attachment. In Locky's case, the attached file was a Microsoft Word document that contained the ransomware code as a macro. When the victim opened the Microsoft Word document, the attacker had to trick the user into launching the macro. The contents of the document appeared to be meaningless garbage. A pop-up message appeared that instructed the victim to enable macros if the data encoding is incorrect. Many users simply enabled macros without considering the impact of that action. Once macros were enabled, the attack sequence started.

The Locky macro actually downloaded and executed the real ransomware. Like CryptoLocker, Locky generates different encryption and decryption keys for each computer it attacks. After creating the encryption/decryption key pair, it sends the decryption (private) key back to the attacker. The private key is required to decrypt your files. After saving the private key back on the attacker's ransomware server, Locky encrypts the victim's files using the public key. The rest of the attack is similar to its predecessor. Another important concept to remember is that many of these attacks are brought into occurrence by a specific attack vector and use a very specific technique to be successful. In many cases, phishing was used to start the ransomware attacks in the first place, which is a form of trickery to get unsuspecting users to enable the attack in the first place by clicking on a malicious link or trigger mechanism.

WannaCry

The WannaCry ransomware attack was launched in May 2017 in a global attack on computers running the Microsoft Windows operating system. Deployed as a worm, WannaCry was able to replicate itself and not rely on unsuspecting victims to launch the payload. **Worms** are standalone malicious software programs that actively transmit themselves without relying on an unsuspecting victim's actions, generally over networks, to infect other computers.

WannaCry attacked a known exploit in the Windows operating system called EternalBlue, which is an exploit on the Windows implementation of the Server Message Block (SMB) protocol. EternalBlue was originally developed by the National Security Agency (NSA) and was kept a secret until it was leaked in April 2017. The SMB protocol defines how resources, such as printers and disk drives, are accessed by other computers on a network. WannaCry exploited a weakness in SMB and automatically infected other computers on the same network that did not have the updated security patches installed. Microsoft released emergency patches that directly addressed the WanaCry ransomware and stopped it from replicating. However, WannaCry still was able to infect more than 200,000 computers worldwide. In spite of the quick response, WannaCry demonstrated that even current operating systems can be vulnerable to sophisticated ransomware attacks.

PrintNightmare

Many of the previous examples of malware were triggered by phishing and led to specific threats, such as the installation of malware that led to ransomware attacks; however, Microsoft Windows systems are vulnerable and can be exploited in other ways as well. One of the most recent major exploits that has caused widespread damage and disruption is from an exploit nicknamed PrintNightmare.

In July 2021, Microsoft released a patch for affected Windows systems to fix a Windows Print Spooler Remote Code Execution Vulnerability that essentially impacted all Windows systems with a printing function. Anything with a print spooler (which is most if not all Windows systems) is affected and, if left unpatched, allows for remote code execution. This type of threat is one that lays dormant in a system due to a bug and exploited when identified. As in the previous examples of ransomware, the vector was clear. However, with the PrintNightmare, this was a widespread threat that was dormant until identified. Once identified, it was exploited until identified and patched. There is a current patch; however, due to widespread deployment of Microsoft Windows systems and that many systems are unpatched or cannot be patched due to their legacy nature, the threat still exists. As we learn when using Microsoft Windows systems, one of the key aspects of security is knowing that it is important to keep systems updated, patched, and tested to ensure that bugs are fixed or, in some cases, removed as a threat with updated code. In this exploit example, the following occur:

- The attacker identifies that a system is vulnerable by running a tool against the system to validate if the print spooler service is running.
- The right tool can also use like a vulnerability scanner, which could identify not only an unpatched system but one with the threat still active. There are many, but one that is time tested and works well with Windows systems is Nessus from Tenable (https://www .tenable.com/).
- Once the threat is identified on the target host, the attacker can connect to it through various methods (locally, remotely,) and gain access.
- The threat with PrintNightmare is that because of many legacy or unpatched systems in the wild, it is easy to exploit the vulnerability due to its widespread nature. The print spooler controls print queues, and an attacker can gain access.
- Once a foothold is obtained, an exploit can be used to gain or elevate system-level privileges.
- Once privilege is granted, arbitrary code can be run to exploit the vulnerability.

The Microsoft Response Center

The Microsoft Security Response Center, or MSRC for short, is the location online where you can go to find the latest information about Windows Security topics revolving around "protection, detection, and response." With security-based incident response, being a good incident responder requires not only knowledge of the role and how to handle an incident properly, but also a trusted source of information and guidance on how to handle specific issues that occur from the software vendor.

As vulnerabilities and exploits are covered in the chapter's text, feel free to do further investigation or, better, use the MSRC to find solutions to exploits you come across in the future.

You can find more online at https://msrc.microsoft.com.

To find system specific vulnerability updates on known issues, you can visit https://msrc .microsoft.com/update-guide.

Discovery-Analysis-Remediation Cycle

A recurring three-step process is followed for addressing attacks. This process is referred to as the discovery-analysis-remediation cycle (**FIGURE 1-3**). This process may occur exclusively within your organization, outside your organization to include cloud-based service providers, or both.

Discovery

The first step in responding to an attack is to know an attack has occurred or is occurring. Discovering an attack is often more difficult than it would seem. Experienced attackers know that the success of an exploit often depends on the amount of time vulnerable systems are exposed. Once an attack starts, a common goal of attackers is to become as

FIGURE 1-3

Discovery-analysis
-remediation cycle.

© Jones & Bartlett Learning.

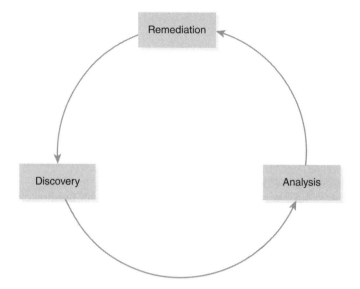

inconspicuous as possible. Keeping a low profile often allows an attack to become more successful as time passes.

To identify an attack, it is important to recognize what "normal" looks like in your environment. Usually, the only way to know something is not right is to compare suspect activity with normal activity, often called a baseline. The most common method of accomplishing this is to use activity and monitoring logs. Log files often contain evidence to detect that something abnormal has happened.

Analysis

Once abnormal activity is identified, the next step is to analyze it. Not all suspect activity is bad. Some activity has a rational explanation. False positives can also possibly create concerns, and these alerts may be due to verbose logging functions, not necessarily an actual threat. Perhaps the database server was under an unusual load due to too many users running large reports. Load balancing could have been disabled so that all network activity was sent through a single device. Both cases are abnormal but do not indicate attacks. Security information and event management (SIEM) tools can make the analysis phase much more efficient. SIEM tools collect and aggregate security-related information from multiple sources and devices and help prepare the data for correlation and analysis. These tools can often cross-reference known vulnerability databases to help identify suspect behavior. The analysis phase includes validating suspect activity as abnormal and then figuring out what is causing it.

The next step is to consult current vulnerability and security bulletin databases to see if others are experiencing the same activity. Many security-related databases serve this purpose, but several repositories are the most popular and commonly used to research vulnerabilities. **TABLE 1-2** lists the most common repositories for security vulnerabilities and exposures.

TABLE 1-2 Popular Repositories for Security Vulnerabilities and Exposures

RESOURCE	ADDRESS	COMMENTS
Common Vulnerabilities and Exposures (CVE)	http://cve.mitre.org/	Dictionary of publicly known vulnerabilities and exposures (focuses on the instance of vulnerability—not the flaw that causes the vulnerability)
National Vulnerability Database	http://nvd.nist.gov/	CVE data plus additional resources
United States Computer Emergency Readiness Team (US-CERT)	http://www.us-cert.gov/	Numerous security alerts and bulletins
Common Weakness Enumeration (CWE)	https://cwe.mitre.org/	A community-developed list of common software security weaknesses (focuses on the flaw that causes a vulnerability)
Full Disclosure	http://seclists.org /fulldisclosure/	Vendor-neutral discussion of vulnerabilities and exploits
Common Attack Pattern Enumeration and Classification (CAPEC)	https://capec.mitre.org/	Dictionary of known patterns of attack

© Jones & Bartlett Learning.

Remediation

The third step in the cycle is to remediate the activity. Simply put, this means to contain any damage that has occurred, recover from any loss, and implement controls to prevent a recurrence.

The particular steps to take in any of these phases depend on the nature of the attack. Most vulnerabilities and exposures that are documented in a public database are accompanied by suggested remediation steps.

It is possible to trace back from the discovery event that indicated abnormal activity occurred. Controls that prevent any new activity that results in the abnormal activity may be a good place to start. Ensure that any new controls comply with operational requirements and don't interfere with critical business processes.

Common Forms of Attack

Attacks on Windows platforms can take on many forms. It is common to see several types of attacks combined to accomplish the attacker's goal. **TABLE 1-3** contains a brief list of the most common types of attacks on any information systems.

TABLE 1-3 Common Information Systems Attack Types

ATTACK TYPE	DESCRIPTION
Phishing	Phishing attacks generally start with a message that contains a link or image to click or a file to open. Taking these actions launches malware attacks.
Malware	Malicious software, also called malware, is software that is designed to carry out tasks that the user would not normally allow.
Denial of service	Any action that dramatically slows down or blocks access to one or more resources.
Remote Code Execution	Remote code execution (also known as arbitrary code execution) allows an attacker to exploit a system in order to run malicious code, gain full control of, or further elevate privileges on a vulnerable system.
Injection attacks	A family of attacks that depend on the ability to send instructions to a software application that cause the application to carry out unintended actions. SQL injection is the most commonly recognized type of this attack.
Unprotected Windows share	A situation that allows attackers to install tools, including malicious software.
Session hijacking and credential reuse	Many online applications set up sessions with valid users providing authentication credentials at the beginning of the session. Attackers often attempt to take over valid sessions or capture the credentials provided to impersonate valid users.
Cross-site scripting	Specially crafted malicious code used to attack web applications.
Packet sniffing	The process of collecting network messages as they travel across a network in hopes of divulging sensitive information, such as passwords.
Buffer overflow attack	The process of overwriting or filling of a systems memory to create a destabilization, corruption, or denial of service.

© Jones & Bartlett Learning.

CHAPTER SUMMARY

Securing Windows operating systems and applications is not easy, but it is possible and necessary for an organization to successfully meet its operational goals.

The first step in securing a Windows environment, and then maintaining a secure environment, is to understand how your computers, devices, and cloud-based services are vulnerable. From there, a study of the most common attacks against vulnerabilities leads to steps on how to respond to threats and make your environments more secure. Learning about past attacks against information systems environments is more than a technical history lesson. It is a study of techniques attackers use to compromise today's IT environments.

In spite of the increasing sophistication of attackers, many of today's attacks are either a resurgence of or a variation on earlier attack methods. Close attention to previous exploits makes you far more agile to respond to the next attack.

KEY CONCEPTS AND TERMS

Administrative control
Attacker
Authorized user
Availability
C-I-A triad
Computer environment
Confidentiality
Corrective control
Defense in depth

Detective control
End-User License Agreement (EULA)
Hacktivist
Integrity
Logical control
Malicious software
Physical control
Preventive control

Ransomware
Risk
Security control
Technical control
Threat
Unauthorized user
Vulnerability
Worm

CHAPTER 1 ASSESSMENT

1. Which of the following is the best description of the defense-in-depth strategy?

   A. Hiding protected resources behind multiple firewalls.
   B. Using multiple layers of security controls to protect resources.
   C. Fully securing the most important resources first.
   D. Staying current on as many known attacks as possible.

2. What is the main goal of information security?

   A. Protect information from unauthorized use
   B. Catch as many unauthorized users as possible
   C. Protect information from unauthorized modification
   D. Stop anonymous users from accessing information

3. Does turning off a computer make the information it contains secure?

A. Yes, because no unauthorized user can access information on a computer that is turned off.

B. No, because the information might be copied somewhere else.

C. Yes, because aggressive actions always result in more secure systems.

D. No, because secure data must still be available to authorized users.

4. Which of the following is the best description of a security control?

A. A mechanism to stop attacks before they occur

B. A rule that defines acceptable use of a computer

C. A mechanism that protects a resource

D. A device that detects unusual activity

5. Which of the following could be classified as a logical control?

A. Firewall

B. Fence

C. Acceptable use policy

D. Smoke detector

6. Which of the following could be classified as a detective control?

A. Password

B. Door

C. Acceptable use policy

D. Log monitor

7. Which of the tenets of information security most directly serves the needs of authorized users?

A. Availability

B. Integrity

C. Confidentiality

D. None of the above

8. Which of the tenets of information security is most related to the need-to-know property?

A. Availability

B. Integrity

C. Confidentiality

D. None of the above

9. Where is the most likely place a database management system would run?

A. Network device   C. Thin client

B. Server   D. Thick client

10. Which Microsoft Windows Server 2019 edition would be most appropriate for large-scale deployment using extensive virtualization?

A. Datacenter

B. HPC

C. Enterprise

D. Web

11. According to the Microsoft EULA, what is the extent of the damages that can be recovered due to a Windows fault?

A. Nothing

B. The price paid for the software license

C. Actual damages incurred

D. Actual damages incurred plus the cost of the software license

12. Which of the following is the best definition of a threat?

A. Any exposure to damage

B. A weakness that allows damage to occur

C. An action that exploits a weakness

D. Any action that could lead to damage

13. What ransomware was released in 2017 and exploited a weakness in SMB to propagate?

A. LockyA

B. Conficker

C. WannaCry

D. CryptoLocker

14. What term describes a malicious software program that users are tricked into running?

A. Trojan horse

B. Worm

C. Virus

D. Phishing message

15. Which of the following defines the cycle used to address Windows threats and vulnerabilities?

A. Plan-do-review

B. Discovery-analysis-remediation

C. Design-implementation-verification

D. Detection-containment-eradication

Security in the Microsoft Windows Operating System

O NE OF THE MORE DIFFICULT TASKS when securing any computer system or
network is identifying where to start. There are many components in any computing
environment. Each component is a potential point of attack. Since the operating system
provides the ability for software and hardware to interact, it is a good starting point for securing
an entire environment. On any computer, the operating system enables software to access
physical resources. For example, it is the operating system that governs how any application
actually reads from, or writes to, a physical disk. Consequently, the operating system is a prime
candidate for attack and a valuable resource to protect.

From an attacker's point of view, a compromised operating system provides easy access
to protected information and resources. Compromising operating system controls gives the
attacker the ability to remove evidence of attacks and "clean up" any leftover log entries or
other traces of the attack. A secure operating system is the basis of a secure environment.

In this chapter, you will learn about the Windows operating system architecture and controls
to ensure system security. You will also learn how attackers search for, identify, and exploit
operating system vulnerabilities. With the knowledge of how attackers operate, you'll be able
to select and implement the right controls to secure your environment.

Chapter 2 Topics

This chapter covers the following topics and concepts:

- What the organization of the operating system components and architecture is
- What the basic Windows operating system architecture is
- What access controls and authentication are
- What security tokens, rights, and permissions are
- What users, groups, and Active Directory are
- What Windows attack surfaces and mitigation are
- What fundamentals of Microsoft Windows security monitoring and maintenance are

Chapter 2 Goals

When you complete this chapter, you will be able to:

- Distinguish operating system components from architecture
- Describe the basic Windows OS architecture
- Discuss access controls and authentication
- Explain security tokens, rights, and permissions
- Research the features of several common security tokens
- Identify the purposes of users and groups
- Discuss the features of directory services
- Analyze the business advantages and challenges of Active Directory
- Describe Windows attack surfaces and mitigation
- Summarize the fundamentals of Microsoft Windows security monitoring and maintenance

Operating System Components and Architecture

In spite of the reference to an "operating system" as a single entity, an operating system is not a single huge program. An operating system is actually a collection of many programs working together, along with data, to provide access to physical resources. The goal of secure information can simply be expressed as simultaneously ensuring both of the following situations:

1. All required information is available to authorized users.
2. No information is available to unauthorized users.

Although these two basic situations appear to be clear and straightforward, simultaneously ensuring both can be challenging. A **control** is any mechanism or action that prevents, detects, or addresses an attack. Once security controls are in place, attackers must identify methods to compromise the controls and gain the privileges of an authorized user. The methods attackers use will rely on one or more vulnerabilities. Your goal is to ultimately harden your operating system from attack; however, if it is compromised, you would need to further identify and then mitigate as many vulnerabilities as possible to deny the opportunity for an attacker to realize a threat vector.

The first step in planning how to secure the operating system is to understand the purpose of various operating system components. In order to do that effectively, understanding the entire attack surface is required. Each operating system component, and the communication between components, can be a potential point of attack. Many different operating systems are in use today, and often multiple versions of each one; however, some components and services are common among them.

The Kernel

The central component of most operating systems is the **kernel**. The kernel is the part of the operating system that may reside partially in memory and provides the backbone of the operating system's services (**FIGURE 2-1**). The classic definition of the kernel states that the entire kernel resides in memory. Today's more complex operating system kernels are made up of both the main memory-resident components and external loadable modules. The use of loadable modules reduces the kernel's memory footprint. The kernel provides access to physical resources and often runs other operating system programs to complete a task. The memory-resident kernel code will directly handle access to the CPU, where efficiency is crucial. In other cases, where flexibility is more important, the kernel will run device driver programs to handle physical resource access. The second approach is slower but makes it easy for the operating system to support a wide variety of hardware devices from different vendors. All that is needed is a device driver program for the operating system to support a new device.

Many current operating systems actually implement microkernel architecture. A **microkernel** only implements the minimal required functionality in the memory-resident portion of the operating system, such as memory management, interprocess communication, and process scheduling. Other necessary functionality is supported by external programs. The main difference between internal and external programs is the privilege level at which each runs. A pure microkernel allows only memory-resident components to run at kernel, or maximum privilege, mode.

> **NOTE**
>
> Of course, each new device driver means a new potential vulnerability and possible point of attack. Ensure your systems do not have device drivers installed for retired devices.

Name	Status	2% CPU	18% Memory	0% Disk	0% Network	Power usage	Power usage tr...
Apps (1)							
> Task Manager		1.7%	15.5 MB	0 MB/s	0 Mbps	Very low	Very low
Background processes (22)							
AggregatorHost		0%	0.6 MB	0 MB/s	0 Mbps	Very low	Very low
Application Frame Host		0%	3.2 MB	0 MB/s	0 Mbps	Very low	Very low
COM Surrogate		0%	2.2 MB	0 MB/s	0 Mbps	Very low	Very low
CTF Loader		0%	3.0 MB	0 MB/s	0 Mbps	Very low	Very low
Host Process for Windows Tasks		0%	2.2 MB	0 MB/s	0 Mbps	Very low	Very low
Microsoft Edge Update (32 bit)		0%	1.0 MB	0 MB/s	0 Mbps	Very low	Very low
Microsoft OneDrive (32 bit)		0%	13.5 MB	0 MB/s	0 Mbps	Very low	Very low
> Microsoft Windows Search Inde...		0%	5.3 MB	0 MB/s	0 Mbps	Very low	Very low
> Runtime Broker		0%	2.8 MB	0 MB/s	0 Mbps	Very low	Very low
> Search (3)		0%	7.1 MB	0 MB/s	0 Mbps	Very low	Very low
> Spooler SubSystem App		0%	3.4 MB	0 MB/s	0 Mbps	Very low	Very low
> Start		0%	15.6 MB	0 MB/s	0 Mbps	Very low	Very low

FIGURE 2-1

Operating system kernel.

© Jones & Bartlett Learning.

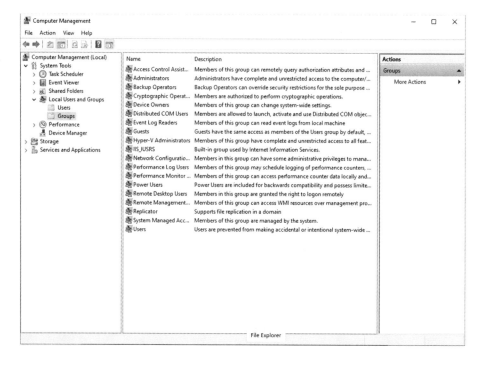

FIGURE 2-2

Windows operating system components.

Courtesy of Microsoft Corporation.

The kernel also includes areas of memory reserved for the operating system data structures. One example of an operating system data structure is the process, or task, table. The process table contains one entry for each running process. Each operating system stores different process properties, but the basic information in the process table is consistent. **FIGURE 2-2** shows a few of the types of information the operating system maintains for processes.

One common process property is the mode in which a process is run. Processes generally run in either **user mode** or **supervisor mode**. You may also see supervisor mode referred to as **kernel mode**. Processes that run in supervisor mode can perform more tasks and access more restricted parts of the computer system. One way for an attacker to access a protected resource is to modify the process table entry and change a user mode process to supervisor mode. The process table is only one example of a kernel data structure that must be secured from unauthorized changes. However, processes running in user mode should be able to view the information in the process table to see what is running at any point in time. The kernel keeps track of what processes can and cannot do.

 NOTE

Some operating system implementations also refer to the maximum privilege mode as supervisor mode or kernel mode.

Operating System Components

Operating systems contain far more than just the kernel. The kernel provides core services of the operating system and calls external programs to provide many more operating system services. **TABLE 2-1** contains a list of general services most current operating systems provide.

TABLE 2-1 Operating System General Services	
OPERATING SYSTEM SERVICE	**DESCRIPTION**
Program/process management	The operating system manages locating, loading, and actually executing all programs. It handles memory allocation, CPU scheduling, and providing the necessary environment for each program.
Input and output	Nearly every program requires input and produces output. The operating system hides the details of the physical hardware and provides programs with the ability to process input and output.
File system	The operating system also provides access to long-term storage, such as disk drives, and helps to organize the information to make it easily and efficiently accessible.
Communication	Programs often need to communicate with other programs, both locally and on other computers. The operating system provides the support for exchanging information between programs.
Error detection and alerts	The operating system is responsible for monitoring activities that occur within the computer and for responding when errors occur.

© Jones & Bartlett Learning.

From a security view, the most important concept of this section is that the operating system is the collection of programs that control access to the physical hardware. Since information is stored and transmitted on physical hardware, ensuring the security of protected information starts with ensuring the security of the operating system.

Basic Windows Operating System Architecture

The Microsoft Windows operating system has changed a lot from the simple personal computer operating system, DOS. It has grown from a single product offering to a full family of products to meet different needs. The current versions of Windows address a wide variety of computing needs, from portable devices and workstations to enterprise-class, high-performance platforms. The Windows operating system is designed to be a modular system to provide the widest variety of services for most platform requirements.

The current versions of client and server Windows operating systems in use today are all based on the legacy Windows NT code base. Windows NT was Microsoft's first operating system designed with security in mind. The first commercial version of Windows NT was version 3.1, released in 1993. At the time, Windows NT was a ground-breaking product from Microsoft. Several versions of Windows share a common ancestry back to Windows NT.

Based on the same kernel, the current Windows operating systems are designed with modified microkernel architectures. The operating system design allows many system functions to be implemented as external programs that run in kernel mode. In a pure

> ● **NOTE**
>
> Windows 7 and Windows Server 2008 R2 are based on the NT 6.1 kernel. Windows 8/8.1 and Windows Server 2012 are based on the NT 6.2 kernel. The most current versions of Windows, Windows 10, Windows 11, Windows Server 2016, Windows Server 2019, and Windows Server 2022, are based on the NT 10.0 kernel.

microkernel architecture, external programs are not allowed to run in kernel mode. Because of the modular nature of Windows, major components can be removed, replaced, or enhanced without having to rewrite the entire operating system. This design allows Microsoft to create different versions of the same base operating system to provide specific services for different client and server environments.

Windows Run Modes

The architecture of the Windows operating system consists of two main layered components—kernel (or supervisor) mode and user mode programs. Kernel mode programs run in a privileged mode, also called kernel or supervisor mode, and interact closely with the physical hardware. User mode programs interact with both users and kernel mode programs. **FIGURE 2-3** shows the basic architecture of a Windows operating system.

Kernel Mode

Programs running in kernel mode have complete access to the computer's hardware and system services. This level of access is needed by the operating system and provides an attractive target for attackers.

TABLE 2-2 shows the main kernel mode program components.

FIGURE 2-3

Basic architecture of a Windows operating system.

© Jones & Bartlett Learning.

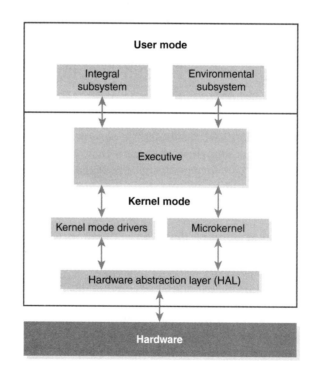

TABLE 2-2 Windows Kernel Mode Components

COMPONENT	DESCRIPTION
Hardware Abstraction Layer (HAL)	The HAL provides the actual access to physical hardware. All other kernel mode programs interact with hardware through the HAL. This allows Microsoft to support multiple hardware platforms by just writing different HAL modules, instead of rewriting all operating system programs.
Kernel mode drivers	Kernel mode drivers provide user programs and other kernel mode programs access to individual hardware devices, through the HAL. These drivers provide the translation to allow other programs to access devices as file objects.
Microkernel	The microkernel is the memory-resident portion of the operating system that provides core functionality, including CPU synchronization, process thread/interrupt scheduling, and exception handling.
Executive	The executive is at the "highest level" of the kernel mode programs. It provides services, such as managing objects, I/O, security, and process management. User mode programs interact with the operating system via the executive.

© Jones & Bartlett Learning.

Technical TIP

One common goal of attackers is to run a program of their choice in kernel mode. At that level of privilege, an attacker can pretty much own a computer. Pay special attention to any vulnerability you encounter that could allow an attacker to escalate privilege to kernel mode.

Windows Server 2022 Kernel Vulnerabilities

With Windows Server 2022 and the movement into cloud computing, many of the newer technologies are aimed at developing server operating systems that can reside in a virtualized architecture. In keeping with the adherence to using kernel mode architecture, these newer technologies can be exploited in the same fashion as on-premise technologies. Two newer exploitable vulnerabilities that are able to gain privilege access based on this older architecture is Windows Kernel Information Disclosure Vulnerability CVE-2022-30162 and Windows Clustered Shared Volume Information Disclosure

Vulnerability CVE-2022-29123. Both of these vulnerabilities have allowed for kernel mode exploitation and have since been patched by Microsoft. It is important, however, to discuss these types of attacks so we can better understand how the underlying architecture is examined by threat actors looking for a way to gain privilege.

When considering Windows Kernel Information Disclosure Vulnerability CVE-2022-30162 and reviewing the threat, it was found quickly and patched by Microsoft so it was not a widespread concern like other vulnerabilities, such as PrintNightmare which we learned about in Chapter 1. Impact from unpatched exploitables help to ensure that the topic of patch management is always considered in any system administration security management plan.

In the case of Windows Clustered Shared Volume Information Disclosure Vulnerability CVE-2022-29123, the threat was a little more concerning in that it exploited the use of containerized applications, which is a newer technology utilized with Windows Server 2022 Azure-based cloud systems. The same kernel mode level **exploit** that attempts to gain privilege through the use of exploiting the weakness and then self-granting access based upon least-privilege will allow access to protected resources. In this threat, the AppContainer execution environment, which is designed to isolate applications to make them more secure, was vulnerable and needed to be patched. Microsoft did respond to the CVE and provided a fix for the exploit in the release of a hotfix.

User Mode

All nonkernel mode programs run under user mode. This includes application programs and the user mode layer of Windows. The Windows user mode layer programs handle all user interaction and processing requests, and pass I/O requests to the necessary kernel mode drivers, using the executive. **TABLE 2-3** lists the two main user mode program components.

TABLE 2-3 Windows User Mode Components

COMPONENT	DESCRIPTION
Environment subsystem	The environment subsystem provides the ability to run programs written for different operating systems, including previous Windows versions and Linux.
Integral subsystem	The integral subsystem handles the user mode functions on behalf of the environment subsystem, including logon and access control, network access, and providing network services.

Access Controls and Authentication

All computer users, including attackers, need to establish access to a computer system before accessing its resources. The operating system is responsible for providing access to authorized users while denying access to unauthorized users. This process of providing and denying access is called **access control**. As developers of operating systems have become more concerned with security issues, access control has matured with each new operating system release. Access control is a multistep process, starting with **identification** and **authentication**. Regardless of the methods used, the operating system needs to identify the user asking for access to a resource. Most often, the user provides a username (or user ID). A username alone is not sufficient to use as a basis for granting access to resources, however. Anyone can claim to be a user. There must be a process that validates that a user is authentic.

The authentication process ensures that users are who they claim to be. There are many methods to authenticate users. The most common method in use is the password. Although anyone can claim to be a particular user, no one else but the real user should know the user's password. The ability to provide both the username and password provides the authentication that the user is valid and authentic.

Authentication Methods

Authentication methods aren't limited to just passwords—they can be one of three types. Each type of authentication is useful in different applications and has strengths and weaknesses. **TABLE 2-4** lists the three authentication types: **Type I**, **Type II**, and **Type III authentication**.

Regardless of the type, or types, of authentication used, the authentication system performs the following tasks:

- Collects identification credentials, such as a username.
- Collects authentication credentials, such as a password.
- Finds the stored information that corresponds to the supplied credentials in the user list, often in an authentication database.
- Compares the stored credentials with the supplied credentials. If they match, the user is authenticated.

> ⚠️ **WARNING**
>
> Attackers know that passwords are common and many people have trouble memorizing the complex ones. So, an attacker will likely explore words and numbers that are easily remembered, such as birthdays, anniversaries, and names of pets or children. Another favorite attack is to walk around an office and look for sticky notes on monitors and under keyboards. Many users write down passwords there.

The strongest authentication comes from using more than one type at the same time. Using two types of authentication is called **two-factor authentication**, and using more than two types is called **multifactor authentication (MFA)**. Any operating system or application that requests more than one response during authentication is using two-factor or multifactor authentication. Using more than a single authentication type strengthens the process by increasing the difficulty of impersonating a valid user.

Multifactor Authentication

With the release of Windows Server 2022 and Microsoft's push toward private, public, and hybrid cloud use, the concepts of MFA should be understood as it grows in use to provide

TABLE 2-4 Authentication Types

TYPE	DESCRIPTION	STRENGTHS	WEAKNESSES
I—What you know	Some pieces of information only a valid user knows. The most common example of Type I authentication is password.	Simple to implement Simple for users	Password overuse—using one password in multiple applications allows a compromised password to provide access to multiple systems. Writing down complex passwords makes them easy to find.
II—What you have	A physical object that contains identity information, such as a token, card, or other device.	More secure than Type I Little or nothing to remember	Can be costly and complex to implement. Risk of lost devices.
III—What you are	Physical biometric characteristics, such as a fingerprint, hand print, or retina characteristic.	Very secure Hard to compromise Nothing to carry or remember	More costly than Type I and II. Difficult to implement. Slow process in some applications.

© Jones & Bartlett Learning.

secure access control. Much like single sign-on (SSO), MFA raises the bar in access control complexity reduction and increased security. As was just discussed in Type I, II and III authentication types, MFA builds on the reduction of exploitation when using, for example, a Type I authentication type such as a password. Although a password can be made and enforced to be complex, it is still something that can be compromised. When you add an additional layer like MFA, you can then create an option to have a code sent to a device to further validate your identity and add an additional (multi) layer of security.

Access Control Methods

Once a user is identified and properly authenticated, the operating system can grant or deny access based on different rule sets. Access control doesn't only apply to users. Any user or program that requests access to a resource is called the access subject. The resource to which the subject requests access is called the access object. Using these terms, access control is the process of granting or denying subjects access to specific objects.

The most common types of access control rules are **discretionary access control (DAC)**, **mandatory access control (MAC)**, and **role-based access control (RBAC)**. DAC strategies are defined primarily at the user, or **subject** level. Each **object** has a defined owner, and the owner has complete control over which users can access the object. In an operating system environment, this means access is granted to resources based on the user's settings. Windows extends this concept to allow object properties that can further restrict access. While this approach is simple to define, it can be challenging to maintain in large environments with many users.

The next main type of access control is MAC. A familiar MAC implementation is used in military and government environments. In such an environment, all data objects are labeled with a specific **classification**. Government classifications are Unclassified, Restricted, Confidential, Secret, and Top Secret. Likewise, all subjects are granted a specific **clearance**. A subject must hold a clearance at, or above, the classification level of the desired object to access it. In most environments, subjects must also demonstrate a specific "need to know." This means even if a subject has the correct clearance, they will not be able to access all of the information at that level unless they have a valid reason to do so.

The final type of access control is RBAC. In one point of view, RBAC extends, or generalizes, DAC. Object access is defined by role, as opposed to individual users. Each user is assigned one or more roles. The roles to which a user is assigned define which objects that user (subject) can access. Most operating systems, including Windows, do not directly use RBAC but use a combination of DAC and RBAC. This combination of access control methods is implemented using both user- and user group–based permissions.

Security Access Tokens, Rights, and Permissions

In a Windows environment, each local system defines local users and groups during the installation process. You can add more local users and groups at any time using the Computer Management tool.

The Local Users and Groups section of the Computer Management tool allows you to add, remove, and manage local users and groups. This tool is most commonly used to create new users and groups, and to associate users with groups. **FIGURE 2-4** shows the Local Users and Groups section of the Computer Management tool.

Technical TIP

Here's how to open the Computer Management tool:

1. Press the Windows + X keys simultaneously to open the Power User menu.
2. Select Computer Management.

Security Identifier

Each local user and group in Windows has a unique **security identifier (SID)**. Windows uses the SID to identify users and groups, not the names. Once you create a local user or group,

Computer Management tool with open Local Users and Groups.

Courtesy of Microsoft Corporation.

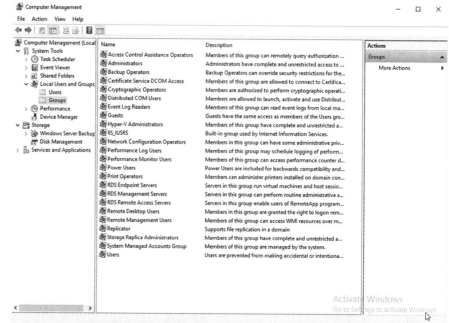

the SID remains the same, even if you change the user or group name. Several well-known users and groups are defined for all Windows machines, but aside from the Microsoft-defined SIDs, all other SIDs are unique to a local machine. **TABLE 2-5** lists a few of the well-known Windows SIDs.

If you create a local user named "Fred" on two different Windows computers, each account will have a different SID. To Windows, the users are completely different, even though they share the same username. This uniqueness between machines makes it difficult to synchronize security settings among multiple standalone computers.

TABLE 2-5 Well-Known SIDs

WELL-KNOWN SID	STRING VALUE	IDENTIFIES
Null SID	S-1-0-0	Group with no members, often used when an SID is not known
World	S-1-1-0	Group that includes all members
Local	S-1-2-0	Users who log on local terminals
Creator Owner ID	S-1-3-0	SID replaced by the SID of the user who created a new object
Creator Group ID	S-1-3-1	SID replaced by the primary group SID of the user who created a new object

© Jones & Bartlett Learning.

Every time a Windows user logs on, the operating system fetches the user's SID and the SIDs for all groups to which the user is assigned. The operating system also looks up any local rights for this computer. All of the SIDs and local rights are written to an ID object called your Security Access Token (SAT). Your session's SAT is attached to all your processes. When you run any process, Windows looks at the SAT and any defined access control information for resources to decide whether to grant or deny access to any requested resources.

Access Rules, Rights, and Permissions

Defining local users and groups is only the first part of the access control implementation process. Windows allows you to associate specific **rights** and permissions to each user that tell Windows what a user can do. User rights define tasks that a user is permitted to carry out, such as take ownership of objects or shut down the computer. **Permissions** define what a user can do to a specific object, such as read or delete the object. Windows stores access rules, or permissions, for resources (objects) in **access control lists (ACLs)**. Each object has an associated ACL and can be used to allow or deny access to the object by user or group. The most common use of ACLs to the general user is to protect files or folders. The Properties dialog box of Files and Folders contains a Security page, which allows you to change the object's access permissions for specific users or groups. The collection of access permissions for each object is called the object's ACL. Windows uses the SAT attached to the currently running process and the ACLs defined for a requested resource to decide whether to grant or deny the requested access. With ACLs, the fundamental building blocks that make one is a list of access control entries (ACE). The list of access control entries is what is used to identify a trustee to derive the rights allowed to grant access, deny access or decide what is auditable. There are two kinds of ACLs, a discretionary access control list (DACL) and a system access control list (SACL). The DACL will be used to identify trustees allowed or that are denied access to an object. The SACL allows an administrator to create log events that can be found in the security event logs within Computer Management, Event Viewer.

Users, Groups, and Active Directory

Today's computing environments are quickly becoming more diverse and geographically separated, but still integrated using networks. Services that are provided by third parties and delivered via the internet are an integral part of many computing environments. These remote services, generally referred to as cloud services, have transformed the way we look at computing infrastructure. Very few of today's computing environments are composed of unconnected workstations or devices. Windows environments, both home and office, are becoming more dependent on internally and externally shared resources. Even the smallest home networks commonly share printers, storage devices, and network access devices. While defining access permissions for small home networks is fairly easy, the same cannot be said for larger business networks.

Workgroups

A business network may contain dozens, hundreds, or even thousands of computers. It is desirable to allow users to access network resources from multiple computers attached to the network. By default, Windows allows computers to share resources by creating a workgroup. A workgroup is a simple peer-to-peer network in which all computers are treated as equals. A workgroup simply allows standalone computers to "see" each other's shared resources. Common shared resources include files, folders, and printers. Each resource can be shared or hidden, and the access to each resource can be controlled by user and group permissions. The main concept behind using a Windows Workgroup is in resource decentralizing. Although this is an easy to set up system that requires little cost, it becomes difficult to manage and secure and is highly discouraged from use.

The main problem with Windows workgroups is that each computer is still defined as a standalone computer. That means users and groups must be defined on multiple computers. In fact, if you want all users to have access on all computers in the workgroup, you have to add the local users on every computer. On small networks, this may seem okay at first, but maintenance can quickly get out of hand. Since all user and group accounts in a workgroup are local accounts, every change to security permissions must be applied to every computer. Administration of workgroups with more than a half dozen computers can quickly become too difficult to remain viable.

Active Directory

Microsoft offered a solution to local users and groups in the original Windows NT operating system. All Windows operating systems since Windows NT have the ability to share user and group definitions with other computers connected to the same network. Many operating systems support a generic capability to share such information, called directory services, which was a flat file architecture. This functionality has matured into a core Windows feature, called **Active Directory**, which is a true hierarchical directory based on tree model that uses LDAP and X.500 structure. Instead of having to define users and groups locally on each computer, Active Directory allows users and groups to be defined once at a central location (centralized vs. the de-centralized workgroup model) and shared among multiple computers. You get to define the limits of how many computers share users and groups by defining domains. A domain can be thought of as a group of computers that can be grouped together for some purpose. The actual database of shared users and groups is stored on one or more computers designated as domain controllers. This shared database makes it easy to maintain users, groups, and permissions in a central location. Microsoft Active Directory has many more features, but its main feature is the ability to define identity and **authorization** permission that can be shared among multiple computers within one or more domains. This capability greatly simplifies security administration in larger networks.

Implementing Active Directory requires more hardware for domain controller computers and network devices. It also requires additional administration time and resources to ensure shared information is protected and available in a timely fashion. In fact, securing Active Directory information ensures its confidentiality, integrity, and availability. An organization that uses Active Directory depends on the security of its information.

The main reason organizations invest in Active Directory resource requirements is not just to make users happy. While implementing a single sign-on capability is a huge benefit for users in a large organization, the real reason to implement Active Directory is to reduce redundant administrative effort. Securing resources across a network, or multiple networks, requires substantial administrative effort. The amount of redundant controls administrators must keep current opens opportunities for attacks on stale controls. Active Directory automates and centralizes many controls, making the entire environment more secure.

Unlike workgroup environments, a domain user or group definition is defined on the domain controller, and its SID will be the same for all computers in the domain. In the workgroup environment, a local user named "Fred" may be defined on each computer, but the SID will be different on each one. Auditing Fred's actions across multiple computers can be more difficult when trying to coordinate multiple SIDs. If the user named "Fred" is defined as a domain user instead, Fred's SID will be stored in the domain controller and be shared with computers in the domain when needed. Fred's SID never changes, regardless of what computer in the domain is being accessed. Active Directory removes the problem of different SIDs on each computer.

Windows Attack Surfaces and Mitigation

Windows, like any operating system, is a collection of services provided to allow users to interact with the physical hardware. Each service provides a specific set of access methods to the hardware and functions that satisfy user requirements. In short, operating system services provide some functionality to users. Each service exposes some part of the computer to external access. Regardless of the care taken to ensure the security of the provided access, there is a risk when exposing any part of a computer to external access. All computing systems can become vulnerable based on lack of hardening, configuration mistakes, bugs, and unknown vulnerabilities—weaknesses that can allow unauthorized access if successfully exploited. The total collection of all possible vulnerabilities that could provide unauthorized access to computer resources is referred to as the **attack surface**. Another way to define the attack surface is the set of all exposed vulnerabilities. The attack surface is further broken down into an **attack tree** and an **attack vector**. An attack tree is what a threat actor will devise, based on vulnerability scanning, testing, and verifying weaknesses, as the blueprint for building the intended attacks. The attack surface is consulted to design the attack tree. The attack vector is considered the road or path the threat actor takes to conduct the attacks. All three are important to know when considering how to create a multilayer defense strategy or apply the concept of defense-in-depth.

Multilayered Defense

The discipline of information security is concerned with minimizing the attack surface of any protected resource. This can be achieved by successfully removing, or substantially reducing, the ability of an attacker to conduct an attack against vulnerability. There are several effective methods to minimize the attack surface. The most secure environments employ a combination of strategies. Most important, a solid overall security strategy avoids monolithic solutions. Relying on a single control to protect a resource increases the probability of a successful attack. Always design a defense strategy that is multilayered, which requires multiple controls be compromised to exploit any vulnerability. Such a strategy is often called a defense-in-depth approach to security. **FIGURE 2-5** shows how a multilayered defense strategy protects resources.

FIGURE 2-5

Multilayered defense.

© Jones & Bartlett Learning.

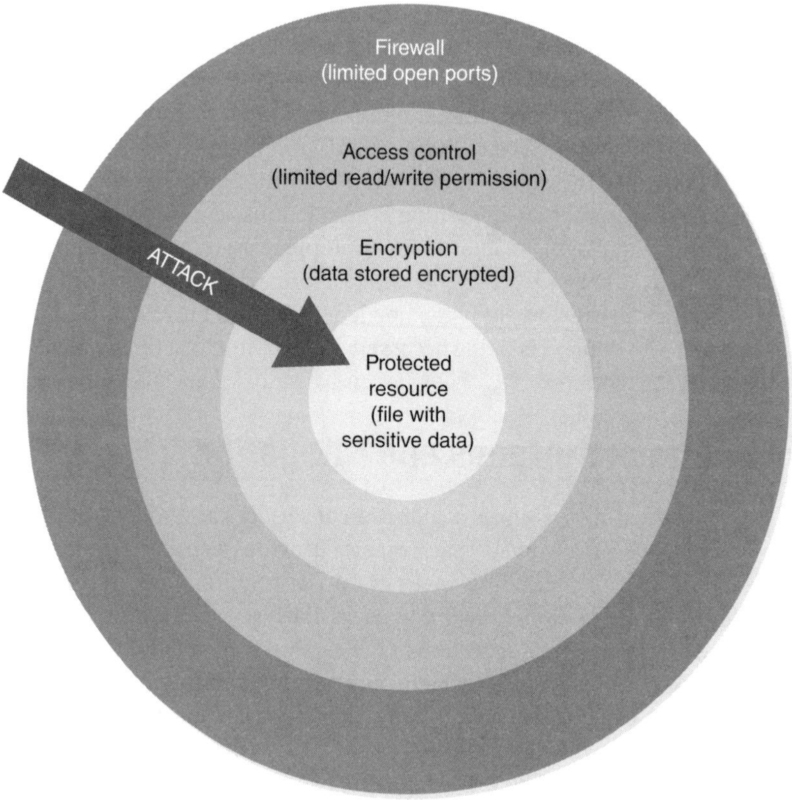

Firewall
(limited open ports)

Access control
(limited read/write permission)

Encryption
(data stored encrypted)

ATTACK

Protected
resource
(file with
sensitive data)

At a high level, the easiest way to reduce the attack surface is to remove functionality. Suppose an attacker wants to exploit an Internet Information Services (IIS) web server vulnerability. The quickest way to deny such an attack is to disable or remove the IIS web server. Although disabling IIS may be easy, it may be an unacceptable solution. What if the server computer in question is a web server in a production environment servicing clients or customers? Disabling IIS in that case is not an option! But in many cases, disabling a web server is perfectly okay if it is not in use—this is also considered hardening a system by removing unused services. What steps you take all depends on the purpose of the server computer and the services it must provide to be functional. Defining the computer role and configuring the operating system for that role is one of the best ways to reduce the attack surface of any computer.

The best way to reduce the need to harden systems is to ensure that when installed, all services needed are known up front and nothing else is added. Proper workstation and server role definition and planning make it easier during the installation process to only install and enable services that are necessary for a particular computer. By installing and enabling only the necessary services, you reduce the operating system's complexity and overall attack surface. Windows Server versions since Windows Server 2008 include the Server Manager tool, which makes it easy to define specific roles for a server. There is even a newer installation option available called Server Core that installs only the basic services to support file and print services, Active Directory, and a few other basic server functions.

The resulting installation takes up less disk space, consumes less memory, and has a much smaller attack surface due to fewer installed services. Server Core doesn't include a Graphical User Interface (GUI) and is primarily managed via PowerShell, so it is the common base image for servers that are managed remotely. PowerShell is a task automation and configuration management program from Microsoft, consisting of a command-line shell and cmdlets that allow you the ability to manually (or use automation) to handle any and all administrative tasks in the Windows Operating System(s).

Here's how to open the PowerShell tool:

1. PowerShell can be accessed by going to the Windows 11 or Windows Server 2022 search bar and typing PowerShell.
2. Once open, type help to see a list of online guidance to get you started.

If you are new to PowerShell, start to use the interface to learn, and search Microsoft documentation online to get specific guidance on commands. Most of the security administration done in Windows Server 2022 core is done via the PowerShell interface.

Mitigation

If you must install and enable a service, such as the IIS web server, you will have to employ measures to protect your system from IIS vulnerabilities. The strategies you will learn to secure any resource, also called mitigating a risk, fall into two main categories:

1. Remove vulnerabilities
2. Stop attacks from exploiting vulnerabilities

Between the two strategies, the former is the better option. Removing vulnerabilities by disabling the service or by updating vulnerable software to a more secure version removes the possibility of a successful attack against a specific vulnerability. However, just applying a security patch doesn't guarantee there is no more vulnerability in the service. That's why a multilayered defense is so important. Never rely on a single control or strategy to protect a resource. Always employ multiple levels of controls. Your goal is to make attackers work very hard to exploit resources on protected computers.

Fundamentals of Microsoft Windows Security Monitoring and Maintenance

The process of securing a Windows computer system and maintaining a secure system is an iterative process. Three main points in a system's life cycle serve as milestones for security management. It is important to maintain a secure system when you do the following:

1. Install the operating system or application software.
2. Monitor the operation of the computer system.
3. Make any configuration changes to the computer system.

The first and third milestones are easy events to identify, at least for small computing environments, and result from some administrative action. Organizations with more than several dozen servers and workstations find that all of the milestones can be challenging.

As any organization grows, policies that result in configuration standards make the administration process easier. It is important to include security concerns in the installation and modification procedures to avoid introducing unintended vulnerabilities. For example, the procedure to upgrade to a new version of SQL Server should include steps to ensure insecure user accounts or demo procedures are not added to the system environment. It is also desirable to carry out validation tasks after any new installations or configuration changes to ensure system security meets stated goals. The second milestone occurs at intervals specified by security administrators for each system. Monitoring can be as frequent or infrequent as necessary. Typically, the monitoring frequency depends on the volatility of the resource and the risk of attacks against the resource.

Security Monitoring

In general, the process of security monitoring involves comparing performance or configuration information with a stated baseline. Microsoft offers several tools and resources to help create and maintain secure systems. The basic process of security monitoring is to follow these steps:

1. Define security goals.
2. Describe secure behavior as a baseline.
3. Sample performance information and compare with the baseline.
4. Report anomalies.

The tools and resources available for Windows operating systems include both the suggested baselines and the tools to compare baselines with system configuration and performance information. System configuration information could include user and group definitions, critical resource permissions, and lists of folders. Baseline information could include a list of known vulnerable users, groups, and folders. Any items in the lists of users, groups, or folders that exist in the baseline could indicate vulnerability. Performance information could include web server log files. SIEM and SOAR tools help collect, manage, and automate the process of monitoring such log files and could show attacks that have been carried out against your system. Security, information, and event management (SIEM) is used to collect and manage security log data, while security orchestration, automation, and response (SOAR) is used to help create responses to the data collected. Or even better, you could see the evidence of a preattack reconnaissance effort. In the case of the latter example, you could use such information to take action to protect your system from an expected future attack.

Identify Vulnerabilities

The idea behind monitoring is to simply consider the current state of a system and help identify any existing security vulnerabilities that may arise from changes in your IT infrastructure. You are proactively taking an approach similar to what an attacker would do in planning an attack. Later in this book, you'll learn about tools that will help you uncover vulnerabilities in your computing environment. After identifying vulnerabilities, you must decide how to address each one. It sounds simple, and it really is at its core. However, putting that goal into practice can be difficult. There are many options to address each vulnerability, and you have to choose the best option for each situation. The process isn't a single occurrence of each step. Security monitoring and responding to the results is a process you'll repeat over and over to keep your systems secure.

CHAPTER SUMMARY

Microsoft Windows is a mature family of operating systems that address the needs of many different types of enterprises and users. The wide variety of information managed by Windows systems and the large number of existing systems that run Windows make the platform an attractive target for attacks. Attackers know that each new Windows release gives security administrators new and improved tools to help secure protected resources and information. They know the only way to stay ahead of the game, and outsmart Windows administrators, is to be as knowledgeable about the operating system and its attack surface as possible. And they know it well.

The best way to defend your systems from attack is to know as much, if not more, about your operating system and its vulnerabilities as attackers know. Think like an attacker, a hacker, or a threat actor. Know where and how they'll likely attempt to compromise your systems. Anticipate their moves, and you'll be better prepared to place deterrents in their path. You have now learned the basics of the Windows operating system architecture.

KEY CONCEPTS AND TERMS

Access control	Discretionary access control (DAC)	Rights
Access control lists (ACLs)	Exploit	Role-based access control (RBAC)
Active Directory	Hardware Abstraction Layer (HAL)	Security identifier (SID)
Attack surface	Identification	Subject
Attack tree	Kernel	Supervisor mode
Attack vector	Kernel mode	Two-factor authentication
Authentication	Mandatory access control (MAC)	Type I authentication
Authorization	Microkernel	Type II authentication
Classification	Multifactor authentication (MFA)	Type III authentication
Clearance	Object	User mode
Control	Permissions	

CHAPTER 2 ASSESSMENT

1. Which of the following is *not* a goal of a secure environment?
   A. All required information is available to authorized users.
   B. No information is available to unauthorized users.
   C. All required information is available to unauthorized users.
   D. No classified information is available to unauthorized users.

2. Which term describes the central component of an operating system?
   A. Kernel
   B. Shell
   C. Hardware Abstraction Layer
   D. Executive

3. What are the two run modes for Windows programs?
   A. Supervisor mode and executive mode
   B. Kernel mode and supervisor mode
   C. User mode and executive mode
   D. Kernel mode and user mode

4. Which of the following Windows components resides in memory to provide the core operating system services?
   A. Kernel
   B. Microkernel
   C. Executive
   D. Hardware Abstraction Layer

5. What is the name of the process that proves you are who you say you are?
   A. Identification
   B. Authorization
   C. Permission
   D. Authentication

6. Which type of authentication is a smart card?
   A. Type I
   B. Type II
   C. Type III
   D. Type IV

7. Which access control method relates data classification to user clearance?
   A. MAC
   B. DAC
   C. RBAC
   D. LDAC

8. What value uniquely identifies a user or group in Windows?
   A. UID
   B. SAT
   C. SID
   D. ACE

9. If the same user is created on three separate Windows computers, which value is the same on all three computers?
   A. SID
   B. User code
   C. Username
   D. SAT

10. Which Windows feature allows users and groups to be "shared" among machines?
    A. Domain controller
    B. Workgroup
    C. SID
    D. Active Directory

11. What defines the limit of how many computers share users and groups?
    A. SID
    B. GUID
    C. Domain
    D. Workgroup

12. Which of the following best describes the term *attack surface*?
    A. All possible vulnerabilities in application software that could be exploited
    B. All possible vulnerabilities that could be exploited
    C. The most likely avenues of attack
    D. Known vulnerabilities that have not been patched

13. When possible, what is the best way to mitigate vulnerability in a specific service?

   A. Remove the service.

   B. Disable the service.

   C. Block access to the service.

   D. Patch the service.

14. When monitoring a Windows system, with what do you compare current system performance to test for security compliance?

   A. The previous monitoring results

   B. A normal performance scan

   C. A stated baseline

   D. A defined security goal

15. Why should you immediately test your system for security compliance after making a configuration change?

   A. Configuration changes generally increase security.

   B. Configuration changes generally decrease security.

   C. Configuration changes may introduce new vulnerabilities.

   D. Configuration changes may remove existing vulnerabilities.

PART II

Managing and Maintaining Microsoft Windows Security

Access Controls in Microsoft Windows

I N THIS CHAPTER, you'll start learning the details of Windows security features and specific steps to make Windows computers more secure.

As in any complex endeavor, it is important to understand the concepts of information systems security before you start making changes and placing controls. Poorly placed security controls can often do more harm than good. A control that is too permissive to be effective does not increase security. Likewise, a control that is too stringent can often reduce usability and increase user frustration. It is important to always keep security goals in mind as you design and implement controls. Always follow the time-tested strategy:

- Think
- Plan
- Design
- Implement
- Evaluate

Follow these steps in order, and you will avoid many of the frustrations encountered from poorly planned actions. The first step in designing and implementing an effective access control strategy is considering the most important access control goals. This chapter will cover access control design strategies and the steps necessary to implement and evaluate them.

Chapter 3 Topics

This chapter covers the following topics and concepts:

- What the principle of least privilege is
- What access models are, including identification, authentication, authorization, ACLs, and more
- What Windows objects and access controls are
- What forms of identification are, including SIDs, GUIDs, and CLSIDs
- What Microsoft Windows access permissions are
- What auditing and tracking Windows access is
- What Microsoft Windows access management tools are, including cacls, xcacls, and Robocopy
- What best practices for managing Microsoft Windows and application vulnerabilities are

Chapter 3 Goals

When you complete this chapter, you will be able to:

- Summarize the principle of least privilege
- Differentiate among identification, authentication, and authorization
- Illustrate the use of Windows ACLs
- Discuss Microsoft Windows objects and access controls
- Identify forms of identification in Microsoft Windows
- Describe Microsoft Windows access permissions
- Examine auditing and tracking Microsoft Windows access
- Research Microsoft Windows access management tools
- Outline best practices for managing Microsoft Windows and application vulnerabilities
- Discuss business challenges of managing vulnerabilities

The Principle of Least Privilege

Here is the goal of access control (and security in general):

> To ensure all authorized users have access to required information on demand, while denying access to unauthorized users.

In the context of access control, security controls must provide object access for all authorized subjects. The easiest way to do that is to grant full access to all objects, for all subjects. In other words, give everybody access to everything. Global access would satisfy the first part of the security goal, but not the second part of the goal. If object access is granted to everyone, it is impossible to prevent access by unauthorized users.

The Orange Book

The solution is to find the best balance between providing necessary access for authorized subjects (users and applications) and denying any unnecessary access. This principle of providing just the necessary access required to carry out a task is called the **principle of least privilege**.

The U.S. Department of Defense Trusted Computer System Evaluation Criteria, DOD-5200.28-STD, also known as the **Orange Book** because of its orange colored cover, was one of the first generally accepted standards for computer security. The Orange

Book has since been replaced by the **Common Criteria for Information Technology Security Evaluation**—an international standard. The Common Criteria extend the concepts stated in the Orange Book. The Orange Book defines least privilege to be a principle that "requires that each subject in a system be granted the most restrictive set of privileges (or lowest clearance) needed for the performance of authorized tasks. The application of this principle limits the damage that can result from accident, error, or unauthorized use."

Least Privilege and Least Privilege User Accounts

In a Windows environment, the principle of least privilege is implemented at the user account level. In fact, Microsoft refers to user accounts defined using this principle as **least privilege user accounts (LUAs)**. All Windows users are associated with one or more **groups**. The majority of permissions in a Windows environment are controlled at the user group level. A common and manageable way to implement least privilege is to create user groups that represent roles in your organization. Every organization is different, and there are many options for creating roles. Groups are effective administration tools because a group can contain a large number of users that can then be managed as a unit. By using groups, you can assign access to a resource, such as a shared folder, to a group instead of each user individually, saving substantial time and effort. You can configure your own groups as you see fit on your network and systems, but most operating systems include a number of predefined groups that you can use as well or modify as needed. Although there are some local default groups, you will most likely encounter Active Directory groups when working with networked Windows computers. **TABLE 3-1** shows a partial list of default Active Directory security groups (https://docs.microsoft.com/en-us/windows/security/identity -protection/access-control/active-directory-security-groups). These groups represent common roles within an organization and provide a starting point for implementing least privilege.

TABLE 3-1 Sample Default Active Directory Security Groups in Windows Server 2016, Windows Server 2019, and Windows Server 2022

GROUP	DESCRIPTION
Account operators	Allows members to create and modify most types of accounts and can log in locally to domain controllers.
Administrators	Members have unrestricted access to the computer, or if the computer is a domain controller, to the entire domain.
IIS_IUSRS	Built-in group used by all versions of Internet Information Services since version 7.0. The IUSR account is a member of this group and provides consistency for web users.

(continues)

GROUP	DESCRIPTION
TABLE 3-1 Sample Default Active Directory Security Groups in Windows Server 2016, Windows Server 2019, and Windows Server 2022 *(continued)*	
Users	General group for normal users that allows users to run applications, access local resources, shut down or lock a computer, and install per-user applications.
Guests	Allows one-time users to log in to a computer in a domain with basic privileges of a regular user. When a member of the Guests groups logs out, the entire profile is deleted.
Backup operators	Members can back up and restore all files on a specific computer, regardless of what permissions are in place for those files.
Remote desktop users	Allows users to establish remote connections to a Remote Desktop Session Host server.

© Jones & Bartlett Learning.

Rights and Permissions

Each group in Windows has the ability to apply rights and permissions to sets of users. Associating users with one or more groups allows the implementation of least privilege in a group setting, as opposed to configuring each individual user account. Securing groups instead of individual users makes the goal of least privilege far more feasible, especially in environments with many users.

> **Technical TIP**
>
> Ensure that you understand the difference between rights and permissions. Rights define what tasks a user can perform on a computer, and permissions define what a user can do to an object. Rights are associated with users, or subjects, and permissions are associated with objects, for example, files.

User rights are defined and maintained through group security policy objects. Permissions apply to specific objects and are maintained through each object's security settings. By defining a list of access control rules for each object, access permissions are defined for specific users or groups. The list of access permissions is called the access control list (ACL) for the object. Since the ACLs that Windows uses are implemented as discretionary access control, the more accurate, but less common, term used for the list of access control rules is a **discretionary access control list (DACL)**. Each entry in the DACL is called an **access control entry (ACE)**. The process of securing resources in Windows starts with creating object DACLs that satisfy your security goals. **FIGURE 3-1** shows a Windows object DACL.

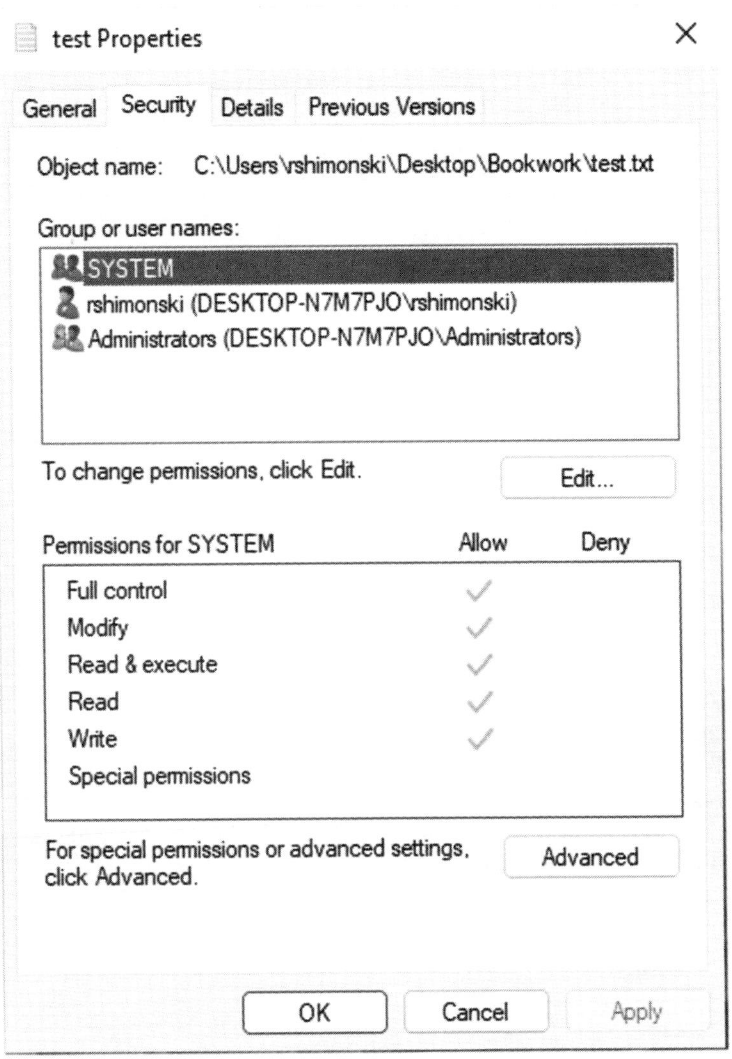

FIGURE 3-1
Windows object DACL.

Courtesy of Microsoft Corporation.

3

Access Models: Identification, Authentication, Authorization, ACLs, and More

When you log on to your computer, Windows follows a specific process to validate you as an authorized user and to decide what you are allowed to do. At the end of the process, Windows has all the information it needs to allow or deny actions based on your security settings. Here are the steps Windows takes to validate a user and build the necessary security information:

1. Windows prompts the user to enter identification and authentication credentials. This can be a prompt for username and password, token entry such as a smart card or a token generated password, or a biometric device, such as a fingerprint reader.

FIGURE 3-2

Windows Security Access Token (SAT).

© Jones & Bartlett Learning.

User's security access token (SAT)

2. Windows looks up the defined user and the associated authentication information. If the supplied information matches the stored information, the user is authenticated.
3. Once a user has been authenticated, the operating system records the user account's security identifier (SID), the SID of each group to which the user is assigned, and the current user's privileges in a token. A token is just a collection of information all stored together. The token that Windows uses to store all the SIDs is called the **Security Access Token (SAT)**. **FIGURE 3-2** shows a Windows SAT.
4. The SAT, with all the user and group SIDs, is attached to each process the user runs.

Technical TIP

Windows gets this information from the local machine for local accounts and from Active Directory for domain accounts. Domain account information stored in Active Directory is delivered to the logon machine, no matter where it is. The ability to share logon and security information among computers in a domain, and perhaps more, is one of the most powerful features of Active Directory.

Windows Server 2016, Windows Server 2019, and Windows Server 2022 Dynamic Access Control

Windows Server 2016, Windows Server 2019, and Windows Server 2022 include extended capabilities to help keep data secure. **Dynamic Access Control (DAC)** describes a collection of features to describe user and data attributes. These attributes help Windows protect files using policies that provide more control over who can access data. DAC includes several features:

- **Identify and classify data**—You can tag data either automatically or manually to tell Windows how to secure different types of data. Automatic tagging can look for special types of data, such as Social Security numbers.
- **Control file access**—Central access policies allow organizations to set global rules on who can access different types of data.
- **Audit file access**—DAC includes central audit policies that provide the ability for auditors and forensic investigators to find out who accessed sensitive information.
- **Apply encryption to sensitive documents**—Automatic **Rights Management Services (RMS)** can encrypt files that contain tagged sensitive data without requiring user interaction.

DAC builds on features introduced in Windows Server 2008 R2. Features available in Windows Server 2008 R2 include the following:

- **File Classification Infrastructure (FCI)** provides the ability to define classification properties for files.
- Automatic classification of files is automatically based on location and content. Windows Server 2012 and newer versions make it easier to identify sensitive files and automatically encrypt file contents.
- Windows Server 2008 R2 allows enforcement of file expiration policies and custom actions based on classification.

Windows Server 2012 and subsequent Windows Server versions add to the capabilities of Windows Server 2008 R2 by automating many of the classified file management utilities. Many of the actions an administrator may take, such as classification and encryption, can be automated in Windows Server 2012 and subsequent Windows Server versions. Windows Server 2012 and later also helps support personnel and investigators by enhancing access denied support. The newest version of Windows Server also provides more capability to identify and respond to actions that result in file access denial.

User Account Control

Members of the Administrators group have additional powers and responsibilities. They each get two-piece, or split, SAT. One part of the SAT is built with the full privileges of the Administrators group. Members of this group enjoy full access to the computer and can perform many tasks that can be harmful to the computer. The other part of the SAT is built to reflect the more limited capabilities of a normal user. All processes initially run using the limited SAT. If a process requires a privilege that is allowed for administrators and the process also contains an administrator SAT, Windows will prompt the user for an escalation confirmation (**FIGURE 3-3**). Windows asks the user to confirm escalating the process to administrator privileges. This confirmation is designed to stop malicious software from making unauthorized changes by running at a higher-than-expected privilege level. This prompt is also extremely helpful in notifying you when something in your system, such as a service or application, is trying to make a change that requires administrative privileges.

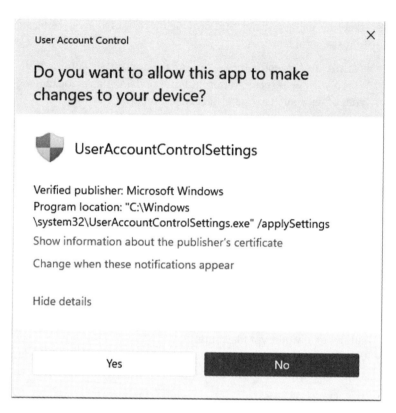

This Windows feature of prompting users before escalating to administrator privileges is
called **User Account Control (UAC)**.

Each time a process needs access to an object, Windows refers to the process's SAT and
the object's DACL to see if the access request is allowed. If the access request is allowed, the
process accesses the object. If the access request is not allowed, Windows returns an error,
and the process cannot complete the requested object access.

Once Windows builds the SAT and attaches it to each process, the SAT becomes the
subject part of the authorization process. Before granting access to an object, Windows must
first authorize the request. Windows uses the DACL defined for an object to decide whether
the access request will be granted or denied. DACLs will be covered in the next section.

Technical TIP

UAC Settings

In previous Windows versions, UAC was often seen as annoying and intrusive. The only options were to
turn UAC on or off. Starting with Windows 7 and Windows Server 2008 R2, users can choose one of four
"comfort levels" of UAC, from "Never Notify" to "Always Notify." You can change this setting in Start
(Windows Menu Icon) > All apps > Windows Tools > Control Panel > User Accounts > User Accounts >
Change User Account Control Settings (**FIGURE 3-4**).

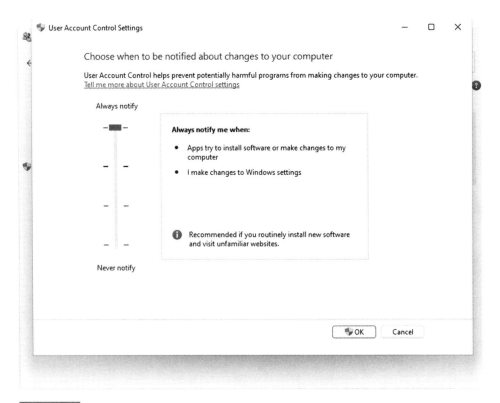

FIGURE 3-4

UAC settings.

Courtesy of Microsoft Corporation.

Sharing SIDs and SATs

The SAT for each process is built from the user's SID and group SIDs. The SAT is specific to a computer in a stand-alone or workgroup environment. Recall that workgroups do not share users or groups. As user and group settings and assignments are customized, synchronizing changes across computers in a workgroup becomes increasingly difficult. This makes Active Directory even more appealing. Active Directory stores the shared necessary information to construct SATs, which are identical for a given user, regardless of the computer where the user logs on.

If the **domain controller** sends security information to the computer where a user logs on, how does Windows stop an attacker from intercepting the SAT information and impersonating an authorized user? Windows extends the concept of authentication to the computer level when constructing SATs. The complete SATs are never shared across a network—only the parts necessary to construct the SAT (**FIGURE 3-5**). The domain controller stores the domain user's SID and the SIDs for all of the domain groups to which the user is assigned. The target server, the server where the resource access resides, already has the local group list of groups to which the user is defined and the local user

© Jones & Bartlett Learning.

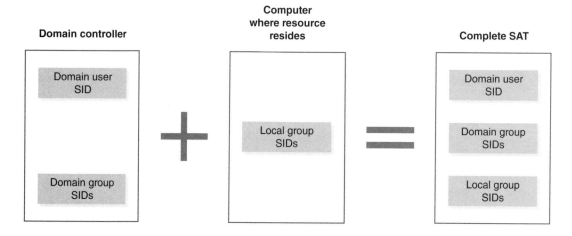

rights definitions. The domain controller sends the domain user and group SIDs to the target server using one of two Windows authentication protocols.

Managed Service Accounts

Windows Server 2012 added support for a new type of account to help administrators manage servers. In previous versions of Windows, administrators had to maintain passwords for multiple system accounts. These accounts provide the credentials that critical Windows services and tasks use. Administrators commonly use multiple accounts to handle the needs of various critical services. For example, backup needs are different from the account for an IIS server. Administrators define each system account with just the permissions required to carry out its tasks. Manually maintaining the passwords for system accounts across many servers was tedious.

Windows Server 2012 and newer includes **managed service accounts**, which can be shared across systems. Administrators create these accounts as managed domain accounts that provide automatic password management. Earlier versions of Windows provided computer accounts and managed server accounts, but neither of these account types could be shared across systems. The new group managed service accounts allow the Windows Server 2012 and newer domain controllers to manage the passwords automatically at the domain level.

Kerberos

The default authentication protocol since Windows 2000 is **Kerberos**. Kerberos is a fast and scalable protocol that allows for secure exchange of information (**FIGURE 3-6**). Each domain controller functions as a Kerberos **key distribution center (KDC)**. One of the most important concepts to understand about the Kerberos protocol and how the KDC functions is understanding how it functions as an authentication service and how tickets

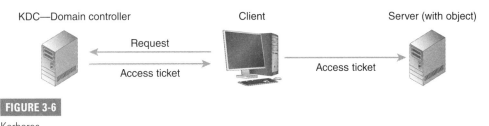

KDC—Domain controller   Client   Server (with object)

Request

Access ticket

Access ticket

FIGURE 3-6

Kerberos.

© Jones & Bartlett Learning.

are handled: first as an authentication service (AS) and then as a Ticket-Granting Service (TGS). The KDC stores all user and computer Kerberos master keys. When a subject requests access to an object, the subject asks the domain controller for an access ticket. The domain controller authenticates the subject. If successful, the domain controller issues the access ticket. The access ticket contains all of the subject's SIDs and is encrypted with the target server's **public key**. The subject then presents the access ticket to the server where the desired object resides. Since the access ticket was encrypted with the server's public key, the server can decrypt it with its private key. Successful decryption means the ticket is valid, and the server evaluates the SIDs for access permission.

Windows Objects and Access Controls

One of the primary security features of Windows is the ability to control access to resources. In a Windows environment, every resource where access can be controlled is defined as a securable object. There are many types of securable objects in Windows, including both named and unnamed objects. The most common securable objects include the following:

- NTFS files and folders
- Pipes, named or unnamed
- Processes and threads
- Registry keys
- Windows services
- Printers, both local and remote
- Network shares
- Job objects

Windows DACLs

A securable object requires a DACL for Windows to control access to the object. Any object with no DACL defined is accessible by any subject—any process, any user. An object's DACL is a collection of individual ACEs and can be modified in the object's Properties dialog box.

The Security page of the object Properties dialog box (**FIGURE 3-7**) allows you to view and modify the security permissions for the selected object. On the Security page, the Group or User Names area lists the users and groups for which ACEs are defined. The Permissions for Users area shows the current permissions for the selected user or group.

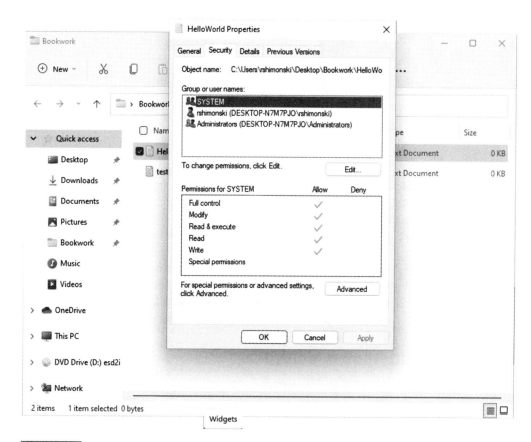

FIGURE 3-7

Object Properties dialog box, Security page.

Courtesy of Microsoft Corporation.

Here's how to display and edit any object's DACL:

1. Open the object's Properties dialog box. Use any one of these procedures:
   a. Right-click the object, then select Properties.
   b. Select the object, press ALT+ENTER.
   c. Hold the ALT key and double-click the object.
2. In the Properties dialog box, select the Security tab.

▶ **TIP**

Choose the Advanced button on the Security page to open the Advanced Security Settings dialog box. To change any permissions settings, choose the Change link next to the Owner.

The Edit button under the Group or User Names area modifies basic permissions for the highlighted user or group. New users, group permissions, or the removal of existing user or group permissions can be modified here. Basic permissions are predefined common groups of individual permissions that make maintaining DACLs easier. Every permission has two checkboxes next to it. Actions can be allowed or modified by using one of the two checkboxes. **TABLE 3-2** lists the basic permissions that can be modified for each user or group.

TABLE 3-2 Basic Windows Object Permissions

PERMISSION	DESCRIPTION
Full Control	Provides no restrictions on access to object
Modify	Allows all modifications to files and folders; cannot delete files or folders, change permissions, or take ownership
Read and Execute	Traverses folders; executes files; lists folders; reads data, basic and extended attributes, and permissions
Read	Lists folders; reads data, basic and extended attributes, and permissions
Write	Creates files and folders; writes data and basic and extended attributes; reads permissions
Special Permissions	Indicates the ACE for this user or group is defined on the Advanced page

© Jones & Bartlett Learning.

DACL Advanced Permissions

The Advanced page provides access to individual object permissions, as opposed to predefined groups of permissions in the general Security page (**FIGURE 3-8**). The Advanced page lists every individual permission for the selected user or group.

To see an example of ACE inheritance, navigate to the following file in File Explorer and open This PC to expose the Local Disk (C:) drive, then view the properties of C:\Windows\System32\drivers\etc\services. Replace C:\Windows with the Windows OS installation folder if Windows was installed to another folder. Once opened, view the Advanced Security Settings of the services file. Notice that the rightmost column, titled Inherited From, shows the original source of each ACE. In this example, the ACEs are all inherited from the parents folder.

You can make several changes in the Advanced Security Settings dialog box. ACEs for specific users or groups can be added or deleted. The ACE inheritance setting can also be modified. Most objects inherit some ACEs from other objects. For example, it is common for file objects to inherit at least some ACEs from the parent folder.

To disable ACE inheritance, first ensure you have the ability to make changes by selecting the Change permissions button in the dialog box. This will prompt you with the UAC service discussed earlier. Select yes, and you will see the dialog box change to now allow changes to take place.

 TIP

If any changes have been made in the Advanced page, one of the Special Permissions boxes will be checked on the Security page to indicate that advanced permissions are defined.

 TIP

Although the Advanced page can be used to set the same permissions as those on the Security page, it should be used only when the basic permissions are not detailed enough to meet current demands. Use the simpler basic permissions when they meet the security objectives. Like basic permissions, special permissions can be allowed or denied by checking one of the two check boxes.

DACL Advanced Security Settings.

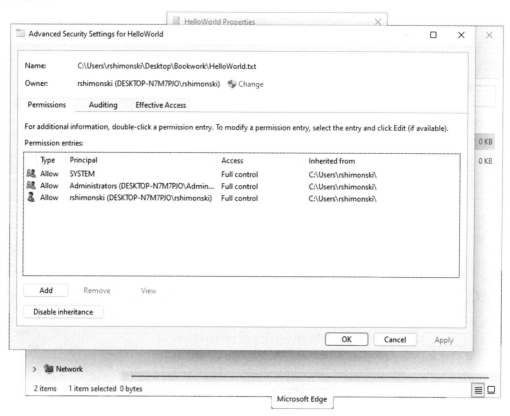

To make a change, first select the Principal you wish to change such as Users and their ability to access and use this resource. Next, click on the "Disable inheritance" button. When disabling the inheritance feature, Windows asks what to do with existing inherited ACEs. There are two choices: Convert inherited permissions into explicit permissions on this object or Remove all inherited permissions from this object. Another way to make these changes would be to select and click on the Add or Remove buttons, which will allow you to become more granular with adding or removing specific basic or advanced permissions. You can also select to remove Principals using the Remove button. If you want to add or remove, you can select each offering as follows:

1. **Add**—Select this option to add all previously inherited ACEs as new explicit ACEs. This option retains the same functionality, but any subsequent changes to the parent's ACEs will not change the current object's permissions.
2. **Remove**—Select this option to simply remove all previously inherited ACEs from this object's DACL.

TABLE 3-3 lists the special permissions available in the Advanced page.

TABLE 3-3 Special Windows Object Permissions

PERMISSION	DESCRIPTION
Traverse Folder/Execute File	Navigates to a folder for folder objects and can execute files for file objects
List Folder/Read Data	Lists the contents of folders for folder objects or reads data for nonfolder objects
Read Attributes	Reads basic object attributes
Read Extended Attributes	Reads extended object attributes
Create Files/Write Data	Creates files in a folder for folder objects or writes data for nonfolder objects
Create Folders/Append Data	Creates new folders for folder objects or appends data to existing nonfolder objects
Write Attributes	Writes basic object attributes
Write Extended Attributes	Writes extended object attributes
Delete	Deletes nonfolder objects
Read Permissions	Reads object permissions
Change Permissions	Changes object permissions
Take Ownership	Becomes the new owner of this object

© Jones & Bartlett Learning.

3

Access Controls in
Microsoft Windows

SIDs, GUIDs, and CLSIDs

In the Windows operating system environment, all users, groups, and computers have unique SIDs. A SID identifies a security subject or group of subjects. Local users and groups are assigned SIDs that are unique to a single computer, while domain objects are assigned SIDs that are unique within the domain. A subject's SID is assigned when the subject is created and never changes throughout its lifetime. A user's name can be changed, but the user's SID remains the same. The use of SIDs gives Windows the ability to record references to users, groups, and computers that remain constant and don't change over time.

As information systems have grown, they have become more diverse and distributed. Many applications now operate as a collection of distributed components running on several different computers. Microsoft uses identification values that are unique across all environments to keep track of objects across many computers. Microsoft assigns many objects a **globally unique identifier (GUID)**, also called a **universally unique identifier (UUID)**, to distinguish objects that may originate from different computers. Originally intended in

Windows to uniquely identify GUI controls, GUIDs are now used to identify many different types of objects, including the following:

- Computers
- Web browsers
- Database records
- Files
- Application components

 TIP

You can go to https://www.guidgen.com/ to generate UUIDs/GUIDs online. If you would rather use a local program, Microsoft provides the UUIDGEN.EXE program with the Platform Software Development Kit (SDK). The UUIDGEN.EXE program is a command line utility you can use to generate UUIDs in several output formats.

There are several ways to generate GUIDs/UUIDs. Performing an internet search for "Generate GUID" or "Generate UUID" will result in references to programs, websites, scripts, and other strategies to create GUIDs/UUIDs on demand. Microsoft offers a tool to create UUIDs called UUIDGEN.EXE. Any strategy that generates a true globally unique ID will provide a UUID that can be used in your own system.

Windows uses GUIDs extensively to keep track of many objects. The Windows Registry uses GUIDs to identify objects and record many of their attributes. When used in this context, the GUIDs are stored as **Class Identifiers (CLSIDs)**. Windows uses CLSIDs to represent a software application or software component. In fact, CLSIDs can represent even more. Using CLSIDs, even basic information, such as an executable filename, can be changed but still refer to the same application. Windows recognizes either the filename or the CLSID for executable objects. For example, follow these steps to launch the Recycle Bin by running its CLSID:

1. Select the Windows icon or press the Windows key, then press "R."
2. Type the following value in the Open box:

   ::{645ff040-5081-101b-9f08-00aa002f954e}

3. Choose OK.

Windows uses CLSIDs to reference software components without having to know the component's name. **TABLE 3-4** lists some common Windows CLSIDs to run programs without referencing the program name. Run any of the listed CLSIDs to open the corresponding program.

Regardless of whether Microsoft refers to objects using a CLSID or the object name, all access control rules must be satisfied before access is allowed. There is no shortcut that uses direct CLSID references to bypass access controls.

Calculating Microsoft Windows Access Permissions

The purpose of access control is to grant and deny access to objects, based on defined rules. Windows supports this goal through definitions of users, groups, and object DACLs. Every object may have a DACL that includes several ACEs. Since an ACE is defined for a specific user or group, it is possible to introduce conflicts. How does the Windows operating system resolve conflicting ACEs?

TABLE 3-4 Common CLSIDs	
CLSID	**DESCRIPTION**
::{20d04fe0-3aea-1069-a2d8-08002b30309d}	My Computer
::{450d8fba-ad25-11d0-98a8-0800361b1103}	My Documents
::{208d2c60-3aea-1069-a2d7-08002b30309d}	My Network Places
::{1f4de370-d627-11d1-ba4f-00a0c91eedba}	Network Computers
::{7007acc7-3202-11d1-aad2-00805fc1270e}	Network Connections
::{2227a280-3aea-1069-a2de-08002b30309d}	Printers and Faxes
::{645ff040-5081-101b-9f08-00aa002f954e}	Recycle Bin
::{d6277990-4c6a-11cf-8d87-00aa0060f5bf}	Scheduled Tasks
::{450d8fba-ad25-11d0-98a8-0800361b1103}\My Folder	Opens My Folder under My Documents; assumes the folder "My Folder" exists

© Jones & Bartlett Learning.

Windows resolves object access requests by following this procedure:

1. Retrieves user and group SIDs from the process's SAT.
2. Examines all ACEs in the object's DACL for requested permission.
   a. If no DACL or ACE is defined for the requested access, Windows allows the access.
   b. If only one ACE exists for the requested access, access is based on whether the ACE is defined as "allow" or "deny."
   c. If multiple ACEs exist for the same requested access, all ACEs must be defined as "allow" for Windows to allow the access. Any ACE defined as "deny" will result in Windows denying the access.
3. Returns an access approval or denial based on permissions.

Since overlapping ACEs can be confusing, Windows makes it easy to see the permissions in effect for any object. The Advanced Security Settings dialog box contains the **Effective Access** page to display calculated permissions for any user or group (**FIGURE 3-9**).

Choose the Select a User link to open the Select User or Group dialog box, type the desired user or group name, and then select OK. Select the View Effective Access button to display the effective permissions calculated for the entered user or group. Any permission checked in the Effective Access display means that permission is allowed for this user or group. An unchecked checkbox means the permission is denied.

Whenever Windows encounters ACE conflicts, "deny" always supersedes "allow." This feature makes it difficult to accidentally grant more access to users than intended.

Windows object
Effective Access.

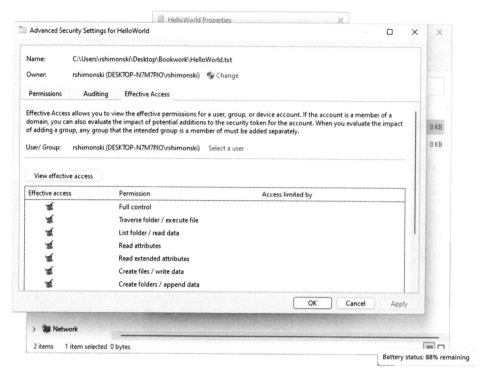

Auditing and Tracking Windows Access

Access control is primarily a set of preventive security controls. Preventive controls are mechanisms that prevent undesired actions from occurring. While it is good to prevent undesired actions, it is also helpful to get information on what the access controls are doing. Viewing access information can help validate access controls and identify any potential issues. Defined access controls may be either too restrictive or too permissive. Collecting performance information for later analysis can help fine-tune controls to make them more effective and precise.

Viewing Effective Access can provide valuable information. It can also be misleading. Viewing the Effective Access for a single group may not tell the whole story. A user who is associated with multiple groups may have less permission than expected at run time if the user is a member of a more restrictive group as well as the one you are viewing.

Auditing is the process of collecting performance information on which actions were taken and storing that information for later analysis. In the context of access control, auditing makes a record of desired, allowed, and denied-access requests. This information can be stored for a long or short time, allowing time to analyze how well access controls are doing their job.

The first step to collecting access control auditing information is to enable auditing. The process of enabling auditing tells Windows to record the events that will be defined for later

 TIP

Before enabling access control auditing, know what information is desired and how long it will be retained. Any auditing activity can create a substantial amount of output and add a performance load to your computer. Audit only events that need to be reviewed.

Technical TIP

To enable auditing for a local machine, log in as a member of the Administrators group, then choose Start > All apps > Windows Tools > Local Security Policy to launch the Local Security Policy maintenance tool (**FIGURE 3-10**). Expand Local Policies in the tree view on the left side of the window, then select Audit Policy. Several auditing options can be enabled. To enable auditing for logon events and object access, double-click Audit Logon Events and Audit Object Access. Each selection gives the option of logging both successful and unsuccessful actions. Unless you want to see a log message for every successful logon and object access, just choose Failure for both.

FYI

To launch the Windows Event Viewer, choose Start > All apps > Windows Tools > Event Viewer. In the Event Viewer, expand Windows Logs from the tree view on the left side of the window; then, select Security. Here you can find the audited events specifically the ones that were just configured for success and failure.

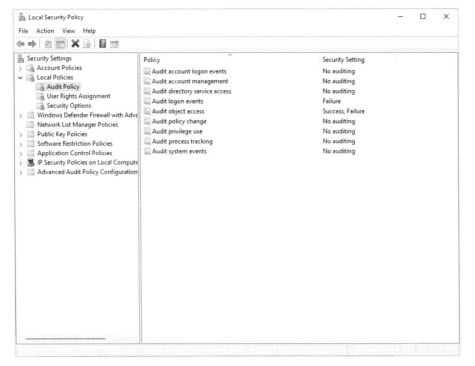

FIGURE 3-10

Local Audit Policy.

Courtesy of Microsoft
Corporation.

analysis. Windows stores audit event notes in event logs and makes it easy to see what has happened on Windows computers.

When enabling auditing for any event category, Windows asks if you want to record successful or failed events, or both. Carefully consider which event types would be beneficial.

> ⚠ **WARNING**
>
> Windows servers commonly provide resource access to many subjects. Consider the auditing needs before auditing any successful events. If you are unsure, try enabling the event category in question, waiting for a short period, and then looking at the audit log files to see how many events have occurred. The number of events will give you an idea of how many audit events to expect.

Each audit event that is recorded requires extra processing to save the event in a log file. Although the effort required for each event is small, it can add up for events that occur frequently. Limit audits to only those events that are needed.

The next step in auditing Windows computers is to view and analyze the log files that contain audit entries. Use the Windows Event Viewer to access audit event records.

Each row in the main Event Viewer window displays a single audit event. Details of the selected row display in the details section at the bottom of the window. The Event Viewer gives you the ability to filter the selected log for ad hoc analysis. You can save filter settings as custom views. The ability to filter events allows you to show only the events that are of most interest without having to scroll through the entire log file.

Expression-Based Security Audit Policy (Windows Server 2012 and Newer)

Windows Server provides administrators with the ability to use expression-based security audit policies. DAC in Windows Server enables administrators to create targeted audit policies by using expressions that are based on user, computer, and resource claims.

Here are two examples of expression-based audit policies that administrators can apply in Windows Server:

- Audit everyone who does not have a high security clearance and attempts to access highly sensitive documents.
- Audit all contractors when they try to access documents that are related to projects that they are not working on.

Policies with specific constraints can help limit the number of audit events and record only the most relevant data or users. Administrators can create expression-based audit policies directly on a file or folder or applied centrally through Group Policy.

Microsoft Windows Access Management Tools

> **TIP**
>
> All the tools listed in **TABLE 3-5** are command-line interface (CLI) tools. You launch these tools from a command prompt. To launch a command prompt window, choose Start > and then enter **cmd.exe** for a standard command prompt, or **powershell.exe** to launch the more powerful PowerShell. We will use PowerShell for examples in this text.

You have seen how to modify object DACLs using the Security page in the Properties dialog box. Although the Properties dialog box is easy to use, it is not effective for managing DACLs for multiple objects. Making bulk DACL changes in the Properties dialog box is a time-consuming process. Suppose you add a new group and want to add group permissions to the DACLs for a large number of objects. How would you do that without opening each object's Properties dialog box?

Fortunately, Microsoft provides several tools that make changing DACLs for a group of objects easy. **TABLE 3-5** lists the main ACL management tools and their uses.

TABLE 3-5 Windows ACL Management Tools	
TOOL	**DESCRIPTION**
Cacls.exe	Control Access Control List (CACLS) utility is a legacy command-line tool to display or modify ACLs for files or folders. **Cacls.exe** is still provided with current Windows versions.
Icacls.exe	Integrity Control Access Control List (ICACLS) utility is a command-line tool intended to replace and extend **cacls.exe**, and another legacy tool, **xcacls.exe**.**icacls.exe**, allows you to list, update, and back up file and folder ACLs.
Robocopy.exe	Robust File Copy (robocopy) is a command-line tool that copies files and folders with or without their associated ACLs.

© Jones & Bartlett Learning.

Cacls.exe

The Control Access Control List, cacls.exe, CLI tool was first introduced in Windows 2000. Although Windows now includes the icacls.exe tool as a newer, updated tool, Windows still includes the cacls.exe tool for those who are used to it and may have batch files that depend on it. The cacls.exe command allows users to list or modify the DACLs for one or more files or folders. A single file or folder can be specified, or wildcards can also be used for multiple files or folders. TABLE 3-6 shows a few cacls.exe examples and what each command accomplishes.

TABLE 3-6 Sample cacls.exe Commands	
COMMAND	**RESULT**
cacls testfile.txt	Lists ACLs for the testfile.txt. The output shows one line for each user or group, along with the permissions assigned to each user/group. Permissions will be one of the following: N—None R—Read W—Write C—Change (write) F—Full
cacls testfile.txt /e /g tpurvis:f	Grants the user "fpurvis" full access to the file testfile.txt.
cacls testfile*.txt /e /g erpusers:r	Grants the members of the "erpusers" group full access to all files that match the pattern "testfile*.txt."
cacls testfile.txt /e /r erpusers	Revokes access permission for members of the erpusers group to the file testfile.txt.
cacls C:\appdocs est /e /t /c /g erpusers:c	Grants the change access permission to members of the erpusers group to all files and folders in the C:\appdocs\test folder and all subfolders.

© Jones & Bartlett Learning.

Icacls.exe

The Integrity Control Access Control List, icacls.exe CLI tool replaces both the cacls.exe and the xcacls.exe tools. The icacls.exe tool enables the listing, updating, and backup of ACLs for both files and folders. You can also find files that belong to a particular user, change the ownership of files and folders, and replace the permissions for one user with permissions of a different user. **TABLE 3-7** shows a few icacls.exe examples and what each command accomplishes.

Robocopy, or "Robust Copy," is a CLI utility that has been available in the Windows Resource Kit for years. Far more than a simple file and folder copy utility, Robocopy provides the functionality to replicate objects and their ACLs in a volatile networked environment. Maintaining a solid access control policy requires keeping defined ACLs intact. Robocopy provides the ability to do just that. Robocopy incorporates many features, including the following:

- Provides the ability to resume copying where it left off in the case of interruption, as in the case of network disruptions
- Preserves attributes, owner information, auditing information, and timestamp information by default
- Copies all ACLs with objects
- Copies a large number of files without having to invoke the tool multiple times
- Copies long file and folder names
- Allows multithreaded copying

TABLE 3-8 shows a few robocopy.exe examples and what each command accomplishes.

TABLE 3-7 Sample icacls.exe Commands

COMMAND	RESULT
icacls C:\windows* /save AclFile /T	Saves the ACLs for all items in C:\windows folder and its subfolders into a file named AclFile
icacls C:\windows\ /restore AclFile	Restores the ACLs for every file within a file named AclFile to any relevant item that exists in C:\windows folder and its subfolders
icacls file /grant Administrator:(D,WDAC)	Grants the user named "Administrator" the Delete and Write permissions to a file named file
icacls file /grant *S-1-1-0:(D,WDAC)	Grants the user or security group whose security identifier is S-1-1-0 the Delete and Write permissions to a file named file
icacls C:\windows\explorer.exe	Displays the access control list for a file named C:\windows\explorer.exe
icacls file /setintegritylevel H	Modifies the mandatory integrity level of an object named file to High

TABLE 3-8 Sample robocopy.exe Commands

COMMAND	RESULT
robocopy C:\source C:\target /E	Copies folder contents recursively (/E) all files in C:\source to C:\target
robocopy C:\source C:\target /COPYALL /E	Copies folder contents recursively (/E) all files in C:\source to C:\target, including all ACL, owner, timestamp, and attribute information
robocopy C:\source \\ backupserver\target /MIR /Z	Mirrors source to target, destroying any files in target that are not present in source (/MIR), copies files in restartable mode (/Z) in case network connection is lost
robocopy C:\source C:\target testfile.txt	Copies the file testfile.txt from directory C:\source to C:\target

© Jones & Bartlett Learning.

Best Practices for Microsoft Windows Access Control

Microsoft provides tools to manage object ACLs and implement solid access control. A secure information system depends on a secure strategy. Best practices for access control center on solid planning and implementing a manageable approach to both subjects and objects. There are many schools of thought related to access control. One particular strategy provides clarity and security. The **AGULP** approach provides a method for managing any number of users predictably. AGULP may appear overly complex for smaller environments, but it really shines when a network has many users. AGULP is an acronym that stands for the following:

- **A**ccounts
- **G**lobal groups
- **U**niversal groups
- **L**ocal groups
- **P**ermissions

The idea behind AGULP is to systematically nest individual user accounts in groups to make securing objects more general. The first step is to create separate user accounts for each user. Creating separate accounts for each user's role adds an extra step of security. In this case, you may have more than one account. User accounts are then added to global groups, according to their shared attributes. These attributes can be geographical or functional, such as manufacturing or human resources. Global groups would then be added to universal groups, or groups that are defined for users in any domain in Active Directory. Global groups and universal groups are then added to local groups on computers that contain resources you want to secure. This strategy avoids the need to add individual users to local groups. Finally, the permissions for secured resources, or objects, are defined for local groups. The AGULP strategy allows you to reduce the number of ACLs for each resource. Regardless of the strategy you decide to use, avoid defining ACLs for individuals. Group-based ACLs are easier and more efficient to maintain.

CHAPTER SUMMARY

Securing information system resources means evaluating each resource request and deciding whether the request should be allowed or denied. While each request can be evaluated on a per-user basis, ease of maintenance often dictates a group-based strategy. Since many users have shared needs for specific resources, it makes sense to group users and assign permissions to resources based on these groups. Windows implements access controls by allowing you to define users, groups, and object DACLs that support your environment. You define the rules, and Windows enables you to enforce those rules.

KEY CONCEPTS AND TERMS

Access control entry (ACE)
AGULP
Auditing
Class Identifiers (CLSIDs)
Common Criteria for Information Technology Security Evaluation
Discretionary access control list (DACL)
Domain controller

Dynamic Access Control (DAC)
Effective Access
File Classification Infrastructure (FCI)
Globally unique identifier (GUID)
Groups
Kerberos
Key distribution center (KDC)
Least privilege user accounts (LUAs)

Managed service accounts
Orange Book
Principle of least privilege
Public key
Rights Management Services (RMS)
Security Access Token (SAT)
Universally unique identifier (UUID)
User Account Control (UAC)

CHAPTER 3 ASSESSMENT

1. Which of the following best describes the principle of least privilege?
   A. Providing the necessary access to carry out any task
   B. Providing access to the least number of objects possible
   C. Providing just the necessary access required to carry out a task
   D. Providing access equivalent to the least populated security group

2. Which type of user account is designed using the principle of least privilege?
   A. LUA
   B. SID
   C. GUID
   D. KDC

3. What structure does the Windows operating system use to store collections of permissions for objects?
   A. ACE
   B. DACL
   C. GUID
   D. CLSID

4. If a regular user is a member of four groups, how many SIDs will be stored in the user's SAT?
   A. 1
   B. 4
   C. 5
   D. 6

5. Which of the following best describes UAC?

A. Prompts users before escalating to administrator privileges

B. Prevents processes from escalating to administrator privileges

C. Terminates programs that attempt to escalate to administrator privileges

D. Alerts users that attempts to escalate to administrator privileges have been automatically denied

6. Which protocol does the Windows operating system use by default to authenticate computers to exchange security information?

A. Kerberos

B. NTLM

C. SAML

D. TCP/IP

7. When viewing an object's DACL, which permission indicates that advanced permissions have been set?

A. Extended permissions

B. Advanced permissions

C. Special permissions

D. Level II permissions

8. Which type of identifier was originally adopted by Windows to identify GUI controls?

A. SID

B. PID

C. CLSID

D. GUID

9. Which type of identifier is used to identify user groups?

A. SID

B. PID

C. CLSID

D. GUID

10. If a user, userA, is a member of groupA and groupB, and groupB allows read access to a file named helloWorld.c, but groupA denies read access to helloWorld.c, can userA read helloWorld.c?

A. Yes, because groupA allows read access to helloWorld.c.

B. No, because groupB denies read access to helloWorld.c.

C. Yes, because userA is a member of groupB.

D. No, because users cannot belong to multiple groups.

11. Why should you carefully design an auditing strategy before turning auditing on?

A. Auditing incomplete information wastes analysis time.

B. Auditing too much information causes excessive overhead.

C. Ad hoc auditing rarely provides useful information.

D. Audit log files only retain limited information without extensive configuration.

12. Which of the following guidelines tends to provide the most useful auditing information?

A. Always audit event success and failures.

B. Never audit both event successes and failures.

C. Generally audit event failures.

D. Do not audit event failures unless you first audit event successes.

13. What tool is most commonly used to view and search audit logs?

A. Windows Event Viewer

B. Windows Log Viewer

C. Windows Audit Viewer

D. Windows ACL Viewer

14. Which of the following Windows tools replaces previous legacy tools and allows ACL modifications?

A. cacls

B. xcacls

C. icacls

D. robocopy

15. When using AGULP, for which entity type are local object permissions defined?

A. User accounts

B. Global groups

C. Universal groups

D. Domain local groups

Microsoft Windows Encryption Tools and Technologies

SECURING DATA BY RESTRICTING access to objects using operating system access controls works well for **data at rest**, or data that is stored at a single location. Access controls limit which subjects can read or write data. This provides a level of security while the data remain on the object's storage device, accessible only through Windows. The problem with this configuration is that functional data tends to be used. Sensitive data are stored in objects that need to be secured. They are also accessed at some point for the purpose of being presented, manipulated, or transmitted to another subject. Once data leaves its protected storage device, you need to provide additional protection to ensure its security is maintained. Along with provided protection, users of sensitive data need to be held accountable for the manner in which they use that data. Security is a team effort.

In this chapter, you'll learn about different strategies Microsoft Windows supports to secure data at rest and **data in transit**. Data that are in transit are being sent from one location to another. **Encryption** is the most common technique used to secure data in transit. Properly used encryption can make unauthorized accessing, viewing, or changing protected data very difficult. You'll also learn how encryption can be used to secure data at rest to provide an additional layer of protection over and above correctly deployed access controls. Encryption is another valuable strategy for securing your information.

Chapter 4 Topics

This chapter covers the following topics and concepts:

- Which encryption methods Microsoft Windows supports
- What Encrypting File System, BitLocker, and BitLocker To Go are
- How to enable file-, folder-, and volume-level encryption
- What encryption in communications is
- What encryption protocols in Microsoft Windows are
- What security certificates are
- What the public key infrastructure (PKI) is
- What best practices for Microsoft Windows encryption techniques are

Chapter 4 Goals

When you complete this chapter, you will be able to:

- Identify encryption methods supported by Microsoft Windows
- Describe EFS, BitLocker, and BitLocker To Go
- Explain setup and enabling of file-, folder-, and volume-level encryption
- Research encryption in communications
- Outline encrypted Microsoft Windows protocols
- Debate the advantages and the disadvantages of encrypted communications
- Describe security certificates
- Examine the public key infrastructure (PKI)
- Outline best practices for Microsoft Windows encryption techniques
- Discuss business challenges of implementing encryption

Encryption Methods Microsoft Windows Supports

Microsoft Windows access controls depend on users using Windows to access the secured objects. But what if an attacker is able to bypass Windows and its access controls? Nearly all of today's computers support multiple **boot devices**. It is not difficult to create a bootable USB device that loads another operating system and completely bypasses controls. Such a boot device could provide direct access to disks and other connected devices without the access controls defined in Windows. In short, an attacker can boot another operating system, effectively bypass all access controls, and gain full access to stored data unless security measures are in place to protect against this type of access.

 WARNING

Just booting a computer using another operating system, such as Linux, is not enough to bypass access controls. The booted operating system has to be configured with drivers and software specifically designed to access New Technology File System (NTFS). It may take a little work, but it's not hard to do.

 WARNING

Since decrypting data depends on having access to the decryption keys, you'll need to carefully protect both the primary and recovery keys. If both sets of keys are damaged or lost, you can't decrypt the data.

Attacking a computer by booting into a different operating system is easy. Windows access controls alone are not sufficient to protect data. This is a prime example that highlights the need for a defense-in-depth strategy. You need additional controls to protect sensitive data. One type of additional control should be physical controls to limit direct access to computers that store sensitive data. By limiting physical access, you make it more difficult for an attacker to insert a disk or USB device and boot a computer from alternate media. You can also deactivate or disable disk insertion or USB ports entirely to remove the ability for these attack vectors to be used. As an example, a cloud-hosted virtual machine in Azure is secure against bootable attacks. Further, bootable attacks are very common to threats originating internally to your network; therefore, having physical security safeguards in place can also help to secure against local bootable attacks. Either way, the best way to secure against this attack type and vector is by encrypting your disks.

Files, folders, and volumes can be encrypted using Windows encryption. Windows-encrypted files cannot be booted into via another operating system. Windows stores the **decryption keys**. An attacker could still potentially boot from alternate media, but the data on the storage devices would be encrypted and useless outside Windows. Whether the encrypted data are stored on a disk or backed up onto other media, they are useless without the decryption keys. Encryption makes stealing backup media far less attractive to attackers. Encryption provides a valuable additional layer in your defense strategy.

Encryption is handy when transferring data between programs. Programs can reside on the same or different computers. It is important to protect sensitive information as it is being transferred from one storage location to another. Commonly, networks are used to transport data. This type of data transport can be vulnerable to attack. Encryption is used to ensure that no unauthorized user can view sensitive data. Encryption also validates both the integrity and the source of the data via the use of digital signatures.

Microsoft provides various programs and methods to secure data with encryption. For securing data at rest, Microsoft includes the following:

> **▶ TIP**
>
> If you need to support multiple operating systems, you'll need to look beyond the Windows-only options presented in this section. For many years, one of the most popular cross-platform encryption products was Truecrypt. This open source utility is still available on multiple operating systems and makes it easy to encrypt files and entire drives. However, Truecrypt was discontinued in 2014 and has not been updated since then. It is recommended that organizations using Truecrypt discontinue its use because the product is not updated with security patches. The most popular alternative solution is Veracrypt. Veracrypt is a fork of Truecrypt and is currently supported. You can find out more about this free product at https://www.veracrypt.fr.

- BitLocker for encrypting entire volumes
- Encrypting File System (EFS) for encrypting files and folders

For securing data in transit, Microsoft provides support for many methods and strategies:

- Secure networking protocols
- Digital certificates
- Public key infrastructure (PKI)
- Virtual private network (VPN)

Encrypting File System, BitLocker, and BitLocker To Go

The Windows operating system supports the ability to encrypt stored data. They include **Encrypting File System (EFS)**, **BitLocker**, and **BitLocker To Go** and are directly a part of the operating system. Each method has its place and should be considered based on specific capabilities. The best choice of data at rest encryption depends on the scope of encrypted data and the location of the data. These three methods are specific to Microsoft Windows operating systems.

FIGURE 4-1

Object properties page.
Courtesy of Microsoft Corporation.

Encrypting File System

Microsoft introduced the EFS in Windows 2000. This feature works only for NTFS file systems. It allows users to encrypt files or entire folders. You can enable the encryption for files or folders simply by selecting a checkbox on the object's properties page. It doesn't require any additional input from the user. **FIGURE 4-1** shows the object property page's encryption setting.

Current versions of EFS use a **symmetric key** partially derived from the user's password. The choice of a symmetric key provides faster encryption and decryption. Previous versions of Windows used Data Encryption Standard-X (DESX) or **Advanced Encryption Standard (AES)** as the default encryption algorithm. The latest versions of both Windows server and client operating systems use a mixed mode of AES, **Secure Hash Algorithm (SHA)**, and **Elliptic Curve Cryptography (ECC)** algorithms. With Windows Server 2022, there are even enhancements on Server Message Block (SMB) utilizing 256 AES encryption. This allows maximum strength and flexibility. The advantage of EFS is its simplicity, transparency, and ability to limit the scope of encrypted data.

The main drawback to EFS is that it is user-based. Each user must choose to enable encryption for specific files or folders. Alternatively,

> ⚠ **WARNING**
>
> If you are using EFS, do not change passwords except through Windows. It's not hard to search the internet and find bootable images that will reset passwords for you. These utilities operate by booting an alternate operating system and modifying system files on your computer. Since this change occurs outside Windows, all EFS encrypted data owned by the user whose password is reset will be lost! Change user passwords only from within Windows.

administrators must define policies that require encryption. The key used to encrypt and decrypt data is based on the user's password. Using any tool that resets passwords outside of Windows will result in your losing all encrypted data for that user.

You must also take care to avoid using single file encryption for sensitive files. When using single file encryption, the file is written in **plaintext**—unencrypted—to the disk and then encrypted. The plaintext file is then deleted. However, many utilities exist that make it easy to recover deleted files. If the data have not been overwritten, you can easily read the unencrypted data.

> ⚠ **WARNING**
>
> Since EFS-encrypted files are written to disk unencrypted first, Windows leaves traces of files that can be vulnerable to attack. To avoid leaving unencrypted data lying around, only use folder encryption. That way, the data in the folder are never stored unencrypted.

BitLocker

A more current encryption method included in Windows is BitLocker Drive Encryption. Windows Vista first introduced BitLocker in the Ultimate and Enterprise versions.

Unlike EFS, BitLocker only has two settings for each volume: on or off. You can't selectively choose which files or folders you want to encrypt. Everything on the selected volume is encrypted. Since entire volumes are encrypted, only administrators can enable or disable encryption. Individual users cannot alter any BitLocker settings. BitLocker also differs from EFS in how it encrypts data. All but one of the BitLocker operation modes depend on the computer's **Trusted Platform Module (TPM)** microchip to manage and protect the key used for volume encryption and decryption. Most computers manufactured within the last several years contain the required TPM hardware to support BitLocker, and this technology is incredibly helpful in allowing vendors to ensure security along with the Microsoft OS in the creation and storage of cryptographic keys.

> ▶ **TIP**
>
> "BitLocker full disk encryption" is a misnomer. Disks refer to physical disk drives. Any computer may have several physical disk drives. Each disk is formatted, and one or more disk volumes are created on each one. A disk volume is normally shown as drive letters such as "C:" or "D:" in the operating system. BitLocker is actually a disk volume encryption tool, since it encrypts entire volumes.

BitLocker offers several authentication modes, based on input requirements for credentials. **TABLE 4-1** lists the BitLocker authentications modes.

BitLocker and EFS solve similar problems but use different approaches. Each approaches the goal of securing data at different levels and with different requirements. **TABLE 4-2** compares the major features of BitLocker and EFS.

EFS is present in the latest newly installed Windows clients and servers. BitLocker is available on Windows workstation computers but is not enabled by default for most Windows Server editions. If you plan to use BitLocker on Windows Server, you must enable it using the Server Manager utility. To launch Server Manager, choose Start > Server Manager. In Server Manager, select Manage > Add Roles and Features from the menu to open the Add Roles and Features Wizard. Select Next three times and then select the Features selection in the open dialog window. Select the BitLocker Drive Encryption checkbox to add BitLocker. **FIGURES 4-2** and **4-3** show the Server Manager and the Add Features Wizard window.

> ▶ **TIP**
>
> One attractive advantage of relying on the TPM hardware is that encryption can occur with no input from the user—the encryption operations are totally transparent.

4

Microsoft Windows Encryption Tools and Technologies

TABLE 4-1 BitLocker Authentication Modes

MECHANISM	AUTHENTICATION MODE	DESCRIPTION
TPM only	Transparent operation	No additional input is required from the user.
TPM + PIN	User authentication	The user is required to enter a PIN before Windows boots.
TPM + PIN + USB key	User authentication	The user is required to enter a PIN, called the Startup PIN, and insert a USB key, called the Startup key, with authentication credentials before Windows boots.
TPM + USB key	User authentication	The user is required to insert a USB key with authentication credentials before Windows boots.
USB key only	USB key mode	The only authentication mode that does not depend on TPM hardware—the user only inserts a USB with authentication credentials before Windows boots.

© Jones & Bartlett Learning.

TABLE 4-2 BitLocker and EFS Feature Comparison

BITLOCKER	ENCRYPTING FILE SYSTEM (EFS)
Encrypts all files on the selected volume	Encrypts only selected files and folders.
Either on or off for all users	Encrypts files based on user actions—each user can encrypt files or folders individually.
Uses TPM or USB key as part of the authentication process	Does not require any special hardware.
Must be administrator to turn BitLocker on or off	Any user can choose to encrypt files or folders.

© Jones & Bartlett Learning.

Before adding BitLocker, Windows will ask you to confirm that you want to continue. Select Next > Install to confirm your choice to add BitLocker. Once BitLocker has been installed, Windows will warn you that you must restart the system. When you select Close, Windows will ask if you want to restart your system now or later. Once you

FIGURE 4-2

Server Manager—Features.

Courtesy of Microsoft Corporation.

FIGURE 4-3

Install new BitLocker
feature.

Courtesy of Microsoft
Corporation.

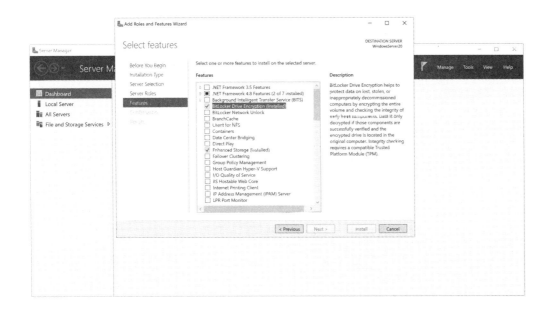

4

Microsoft Windows Encryption
Tools and Technologies

NOTE

In some deployments of Windows Server, you will find BitLocker enabled by default. For example, an Azure cloud-hosted Windows Server 2022 Datacenter system comes with the host enabled with BitLocker by default. If you would like, you can uninstall the feature, reboot, and then reinstall it in order to complete the exercises.

restart Windows, the BitLocker feature will be available for all volumes. **FIGURES 4-4**, **4-5A**, and **4-5B** show the confirmation and completion windows.

Microsoft added new features to BitLocker starting with Windows 8 and Windows Server 2012. The added features make it even easier to encrypt files on a Windows computer. Here is a list of the BitLocker features used in Windows:

- **BitLocker provisioning**—In previous Windows versions, BitLocker could be enabled only after installing the operating system. Now, administrators can enable BitLocker as part of the Windows workstation installation process. This allows administrators to deploy Windows workstations in an encrypted state.

- **Encrypt only used disk space**—BitLocker now allows administrators to encrypt only blocks in a volume that are used to store data. When using this option, BitLocker will not encrypt unused blocks. This option can dramatically reduce the time required to initially encrypt an existing volume.

- **Allow regular users to change BitLocker PIN or password**—Regular users can change the Windows workstation BitLocker PIN or password for operating system volumes. Regular users can also change the Windows workstation BitLocker for fixed data volumes. These features make it easier for administrators to deploy BitLocker to a large number of computers without having to use only generated PINs and passwords.

FIGURE 4-4

Confirm BitLocker installation.

Courtesy of Microsoft Corporation.

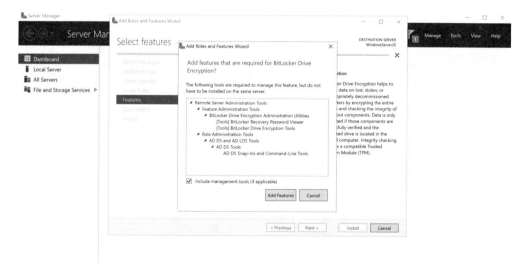

FIGURE 4-5

Completed BitLocker installation.

Courtesy of Microsoft Corporation.

A

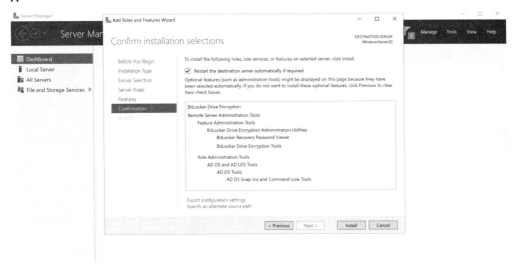

B

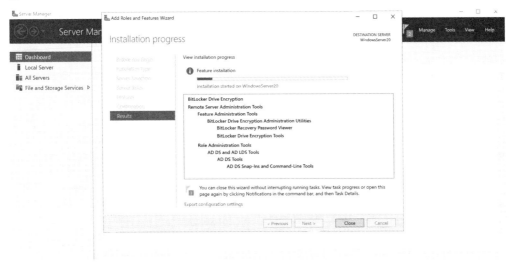

- **Network unlock**—The current Windows Server feature allows desktop and server computers to automatically unlock operating system volumes when they boot. To use this feature, computers must be connected to a trusted wired network.
- **Support for encrypted hard drives**—Bitlocker is a software solution that provides **Full Volume Encryption (FVE)**. Another encryption method gaining popularity is **Full Disk Encryption (FDE)**. In FDE, the disk controller encrypts each block. FDE is faster than FVE,

since it occurs at a lower level than the operating system. BitLocker since Windows 8 and Windows Server 2012 supports encrypted hard drives that use FDE.

BitLocker To Go

BitLocker To Go is an extension to BitLocker that protects removable storage devices, such as USB keys. Since removable storage devices may be used to transport sensitive data from one computer to another, it is important to ensure the data are secure as they are being transported. BitLocker To Go makes it easy to encrypt an entire device. When you turn on BitLocker To Go for a device, Windows asks whether to use a password or a **smart card** to encrypt the data.

 TIP

Since removable devices routinely transport files among computers, it wouldn't make much sense to store encryption keys on one computer's TPM hardware. That would make the device usable only on that computer. For that reason, TPM encryption isn't an option for BitLocker To Go.

Once initialized, all data on the removable device are encrypted. You'll need to enter the same password or use your smart card to access the media's contents on the other computer (based on which option you selected when you enabled BitLocker To Go). As long as the other computer is running Windows 7 or later, you'll just be prompted for the password or smart card.

Enabling File-, Folder-, and Volume-Level Encryption

Enabling EFS, BitLocker, and BitLocker To Go is easy. All you have to do is open the Properties dialog box for the desired object and select the appropriate option. Here's how to enable each type of encryption.

Enabling EFS

The first step to enabling EFS is deciding what to encrypt. Remember that individual files are stored on disk in plaintext form—unencrypted—before being encrypted. After being encrypted, the plaintext files are deleted, but not totally removed. To avoid any traces of plaintext files being left, it is recommended that you use folder encryption. Once you decide what to encrypt, open Windows Explorer and navigate to the file or folder. To encrypt the object, open the context menu by right-clicking on the object, and select Properties. From the Properties dialog box, choose the Advanced button. In the Advanced Attributes dialog box, select the "Encrypt contents to secure data" checkbox, choose OK, then choose OK again to close the Properties dialog box. The object is now stored as an encrypted object. No further action from the user is necessary. **FIGURE 4-6** shows the Properties and Advanced Attributes dialog boxes.

Enabling BitLocker

Enabling BitLocker is just as easy as EFS. First, however, ensure that you are logged on as an administrator user. To enable BitLocker, open Windows Explorer and navigate to Computer. Open the context menu of the selected volume by right-clicking on the desired volume, and select Turn On BitLocker. **FIGURE 4-7** shows the BitLocker option on the object's context menu.

FIGURE 4-6

Object properties—Advanced attributes.

Courtesy of Microsoft Corporation.

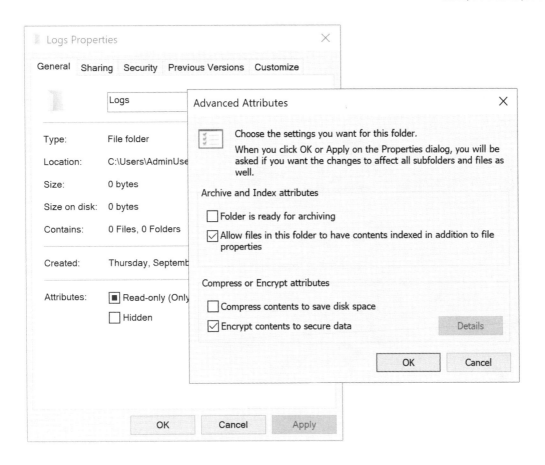

Alternatively, you can launch the BitLocker management tool to view and manage BitLocker for all volumes. Open the Control Panel by selecting Start > Control Panel. Select System and Security, then BitLocker Drive Encryption. The BitLocker management tool displays all volumes, along with an option to turn BitLocker on or off for each volume. **FIGURE 4-8** shows the BitLocker management tool.

After selecting to enable BitLocker, Windows asks you to pick an authentication method. The authentication method tells Windows what information is required to access an encrypted volume. **FIGURE 4-9** shows the BitLocker Authentication options.

▶ **TIP**

Note that you can select more than one BitLocker Authentication option. Selecting more than one option requires a user to provide more than one type of authentication before Windows boots and allows access to the encrypted volumes.

FIGURE 4-7

Enabling BitLocker.

Courtesy of Microsoft Corporation.

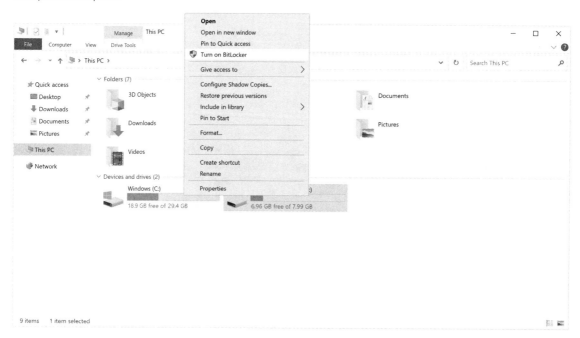

FIGURE 4-8

BitLocker management tool.

Courtesy of Microsoft Corporation.

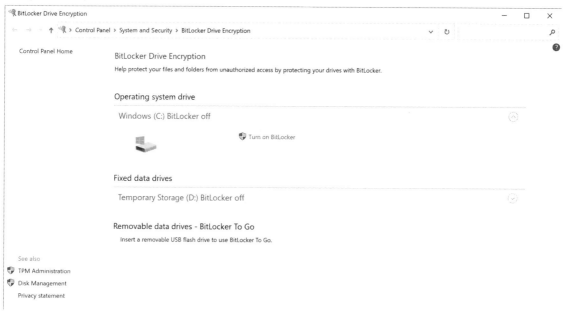

FIGURE 4-9

BitLocker authentication options.

Courtesy of Microsoft Corporation.

×

← 🖭 BitLocker Drive Encryption (D:)

Choose how you want to unlock this drive

☐ Use a password to unlock the drive

    Passwords should contain uppercase and lowercase letters, numbers, spaces, and symbols.

    Enter your password

    Reenter your password

☐ Use my smart card to unlock the drive

    You'll need to insert your smart card. The smart card PIN will be required when you unlock the drive.

        Next   Cancel

4

Microsoft Windows Encryption Tools and Technologies

Once you select the desired authentication options, Windows will ask where to save a **recovery key**. If you lose the ability to access the primary encryption key, you'll need the recovery key to decrypt the volume. Windows provides the following options for storing the recovery key:

- Save the recovery key to a USB flash drive.
- Save the recovery key to a file.
- Print the recovery key.

Enabling BitLocker To Go

Enabling BitLocker To Go is very similar to enabling BitLocker. The big difference between the two is that BitLocker works to encrypt system disks while BitLocker To Go focused on removable media such as SD cards, removable drives and other removable media. Before starting the procedure, ensure your removable

> ⚠️ **WARNING**
>
> Ensure your recovery key is secure and available in case of a failure. For example, a motherboard hardware failure makes the primary key unavailable. If you save the recovery key to a file, don't save it to the volume that is being encrypted.

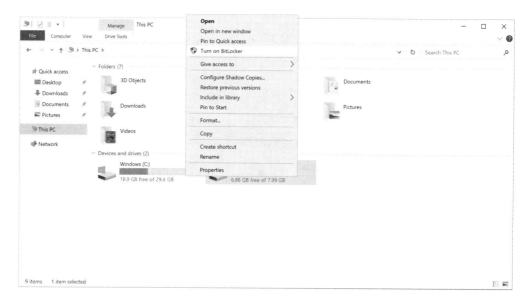

▶ **TIP**

Notice that there is no "Administrator required" icon next to the "Turn On BitLocker" as there was for fixed drives. That is because any user can enable BitLocker To Go. You don't have to be an administrator to enable BitLocker To Go on removable devices.

device is attached. First, open Windows Explorer and navigate to Computer. Open the context menu of the selected removable volume by right-clicking on the desired volume, and select Turn On BitLocker. **FIGURE 4-10** shows the BitLocker To Go option on the object's context menu.

The rest of the process for enabling BitLocker To Go is identical to enabling Bitlocker.

Encryption in Communications

Encryption is commonly used for more than just data at rest. It can be used to keep data secure as they are transferred from one place to another. You have already seen how BitLocker To Go can encrypt data on removable media. This is a combination of data at rest and data in transit. BitLocker To Go encryption is technically just encryption of data at rest. A common use of removable media is to transport data from one computer to another. Encryption protects the data by making the data unreadable by anyone who does not possess a valid decryption key. If the removable device is lost or stolen, the contents are unreadable without a decryption key.

Communication data encryption is similar to the concept of BitLocker To Go. Data are encrypted as they are placed on the transmission media. Data are transmitted from the sending process to the receiving process. Here, they are decrypted and used as normal data. **FIGURE 4-11** shows the encryption process when used for data transmission.

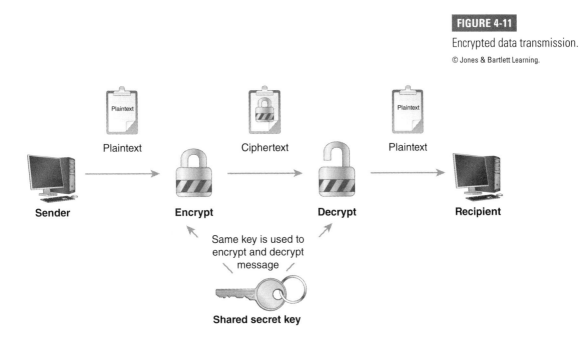

FIGURE 4-11

Encrypted data transmission.
© Jones & Bartlett Learning.

Many methods are available for secure data transfer. You can encrypt individual messages or create an encrypted connection, or tunnel, to encrypt all data between a sender and a receiver. Regardless of the method or protocols you choose, the goal of communication encryption is to make it very difficult for unauthorized users to access the contents of a message.

The most common perception of encryption is to ensure confidentiality. Encryption provides the ability to "hide" data from unauthorized users. It also provides integrity and nonrepudiation. Integrity is provided by ensuring data have not been modified since they were encrypted. This is often accomplished by calculating hash or checksum values. These values are then sent along with the data. **Nonrepudiation** means that a receiver can verify the source of a message. Additionally, the sender cannot deny sending the message. Windows supports the use of digital signatures to provide nonrepudiation. You'll learn about several ways Windows uses encryption in the following sections.

> **TIP**
>
> Encryption should never be the only control in place to protect data. Good physical controls are important to protect physical media. Other technical controls, such as a firewall, should be in place to provide additional barriers to attackers. Encryption should be necessary only if other controls have failed to keep unauthorized subjects away from sensitive information.

4

Microsoft Windows Encryption Tools and Technologies

Encryption Protocols in Microsoft Windows

Windows includes support for several protocols to provide the infrastructure for encrypted communication. Since encryption can be invoked at several different levels, Windows includes a rich set of protocols to support various encryption needs.

Transport Layer Security

One of the most common types of encrypted communication is the **Transport Layer Security (TLS)**. TLS was formerly called **Secure Sockets Layer (SSL)**. It was originally introduced to secure web application communication. TLS provides the secure channel for the Hypertext Transfer Protocol Secure (HTTPS) protocol for secure webpages. TLS creates an encrypted tunnel between a web client, most commonly a web browser, and a web server. All data sent back and forth between the server and the client are encrypted. The client and server negotiate a **cipher** and then exchange a key using **public key cryptography**. Once the key has been securely exchanged, both sides use the symmetric key for subsequent communications. **FIGURE 4-12** shows a secure connection between a web client and a web server. TLS is especially useful in wireless environments where it is easy to snoop packets by using readily available hardware and software.

Although SSL/TLS was created for web application communication, it is commonly used in many applications, including Remote Desktop, database connections, and any network connections that require exchanging encrypted data.

> **Note**
>
> With newer versions of Windows and the release of Windows Server 2022, new communication protocol security is at the forefront of protecting information with encryption. When it comes to secure connectivity and the transport of data, HTTPS and TLS 1.3 are enabled by default. It should be noted that this means for backward compatibility with older clients, you may need to perform some additional maintenance to allow connectivity.

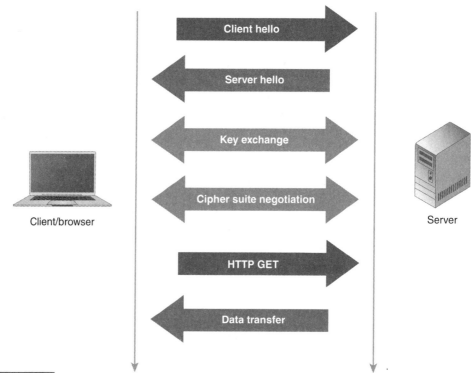

FIGURE 4-12

Secure web application connection.

© Jones & Bartlett Learning.

Internet Protocol Security

Internet Protocol Security (IPSec) is another secure network protocol suite. IPsec operates at a lower level than SSL/TLS and is used to provide encryption for IPV4 traffic. IPSec can be used to encrypt traffic between hosts (host-to-host), two networks (network-to-network), or between a gateway and a host (network-to-host). IPSec authenticates each endpoint and then encrypts all IPV4 traffic between the endpoints. IPSec was designed to overcome the weaknesses of IPV4, is recommended for use anytime IPV4 traffic needs to be secured, and is integrated into Active Directory. Administrators can set up and manage IPSec through Local or Group Policies.

Virtual Private Network

Another type of encrypted communication is a **virtual private network (VPN)**. This type of communication exists between a client and a server or between two servers. Once the VPN is established, all messages exchanged between the computers are encrypted. The difference between a VPN and a standard TLS connection is the number of applications each can handle. The TLS connection is generally limited to a single application, while the VPN may transport data from many different applications.

A client must initiate a VPN. During negotiation, the client and the server agree on a protocol and other connection settings, a **pre-shared key (PSK)**, and set up an encrypted tunnel. The tunnel looks like a regular network connection to local applications and doesn't require any special processing. Applications send unencrypted messages to one another while the VPN endpoints take care of the encryption and decryption. **FIGURE 4-13** shows a VPN.

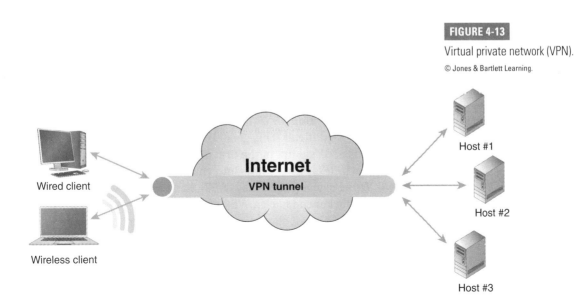

FIGURE 4-13

Virtual private network (VPN).

© Jones & Bartlett Learning.

WARNING

Depending upon the VPN configuration, PPTP VPNs need ports TCP/1723 and UPD/500 open to operate. L2TP needs ports TCP/1701 and UDP/500 open to operate. If any network device between the client and server blocks traffic on any of these ports, the VPN will not work. If they don't work, talk to your organizations firewall administrator.

 TIP

The VPN protocols discussed so far are all supported directly by the Windows operating system. Another popular VPN protocol is an open-source VPN named OpenVPN. OpenVPN requires external software that must be downloaded for both the server and the client but provides point-to-point and site-to-site secure connections and works across many platforms. OpenVPN is a newer VPN protocol that is very secure due to its use of the latest encryption standards.

Several protocols are commonly used in VPNs. The most common VPN protocol pair is the IPSec with **Layer 2 Tunneling Protocol (L2TP)**. This protocol pair, often referred to as L2TP/IPSec, provides end-to-end tunneling with optional encryption and is supported both with and without a pre-shared key option. Internet Key Exchange (IKEv2) is a tunneling protocol based on IPSec. Version 2 was developed by Microsoft and Cisco and is part of the Windows operating system. IKEv2 doesn't support as many platforms as other popular VPN protocols, but it is very secure and fast. The other common VPN protocol used in legacy systems is the **Point-to-Point Tunneling Protocol (PPTP)**. Windows supports both IPSec/L2TP and PPTP when setting up VPNs. One drawback to both protocols is that they can have problems with **firewalls** and **web proxies**, among other things. Each of these protocols uses specific ports that must be open through network devices for the protocol to work.

Microsoft introduced a new VPN protocol for Windows Vista Service Pack 1 and Windows Server 2008—**Secure Socket Tunneling Protocol (SSTP)**. It establishes an encrypted tunnel over an SSL/TLS connection. The advantage of using SSL/TLS is that only port TCP/443 is required for the protocol to operate. Since this is the same default port for secure webpages using SSL/TLS protocol, it is commonly open through most network devices that connect to the outside world. Although SSTP provides more flexibility than the other two common protocols, it does not support site-to-site tunnels.

Wireless Security

More and more devices are connected to a network using wireless connections. These connections are often temporary. They allow authorized users to connect to enterprise resources from insecure locations, such as coffee shops. Although VPNs can secure all traffic flowing between the client computer and enterprise network, all other traffic will be transmitted in the clear unless another form of encryption is employed.

It is cumbersome to enable encryption for transient public wireless networks because it makes connecting more difficult. This generally conflicts with the provider's purpose of installing a wireless access point in the first place. Despite this, you should use encryption for all wireless entry points into your network. The original wireless security protocol, **Wired Equivalent Privacy (WEP)**, has been shown to be easily compromised. A determined attacker can hack a WEP key in just a few minutes. Today, it is highly discouraged to use WEP, and it should, in fact, never be used due to its simplistic ability to be exploited. The successor to WEP is **Wi-Fi Protected Access (WPA)**.

The original WPA implemented only a portion of the IEEE 802.11i standard. The successor to WPA, WPA2, is a full 802.11i implementation. While the full WPA2 protocol requires an 802.11X server, the PSK mode bypasses the complexity of the authentication server. Simpler WPA implementations, including most homes and small businesses, use WPA-PSK or WPA2-PSK. The Wi-Fi Alliance has announced the availability of WPA3, the latest technology to secure wireless communication. WPA3 focuses on making general use devices on wireless networks easier to secure and harder to compromise. WPA3 raises the bar with a more secure handshake, stronger security through larger key sizes, and the ability to stop basic attacks.

Microsoft Windows and Security Certificates

There are two main types of encryption algorithms: symmetric and asymmetric. Symmetric algorithms use the same key to encrypt and decrypt data. **Asymmetric algorithms** use two related keys—one key to encrypt data and another key to decrypt data. In general, symmetric algorithms are faster than asymmetric algorithms of the same strength. For large amounts of data or frequent encryption/decryption cycles, symmetric algorithms are preferable to asymmetric algorithms because of the faster execution time.

The main problem with using symmetric algorithms in distributed applications, such as web applications or VPNs, is getting the same key to both server and client. If you can't get the encryption key to a client in a secure manner, then you can't create a secure connection. One approach to the problem is to only use asymmetric encryption. Asymmetric encryption is slower and requires substantial overhead to maintain connections.

A novel solution is to use asymmetric encryption to exchange a symmetric key. The receiver receives a message containing the symmetric encryption key that has been encrypted using the sender's private key. The receiver can decrypt the message with the sender's public key. Once the key is properly exchanged, all subsequent communication can use the faster symmetric encryption. One problem with this approach is ensuring there is trust when negotiating and exchanging encryption keys during connection setup. You have to trust that the sender is who he or she claims to be and not an imposter.

A **security certificate**, also called a **digital certificate**, is used to deliver a trusted public key that can be used with assurance that it belongs to the stated owner. In other words, a digital certificate is used to authenticate the identity of the certificate's owner to others. A security certificate is a document that contains identity information and a public key, along with other descriptive information. The document is then encrypted with the private key of a trusted entity. A digital certificate can be decrypted using the public key of the trusted entity—if it came from the trusted entity. Once successfully decrypted, the document will contain the public key from a source that can be trusted—at least you can trust that the key came from the stated source. The most commonly used format for digital certificates is defined by the **International Telecommunications Union (ITU-T)** and **X.509** standard. **TABLE 4-3** shows the most common types of digital certificates and how each one is used.

TABLE 4-3 Main Types of Digital Certificates	
CERTIFICATE TYPE	**DESCRIPTION**
TLS/SSL Server certificate	A certificate presented by a TLS/SSL server to authenticate that server during a TLS/SSL connection setup.
TLS/SSL Client certificate	A certificate presented by a TLS/SSL client during TLS/SSL connection setup when bidirectional (server and client) authentication is required.
Email certificate	The S/MIME secure email protocol uses an email certificate for the message recipient to acquire the recipient's public key and uses it to encrypt email messages for that recipient.
Code Signing certificate	A certificate used to validate signatures of compiled programs used to detect any unauthorized changes made after signing.
Qualified certificate	A certificate that identifies an individual and is commonly used with electronic signatures.
Self-signed certificate	A certificate signed by the issuer. When a certificate is not issued by a trusted authority, the value of the self-signed certificate relies on the trust a certificate user has for the issuer. Generally regarded as untrusted, self-signed certificates are sometimes called snake oil certificates.

© Jones & Bartlett Learning.

Public Key Infrastructure

The general approach to handling keys using trusted entities and digital certificates has been formalized into a strategy called the **public key infrastructure (PKI)**. PKI is the collection of hardware, software, policies, and procedures needed to manage digital certificates. The PKI process starts with a list of trusted entities and their public keys. A trusted entity is generally a **certificate authority (CA)** or a defined **trusted source**. Each computer system contains a list of public keys of trusted entities. A document that is encrypted with a trusted entity's private key can be decrypted with the same entity's public key.

When setting up a connection, you would first obtain a security certificate from a trusted entity. The formal PKI process would require you to request a certificate for the connection's target, or other end, from the PKI **registration authority (RA)**. The RA authenticates you and directs the CA to issue the certificate. You would decrypt the certificate using the CA's public key. The certificate contains the public key for the target. Once the target's public key is obtained, you can use it to encrypt messages that only the target can decrypt with its private key.

Best Practices for Windows Encryption Techniques

Many options and strategies should be considered when implementing encryption in Windows. Encryption can provide a valuable layer of protection for data, but it does come with a cost. Encrypting and decrypting data is slower than storing the data in unencrypted format. While the performance impact may not be noticeable, you must investigate its impact on your environment before encrypting large amounts of data. Encryption also increases the amount of administrative effort required to maintain system health. Policies must be kept up to date, and you should maintain recovery keys to use with encrypted objects if the primary keys become unusable. Maintaining recovery keys can require a significant amount of time for large organizations with many users. Before implementing encryption of any type, you must assess the cost to both performance and maintenance effort.

While no single set of rules or guidelines is the "best" for any specific environment, following some general best practices should result in a secure environment. Following is a list of best practices for implementing encryption in a Windows environment:

- Change your passwords periodically. The longer passwords remain unchanged, the higher the probability they will be compromised. Change passwords at least every 6 months.
- Rotate your encryption keys at least every 6 months for meeting compliance and maximizing your security posture.
- Do not write down passwords. Use passwords that can be remembered. Passwords that are written down are easier for an attacker to find and use.
- Export recovery keys to removable media and store the media in a safe place. EFS or BitLocker recovery information should be physically stored in a separate, safe location.
- Encrypt the Documents folder for all users. Since most people use Documents for most document files, encrypting this folder will protect the most commonly used file folder.
- Never encrypt individual files—always encrypt folders. This keeps any sensitive data from ever being written to the disk in plaintext.
- Designate two or more recovery agent accounts per organizational unit. Designate two or more computers for recovery, one for each designated recovery agent account.
- Avoid using print spool files in your print server architecture, or make sure that print spool files are generated in an encrypted folder. This keeps sensitive information from being stored in plaintext on a print server.
- Use multifactor authentication when using BitLocker on operating system volumes to increase volume security.
- Store recovery information for BitLocker in Active Directory Domain Services to provide a secure storage location.
- Disable standby mode for portable computers that use BitLocker. BitLocker protection is effective only when computers are turned off or in hibernation.
- When BitLocker keys have been compromised, either format the volume or decrypt and encrypt the entire volume to remove the BitLocker metadata.

- Require strong passwords for all VPN connections.
- Use the strongest level of encryption and algorithm that your situation allows for VPNs.
- Use SSTP for VPNs when possible.
- Disable SSID broadcasting for wireless networks.
- Never use WEP for wireless networks—only use WPA/WPA2/WPA3.
- Trust only certificates from CAs or trusted sites. Train users to reject certificates from unknown or untrusted sites.

CHAPTER SUMMARY

A solid security strategy depends on having multiple layers of controls to protect each object. In this chapter, you learned how additional layers of controls using encryption can increase the security of sensitive data. Windows includes the ability to encrypt data at rest using EFS, BitLocker, and BitLocker To Go. Windows also supports encryption of data in transit through the use of several protocols and methods.

Selecting the best mix of encryption methods and applying best practices when using those methods will make your data more secure. Effective use of Windows encryption provides a greater level of security for data at rest and in transit by adding a solid layer of protection to a multilayered security strategy.

KEY CONCEPTS AND TERMS

Advanced Encryption Standard (AES)
Asymmetric algorithms
BitLocker
BitLocker To Go
Boot devices
Certificate authority (CA)
Cipher
Data at rest
Data in transit
Decryption keys
Digital certificate
Elliptic Curve Cryptography (ECC)
Encrypting File System (EFS)
Encryption

Firewalls
Full Disk Encryption (FDE)
Full Volume Encryption (FVE)
International Telecommunications Union (ITU-T)
Internet Protocol Security (IPSec)
Layer 2 Tunneling Protocol (L2TP)
Nonrepudiation
Plaintext
Point-to-Point Tunneling Protocol (PPTP)
Pre-shared key (PSK)
Public key cryptography
Public key infrastructure (PKI)
Recovery key

Registration authority (RA)
Secure Hash Algorithm (SHA)
Secure Socket Tunneling Protocol (SSTP)
Secure Sockets Layer (SSL)
Security certificate
Smart card
Symmetric key
Transport Layer Security (TLS)
Trusted Platform Module (TPM)
Trusted source
Virtual private network (VPN)
Web proxies
Wi-Fi Protected Access (WPA)
Wired Equivalent Privacy (WEP)
X.509

CHAPTER 4 ASSESSMENT

1. Which of the following is the strongest reason why operating system access controls are insufficient to secure objects?

A. It's possible to boot into another operating system and format the disk.

B. Strong passwords longer than 24 characters are not common.

C. It's possible to boot into another operating system and bypass access controls.

D. It is often possible to find a user's password written down.

2. What piece of information is necessary to encrypt and decrypt data?

A. Key

B. Salt

C. TPM

D. Recovery agent

3. Which Windows feature allows you to encrypt entire volumes?

A. EFS

B. Veracrypt

C. BitLocker

D. AppLocker

4. Which Windows feature uses keys based on a user's password?

A. EFS

B. Veracrypt

C. BitLocker

D. AppLocker

5. Where does BitLocker store encryption keys for transparent mode?

A USB key

B. Recovery file

C. EFS

D. TPM

6. Which version of the Windows operating system has TLS1.3 enabled by default?

A. Windows Server 2022

B. Windows XP

C. Windows 10 Professional

D. Windows 10 Home

7. Which of the following services does communication encryption *not* provide?

A. Confidentiality

B. Nonrepudiation

C. Integrity

D. Availability

8. Which protocol commonly provides a secure channel for HTTPS?

A. TLS/SSL

B. PPTP

C. S-PPTP

D. L2TP

9. Which VPN protocol has the fewest issues with Nats and firewalls?

A. L2TP

B. SSTP

C. IPSec

D. PPTP

10. Which of the following is the weakest wireless protocol (and should never be used)?

A. WPA

B. PSK

C. WEP

D. SSID

11. Which type of encryption algorithm uses two related keys?

A. Symmetric

B. Balanced

C. Private

D. Asymmetric

12. Which of the following is used to deliver a trusted public key that can be used with assurance it belongs to the stated owner?

A. Digital signature

B. Digital certificate

C. Certificate authority

D. Private key

13. What is a general approach for handling keys using trusted entities and digital certificates?

   A. PKI

   B. IPSec

   C. WPA-PSK

   D. SSTP

14. Which common folder should be encrypted for all users?

   A. Windows

   B. Program Files

   C. Documents

   D. My Secure Files

15. Why is it recommended to encrypt folders instead of files?

   A. Individual files are written to disk unencrypted before being encrypted.

   B. Folder encryption is faster.

   C. Folder encryption results in less disk usage.

   D. Individual files are encrypted first and then written to disk.

Protecting Microsoft Windows against Malware

© Ruslan Gi/Shutterstock

NFORMATION SECURITY EFFORTS are often focused on protecting data from unauthorized people. While the concepts are generally stated in terms of users and not people, it is common to relate the two. What if an attacker is not a person? Programs can carry out attacks on behalf of people. It is important to consider controls to prevent programs from violating the confidentiality, integrity, and availability of data as well as just preventing human attacks.

In this chapter, you'll learn about the different types of software that can violate the security of your information systems. Software designed to infiltrate a target computer and carry out the attacker's instructions is referred to as malicious software. Malicious software of all types is generally referred to as malware. You'll also learn techniques to prevent malware attacks, search for the presence of suspect software, and remove any software you have identified as malicious. Diligence is required to fully protect an information system environment from malware attacks, and you'll learn what to do to keep your systems secure.

Chapter 5 Topics

This chapter covers the following topics and concepts:

- What the purpose of malware is
- What different types of malware are
- What antivirus and anti-spyware software are
- Why updating software is important
- What maintaining a malware-free environment is
- What scanning and auditing malware are
- What tools and techniques for removing malware are
- What best practices for malware prevention are

Chapter 5 Goals

When you complete this chapter, you will be able to:

- Explain the purpose of malware
- Explain the effects of malicious code
- Classify malicious code
- Describe how malicious code spreads and operates, and where it resides
- Explain how antivirus and anti-spyware software work
- Discuss the importance of timely updates, testing, and deployment
- Identify strategies for maintaining a malware-free environment
- Recognize the importance of scanning regimes
- Analyze tools and techniques for malware cleanup
- Outline best practices for malware prevention

The Purpose of Malware

The term **malware** refers to a collection of different types of software that share the goal of infiltrating a computer and making it do something harmful to the system, its data, or the user. It is often called malicious software. In many cases, malware does something undesired and operates without the explicit consent of the owner. This is not always the case, however. Some types of malware are downloaded and installed with the owner's full knowledge.

Malware was first introduced to computers and networks as "harmless" experiments or pranks. In fact, the earliest examples of programs that later came to be known as malware really were not malicious at all. The earliest malware developers were mostly interested in learning what novel computer programs could accomplish. Today, most malware satisfies more dubious purposes. Current malware generally exists to fulfill one or more of the following purposes:

- **Disrupt computer operations**—Malware programs can overwhelm a computer's ability to run other programs or communicate with other computers or devices. They can also damage, deny access to, or even remove files or critical operating system components that other programs need to operate. Malware can also alter or delete memory content or disk content that programs need to run. Most of the actions malware takes to disrupt computer operations results in unexpected conditions that programs cannot handle. The result is unexpected program behavior or even crashed programs.
- **Gather sensitive information**—Many types of malware programs operate without announcing themselves. They search for sensitive data, such as financial data and personal identification data. They store any data they find or send the data to the

malware creator using the computer's network connection. There are many places users store sensitive information, including browser cache, files on disk, and even in memory. Malware programs are programmed to know where to look for the most common sensitive data.

- **Gain unauthorized access to restricted computer resources**—The third main purpose of malware is to provide a way for attackers to access computers and other network resources. Malware written for this purpose exploits vulnerabilities to get inside a protected network. It then takes some action that results in a new access method for an attacker, commonly referred to as a backdoor. In effect, this type of malware opens a new door to a restricted computer. A serious threat to internal systems is when malware is used to penetrate and then hide within the confines of an infrastructure undetected for the purposes of intelligence gathering or worse. The worst of these types of threats are known as APTs or an advanced persistent threats.

- **Generate financial gain**—A fourth purpose of malware is to generate financial gain for the attacker. One common example of this is malware known as a crypto malware/crypto mining malware, which infiltrates a victim computer and then uses that computer's resources to mine for cryptocurrency, for the financial gain of the attacker. Another common example is ransomware, which is a type of malware where the attacker will encrypt all of the data on the victim computer, so it is not useable and then charge the victim a fee in order to have that data decrypted and safely returned.

Malware may exist to carry out specific attacks or to accomplish only one step in more complicated attacks. For example, malware can often help attackers identify likely victims for a subsequent attack. Attackers routinely use many types of tools to carry out attacks. Malware is just one tool in their arsenals.

Types of Malware

Attackers can choose different types of malware to meet the goals of their attacks. The best type of malware for any situation depends on the type of attack. Malware can be loosely divided into two main categories: programs that spread or infect and programs that hide.

Programs that spread or infect actively attempt to copy themselves to other computers. Their main purpose is to carry out instructions on new targets. Malware of this type includes viruses and worms.

Other malware hides in the computer to carry out its instructions while avoiding detection:

- Trojan horses
- Ransomware
- Rootkits
- Spyware
- Adware
- Keyloggers
- Crypto malware

Understanding these nine basic types of malware and how to protect your systems from them is an important component of a solid security plan. The following sections describe each malware type.

FYI

As far back as 1962, developers at Bell Labs actually created a game called Darwin that contained virus-like behavior. The game allowed "creatures" to grow, thrive, and overtake each other. One of the developers, Robert Morris, Sr., created a lethal beast that used virus-like tactics to infect areas of the playing arena. It was constrained to a single computer but set the stage for future malware. In 1988, his son, Robert Tappen Morris, developed the first computer worm malware, the Morris Worm, which then infected 6,000 computers. Morris Jr. was convicted for violating the "Computer Fraud and Abuse Act" and was sentenced to 3 years probation, 400 hours of community service, and a $10,000 fine. More on the Morris worm further in this chapter.

Virus

A computer **virus** is a software program that attaches itself to, or copies itself into, another program. It causes the computer to follow instructions not intended by the original program developer. A virus "infects" a host program and may cause that host program to replicate itself to other computers. The term "virus" is used to describe malware that acts in a similar fashion to biological viruses. The virus cannot exist without a host, similar to many parasites. It can spread from host to another host in an infectious manner.

The Creeper was the first reported intercomputer virus recorded. It was written by Bob Thomas in 1971. The Creeper would copy itself to other networked computers and display the message "I'm the creeper, catch me if you can!" It was designed as an experimental self-replicating program to see how such programs would affect computers on a network. Shortly after the Creeper was released, the Reaper program was unleashed to find and eradicate the Creeper.

Today, there are thousands of known viruses that infect programs of all types. The main concern with viruses is that they often attach themselves to commonly run programs. When users run these infected programs, they are actually running virus code with their user credentials and authorization. The virus doesn't have to escalate privileges. Users who run the infected program provide the virus with their authenticated credentials and permissions.

Worm

A worm is a type of malware that is self-contained. It is a program that replicates and sends copies of itself to other computers, generally across a network. The worm may take other actions, or its purpose may just be to reduce availability by using up network bandwidth. The main difference between a virus and a worm is that a worm does not need a host program to infect; the worm is a stand-alone program. Since worms don't rely on hosts, they generally can spread faster and farther. Worms tend to be somewhat platform specific, since they are stand-alone programs.

The first worm reported to spread "in the wild" was the Morris worm. It was designed to spread across the internet and infect computers running versions of the UNIX operating system. The original intent of this worm was to estimate the size of the internet, but the worm spread faster than its author expected. The worm ended up infecting computers multiple times and eventually slowed down each infected computer until it became unusable.

Since the Morris worm, attackers have released many other notable worms, such as Melissa, the Love Bug, Stuxnet, Code Red, Nimda, SQL Slammer, Sasser, and Conficker. Worms tend to thrive in environments where users run them without thinking about the potential consequences. In the past, many worms were transported in email messages. In the near future, expect to see a substantial increase in worms spreading through social networking. The fast pace of communicating through social media mechanisms opens new opportunities for both attackers and security administrators.

> **NOTE**
>
> The Morris worm exploited **the buffer overflow** vulnerability. A buffer overflow is a condition in which a running program stores data in an area outside the memory location set aside for the data. By storing more data than a program expects, it is possible to put instructions into a program that alter its behavior at run time. Buffer overflows are numerous and always result from a programmer neglecting to validate input data.

Trojan Horse

The **Trojan horse**, also called a Trojan, is malware that either hides or masquerades as a useful or benign program. The name derives from the story of the Trojan horse in *The Aeneid*. In the story, after 10 years of war with Troy, the Greeks constructed a large wooden horse. The Greeks left the horse and sailed away. The gift was seen as a victory offering and was brought into the city. That night, Greek soldiers hidden inside the hollow horse opened the city gates and let the rest of the Greek army, which had returned after dark, into the city. The Greeks soundly defeated Troy that night.

Trojan horse programs use their outward appearance to trick users into running them. They are disguised as programs that perform useful tasks, but they actually hide malicious code. Once the program is running, the attack instructions execute with the user's permissions and authority. In essence, the Trojan horse developer has tricked a user into running an attack program.

The first known Trojan was Animal, released in 1974. The program was disguised as a simple quiz game in which the user would think of an animal and the program would ask questions to attempt to guess the animal. In addition to just asking questions, the program would actually copy itself into every directory where the user had write access. Today's Trojans do far more than just save copies of themselves. Trojans can hide programs that collect sensitive information, open backdoors into a computer, or actively upload and download files. The list of possibilities is endless.

Rootkit

A **rootkit** is a type of malware that modifies or replaces one or more existing programs to hide the fact that a computer has been compromised. It is common for rootkits to modify parts of

TIP

Rootkits often work with other malware. Suppose a program, malware.exe, is running on a Windows system. A simple rootkit example would be to replace the Windows Task Manager with a modified version that does not list any program named malware.exe. Administrators would not know the malware program is running.

the operating system to conceal traces of their presence. Rootkits can exist at any level, from the boot instructions of a computer up to the applications that run in the operating system. Once installed, rootkits provide attackers with access to compromised computers and easy access to launching additional attacks.

Rootkits are newer than other types of malware and did not appear until around 1990. They can be difficult to detect and remove since their main purpose is to hide their own existence. But identifying and removing rootkits is crucial to maintaining a secure system.

Spyware

The next type of malware is **spyware**, software that covertly collects information without the user's knowledge or permission. The information collected can be sensitive personal information, such as a password or credit card number, or information used to build profiles for future action. Spyware is commonly used by aggressive marketers to collect specific information about customers and their preferences.

Most spyware programs piggyback onto other legitimate programs. They are installed along with the intended programs. Although the primary purpose of most spyware is to collect and report on information, the process of doing just that can cause other problems. Spyware causes additional processes to run to collect the pieces of information. This adds more processes, uses more memory, and can generally slow down a computer. Computers that have many spyware programs installed can run noticeably more slowly than a clean computer.

Spyware has been around since the late 1990s but became more common after 2000. The rapid growth of the internet enabled attackers to collect useful information from unsuspecting users. Use of the information collected by spyware can range from customized suggestive selling to identity theft. The main goal of spyware is to collect and deliver information—especially private information. When successful, spyware violates the privacy of information and provides easy access to unauthorized users. Private information should stay private. Spyware is a type of malware that specifically threatens the confidentiality of information.

Adware

Another type of malware is adware. Like spyware, adware is more of an annoyance than a concerning threat. However, like spyware, adware does in fact create a concern for those who want to keep their systems secure. For example, browser hijacking can take place from adware. Adware, which is simply "advertising" developed software mostly used in a web browser, is mostly used to create income from those who visit websites and either click on links or the software sometimes run in the background without the user's knowledge. Adware by nature isn't highly malicious; however, if a browser is hijacked, it can create a performance (or denial) issue, it can create privacy concerns, or in its worse form, it can install a virus when the browser is hijacked.

Keylogger

Another type of malware is a keylogger, which is similar to a Trojan in that is will be installed without the user knowing, lay dormant if undetected, and collect intelligence when it's in use without the users consent or knowledge. A keylogger does exactly what it sounds like it does—it logs keystrokes and collects (or sends) them for malicious use and intent. When recorded keystrokes are captured, a threat actor can glean useful information like usernames, passwords, financial information like account numbers, and much more.

Ransomware

Another type of malware that attempts to generate funds directly from a computer user is known as **ransomware**. Ransomware is typically seen as a Trojan in its initial form, trying to remain undetected, but once activated, it absolutely wants you to know it exists. Ransomware attacks a computer and limits the user's ability to access the computer. It can limit access by slowing down the computer, denying access for authorized users, or blocking access to specific programs or resources. Some ransomware operates by encrypting important files, or even the entire disk, and making them inaccessible. The attacker generally alerts the users to the restrictions and demands a payment to restore full access. This is when the unsuspecting malware lets you know it is in fact installed, when your system is unusable until you pay the ransom to release it back to you for use. The payment, or ransom, gives this type of malware its name. The attacker promises to decrypt the user's data or remove any mechanisms that block access once the ransom is paid. Most computer users rely on their computers and the data they store. Few computer users can lose access to their data and other resources without encountering ongoing frustration.

Business users may find ransomware to be far more than a simple annoyance. The inability to access key parts of a business computing system can have the same effect as a denial of service (DoS) attack. Ransomware can cause organizations to lose large profits in a very short period. Attackers who launch ransomware attacks expose themselves to huge risks but also can realize large profits. Ransomware is a growing trend in malware. User reliance on mobile devices makes such devices attractive targets. As Windows computers and devices become more mobile, they become even more vulnerable to potential ransomware attacks.

> **NOTE**
>
> Another newly deployed type of malware is closely related to ransomware. **Cryptojacking** malware can be distributed several ways, but has the goal of using the victim's computing power to mine cryptocurrency. Cryptojacking can infect a computer as a virus, worm, Trojan, or even as JavaScript that is run when the user visits a website. In many cases, victims only notice that their computer or device just runs more slowly than before being infected. The good news is that hackers are finding out that cryptojacking doesn't provide a high return on investment, so its use is beginning to decline.

Malware Type Summary

Most current malware tends to be complex and possess characteristics of several of the basic types discussed in this section. Modern malware is commonly a hybrid of two or more types, allowing it to be more effective and harder to combat. Even though hybrid malware is becoming more common, it is still important to understand the basic types

TABLE 5-1 Common Types of Malware	
MALWARE TYPE	**PROMINENT CHARACTERISTIC**
Virus	Attaches to or "infects" a host program
Worm	Stand-alone program—does not need a host
Trojan	Hides or masquerades as a harmless program, tricking users into running the malware
Rootkit	Modifies programs, possibly even operating system programs, to hide traces of its own existence
Spyware	Covertly collects information and sends it to a collector
Adware	Can hijack a web browser and install malware
Keylogger	Lays dormant and can conduct intelligence gathering through the capturing of keyboard strokes
Ransomware	Limits access to the infected computer and demands a ransom to be paid to the attacker to restore full access

© Jones & Bartlett Learning.

and how to protect your systems. Protection from more complex malware often includes protecting systems from a combination of basic malware types. **TABLE 5-1** compares the six basic types of malware and their most prominent characteristics.

Anti-Malware Software

The success of any malware program lies in its ability to avoid and resist detection and removal. The basic design of malware makes the process of keeping your computers clean more difficult. It is nearly impossible to manually identify and remove all traces of malware—there is just too much active malware threatening any computer connected to a network.

The only reasonable approach to addressing the problems of malware is to use a collection of programs specially designed to combat malware. Such programs include antivirus and anti-spyware software. Collectively, these software packages are also called anti-malware software. While there are some overlapping features, each type of software generally performs different functions. Both types of software are necessary to create and maintain a secure computer system.

WARNING

A computer does not have to be connected to a network to be infected with malware. Malware can travel from computer to computer via removable media as well as via networks. Any DVD, USB device, Bluetooth device, or other removable device has the potential to transport infected programs to a target machine. Don't neglect removable media and devices when you develop an anti-malware policy.

Antivirus Software

Antivirus software can help detect and mitigate some types of malware. Many antivirus programs are available to identify many known types of malware and help respond to the threats malware programs present. Most antivirus software focuses on viruses, worms, and Trojan horses but may also address rootkits and spyware. Current antivirus software provides the ability to prevent, detect, and remove malware instances.

Many quality antivirus software products are available. **TABLE 5-2** lists several of the more commonly used antivirus products for Windows. Note that Table 5-2 is just a sample list of some common antivirus products.

The most common method used to identify malware is to compare known malware code with processes running in memory or files stored on disk. Each instance of malware has a unique set of instructions, called the malware's **signature**, which identifies any copies of the malware on your system. The organized collection of known malware signatures is stored in a **signature database**. The antivirus software uses the signature database for signature matches when scanning processes or files. Any process or file that contains instructions that match a known malware signature is flagged as malware.

Another method some antivirus software uses to identify malware is called **heuristics**. Heuristics is the practice of identifying malware based on previous experience. The actions malware programs tend to carry out are stored in a database.

> ⚠ **WARNING**
>
> Regardless of how good your anti-malware software is, it can't catch everything. Never rely on any single control to do all the work. Always use the defense-in-depth strategy to ensure multiple controls protect each resource.

TABLE 5-2 Common Antivirus Software for Windows

PRODUCT	WEBSITE
Microsoft Defender Antivirus	https://www.microsoft.com/en-us/windows/comprehensive-security
Bitdefender Internet Security	http://www.bitdefender.com/
Kapersky Internet Security	http://www.kapersky.com/anti-virus
Norton Security	http://us.norton.com/antivirus/
McAfee Antivirus	https://www.mcafee.com/en-us/index.html
Comodo Internet Security	https://www.comodo.com/home/internet-security/free-internet-security.php
F-Secure Safe	http://www.f-secure.com
G Data Internet Security	https://www.gdatasoftware.com/
Bullguard Internet Security	https://www.bullguard.com/products/bullguard-internet-security.aspx
Panda AntiVirus	http://www.pandasecurity.com/usa/homeusers/solutions/antivirus/
Avast AntiVirus	http://avast.en.softonic.com/
Avg AntiVirus	http://www.avg.com/us-en/buy-antivirus

© Jones & Bartlett Learning.

5

Protecting Microsoft
Windows against Malware

PRODUCT	WEBSITE
Microsoft Defender Antivirus	https://www.microsoft.com/en-us/windows/comprehensive-security
SpyBot Search and Destroy	http://www.safer-networking.org/
SUPERAntiSpyware	https://www.superantispyware.com/
Malwarebytes AdwCleaner	https://www.malwarebytes.com/adwcleaner/
EnigmaSoft SpyHunter	https://www.enigmasoftware.com/products/spyhunter/

TABLE 5-3 Common Anti-Spyware Software for Windows

© Jones & Bartlett Learning.

When searching for malware, a heuristic scanner compares observed behavior with stored malware behavior. A match indicates the process in question is malware. The heuristic approach is more complex and slower than signature matching, but it can detect previously unknown malware if its behavior is similar to a known malware instance.

Anti-Spyware Software

Anti-spyware software is another type of anti-malware software. It helps detect and mitigate malware. As the name implies, the primary target is spyware. While many antivirus software suites may include an anti-spyware component, there is value to using one or more additional stand-alone anti-spyware products. There are so many spyware instances that it makes sense to use multiple anti-spyware software products to ensure you identify as many instances on your computers as possible.

Many good anti-spyware software products are available. **TABLE 5-3** lists several of the more commonly used anti-spyware products for Windows.

Malware Mitigation Techniques

There is no single action you can take to protect your computers and devices from malware. Attackers know that malware can be very effective in meeting their goals. They also know that their success just depends on vulnerable targets. Those targets aren't always just computers. Users can be, and often are, the most vulnerable targets for attackers. The best strategy to protect yourself from malware is to be proactive, implement multiple levels of controls on all of your computers and devices, and learn as much as possible about how to avoid becoming a victim. While this sounds like a large task, it really boils down to just being consistent in making sure that several controls are in place and effective.

Here is a brief list of malware layers of defense:

• Install anti-malware software on all computers and devices to maintain malware-free environments.
• Enable real-time protection options available in anti-malware software.
• Ensure that all anti-malware software is continuously kept up to date.
• Run frequent scans for malware that may have evaded real-time protection shields.

- Aggressively isolate and remove any malware that you find on any computer or device.
- Periodically review and update security policies to incorporate anti-malware best practices.
- Limit the number of devices that hold sensitive information.
- Use software solutions to limit user browsing to secure websites.
- Keep data backups of important business information on offsite servers

The following sections provide details of several layers of defense that work together to protect computers and devices from the continuous onslaught of malware.

Importance of Updating Your Software

Attackers introduce new malware on a daily basis. Eugene Kapersky of Kapersky Lab reports that there are currently around 360,000 new virus, Trojan, and other malicious files processed by Kapersky's detection technologies every day. That represents a dramatic increase from just a few years ago. Today's malware creators commonly use automated tools to craft new malware threats by automatically making small changes to existing malware. Essentially, the signature database downloaded last week can't protect you from new threats that have emerged this week. If you update your antivirus or anti-spyware software only once a week, you could potentially be vulnerable to many new threats that attackers launched since you last downloaded the malware signature database.

When an attacker releases a new malware instance, the race against the clock begins. From the beginning, heuristic-based software may detect the activity and identify the software as malware. If the attacker designed a clever malware program, it could fool heuristic-based tools. Signature-based anti-malware tools will not identify this new threat until a signature for the threat is added to a signature database.

The largest number of potential victims occurs during a **zero-day attack**. A zero-day attack is malware that is actively exploiting an unknown vulnerability and one or more of the following is true:

- The malware's actions have not been noticed, and the vulnerability has not been discovered.
- The malware's actions have been noticed but not identified as an attack.
- The malware and the vulnerability have been identified, but no fix is available yet.

Organizations that produce anti-malware software strive to stay up to date on emerging threats, create rules and signatures to identify new threats, and develop mitigation actions for each threat. Each of these steps takes time. By the time a new signature database is released, several days or weeks could have elapsed since the malware was on the rampage. Because brand-new signature databases are several days behind zero-day attacks, it is vitally important that your anti-malware software and data be kept as current as possible.

Most antivirus and anti-spyware software have an option to automatically update the software and data. Ensure that you have enabled the automatic update option and have selected the minimum reasonable update frequency. Frequent updates will help keep your protection from malware at its highest level.

TIP

In most environments, daily updates should be sufficient. Ask your antivirus and anti-spyware software vendors when they release updated signature databases. Then, schedule your updates to occur shortly after the new information is released.

NOTE

Many anti-malware software products give options for enabling or disabling the shield function, also called real-time scanning, for different types of information. Unless you have a specific reason to disable the shield for a specific type of information, leave it enabled for all types.

Maintaining a Malware-Free Environment

The key to keeping malware out of your computer system is to start with a clean structure and diligently protect it from becoming infected. Your anti-malware software contains several components that work together to keep your computer free of malware. **TABLE 5-4** lists the common components of anti-malware software needed to keep a system malware-free.

The first step in staying malware-free is to install one or more anti-malware software products and scan your system. You'll learn more about the scanning process in the next section, but for now, scanning searches your computer for malware. The scanning process uses the scanner and signature database components to find any malware programs. If the software does find any malware, it will need to be removed. You'll learn more about malware removal in a later section. The removal process may use the vault component in the cleanup process.

Once the computer is free from detected malware, you need to ensure it stays clean. The remaining common component of anti-malware software is the **anti-malware shield**. The shield is software that intercepts and scans incoming information for malware. Some shield software can also scan outgoing information for malware. The shield helps protect a computer from new malware or from sending malware to another computer if you have enabled outgoing scanning.

Malware can move from computer to computer in many ways, so anti-malware shield software often intercepts information, such as the following:

- Internet email messages
- Local email client messages
- Social media messages
- Web traffic

TABLE 5-4 Common Anti-Malware Software Components

COMPONENT	DESCRIPTION
Signature database	Collection of identifying instructions for known malware used to detect malware in existing programs and files
Scanner	Software that compares existing file contents with a signature database to identify malware
Vault	Secure location on disk used to store identified malware
Shield	Software that intercepts all incoming—and optionally outgoing—information, scanning each message or file for malware content

- Other application network traffic
- P2p traffic

The shield function of your anti-malware software will go a long way toward keeping your computers malware free, but it should not be the only control in place. Always remember the defense-in-depth strategy when protecting resources. A good anti-malware shield is only one part of an overall security plan to keep computers malware-free.

Scanning and Auditing Malware

Anti-malware software can fail to detect very new malware. Don't rely only on an anti-malware shield to keep your computers clean. Recall that even the latest version of a signature database will not have zero-day attack signatures. It is important to periodically scan the contents of your computers to detect any malware that the shields have missed.

The scan process is simple: the anti-malware scanner opens files that have been selected and searches them for malware. The scanner looks for copies of known malware signatures from the signature database in files selected for scanning. This can be a time-consuming process. It is important to carefully plan your scanning schedule and select the most efficient options for each scan. **TABLE 5-5** lists the most important questions to consider when scheduling a malware scan for your computers. Each anti-malware software package has specific options that may differ among vendors, but the general questions you must answer are common among most anti-malware software.

TABLE 5-5 Malware Scanning Options

QUESTION	POTENTIAL IMPACT
Scan which drives?	Scanning physical disk drives takes longer and can degrade overall computer performance. For frequent scans, scan only the disks that are frequently used by users and applications.
Scan removable media?	For the best security, scan all removable media when it is inserted. This may cause excessive scan activity. Another option is to only require removable media scanning for any media introduced from outside your controlled organization.
Full or quick scan?	Quick scans generally only scan files that are likely to contain malware, such as executable files. Quick scans can reduce the negative performance impact on computers. Ensure full scans occur periodically, such as weekly.
Scan when?	Computers should be scanned for malware under any of the following circumstances: • You suspect that malware is present. • You have installed new software or upgraded existing software. • Sufficient time has passed since the last scan. Each organization should develop a schedule for malware scans.

Tools and Techniques for Removing Malware

Despite the best efforts to keep malware away from your computers, you may find active malware during a scan process. Once you have identified malware, what do you do? The answer to that question is simple: follow your malware eradication plan. That means you should have already planned your actions. The time to think through the best way to handle malware infection is before the infection occurs.

There are two primary resources you should consult as you develop a malware eradication plan. Become familiar with these resources. They can help you avoid reinventing the wheel when developing your plan to handle malware infections.

1. Your anti-malware software's support resources
2. Microsoft's online resources—specifically, the Microsoft Malicious Software Removal Tool (MSRT)— https://www.microsoft.com/en-us/download/details.aspx?id=14591

In many cases, anti-malware software will suggest an action for each malware instance it finds. You can accept the suggestion or override the suggestion with your own action. Most anti-malware software provides links to follow for more information if you don't have enough information to make a decision.

If you detect malware soon after installing or updating software, the easiest fix may be to uninstall or downgrade the offending software. Make sure you initiate another scan after taking any action to ensure your action actually fixed the problem.

 WARNING

Don't just choose the default action when presented with malware. Carefully read the explanation your software provides and do some research. In many cases, the action your software suggests is the best action, but you always need to make an informed decision. Always read the anti-malware's explanation before responding.

If the options provided by your anti-malware software are not sufficient to remove the detected malware, the next step is to employ the Microsoft Malicious Software Removal Tool (Msrt). Visit the link provided earlier in this section to download the Microsoft Msrt. Install the tool and run it to help in removing some common malware found on Windows computers. Note that with the release of newer Windows systems like Azure based cloud-hosts, Windows 11, and Windows Server 2022, the focus to providing security for these systems relies on Microsoft Defender.

If the detected malware still persists after taking the actions suggested previously, the best course of action is to isolate the infected computer and explore more aggressive actions. Follow as many of these steps as are practical:

1. Disconnect the infected computer from your network.
2. Download at least one alternate anti-malware using another computer connected to the internet. This chapter includes a list of suggested anti-malware software packages.
3. Install the additional product(s) on the infected computer.
4. Use the new tool(s) to scan the infected computer.
5. Follow instructions presented to remove any detected malware.

If using additional anti-malware tools still does not remove the infection, you should seek additional assistance to clean the computer. It is possible at this point that you'll need to reinstall the operating system to fully remove all malware.

Malware Prevention Best Practices

Removing malware and cleaning up after an infection can be time consuming. Although the process of protecting computers from malware may seem to be tedious, it is far better to prevent malware than to clean up after a malware infection. Develop a malware prevention strategy as well as malware mitigation procedures.

⚠️ **WARNING**

In some circumstances, especially in the case of certain rootkits, the only way to completely clean a computer is to reformat the disks and perform a full operating system install. This option is extreme and should only be used as a last resort.

Aggressive malware prevention strategies will likely include some of the following:

- Frequent media scans
- Multiple anti-malware software shields
- Frequent signature database updates
- Restrictive software installation policy
- Restrictive download policy
- Restrictive removable policy
- Limited web browser functionality
- Not running in Administrator mode unless necessary
- Scanning incoming emails

While each item on this list does reduce the probability of malware infections, it reduces the computer's usability. Overly aggressive malware prevention measures can become so intrusive that they can interfere with business functions. Weak malware prevention can allow infections that can also interfere with, or even prevent, business functions.

The best solution is a balance between the two extremes. The following best practices employ a good measure of malware prevention without being overly intrusive. Follow these suggestions to develop a solid malware prevention strategy:

- Install antivirus and anti-spyware software on all computers.
- Enable all real-time scanning (shield) options.
- Update signature databases and software daily.
- Perform a complete scan of all hard drives at least weekly.
- Perform a quick scan after installing or updating any software.
- Enable boot time virus checking, including boot sector and memory scan at startup options.
- Remove administrator rights from all normal users.
- Apply software and operating system security patches.
- Educate users on the dangers of malware and how to avoid becoming a victim.
- Block outbound network connections that are not required for your applications.
- Establish incident response capabilities.
- Back up your files.
- Scan incoming email attachments and links

CHAPTER SUMMARY

Malware is already a big problem for organizations. The problem is growing at an increasing pace. McAfee Threats Report has stated that there were more than 700 million unique malware strands as of the end of 2018 Q1. The report has also indicated that the number of malware strands grew by more than 66% just since the beginning of 2016. Malware is becoming more sophisticated and more difficult to contain. The potential payoff for a successful attack can be quite lucrative, and the lure of a big score attracts more and more attackers.

Malware gets in the way of normal computer operation and threatens the security of information stored on the computers. Results of malware infestation can range from annoying to destructive and cause substantial loss for any organization. Each incident requires effort and personnel to react to the incident and repair any damage. Such activity requires time and money. Preventing incidents is nearly always less expensive than repairing the damage. Maintaining a secure computer system requires an understanding of the malware threat and the knowledge of how to combat it.

The two most important concepts when combating malware are defense in depth and prevention. A layered approach to securing systems against malware is crucial. No single control will prevent all malware instances, so you need multiple layers. When planning to manage malware threats, prevention efforts are more productive than eradication. Malware is manageable if you plan ahead wisely.

KEY CONCEPTS AND TERMS

Anti-malware shield	Heuristics	Signature database
Anti-spyware software	Malware	Spyware
Antivirus software	Ransomware	Trojan horse
Buffer overflow	Rootkit	Virus
Cryptojacking	Signature	Zero-day attack

CHAPTER 5 ASSESSMENT

1. Which type of malware is a stand-alone program that replicates and sends itself to other computers?

   A. Worm
   B. Virus
   C. Rootkit
   D. Trojan

2. Which type of malware modifies or replaces parts of the operating system to hide the fact that the computer has been compromised?

   A. Worm
   B. Virus
   C. Rootkit
   D. Trojan

3. Which type of malware disguises itself as a useful program?

A. Worm
B. Virus
C. Rootkit
D. Trojan

4. Which term describes a unique set of instructions that identifies malware code?

A. Fingerprint
B. Signature
C. Rule set
D. Heuristic

5. Which of the following terms means identifying malware based on past experience?

A. Heuristic analysis
B. Log file analysis
C. Signature analysis
D. Historical analysis

6. A signature database that is 1 month old may potentially expose that computer to how many new threats?

A. 360,000
B. 2,500,000
C. 1,080,000
D. 10,800,000

7. Which of the following terms describes a secure location to store identified malware?

A. Safe
B. Vault
C. Signature database
D. Secure storage

8. Which of the following anti-malware components is also referred to as a real-time scanner?

A. Shield
B. Scanner
C. Heuristic engine
D. Antivirus software

9. Which anti-malware tool is included with Windows 10?

A. Windows Antivirus
B. Windows Doctor
C. Windows Defender
D. Windows Sweeper

10. Which of the following best describes a zero-day attack?

A. Malware that no longer is a threat
B. Malware that can exploit a vulnerability but has not yet been released
C. Malware that is actively exploiting vulnerabilities on computers that have not applied the latest patches
D. Malware that is actively exploiting an unknown vulnerability

11. What is the best first step to take when malware is discovered soon after installing new software?

A. Uninstall the new software.
B. Scan for malware.
C. Update the new software.
D. Install additional anti-malware software.

12. What is the best first step to take if initial actions to remove malware are not successful?

A. Install additional anti-malware software.
B. Rescan for malware.
C. Update the signature database.
D. Disconnect the computer from the network.

13. The Morris worm exploited this vulnerability: _____.

14. Which type of malware covertly primarily collects pieces of information?

A. Spyware
B. Trojan
C. Virus
D. Rootkit

15. Why is a rootkit so difficult to detect?

A. Most anti-malware tools don't scan for rootkits.
B. A rootkit gives administrator privileges to an attacker.
C. A rootkit does not run in memory.
D. A rootkit may have modified the tools used to detect it.

Group Policy Control in Microsoft Windows

© Ruslan G/Shutterstock

MICROSOFT PROVIDES MORE EFFECTIVE security controls and countermeasures with each new Windows release. This protects computers from new and improved methods of attacks. It can be difficult and confusing to keep track of all the individual security rules as the number of new features continues to grow. Windows provides administrators with the ability to configure many security rules in a central location. The **Group Policy** feature of Windows organizes collections of security rules that control different aspects of how Windows operates. To make administration easier, collections of Group Policy settings can be stored in named objects called **Group Policy Objects (GPOs)**. GPOs can be associated with one or more users and across multiple computers to enforce settings without having to edit each user's individual settings.

In this chapter, you'll learn about Group Policy and GPOs and how to maintain them in Windows. You'll learn how to use GPOs to control what your users can and cannot do. You'll also learn how to do more than just change settings—you'll learn how to design GPOs that satisfy your organization's security policy.

Chapter 6 Topics

This chapter covers the following topics and concepts:

- What Group Policy and GPOs are
- How to make Group Policy conform to security policy
- Which types of GPOs are in the Registry
- Which types of GPOs are stored in Active Directory
- What designing, deploying, and tracking Group Policy controls are
- How to audit and manage Group Policy
- What best practices for Microsoft Windows Group Policy and processes are

Chapter 6 Goals

When you complete this chapter, you will be able to:

- Explain Group Policy and GPO
- Recognize the relationship between Group Policy and security policy
- Illustrate how to make Group Policy conform to security policy
- Describe GPOs in the Windows Registry
- Describe GPOs in Active Directory
- Design Group Policy controls
- Analyze techniques to deploy and track Group Policy controls
- Examine auditing and managing Group Policy
- Outline best practices for Group Policy and processes
- Discuss business challenges of Group Policy

Group Policy and GPOs

> **NOTE**
>
> Starting with Windows Server 2012, Microsoft included a new feature, called the Remote Group Policy Update, to make applying GPOs easier. Instead of waiting for individual computers to pull GPO changes, Windows Server 2012 and later computers can force GPOs to refresh. All of the selected computers will receive the new or changed GPOs within 10 minutes. You can also use another feature available starting in Windows Server 2012 called GPO caching. If GPO caching is enabled, selected computers will save GPOs locally and use those for the next restart. The advantage is that computers using cached GPOs will start faster. The drawback is that any GPO changes that occurred while a computer is offline will be sent to that computer at a regular interval after that computer starts, and not at start time.

The Windows Group Policy feature provides a centralized set of rules that govern the way Windows operates. It provides the ability to define and apply both general and security configuration changes to one or more computers. You can define both Local Group Policy settings and Group Policies in Active Directory. Local Group Policies control the behavior of a single computer. Active Directory Group Policies can apply to any users on any computers defined in Active Directory. Using Group Policy can make administration tasks easier than having to write scripts or individually configure basic security settings.

When booting a computer or logging on, Windows looks up and applies the GPOs for that computer and user. Group Policy uses a "pull" technology, which means that Windows periodically searches for any updated GPOs. If it finds a new GPO, it downloads and applies the changes to the existing environment. It pulls new or changed GPOs to the local computer and ensures that the settings are current. By default, Windows checks for new or updated GPOs at a random interval from 90 to 120 minutes. This automatic update feature ensures that Windows applies any new or updated GPOs, often without requiring that users log off or reboot computers.

Group Policy Settings

GPOs make it easy to enforce standard behavior across multiple users or computers. For example, GPOs can easily set firewall settings on multiple computers, define consistent desktop layouts, run scripts when users log on and log off, and redirect folders to network folders. These are only a few of the uses for GPOs. **TABLE 6-1** lists additional category settings using GPOs.

Group Policy is a central method to customize computer and user settings (**FIGURE 6-1**). Most operating systems, including Windows, provide the ability to create boot and logon scripts that run when a computer boots or a user logs on. Group Policy extends this

TABLE 6-1 Categories of Settings in GPOs

CATEGORY	DESCRIPTION
Password Policy	Sets requirements for password strength, age, history, and storage
Account Lockout Policy	Determines how Windows handles accounts locked after failed logon attempts
Kerberos Policy	Sets lifetime limits for Kerberos tickets and clock synchronization
Audit Policy	Defines events Windows should record in audit files
User Rights Assignment	Assigns individual user rights that define what general actions users can perform, such as "Access this computer from the network" or "Change the system time"
Security Options	Offers options granting rights that define what security-related actions users can perform, such as "Allowed to format and eject removable media" or "Require smart card"
Event Log	Defines maximum size, retention settings, and guest access settings for event logs
Restricted Groups	Lists users in security-sensitive groups and to what other groups the restricted group can belong
System Services	Defines startup mode and access permissions for system services
Registry	Defines access permissions and audit settings for Registry keys
File System	Defines access permissions on discretionary access control lists (DACLs) and audit settings for system access control lists (SACLs)

FIGURE 6-1

Group Policy.

© Jones & Bartlett Learning.

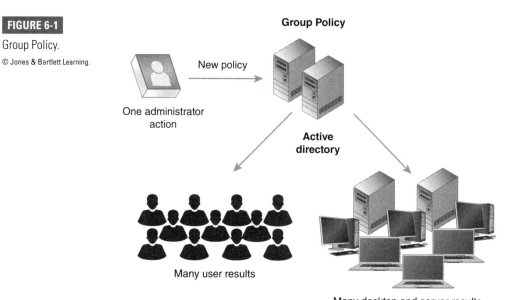

capability by maintaining the commands from a central location. You don't have to make changes to scripts and copy them to each computer or user's directory. Group Policy changes are automatically distributed to the right locations. Another benefit that bears a closer look is the periodic update feature of Group Policy. Boot and logon scripts take effect only when you reboot the computer or log off and log on again. Group Policy applies many settings to the current session. This feature causes changes to take effect faster than with using other configuration options.

Technical TIP

Microsoft publishes a handy spreadsheet listing all of the Group Policy settings included when installing an operating system. Microsoft includes several template files with each Windows version that define many settings. The spreadsheet can be found by visiting the website https://www.microsoft.com/en-us/download/details.aspx?id=104005 and downloading the provided template. As you will note, all previous versions of operating systems have been consolidated to this single template and can be used for Windows 11, Server 2022, and all currently supported versions of the operating system. Microsoft provides several versions of the spreadsheet to cover different Windows releases; however, most of what you need can be found in a single reference. Download the version provided and loo on the security tab and then the "supported on" column to verify if your current OS version is supported. This reference contains descriptive information you can use to create and modify GPOs to meet your organization's security needs. and it's highly recommended that it's reviewed.

GPO Linking

You can link GPOs to specific users to customize settings for groups of users or even individual users. Users who log on anywhere in the Active Directory domain will get GPOs linked to their user account. You can also link GPOs to **organizational units (OUs)**. In fact, you must link GPOs to at least one computer, domain, or OU for the GPO to be active. GPOs that aren't linked to a computer, domain, or OU are defined but inactive. You can define OUs to logically group computers into functional groups, such as "Accounting," "Manufacturing," and "Distribution." Once you define one or more OUs, you can add computers to each OU to logically group them together. When you link GPOs to OUs, Windows will download and apply only the appropriate GPOs for the computer and the user logging on.

 NOTE

You may define a desktop with icons related to manufacturing applications for the Manufacturing OU. A user who logs on to a computer in the Manufacturing OU will see the desktop specific to manufacturing. Users who log on to a computer that is not in the Manufacturing OU will see a different desktop.

Making Group Policy Conform to Security Policy

Group Policy is a functional feature of Windows that has little meaning by itself. It is a mechanism used to apply controls enforcing your security policy. For example, should you set a maximum password age for all the computers in your environment? The answer is: "It depends." Setting a maximum password age is generally a good idea, but not something you should arbitrarily enforce. Your security policy should direct any settings you add to GPOs. In fact, the GPOs you define and use should conform to your security policy. There are a few main reasons for making Group Policy conform to your security policy: to allow management to meet security responsibilities, and to ensure that your security policy has no gaps and also doesn't contain extra controls.

Security Responsibility

First, it is management's responsibility to ensure the security of an organization's assets, including information. All actions IT security personnel take to secure information occur within the authority granted by management to do the job. IT security controls that exceed management's security goals also exceed granted authority. Technically, management authorizes IT security to do only what the security policy states. It is important that management include all necessary security goals in your organization's security policy. The policy provides the direction for creating controls to secure information. A strict security policy interpretation means that any control that the security policy does not address is not important to the organization.

 WARNING

Your organization's culture should provide guidance on interpreting the security policy. A strict security policy interpretation means that no security controls exist unless they are directed by the policy. A less strict interpretation is more common. It allows IT security to exercise some discretion to implement best practices that may not be explicitly defined in the security policy.

Security Policy and Group Policy

Second, your Group Policy definition should satisfy your security policy goals while not adding any arbitrary controls. Your primary goal for designing Group Policy should be to ensure your Group Policy does not leave any gaps in your security policy. The GPOs you create and implement should meet all the goals in your security policy. It shouldn't add any controls that are not covered in the policy. When your environment's Group Policy conforms to your security policy, you create a validation method of your security policy. You can record the existence and performance of GPOs as evidence that you are complying with your security policy. You'll learn how to audit how your Group Policy is functioning later in this chapter.

Making Group Policy conform to your security policy is a three-step process. First, examine a list of GPO settings that already exist in the default Windows templates. As noted earlier in the downloaded spreadsheet reference, the Group Policy Settings Reference from Microsoft is an excellent resource for this task. Identify any GPO settings that satisfy parts of your security policy. Activate all settings that are appropriate for your policy.

The second step is to identify any elements in your security policy that do not already exist in default Windows templates. Then, list the elements that new GPO settings can address. For example, suppose you want to hide the Recycle Bin on every user's desktop. You can easily create a new GPO with this setting.

The third step in making Group Policy conform to your security policy is to create new GPOs for each of the remaining goals in your security policy that you identified in the second step.

Group Policy Targets

Group Policy allows you to define the specific targets for each rule. Some rules on your security policy apply to all users on all machines while others do not. For example, the rule "All users must create passwords for user accounts that conform to the strong password policy" applies to all users. The rule "Members of the Database Administrator group must change passwords at least every 90 days" applies only to users who are members of the Database Administrator user group. Windows provides you with the ability to specify GPO scope, which defines how Windows enforces security rules.

Active Directory provides the ability to define Group Policy at different levels. Windows looks up all applicable GPOs when a computer boots or a user logs on. Windows applies multiple GPOs in the following order (lowest priority to highest priority) (**FIGURE 6-2**):

- **Local GPOs**—GPOs defined and stored on the local computer
- **Site GPOs defined in Active Directory (AD)**—GPOs defined in AD for a specific site
- **Domain GPOs**—Domain-wide GPOs defined in AD
- **Organizational unit GPOs**—OU GPOs defined in AD

Any setting in a higher-level GPO will override a lower-level GPO setting. For example, a setting in a domain GPO will override a conflicting setting in a local GPO. This behavior applies only if a GPO setting contains a specific value. If the higher-level GPO setting value is "Not Configured," then Windows applies the value of the lower-level GPO setting.

Creating GPOs that conform to your security policy enables you to validate and evaluate each part of the policy. You'll learn later in this chapter how to list and audit GPOs. Reporting on GPOs makes it easy to evaluate how well your organization is complying with your security policy.

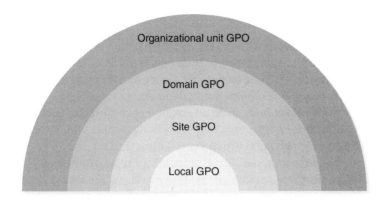

FIGURE 6-2

Group Policy Object order.

Types of GPOs in the Registry

Windows stores many Group Policy settings in the Registry. The **Registry** is a database on each Windows computer that stores configuration settings for the computer and users. The Group Policy Settings Reference spreadsheet lists the key locations for settings stored in the Registry. The Registry stores Group Policy settings either in HKEY_CURRENT_USER (HKCU) or HKEY_LOCAL_MACHINE (HKLM). HKCU keys define settings that are specific to each user. HKLM keys define settings that apply to the computer, regardless of who is logged on.

Technical TIP

Recall that Microsoft publishes a handy spreadsheet that lists all of the Group Policy settings included when you install your operating system. Microsoft includes several template files with each Windows version that define many settings. You can go to https://www.microsoft.com/en-us/download/details .aspx?id=104005 and download the spreadsheet we will work with in this chapter. Microsoft provides several versions of the spreadsheet to cover different Windows releases; however, you will find that within each sheet, most supported OS versions are covered by a single template. This reference contains descriptive information you can use to create and modify GPOs to meet your organization's security needs.

Open the spreadsheet, select the "Security" tab at the bottom, and examine the "Policy Path" column to find the key for settings stored in the Windows Registry.

Technical TIP

You can open the Local Group Policy Editor using these steps:

1. Choose the Windows Start button.
2. Type gpedit.msc in the Run box.
3. Press the Enter key.

Local Group Policy Editor

It is easy to view and edit Group Policy settings with the Group Policy Editor. There are two main types of Group Policy settings: Local Group Policy settings and Active Directory Group Policy settings, which you'll learn about in the next section. You define local Group Policy settings on each computer, and Windows stores the settings on that computer. All of the local Group Policy settings apply to a single computer. When you first open the **Local Group Policy Editor**, you see the two main groups of settings, "Computer Configuration" and "User Configuration" settings. **FIGURE 6-3** shows the Local Group Policy Editor.

Notice the two main categories of settings in the Local Group Policy Editor. The settings under the Computer Configuration category are stored in the Registry under the HKLM entry. The settings under the User Configuration category are stored under the HKCU entry. Although the Windows Registry Editor can be used to modify Group Policy settings, the Local Group Policy Editor is easier and safer. The Local Group Policy Editor allows you to change only Group Policy settings and ensures the settings are stored properly and in the correct location in the Registry. Changing Group Policy settings in the Local Group Policy Editor is easy. Find the setting you want to change, choose Edit, and change the setting to the value you choose. **FIGURE 6-4** shows the modified value for the Turn Off user-installed desktop gadgets setting. When you enable this setting, users will not be able to launch any of their own user-installed gadgets in the sidebar of their desktop.

You can follow these steps to change the same setting you see in Figure 6-4.

1. In the Local Group Policy Editor, expand the Computer Configuration, Administrative Templates, and Windows Components items.
2. Select Desktop Gadgets.

FIGURE 6-3

Local Group Policy Editor.

Courtesy of Microsoft Corporation.

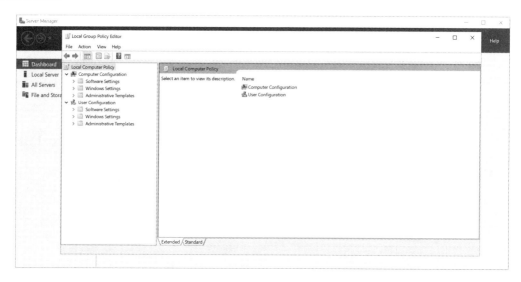

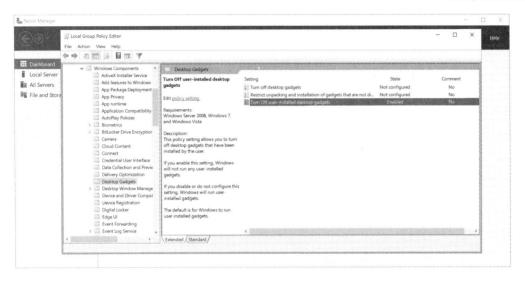

FIGURE 6-4

Changing a setting in the
Local Group Policy Editor.

Courtesy of Microsoft Corporation.

3. On the right side of the window, select Turn Off User-Installed Desktop Gadgets.
4. Right-click to open the context menu and select Edit.
5. Choose the Enabled option button to enable the setting.
6. Choose OK to save the setting and close the Setting Editor dialog box.

GPOs in the Registry Editor

Since Group Policy settings are stored in the Registry, they can be edited directly using the **Registry Editor**. Windows stores all currently active GPOs in the Registry under the HKCU entry. When a user logs on, and every 90–120 minutes thereafter, Windows will update the HKCU hive with the most current GPOs that apply to the current user. This updater will also occur within 10 minutes if a Windows Server computer refreshes GPOs with the Remote Group Policy Update. Each GPO has a globally unique identifier (GUID) that uniquely identifies it as a Windows object. The GPO GUID is the key Windows uses to store the GPO in the Registry. Windows stores current GPOs under the key:

HKEY_CURRENT_USER\Software\Microsoft\Windows\ CurrentVersion\Group Policy Objects\. **FIGURE 6-5** shows the GPO setting for "Turn Off User-Installed Desktop Gadgets" from the previous example in the Registry Editor.

 WARNING

Be very careful when using the Registry Editor. Changing the wrong Registry data in the Registry Editor can make your computer unstable. When another editor is available to edit data, such as the Local Group Policy Editor, use it instead of the Registry Editor. Always attempt to make a backup of the Registry prior to making changes so that if any issues occur, you can resolve the issues quickly.

FIGURE 6-5

Group Policy setting in
the Registry.

Courtesy of Microsoft Corporation.

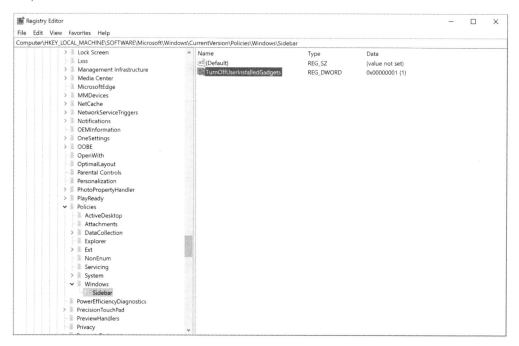

You can follow these steps to view the same setting you see in Figure 6-5.

1. Select the Windows Start button.
2. Type regedit.exe in the Run box; then, press the Enter key to run the Registry Editor.
3. Select Edit > Find from the menu bar.
4. Type Turn Off User-Installed Gadgets; then, choose Find Next.
5. Examine the full path to the GPO setting in the status area at the bottom of the Registry Editor window.

If you don't see a path in the status bar, choose View > Status Bar from the menu bar.

Types of GPOs in Active Directory

Although defining local GPOs provides positive control over single computers, the real power of Group Policy is in AD. Defining GPOs in AD gives you the ability to centralize security rules and control how Windows applies each rule. You create AD GPOs on a domain controller. Windows stores GPOs in AD in such a way that the domain controller automatically replicates the GPOs to other domain controllers. This feature reduces the workload of administrators. Using Group Policy in AD relieves the need to define security rules on multiple computers one at a time.

Group Policy Management Console

AD GPOs are created on the domain controller using the **Group Policy Management Console (GPMC)** (FIGURE 6-6). Note that the GPMC is only available on domain controllers. The GPMC looks a lot like the Local Group Policy Editor, but it allows you to do far more than just create GPOs and maintain their settings. Here is a list of some of the actions you can perform in the GPMC:

- Create and edit GPOs.
- Import and export GPOs.
- Copy and paste GPOs.
- Backup and restore GPOs.
- Search for GPOs.
- Create reports on GPOs.

Although GPOs can be created multiple ways, the most common method is to create them under the desired domain in the GPMC. New AD GPOs don't actually do anything until you link them with some entity. You'll learn about GPO linking later in this chapter.

When you promote a server to a domain controller, Windows automatically installs the GPMC on that server. You can follow these steps to open the GPMC:

1. Choose the Windows Start button.
2. Select Windows Administrative Tools > Group Policy Management.

FIGURE 6-6

Group Policy
Management Console.

Courtesy of Microsoft Corporation.

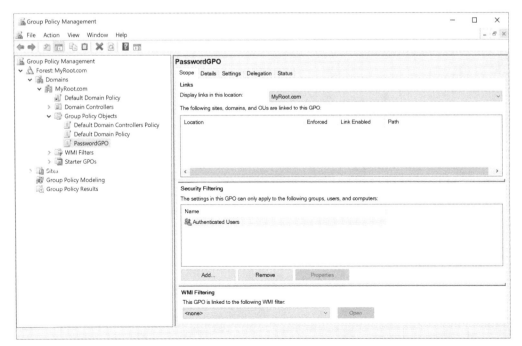

You can also follow these steps to open the GPMC:

3. Choose the Windows Start button.
4. Type gpmc.msc in the Run box.
5. Press the Enter key.

GPOs on the Domain Controller

Windows stores AD GPOs in a folder on the domain controller. Computers that are in a domain retrieve all the GPOs that apply to that computer when a user logs on using a domain account or when a computer connects to the domain. The domain controller searches for the appropriate GPOs and sends them to the computer. Of course, the computer and user must first successfully authenticate to the domain controller. Then, every 90–120 minutes the remote computer asks the domain controller if any GPOs have changed. If they have, the domain controller sends the new or updated GPOs and the remote computer applies them.

 WARNING

If you installed Windows in a directory other than C:\Windows, then the path to Policies for your computer will be different. Just replace C:\Windows with your Windows install folder to get the correct path to the Policies folder.

The domain controller stores AD GPOs in a folder named Policies (**FIGURE 6-7**). Windows creates a Policies folder for each domain. For example, the full pathname for the Policies folder for a domain named corp.domain.com is C:\Windows\sysvol\sysvol\corp.domain.com\Policies.

Windows stores each GPO in a subfolder under Policies. The name of each subfolder under Policies is the GUID for the GPO. You can navigate to the GPO in Windows Explorer to see where Windows stores the GPO settings. Each GPO folder, or GPO shell, contains two subfolders named Machine and User. These subfolders contain the GPO settings for

FIGURE 6-7

GPOs in the Policies folder.

Courtesy of Microsoft Corporation.

FIGURE 6-8

Linking AD GPOs in the GPMC.

Courtesy of Microsoft Corporation.

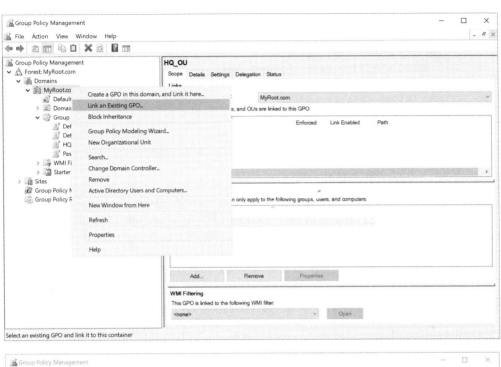

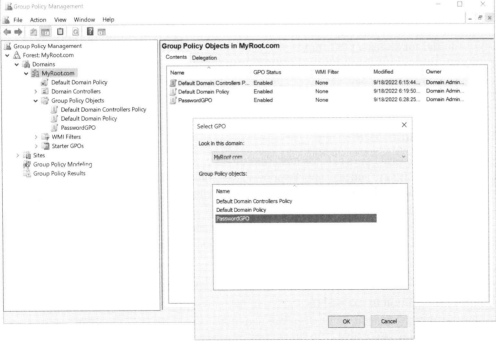

Technical TIP

Follow these steps to link a GPO to an object:

1. In the GPMC, select a container or object. For example, select MyRoot.com.
2. Open the context menu by right-clicking on MyRoot.com.
3. Choose Link an Existing GPO.
4. Select the desired GPO from the list of defined GPOs.
5. Choose OK.

---

both the machine-wide and user-specific settings. Each subfolder contains policy files for defined GPOs that apply to a domain.

Unlike Local GPOs, AD GPOs do nothing until you link them to one or more containers. An AD **container** can be a site, a domain, or an Ou. The Group Policy Objects section of the GPMC lists all defined GPOs. You can edit existing GPOs or add new GPOs. You must link GPOs to one or more sites, domains, or OUs to make the GPOs do anything (**FIGURE 6-8**). A single GPO may be linked to multiple containers, and each container can have multiple GPOs linked to it. The easiest way to link GPOs to containers is from the context menu of the container or object.

Designing, Deploying, and Tracking Group Policy Controls

One of the most important considerations when designing GPOs is efficiency. You want to define and link the minimum number of GPOs to satisfy your security policy. Creating too many GPOs will increase the time and effort you'll need to administer and maintain your security policy. Having too many GPOs also increases the possibility of errors and opportunities for attackers to compromise your systems. The simplest environment would be one in which you define one set of GPOs that applies to all computers and all users in all domains. Unfortunately, few environments end up being that simple. Functional demands often require different controls for various computers and users.

GPO Application Order

You can define several layers of GPOs that work together to ensure you enforce your security policy for all computers and all users. Windows gives you the ability to create high-level GPOs that enforce large-scale security settings and more specific GPOs that allow you to fine-tune settings for specific situations. Recall from earlier in this chapter that Windows applies GPOs in a specific order. Knowing this order lets you put more generic settings in GPOs that Windows applies first, and more specific settings in GPOs that Windows applies later in the process.

Recall that Windows applies GPOs in this order:

- **Local GPOs**—GPOs defined and stored on the local computer
- **Site GPOs defined in AD**—GPOs defined in AD for a specific site
- **Domain GPOs**—Domain-wide GPOs defined in AD
- **Organizational unit GPOs**—OU GPOs defined in AD

Design your GPOs with this order in mind. Since Windows applies OU GPOs last, any global GPO settings should go here. Identify any settings you want to enforce for all computers and users and define GPOs that you link to one or more OUs. Then, you can define GPOs and link them to lower-level containers for settings that do not apply to all computers or users. Since OU GPOs have the largest scope, they are the easiest to implement and maintain. Start by reviewing your OU structure. You should ensure your OU structure realistically represents your functional organizational structure as closely as possible. OU designs that closely represent functional structures make it easier to create appropriate OU-level GPOs that satisfy your security policy. For example, suppose your security policy requires specific application and object access for members of the Human Resources (HR) Department. If you define all users in the HR Department in the HR OU, it is easy to create GPOs for the OU that affect all HR Department users.

> **⚠ WARNING**
>
> OU GPO settings will override any settings that exist in lower-level GPOs. For example, if a setting exists in both a site GPO and an OU GPO, the OU GPO setting will override the site GPO setting. Don't include settings in OU GPOs that may require local overrides.

All security control design starts with your security policy. Once you validate your OU design and identify the controls you'll need to satisfy your security policy, you can define the control scope. In the context of GPO settings, the scope of any control is the group of computers or users to which each GPO applies. Settings scoped to the OU level should exist in OU GPOs. You can define any settings that apply only to some computers or users in local, site, or domain GPOs. You can also define limited scope GPOs at the OU level and use filters to limit the scope. You'll learn about GPO filters later in this chapter. As a general rule, define GPO settings either at the lowest level that includes all of the desired computers and users or at the OU level using filters when the OU approach meets your needs. For example, you can define any settings that apply to all users for a specific computer in either a local GPO, site GPO, or a filtered OU GPO. The main difference is that Windows stores local GPOs on the affected computer and stores site and OU GPOs in AD. OU GPOs also make administration simpler since you define and link GPOs at a single level.

Security Filters

Windows applies GPOs to all computers and users in a container by default. That means all computers and users in an OU will inherit any OU GPOs defined for that OU by default. You can change that behavior with **security filters** (**FIGURE 6-9**) if you want an OU GPO to apply only to some computers or users in the OU. The GPMC allows you to add as many security filters for GPOs as necessary to satisfy your security policy. You can limit a GPO to users, groups, or computers. Once you define a security filter, Windows will apply that GPO only to subjects defined in the filter. This option gives you much more control over how Windows applies GPOs you define at the OU level.

> **⚠ WARNING**
>
> The GPMC creates new GPOs that apply to all authenticated users. If you create filters to limit the scope of a GPO, make sure you delete the default filter of "Authenticated Users."

GPO Windows Management Instrumentation Filters

Windows Management Instrumentation (WMI) is the infrastructure Windows uses to maintain and exchange management and operations data. **WMI filters** give you even more control over when and where GPOs apply. You can create multiple WMI filters for each domain and then, link each filter to one or more GPOs. You can link only one WMI filter to each GPO. Windows

FIGURE 6-9

GPO security filters.

Courtesy of Microsoft Corporation.

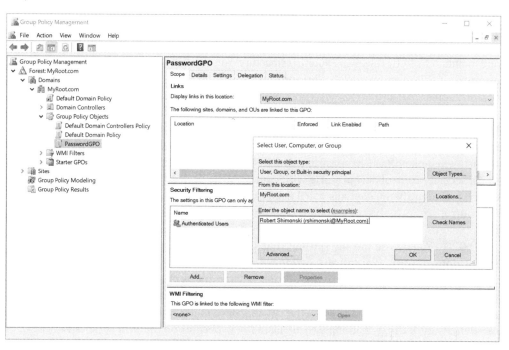

Technical TIP

Follow these steps to define a security filter for an OU GPO:

1. In the GPMC, select and expand a domain.

2. Expand Group Policy Objects and select a GPO.

3. Select the Scope tab in the right panel and then select Add in the Security Filtering section.

4. You have the option to change the type of objects and the location Windows uses to build the filter options. The defaults will allow you to select Users, Groups, or Built-In Security Principles from the domain you selected in Step 1. You can select the Object Types button and select the Computers check box to define a filter for specific computers.

5. Enter the user, group, or computer name for this filter. Choose Check Names to validate the object name you entered.

6. Choose OK to create the new filter and return to the GPMC.

evaluates the GPO's WMI filter before applying a GPO and proceeds only if the WMI filter expression evaluates to TRUE. WMI filters allow you to query the target environment and apply security settings only in certain situations.

For example, suppose you want to apply a GPO only for computers that are running Microsoft Windows 10 or Windows 11. You could define a WMI filter that would restrict the GPO to the desired machines. Windows uses the **WMI Query Language (WQL)** to define the queries for the filters. WQL is a subset of the SQL language many database engines use to query data. The following WQL query will return TRUE when the target computer is running Microsoft Windows 8.1 Pro:

Select * from Win32_OperatingSystem where Caption = Microsoft Windows 8.1 Pro.

Technical TIP

You can find more information on WMI, WQL and more on Microsoft.com at https://learn.microsoft .com/en-us/windows/win32/wmisdk/wmi-start-page.

If the target computer is running Microsoft Windows 8.1 Pro, Windows will apply the GPO. This additional feature gives administrators the ability to define GPO scope at a very specific level of detail. Once you define the WMI filter in the GPMC, you can link the filter to any GPO by just selecting the desired WMI filter from the drop-down list in the GPO's WMI Filtering section (**FIGURE 6-10**).

FIGURE 6-10

WMI filters.

Courtesy of Microsoft Corporation.

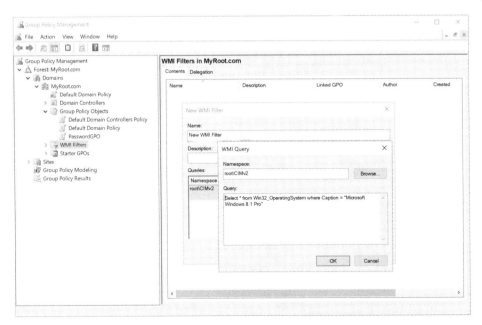

Deploying Group Policy

Windows ensures that new and changed GPOs get distributed and applied every 90–120 minutes. In some cases, you may want to force GPO distribution. In Windows Server 2012 and newer, you can force a GPO refresh from within the GPMC. For all versions of Windows, you can use the **Group Policy Update tool** to accomplish this task. The tool also provides the ability to force user logoff or system boot when setting changes require these actions. You can use the Group Policy Update tool whenever you want to ensure that settings are in place on target computers.

Technical TIP

Follow these steps to define a WMI filter and link it to an existing GPO:

1. In the GPMC, select and expand a domain.
2. Expand WMI Filters, open the context menu and choose New.
3. Type the desired name and description, then choose Add.
4. Type the following text into the query editor: Select * from Win32_Operating System where Caption = "Microsoft Windows 8.1 Pro"
5. Choose OK; then, Save to create the new WMI filter and return to the GPMC.
6. Expand Group Policy Objects and select a GPO.
7. Open the drop-down list in the WMI Filters section and select the newly created WMI filter.

Follow these steps to run the Group Policy Update tool:

1. Open a PowerShell window—Choose the Windows Start button > type **powershell.exe**.
2. Enter the following command: **gpupdate.exe**.

The Group Policy Update tool supports several options that change the scope of targets or additional actions. **TABLE 6-2** lists the most common options for gpupdate.exe.

TABLE 6-2 Gpupdate.exe Options

OPTION	DESCRIPTION
/target:{Computer | User}	Limits the target of the update to only user or computer policy settings.
/force	Reapplies all settings. The default is to apply only new or changed settings.
/wait:value	Sets wait time for the specified number of seconds for the processing to finish. A value of −1 means wait forever.
/logoff	Forces a user logoff after the update processing completes.
/boot	Forces a system reboot after the update processing completes.
/sync	Synchronously applies the next logoff or boot policy setting.

Auditing and Managing Group Policy

Once you design and deploy GPOs to support your security policy, it is important to validate your Group Policy to ensure that you have defined the right GPOs. Auditing Group Policy ensures the GPOs you have in place satisfy your security policy. As you change users and computers in your organization, you may find that your GPOs no longer satisfy your security policy. It is important to audit Group Policy periodically to ensure that any changes in your organization have not reduced your GPO's effectiveness.

Microsoft provides two main tools you will use to audit Group Policy: Group Policy Inventory and Resultant Set of Policy tool. The first tool, Group Policy Inventory (also known as Gpinventory), provides an inventory list of GPOs and many other computer and user settings. You must download this program from Microsoft's website and install it on your computer—it isn't included when you install Windows. You can get this tool by going to https://www.microsoft.com/en-us/download/details.aspx?id=14126. The second tool is included with Windows. The Resultant Set of Policy tool shows what settings Windows applies to a specific user on a specific computer.

Group Policy Inventory

The first step in using the **Group Policy Inventory tool** (GPInventory.exe) is to download and install it on your computer. GP Inventory queries the computers you select for system and GPO information and then displays the results in a single window. This tool makes it easy to collect information from many computers across a domain to ensure that your Group Policy is deploying the way that you expect. Follow these steps to run GP Inventory:

> **NOTE**
>
> Windows Server 2012 added a new tab to the GPMC. The new Status tab shows the current replication status of the selected GPO. This option makes it easier to see the deployment status of your GPOs.

1. **Open a PowerShell window**—Choose the Windows Start button > type powershell.exe.
2. **Change directories to the install directory for the GP Inventory tool**—Enter: **cd C:\<browse** to where you installed or downloaded the GPInventory.exe file>.
3. **Run Gpinventory**—The command is GPInventory.exe.
4. **Choose the computers to query**—Query > Select Computers to Target using Active Directory.
5. **Choose the information you want to gather**—Query > Select Information to Gather.
6. **Execute the query**—Query > Run Query.

Technical TIP

You must download and install the Group Policy Inventory tool before you can use it. You can get the tool from the Microsoft website. Go to http://www.microsoft.com/en-us/download/details .aspx?id=14126 to download the tool.

After Group Policy Inventory gathers the information you requested, it displays the results in the main window. You can view the details and save the information to analyze later. The Group Policy Inventory tool will save the results in an XML file or a text file. Use the Results menu item to save the results in either format. Group Policy Inventory is an important tool to provide validation of Group Policy in your domain. Use it after any GPO change and periodically to ensure computers and users are operating with the settings you define to comply with your security policy.

Analyzing the Effect of GPOs

The other common tool you will use to audit GPOs is the **Resultant Set of Policy (RSOP) tool**. The RSOP tool is included in Windows and shows the specific settings that will result from applying GPOs to a specific user logged on to a specific computer. The Group Policy Inventory tool can include some RSOP results, but the stand-alone RSOP tool provides access to more details. RSOP is a great way to analyze the effect of any GPO changes. RSOP provides two modes of operations—logging mode to show existing GPOs and planning mode that shows the effect of planned GPO changes.

You can run RSOP using two methods. The first method runs RSOP in logging mode that defaults to the currently logged-on user on the current computer. After the initial information displays, you can easily change the user or computer and generate updated GPO information. Follow these steps to run RSOP in logging mode:

1. Choose the Windows Start button.
2. Type **RSOP.msc** in the Run box, and then, press Enter.
3. The Resultant Set of Policy window displays the current settings for the user who is currently logged on. The display looks like the GPMC, but you can't change any settings here.
4. If you want to run RSOP for another user or computer, open the context menu (by right-clicking) on the main item in the left panel. This item will be your username and computer name.
5. On the context menu, select Change Query.
6. Select the desired computer and user on the next two dialog boxes.
7. RSOP will calculate the effective settings using the new user and computer you provided.

RSOP also runs in a powerful planning mode. The planning mode is useful when you want to analyze the effects of a GPO change before deploying the change. Follow these steps to run RSOP in planning mode:

1. Choose the Windows Start button > Windows Administrative Tools > Active Directory Users and Computers.
2. Open the context menu of the desired object by right-clicking the desired computer, user, domain, or OU.
3. Select All Tasks > Resultant Set of Policy (Planning).
4. The next several screens ask you to provide information that describes the planned target environment. RSOP will evaluate the GPOs based on the information you provide here. You can provide the following information:
   a. **User and Container**—Run RSOP for any user for any container.
   b. **Advanced options**—Set advanced simulation conditions.
   c. **Groups**—Analyze the effects of adding or removing group assignments.
   d. **WMI Filters**—See what effects different WMI filters produce.

Group Policy Inventory and RSOP help you validate the Group Policy you have in place and evaluate how changes will affect your environment. Both tools are important components of a complete administrator's toolbox.

Best Practices for Microsoft Windows Group Policy and Processes

Group Policy is an important component of secure Windows environments. Many resources are available to help you follow established best practices for secure systems. You'll learn about a few of the recommended guidelines and available resources in this section.

Group Policy Design Guidelines

While Group Policy for your organization can be designed many ways, a few guidelines can help focus your efforts. Follow these guidelines to design a Group Policy that will minimize administrative effort while satisfying your security policy. Most important, don't make your Group Policy overly complex. Simplicity is always an asset in any policy. Keep your security policy and Group Policy as simple as possible while still fulfilling your goals. Here are a few additional guidelines that should result in simple and effective Group Policy:

- Define OUs that reflect your organization's functional structure.
- Create OU GPOs for controls required in your security policy.
- Use meaningful names for GPOs to make maintenance and administration easier.
- Deploy GPOs in a test environment before deploying to your live environment.
- Use security filtering and WMI filters to restrict settings when necessary.
- Back up your GPOs regularly.
- Do not modify the default policies—instead, create new GPOs.
- Periodically audit your group policies to ensure they reflect new organizational goals.
- Increase GPO processing speed by disabling unused computer and user configurations.

Ensure your Group Policy is both effective and easily maintainable. Only define and deploy the GPOs you actually need to meet the goals of your security policy. Extra GPOs will only complicate administrative tasks and may get in the way of completing primary business functions. The process of migrating from an environment with few controls to a secure environment can be frustrating both for end users and administrators. Make sure you test all GPOs before deploying them to a live environment. Conduct tests that will allow you to evaluate how each GPO will affect your users' abilities to do their jobs. New security settings that stop people from doing their jobs are harmful to your business. Be aware of any new policies that may result in a negative business impact. When security requirements conflict with business requirements, it is up to the organization's management to resolve the conflict. The best security solutions always support both security and business concerns.

Several other resources are listed in **TABLE 6-3** that make designing and implementing Group Policy across a domain easier. Use these resources as well as the tools and resources you have already seen. They keep you from reinventing the wheel. They also provide input on solving issues that you may not have encountered yet.

TABLE 6-3 Group Policy Best Practices Resources

RESOURCE	DESCRIPTION	WHERE TO FIND IT
Group Policy Best Practices Analyzer	Helps you identify Group Policy configuration errors or dependency issues that may prevent settings from functioning as you expected.	In Server Manager, Roles and Server Groups, select a server role group. Once selected, you can scroll down to find the Best Practices Analyzer, click on Tasks and select Start Bpa Scan. A dialog opens to confirm the server and then you can start the scan.
Group Policy Settings Reference	Spreadsheets that list the policy settings included in the Administrative template files that are delivered with the Windows operating systems.	https://www.microsoft.com/en-us/download/details.aspx?id=104005
Windows 8.1 and Windows Server 2012 R2 Security Baseline	Resources for planning, deploying, and monitoring the security baselines of servers running Windows 8.1 and Windows Server 2012 R2.	https://learn.microsoft.com/en-us/archive/blogs/secguide/security-baselines-for-windows-8-1-windows-server-2012-r2-and-internet-explorer-11-final
Windows 10 and Windows Server 2016 Security Baseline	Resources for planning, deploying, and monitoring the security baselines of servers running Windows 10 and Windows Server 2016.	https://docs.microsoft.com/en-us/windows/security/threat-protection/windows-security-baselines
Windows 10 v1809 and Windows Server 2019 Security Baseline	Resources for planning, deploying, and monitoring the security baselines of servers running Windows 10 v1809 and Windows Server 2019.	https://techcommunity.microsoft.com/t5/microsoft-security-baselines/security-baseline-final-for-windows-10-v1809-and-windows-server/ba-p/701082
Windows 11 and Server 2022 (as well as all other products) Security Baseline Guidance	Covers new and supported technologies.	https://techcommunity.microsoft.com/t5/microsoft-security-baselines/bg-p/Microsoft-Security-Baselines
Security Compliance Toolkit (Sct)	A set of tools used to acquire, test, and deploy configuration baselines recommended by Microsoft. The security guides in the toolkit recommend Group Policy configurations and Security Template configurations that are enforced via Active Directory Domain Services.	https://docs.microsoft.com/en-us/windows/security/threat-protection/security-compliance-toolkit-10

CHAPTER SUMMARY

Group Policy is one of the most important security and administrative features in Windows. It enables administrators to effectively implement a security policy across a network of computers. Group Policy and Active Directory provide a centrally controlled environment to define and deploy changes to security and other configuration settings. Although Group Policy is most often discussed in security contexts, it is an efficient way to enforce standard settings across a diverse environment. You can use Group Policy to enforce password aging settings and a default screen saver. Group Policy uses are nearly endless. A good Group Policy design can reduce the workload of administrators and greatly enhance their abilities to enforce organizational standards in a consistent manner.

KEY CONCEPTS AND TERMS

Container
Group Policy
Group Policy Inventory tool
Group Policy Management Console (GPMC)
Group Policy Object (GPO)
Group Policy Update tool

Local Group Policy Editor
Organizational unit (OU)
Registry
Registry Editor
Resultant Set of Policy (RSOP) tool
Security filter

Windows Management Instrumentation (WMI)
WMI filter
WMI Query Language (WQL)

CHAPTER 6 ASSESSMENT

1. The Windows Group Policy feature provides a centralized set of rules that govern the way Windows operates.

   A. True
   B. False

2. Windows checks for new or updates GPOs every _____ minutes.

3. Which of the following statements best describes the relationship between security policy and Group Policy?

   A. Security policy should implement Group Policy.
   B. Security policy is derived from Group Policy.

   C. Group Policy should implement security policy.
   D. Group Policy supersedes security policy.

4. Who holds the primary responsibility to ensure the security of an organization's information?

   A. IT security
   B. Management
   C. Information system users
   D. Human Resources

5. Which tool would you most likely use to edit Group Policy settings in a stand-alone computer?

   A. Local Group Policy Editor
   B. Registry Editor

C. Group Policy Management Console
D. Resultant Set of Policy Editor

6. You can only edit user-specific Group Policy settings in the Windows Registry Editor.

A. True
B. False

7. Defining GPOs in _____ gives you the ability to centralize security rules and control how Windows applies each rule.

8. Which folder does Windows use to store AD GPOs on the domain controller?

A. Windows
B. Policies
C. GPO
D. ADdata

9. Windows stores each GPO in a subfolder with the same name as the _____ of the GPO.

10. Which of the following features allows you to restrict the groups to which a GPO applies?

A. Security filter
B. WMI filter
C. GPO link
D. OU list

11. Which of the following features allows you to restrict the types of operating systems to which a GPO applies?

A. Security filter
B. WMI filter

C. GPO link
D. OU list

12. Windows will automatically cause a user logoff or system reboot after applying new or changed GPOs.

A. True
B. False

13. Which of the following tools lists information about deployed GPOs and other computer-specific attributes?

A. Gpupdate.exe
B. RSOP
C. Gpedit.msc
D. Gpinventory.exe

14. You can use the _____ tool to view the effective settings after all current GPOs are applied to a specific user.

15. Which of the following resources is installed with Windows?

A. Group Policy Settings Reference
B. Security Compliance Management Toolkit
C. Group Policy Best Practices Analyzer
D. GPOAccelerator

Microsoft Windows Security Profile and Audit Tools

T HE GOAL OF INFORMATION SECURITY is to prevent loss by protecting the confidentiality, integrity, and availability of information. Security controls protect resources and manage control in a larger environment using group policy. How do you know if your system is meeting your security goals? You can verify that controls are functional, but how do you know if they are working and getting the job done by securing your systems? Are your systems configured with similar controls using recognized best practices? Is your environment clear of risks that may be surfaced by the use of industry leading tools created to expose vulnerabilities?

In this chapter, you'll learn how to analyze your current computer settings. You'll learn how to compare them with established settings and goals. You'll learn how to identify differences between your desired settings or overall security goals and your current configuration. You'll also learn how to test and then fix any issues that you identify and how to monitor your environment's behavior over time to ensure that you're staying secure.

Chapter 7 Topics

This chapter covers the following topics and concepts:

- What profiling Microsoft Windows security is
- What the Microsoft Baseline Security Analyzer (MBSA) is
- What OpenVAS vulnerability management framework is
- What Nessus Essentials and Burp Suite security analyzers are
- What a Microsoft Windows security audit is
- What Microsoft Windows security audit tools are
- What best practices for Microsoft Windows security audits are

Chapter 7 Goals

When you complete this chapter, you will be able to:

- Describe the need for profiling the security of a Windows system
- Explain how to use common Windows security profiling tools
- Explain the process of auditing Windows security
- Describe how to use Windows security audit tools

Profiling Microsoft Windows Security

It is difficult to know if your controls are correct without the ability to compare other configurations. You want to be able to compare configuration settings of your systems with the configurations of systems you know to be secure. System administrators often collect reported configuration settings for comparison with similar settings. A collection of configuration settings is called a **baseline** and can take on many forms. Each baseline generally contains a collection of configuration settings intended for a specific purpose. For example, a collection of security-related settings is commonly referred to as a security baseline.

Profiling

Once you have a baseline, or snapshot, of one or more of your computers, what do you do with it? One of the most effective uses of baselines is to compare them with known "good" baselines. There are many definitions for a "good" baseline. It generally means a baseline of a secure system. The process of comparing configuration settings of a computer with a collection of secure configuration settings makes it easy to see the differences. An alternate approach would be to define an insecure baseline and look for similarities or differences with your systems.

The process of comparing real computer configurations to known baselines is called **profiling**. Profiling, in general, means extracting information about someone or something based on known attributes. Many movies contain plot devices that depend on profiling. Westerns provide a great example of character profiling. In many old Westerns, the good guys wore white hats. The bad guys wore black hats. It was easy to tell who was good and who was bad. The process of comparing the known wardrobe characteristics with what a specific character wears is called profiling the character.

While profiling is not accurate in all cases, it quickly identifies attributes or characteristics associated with a subject of a predefined group. In old Western movies, wearing a black hat doesn't make a character bad, but it makes the audience suspicious of that character. Profiling in the operating system security context is really no different. The idea of profiling is to define a baseline of a known configuration. In most cases, the baseline is that of a secure configuration. Once you have a defined baseline, it can be compared with existing system configurations, reporting any differences. You can investigate the differences and take appropriate action to make your computers more secure.

Profiling also allows you to compare snapshots, or baselines, of your systems over time. Comparing two snapshots of the same computer taken at two different times helps you see configuration changes over time. While some changes may be normal, other configuration changes may indicate unauthorized changes to your environment.

Profiling Windows Computers

Microsoft provides a few tools that make profiling Windows easy. The **Security Configuration and Analysis (SCA)** tool helps administrators do several things. It allows you to analyze a computer and compare its configuration settings with a baseline. The SCA can also apply a baseline to force current computer settings to match the settings defined in the baseline. This tool is handy anytime you want to overwrite existing settings and revert to a known configuration. The SCA uses **security templates** to store the settings that make up baselines (**FIGURE 7-1**). A security template is a text file that contains a list of configuration settings.

FIGURE 7-1

Security templates.

Courtesy of Microsoft Corporation.

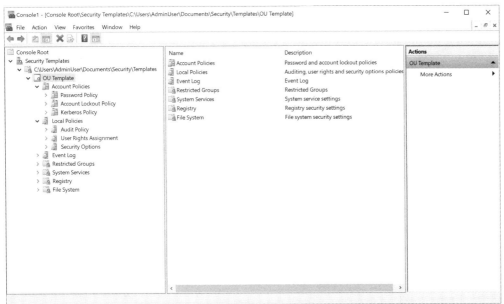

Technical TIP

To open a new Microsoft Management Console (MMC) and use the Security Templates and add the snap-in in the MMC:

1. Open the MMC. Choose the Windows Start button and enter **mmc/a** in the Run box.
2. From the MMC menu, select File, Add/Remove Snap-in.
3. Select Security Templates from the list of snap-ins on the left.
4. Choose Add, OK, to add the Security Templates snap-in.
5. Select the first path under Security Templates and open the context menu by right-clicking on the path.
6. From the menu, select New Template.
7. Enter a name and description for the new template and choose OK. To use this example in PowerShell later in the chapter, select the name OU Template.
8. Expand sections of the new template and edit any desired settings.

 NOTE

Windows Server operating systems, up through Windows Server 2012 R2, include another tool that is helpful in profiling a Windows server. The Security Configuration Wizard (SCW) analyzes a server and makes recommendations to improve its security. SCW was retired after Windows server 2012 R2 and is not available in Windows Server 2016 or later.

Older versions of Windows included a collection of security templates. Since Windows computers operate in a wide variety of use cases, current versions of Windows do not include an assortment of specific templates. Microsoft decided that attempting to address so many workstation and server roles would be difficult and wouldn't end up providing much value. Creating vendor-supplied generic default security templates becomes more difficult as the number of configuration roles and options grow. A good way to create a baseline for profiling use is to create your own security template that corresponds to your organization's security policy. The process of editing template settings is very similar to editing Group Policy Object (GPO) settings.

Microsoft provides the Security Configuration and Analysis tool **snap-in** (**FIGURE 7-2**) to the **Microsoft Management Console (MMC)**, which helps you to create and manage security profiling. The SCA tool can be used to profile a Windows computer. The SCA tool allows you to analyze a computer using either a default template or a custom template you created using the Security Templates MMC snap-in. You can also use security templates you have acquired from some other source. You can conduct a security analysis, also called profiling a system, using either the SCA MMC snap-in or the SCA command-line tool. The security analysis compares the current system settings with the template loaded representing the baseline. Once a baseline template is created, use the SCA command-line tool to report any differences between the current computer settings and the baseline. Although the same information is available in the SCA MMC snap-in, the SCA command-line tool produces text output. This makes it easier to spot differences

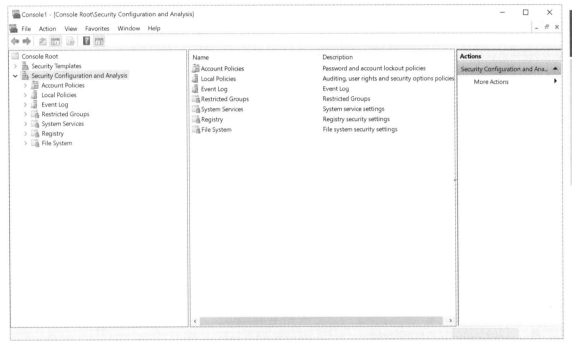

without having to navigate through multiple windows. You can even use SCA to change
current settings to match the baseline template.

Microsoft Baseline Security Analyzer

Microsoft in the past provided a free tool for several versions of Windows that analyzes
computers to identify insecure configurations. The **Microsoft Baseline Security Analyzer
(MBSA)** is an easy-to-use legacy tool. However, MBSA isn't the latest analysis tool available,
and with each new version of Windows, it looks for fewer and fewer vulnerabilities. At
the time of this writing, it no longer supports the most current versions of the Window
operating systems, including Windows 11 and Windows Server 2022. The last known
supported versions were for Windows 8.1 and Windows Server 2012R with minimal
support still available for Windows 10 and Windows Server 2016. Support for the tool has
officially ended with the most current versions, and the MBSA is no longer found on the
Microsoft official website for download. Because there is still a gap between those who are
on new older systems and those who have not upgraded their systems to Windows 11 and
Windows Server 2022, the tool is still useful for legacy system security testing. The latest
(and last) version of MBSA is version 2.3. If your environment includes computers running

NOTE

Although each new version of MBSA scans for fewer vulnerabilities than previous versions, it still has value. MBSA can help you find the most obvious security issues that can be easy to address. It is recommended that every organization use multiple toolsets to comprehensively analyze Windows computers for security issues. You'll learn about other tools available to help keep Windows computers secure in this chapter.

previous versions of Windows, you can consult the MBSA release notes or download page to ensure that your version of MBSA supports all your Windows computers. Since MBSA does not install with Windows, you must download and install it yourself. It is well worth the small amount of time and effort to acquire and install this tool.

The MBSA evaluates part of the current security state of computers in accordance with Microsoft security recommendations. It not only identifies problems but also ranks them by severity and provides recommendations to fix each one. Although MBSA isn't as comprehensive as it used to be, it does a good job of finding much of the "low hanging fruit."

Technical TIP

The SCA snap-in in the MMC profiles a Windows computer. To add the SCA snap-in:

1. Open the MMC. Choose the Windows Start button and enter **mmc/a** in the Run box.
2. From the MMC menu, select File, Add/Remove Snap-in.
3. Select Security Configuration and Analysis from the list of snap-ins on the left.
4. Choose Add, OK, to add the SCA snap-in.

The SCA snap-in compares your current computer's settings with the baseline in an SCA database. The next step is either to load the baseline template into a database or to open an existing database. Follow these steps to open a database:

5. Select SCA and right-click to open the context menu.
6. Select Open Database.
7. Enter the name of a new database or navigate to an existing database and choose Open. If you want to test this in PowerShell, select the name of the template created earlier in the chapter and make the log name **SCADB.sdb**.
8. Select the template you want to use for the profiling session and choose Open.
9. Right-click to open the context menu for SCA.
10. Select Analyze Computer Now.
11. Enter the fully qualified pathname for the analysis error log file and choose OK. To use this in the PowerShell example, the log name selected post scan should be SCALog.log.
12. To view the results of the analysis, select the desired policy element. Expand a parent node to see the desired policy elements. The SCA snap-in displays each policy setting along with the baseline setting and the current computer setting (**FIGURE 7-3**).

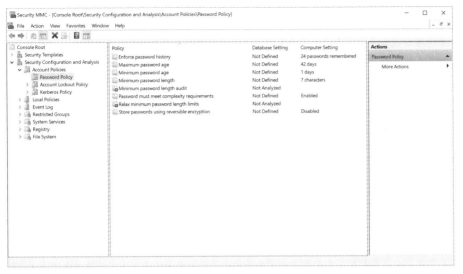

FIGURE 7-3

SCA snap-in analysis results.

Courtesy of Microsoft Corporation.

FIGURE 7-4

SCA command-line tool.

Courtesy of Microsoft Corporation.

The SCA command-line tool can be used to profile a Windows computer. Follow these steps:

1. Open a PowerShell window. Choose the Windows Start button and select PowerShell and Run as an administrator.

2. Enter the following command to profile a Windows computer using the SCADB.sdb database, loading the OUSettings.inf and the SCALog.log file for the output log file:

   Secedit /analyze /db SCADB.sdb /cfg "OU Template.inf" /Log SCALog.log /verbose

3. If you have already loaded a template into a database, you can use this command instead to use an existing database:

   Secedit /analyze /db SCADB.sdb /Log SCALog.log /verbose

4. Open the SCALog.log file to review the analysis results (**FIGURES 7-4** and **7-5**).

7

Microsoft Windows Security
Profile and Audit Tools

SCA command-line tool
analysis results.

```
SCALog - Notepad                                                   —    □    ×
File  Edit  Format  View  Help
Saturday, September 24, 2022 1:18:09 PM
----Analysis engine was initialized successfully.----

----Reading Configuration Info...

----Analyze User Rights...
        Analyze SeNetworkLogonRight.
Not Configured - SeNetworkLogonRight.
        Analyze SeTcbPrivilege.
Not Configured - SeTcbPrivilege.
        Analyze SeMachineAccountPrivilege.
Not Configured - SeMachineAccountPrivilege.
        Analyze SeBackupPrivilege.
Not Configured - SeBackupPrivilege.
        Analyze SeChangeNotifyPrivilege.
Not Configured - SeChangeNotifyPrivilege.
        Analyze SeSystemtimePrivilege.
Not Configured - SeSystemtimePrivilege.
        Analyze SeCreatePagefilePrivilege.
Not Configured - SeCreatePagefilePrivilege.
        Analyze SeCreateTokenPrivilege.
Not Configured - SeCreateTokenPrivilege.
        Analyze SeCreatePermanentPrivilege.
Not Configured - SeCreatePermanentPrivilege.
        Analyze SeDebugPrivilege.
Not Configured - SeDebugPrivilege.
        Analyze SeRemoteShutdownPrivilege.
Not Configured - SeRemoteShutdownPrivilege.
        Analyze SeAuditPrivilege.
Not Configured - SeAuditPrivilege.
        Analyze SeIncreaseQuotaPrivilege.
Not Configured - SeIncreaseQuotaPrivilege.

                           Ln 1, Col 1        100%   Windows (CRLF)    UTF-16 LE
```

Technical TIP

You can download MBSA 2.3 from this link:

https://www.techspot.com/downloads/3886-microsoft-baseline-security-analyzer.html.

Once you download MBSA, open the downloaded file and follow the directions to install MBSA on your computer. Although Microsoft does not officially offer the tool on its website, this website is considered reputable and verifiable.

MBSA Graphical User Interface

You can run the MBSA using the graphical user interface (GUI) or the command-line interface. The **GUI** provides an intuitive way to select the types of resources MBSA will analyze. The GUI is the most common interface to use when learning about MBSA. To run MBSA, launch the program, select the scan scope and options, and then start the scan. The scan report contains lots of information on what was found and what you should do about it. You choose to address or ignore each identified issue. It's really that simple. The MBSA will scan your selected computers for just the types of vulnerabilities that interest you. In addition to looking for specific security vulnerabilities, MBSA will alert you if operating system or application updates exist that you haven't installed.

Technical TIP

Follow these steps to use the MBSA GUI (**FIGURE 7-6**) to scan your computer for vulnerabilities:

1. Open MBSA. Choose the Windows Start button and then, select Microsoft Baseline Security Analyzer 2.3.
2. Select the desired operation mode:
   a. Select Scan a Computer to scan a single computer.
   b. Select Scan Multiple Computers to scan more than one computer in a single session.
   c. Select View Existing Security Scan Reports to view the results of previous scans.
3. If you chose to scan one or more computers, enter the computer or domain name or IP address(es).
   a. For single computer scans, enter either a computer name or IP address.
   b. For multiple computer scans, enter a domain name or a range of IP addresses.
4. Select the checkboxes next to the desired scanning options (**FIGURE 7-7**). In many cases, leaving all options checked provides the most extensive analysis.
5. Choose Start Scan to begin the scanning process.
6. Whether you selected the scan option or selected an existing security scan report, MBSA presents the results (**FIGURE 7-8**) in a user-friendly report. Each report issue includes a description of what was scanned, details of the result, and in many cases, descriptive information on how to resolve the issue.
7. Choose OK to close the report viewer and return to the MBSA main window.

FIGURE 7-6

MBSA GUI.

Courtesy of Microsoft
Corporation.

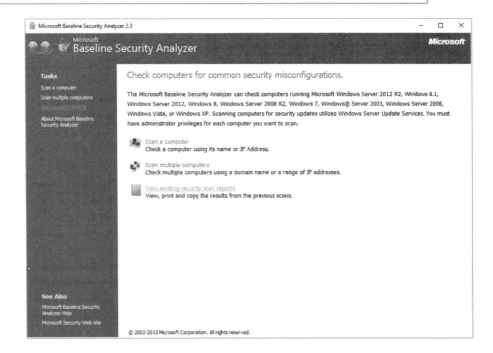

FIGURE 7-7

MBSA scan options.

Courtesy of Microsoft
Corporation.

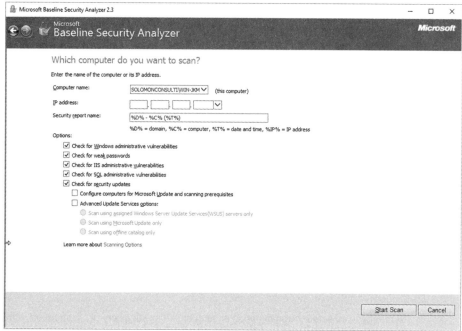

FIGURE 7-8

MBSA scan results.

Courtesy of Microsoft
Corporation.

MBSA Command-Line Interface

Microsoft also provides a command-line interface for MBSA (**FIGURE 7-9**). The MBSAcli. exe command performs the same scan as the MBSA GUI (**FIGURE 7-10**) but with the added flexibility of starting the scan from the command line. Calling an MBSA scan from the command line gives you the ability to use batch files to scan computers for vulnerabilities. You can schedule batch files to run scans unattended at any time.

The MBSA command-line interface supports the same functions as the GUI. In fact, there are advanced options that give you more flexibility than the GUI. **TABLE 7-1** shows the most common MBSA command-line interface options.

Microsoft SCA and MBSA aren't the only profilers. Other products can help you identify security vulnerabilities and keep your computers as secure as possible. You'll learn about other products that extend and complement SCA and MBSA in the next sections.

7

Microsoft Windows Security Profile and Audit Tools

FIGURE 7-9

MBSA command-line interface.

Courtesy of Microsoft Corporation.

FIGURE 7-10

MBSA command-line interface scan results.

Courtesy of Microsoft Corporation.

TABLE 7-1 Common MBSA Command-Line Interface (mbsacli.exe) Options

OPTION	DESCRIPTION
/target	Computer to scan. Target can be a domain or computer name or an IP address.
/d	Domain to scan. Use NetBIOS-compatible domain names instead of fully qualified domain names. For example, use "CorpDomain" instead of "CorpDomain.com."
/r	Range of IP addresses of computers to scan. Beginning and ending IP addresses should be separated by a hyphen. For example, use "192.168.141.130-192.168.141.254."
/listfile	Filename of a text file that contains computer names or IP addresses of computers to scan. Each computer name or IP address should be on a separate line.
/n	Scan options that MBSA should *not* perform. Excluded options may consist of:OS—Windows administrative vulnerabilitiesIIS—Internet Information Services administrative vulnerabilitiesSQL—SQL Server administrative vulnerabilitiesUpdates—Missing security updatesPassword—Check for weak passwords. You can combine options with the "+" operator. For example, "/n os+iis+sql+password" would scan only for missing updates. MBSA excludes all options you supply.

© Jones & Bartlett Learning.

Technical TIP

Follow these steps to use the MBSA GUI to scan your computer for vulnerabilities:

1. Open the PowerShell window. Choose the Windows Start button and select PowerShell.

2. Enter the following command to scan a single computer named "generic" for all vulnerabilities and store the results in a file named mbsaout.txt:

   mbsacli /target generic >mbsaout.txt

3. Enter the following command to scan a single computer named "generic" only for missing updates and store the results in a file named mbsaout.txt:

   mbsacli /target generic /n os+iis+sql+password >mbsaout.txt

   This command uses the /n option to "Not scan" for "OS," "IIS," "SQL," and "Password" vulnerabilities.

4. Enter the following command to scan a range of computers using IP addresses only for missing updates and store the results in a file named mbsaout.txt:

   mbsacli /r 192.168.141.130-192.168.141.254 /n os+iis+sql+password >mbsaout.txt

   This command uses the /n option to "Not scan" for "OS," "IIS," "SQL," and "Password" vulnerabilities.

The results for each scan are reported in two locations. The mbsacli command produces text output and also creates a descriptive results report in the C:\users\username\ Securityscans folder. This is the same folder that the MBSA GUI uses and the report is in the same format. You can use the MBSA GUI to view and analyze the output of the command-line MBSA just as if the output were generated from the GUI.

Technical TIP

MBSA and SCA primarily focus on the core Microsoft operating system settings, and settings of some older Microsoft application software products. The following tools are not only concerned with Microsoft products, they can search for vulnerabilities in the operating system as well as in software developed by organizations other than Microsoft.

OpenVAS

The Open Vulnerability Assessment System (OpenVAS) is an open source framework of a collection of tools and services. These tools and services work together to scan multiple computers, identify known vulnerabilities on these computers, and provide a set of tools for reporting on and managing the mitigation of identified vulnerabilities. Many vulnerability assessors, auditors, penetration testers, and hackers use OpenVAS to search for security vulnerabilities. The OpenVAS framework is free to use and is frequently updated to identify the latest vulnerabilities. You can use OpenVAS to scan many computers, including those running Microsoft and non-Microsoft operating systems. The framework is very good at identifying the underlying operating system for any target and then tailoring the scans for that operating system.

OpenVAS originally began its life as a fork of the popular Nessus vulnerability assessment software package. Tenable Security, who owns Nessus, decided to change the Nessus open source license to a closed proprietary license model in 2005. A group of penetration testers took a fork of the Nessus open source product and created GNessUs, which was a contrived name that indicated the new product was Nessus under the GNU General Public License (GPL). The product was eventually renamed to OpenVAS and is currently developed and provided by Greenbone Networks GmbH. Nessus remains as a viable commercially available vulnerability assessment framework, but many organizations choose to use the somewhat less comprehensive OpenVAS product to avoid commercial license fees.

Unlike most other software products that support vulnerability scanning, OpenVAS isn't packaged as a downloadable executable file that you can just install on a Windows computer. You can get OpenVAS several different ways:

- **Live demo**—This is a live environment that allows users to connect to an OpenVAS scanner via a website and conduct scans on a set of provided target systems.
- **Virtual appliance**—OpenVAS is available in a prebuilt virtual appliance that is compatible with VirtualBox, VMware ESXi, and Hyper-V virtualization managers. If you already have a virtualization manager installed, you can simply add this to it and get it up and running.

- **Source code**—Greenbone makes all of the OpenVAS source code available for anyone to download and compile on their own systems. This option allows organizations to customize OpenVAS as needed for their own environments.
- **Install packages**—Third-party providers offer prebuilt installable packages for various operating systems. The most popular install target operating system is Linux. In fact, you can even install OpenVAS in the Windows Subsystem for Linux.

Regardless how you acquire OpenVAS, the steps to run scans is the same. (Following is just a simple list of steps—OpenVAS supports many more options to identify and manage vulnerabilities).

- Launch the Greenbone Security Assistant (GSA). After starting the OpenVAS engine (see the documentation that came with OpenVAS on how to do this—it is often the command **openvas-start**) launch a web browser and enter the address **https://127.0.0.1**.
- Log in using the default userid of admin and the password that was generated when you installed OpenVAS.
- Select Scans -> Tasks from the menubar, Click on the "Task Wizard" icon. This icon is a magic wand in a purple square. That will launch the task wizard to help you configure a new scan.
- Enter an IP address you want to scan and select Start Scan.

FIGURES 7-11 and 7-12 show how to set up a single node scan in OpenVAS. FIGURE 7-13 shows the results from the last OpenVAS scan.

FIGURE 7-11

Greenbone Security Assistant (OpenVAS) main dashboard.

Used with permission from Greenbone Networks GmbH.

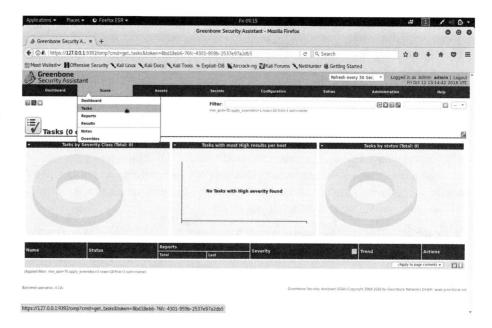

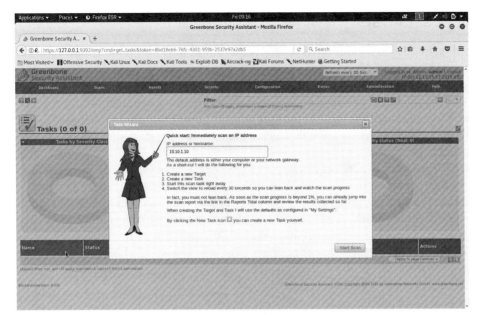

FIGURE 7-12

OpenVAS Task
Wizard.

Used with permission from
Greenbone Networks GmbH.

7

Microsoft Windows Security
Profile and Audit Tools

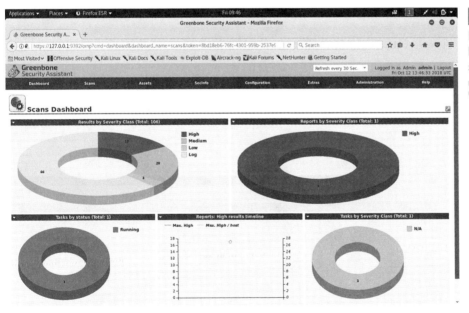

FIGURE 7-13

NetChk Protect
Limited OpenVAS
scan results.

Used with permission from
Greenbone Networks GmbH.

Technical TIP

You can visit http://www.OpenVAS.org/ for complete OpenVAS product descriptions, requirements,
and product support.

Nessus Essentials

Although OpenVAS is a popular open source vulnerability scanner, Tenable now offers its Nessus scanner product in three versions. You can purchase a Nessus Professional license as a one-time purchase or as a subscription. The Nessus Professional license includes one of the most advanced and up-to-date vulnerability scanning solutions available. Tenable also offers the Nessus Essentials license. The Essentials license is free to use for up to 16 IP addresses and makes it a great option for students and entry-level security practitioners.

Nessus makes it easy to conduct many types of vulnerability scans with options that fit almost any security practitioner's needs. You can conduct and agent and an agentless scan, where the agent-based can produce more granular results. The Essentials license doesn't include some of the more advanced options, but it will show you what the more advanced licenses can do for you. The Nessus product relatively straightforward to use. Unless you need to modify specific settings, you select the type of scan you want, tell Nessus what target IPs to scan, and then start the scan. Nessus carries out the requested scans and provides detailed results of what it finds.

FIGURE 7-14 shows the Nessus Essentials desktop.

FIGURE 7-15 shows the results of an advanced scan with summary information listed for each target, and **FIGURE 7-16** shows a sample page form the Nessus Essentials exported summary report.

Technical TIP

Go to https://www.tenable.com/products/nessus to see more Nessus product and license information.

FIGURE 7-14

Nessus Essentials desktop.

Reprinted with permission from Tenable, Inc.

FIGURE 7-15

Results from a Nessus Essentials advanced scan.

Reprinted with permission from Tenable, Inc.

7

Microsoft Windows Security Profile and Audit Tools

Burp Suite Web Vulnerability Scanner

Some Windows servers perform specialized functions and need to be assessed accordingly. For example, you should scan your web servers for general security vulnerabilities, but also scan them for vulnerabilities that are specific to web applications. The Burp Suite Web Vulnerability Scanner does just that. Burp Suite focuses on vulnerabilities found in web applications and makes it easy to scan for those weaknesses. Depending on your needs, you can get Burp Suite as Enterprise, Professional, or Community licenses. Each license provides different levels of service. The Community edition is free, but lacks the powerful Web Vulnerability Scanner. Not only does the vulnerability scanner identify vulnerabilities, it provides a lot of useful supplemental information. For example, rather than just ranking vulnerabilities based on severity, it also rates them based on confidence level, allowing you to focus on vulnerabilities that have a low chance of being false positives. Burp Suite also provides information like CVE IDs, descriptions, and proofs of concept (POC) on how the exploit was performed. This allows you to gather extra information regarding the vulnerability, and the POC will show you how you can recreate that exploit yourself so that you can be confident that it isn't a false positive. To get the scanner, you'll need at least the Professional license. **FIGURE 7-17** shows the defined web server target for a vulnerability scan. **FIGURE 7-18** shows the results of a web vulnerability scan. **FIGURE 7-19** shows an Executive Report that Burp Suite created based on the previous scan.

Technical TIP

Visit https://portswigger.net/burp/ for complete Burp Suite product descriptions, requirements, and capabilities.

10.0.0.1

0	0	1	3	27
CRITICAL	HIGH	MEDIUM	LOW	INFO

Vulnerabilities — Total: 31

SEVERITY	CVSS	PLUGIN	NAME
MEDIUM	6.4	51192	SSL Certificate Cannot Be Trusted
LOW	3.3	10663	DHCP Server Detection
LOW	3.3	11197	Multiple Ethernet Driver Frame Padding Information Disclosure (Etherleak)
LOW	N/A	69551	SSL Certificate Chain Contains RSA Keys Less Than 2048 bits
INFO	N/A	45590	Common Platform Enumeration (CPE)
INFO	N/A	54615	Device Type
INFO	N/A	19689	Embedded Web Server Detection
INFO	N/A	35716	Ethernet Card Manufacturer Detection
INFO	N/A	86420	Ethernet MAC Addresses
INFO	N/A	84502	HSTS Missing From HTTPS Server
INFO	N/A	43111	HTTP Methods Allowed (per directory)
INFO	N/A	10107	HTTP Server Type and Version
INFO	N/A	24260	HyperText Transfer Protocol (HTTP) Information
INFO	N/A	10114	ICMP Timestamp Request Remote Date Disclosure
INFO	N/A	106658	JQuery Detection
INFO	N/A	11219	Nessus SYN scanner
INFO	N/A	19506	Nessus Scan Information
INFO	N/A	11936	OS Identification
INFO	N/A	50845	OpenSSL Detection

10.0.0.1 4

FIGURE 7-16

Sample page from a Nessus Essentials exported summary scan report.

Reprinted with permission from Tenable, Inc.

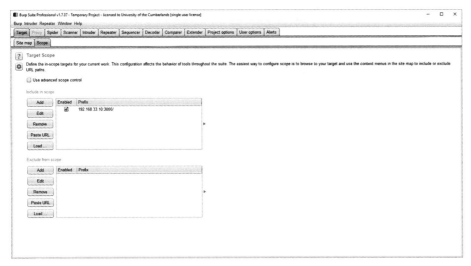

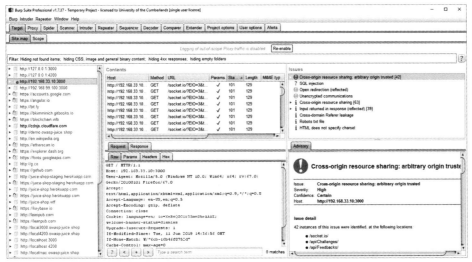

Microsoft Windows Security Audit

An *audit* is an evaluation of a collection of one or more objects. The objects can be people, things, processes, or organizations. An audit can be an evaluation of pretty much anything. The purpose of an audit is to determine if the objects of the audit meet some criteria. An audit is more than just collecting information about things. You must compare the collected information with some standards or guidelines and then determine if your collected information is similar to, or different from, the standard information. In most cases, an audit doesn't focus only on a point in time. Most audits consider information

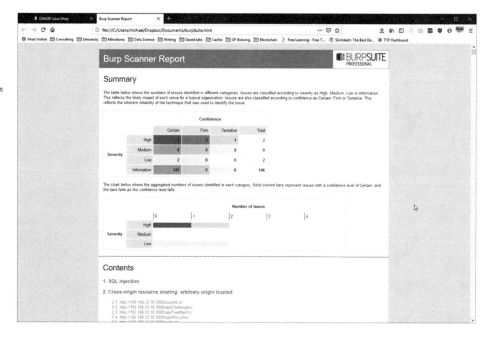

gathered over a specific period. In this way, audits can reveal patterns of performance when compared with standards.

A security audit in a Windows computer environment is a collection of configuration and performance information compared with information contained in your security policy. The purpose of a Windows security audit is to measure how well the audited computer operation complies with your security policy. This process may seem similar to profiling a Windows computer. Although there are similarities, and profiling is often a part of a security audit, the two processes differ. Profiling is the process of comparing computer security settings with a baseline. Windows security auditing is a larger process of comparing computer security settings and performance with your security policy, typically over a defined period. As a general rule, the scope of an audit is larger than just profiling a collection of computers.

A Windows security audit involves several activities. These activities are related and may occur multiple times throughout an audit. Each audit may take different paths but the basic process (**FIGURE 7-20**) includes the following:

- Verifying that security controls comply with the security policy
- Collecting configuration and performance information
- Creating initial and subsequent baselines
- Recognizing and analyzing configuration or performance information changes

Collecting initial and subsequent baseline information involves more than just saving analysis reports. You will likely include various audit log files to track access to sensitive

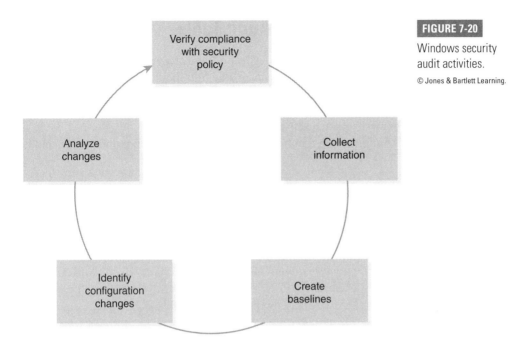

FIGURE 7-20

Windows security
audit activities.

© Jones & Bartlett Learning.

7

Microsoft Windows Security
Profile and Audit Tools

resources. Most log file entries of interest will likely be data access for sensitive data and to execute events for administrative programs that can cause damage if used improperly. Log files can provide a wealth of performance information. They can help isolate problems and identify behaviors that both support and violate security policy.

Carefully consider what items you want to audit. Auditing too many events for too many objects can cause your computers to run more slowly and consume more disk space to store the audit log file entries. Consider logging only access failures for most objects you choose to audit. You can audit both access successes and failures for resources that are critical to your organization, but don't track audit information for all resources unless absolutely necessary. The rule of thumb is to consider the most sensitive areas that directly impact your ability to secure your systems such as login attempts. If you find multiple failed logins against disabled accounts set as honeypots, you may want to consider that your system may be under attack and other security measures must be taken. This is a strategy to help focus your auditing plan instead of just turning auditing on for everything.

Another important consideration is being consistent. The way you conduct an effective audit is to establish a consistent process. Define the information you'll need for the analysis phase and then ensure that you are collecting and storing the necessary information. Planning audit activities improves the likelihood that you'll capture all the information you need. Auditing should not be viewed as activities that attempt to uncover problems. It should be a continuous process of improving the security standing of your computing environment. In other words, make sure auditing is proactive in problem-solving and not just reactive.

Microsoft Windows Security Audit Tools

A Windows security audit involves identifying, collecting, and analyzing information. You'll need a plan and some tools to make the task manageable. You should plan ahead for any audit information needs and start the collection process as soon as possible. Your goal is to use the tools at your disposal to collect every bit of information that an auditor can use to verify compliance or research unusual activity.

Collecting every bit of information that may be needed can seem impossible and become

---

Technical TIP

You can download the SomarSoft utilities from http://www.systemtools.com/somarsoft/?somarsoft.com.

You can download MSAT from http://www.microsoft.com/en-us/download/details.aspx?id=12273.

You can download the Microsoft SCT from https://www.microsoft.com/en-us/download/details .aspx?id=55319.

---

overwhelming. It is also difficult to do without collecting lots of unneeded information. The goal should be to collect as much information as possible that is likely to be useful for auditing. **TABLE 7-2** lists some Windows auditing-related tools you can use and the information they help you retain.

The tools listed in Table 7-2 are a great starting point for collecting audit information. Develop a naming convention and storage location for the tools' output. A good naming convention includes information, such as the computer name, date, time, and type of information in the file. Here is a suggested audit file-naming convention:

Computer_name.file_contents.yyyymmddhhmmss.txt
Example: SCILaptop.sec_evt_log.20100401113533.txt

- **Computer_name**—Name of the computer
- **File_contents**—Abbreviated identifier that represents the contents of the file, such as sec_evt_log or registry
- **Date and time**—Creation date and time of the file
  - **yyyy**—Four-digit year
  - **mm**—Two-digit month
  - **dd**—Two-digit day of the month
  - **hh**—Two-digit hour in 24-hour format
  - **mm**—Two-digit minute
  - **ss**—Two-digit second

Use the Windows auditing tools at your disposal to create periodic baselines and store event log files. You should decide what frequency works best for your organization. Monthly or quarterly baselines generally provide a good starting point for auditors. Be sure to consult both your internal security policy and any security related compliance

TABLE 7-2 Windows Auditing Tools	
TOOL	**DESCRIPTION**
SCA snap-in	GUI snap-in to the MMC that compares a computer's settings with a predefined template. The SCA is useful to quickly identify any differences from standard settings.
Secedit.exe	Command-line version of SCA. Secedit performs the same basic functions of SCA but produces a text file as output. The command-line format allows you to use secedit in batch files for automatically scheduled audits.
MBSA	GUI auditing tool that checks one or more computers for missing patches, weak passwords, and other common security vulnerabilities. Supports older versions of Windows to include Windows 8.1 and Windows Server 2012 R2.
Mbsacli.exe	Command-line interface for MBSA. Mbsacli makes it easy to run MBSA on a schedule and store output text files for later analysis.
Microsoft Security Assessment Tool (MSAT)	Legacy tool to measure current system security and provide recommendations to mitigate vulnerabilities. MSAT supports Windows versions through Windows 7 and Windows Server 2008.
Microsoft Security Compliance Toolkit (SCT)	A set of tools to help enterprise administrators assess Microsoft-recommended security baselines for Microsoft products.
DumpSec	The SomarSoft utility that dumps permissions and audit settings for the file system, Registry, and printers, and shares the information to a text file; a command-line utility to use in batch files to schedule audit tasks.
DumpEvt	The SomarSoft utility that dumps the Windows event logs to text files. DumpReg is a command-line utility you can use in batch files to schedule audit tasks.
DumpReg	The SomarSoft utility that dumps part or all of the Windows Registry to text files. DumpReg is a command-line utility you can use in batch files to schedule audit tasks.

© Jones & Bartlett Learning.

requirements you may have when deciding on a frequency. Also, consider creating baselines more frequently in environments that regularly change. The baselines show a snapshot of your computers at a point in time, and the event logs show how settings changed from one baseline to another. Taken together, baselines and event log files can provide the information to better understand your Windows environment and make it compliant with your security policy.

Best Practices for Microsoft Windows Security Audits

A solid Windows security audit strategy is one that collects just enough information to satisfy audit needs and no more. Collecting too much information slows down your computers and wastes disk space. It also makes the auditing task harder with excessive information to review. You want to continually refine the audit information collection process to add collectors for information you need and remove collectors for information that is irrelevant.

Here is a list of Windows security audit best practices that will help you design, develop, and maintain an audit process that is efficient and effective. Modify these guidelines to suit your organization but pay attention to the suggestions—they can help you avoid wasting time and resources.

- Create initial baselines that represent a "secure" starting point for each computer. Develop security templates in SCA that contain the security settings for each type of workstation and server. Change the templates as needed and use them when building new computers. You can apply up-to-date templates to new Windows installations to quickly configure a new computer to your security standards.
- Run SCA/MBSA using command-line interface options to compare computer settings and configurations with your standards. Schedule scans to run periodically, such as weekly or monthly, and review the resulting output files for any identified problems.
- Develop batch files (or other automation methods) to run scans and collect ongoing operational information. Collect information using a set daily, weekly, or monthly schedule, and archive collected data files.
- Maintain current backups of all audit information, so you can recover historical audit information in the case of a disaster. Also make sure you back up your templates and other key data so you have spare copies if needed. Make sure these copies are also secured.
- Enable Windows auditing only for sensitive or critical resources. Use a strategic approach to audit what is most sensitive, priority areas or likely to be a risk you want to reduce. Turning auditing on for everything can be difficult to validate (too many false positives) and tax your system performance.
- Do not enable Read or List auditing on any object unless you really need the information. Read/List access auditing can create a tremendous amount of auditing information.
- Do not enable Execute auditing on binary files except for administrative utilities that could be used in an attack.
- Limit enabling all auditing actions to files, folders, programs, and other resources that are important to your business functions. Don't be afraid to enable auditing for any object—just ensure you need the information you'll be saving.
- Enable auditing for all change actions for your Windows install folder and any folders you use in normal business operation. It is also a good idea to audit changes to the Program Files folder.

- Audit all printer actions. You may need to be able to know who printed a document that found its way into the wrong hands.
- Ignore Read and Write actions for temporary folders but do audit Change Permissions, Write Attributes, and Write Extended Attributes actions. These actions can help identify attacker activities.
- Develop Windows policies and Group Policy Objects that are as simple as possible and still satisfy your security policy. Complex policies are difficult to verify.
- Develop clear guidelines to evaluate each element of your security policy. An audit should be a structured process to verify your security policy, not an unorganized hunt for problems. Know what you will be looking for before you search through lots of audit data.
- Limit the number of people who can edit or delete audit logs. Audit logs/information is meant to be a perfect record of what occurred on a system; in order for it to be valuable, you must be confident that it has not been modified in anyway. Therefore, in most instances audit logs should only be readable and not edited or deleted outside of scheduled deletions.
- Create clear labelling for all your log file storage. You want to make it as easy as possible to find the audit logs that pertain to certain resources. This is important not just for general auditing but also for investigations during a potential cyberattack/data breach.
- Have tools/scripts ready to parse log file data. Log files are usually too large in number to manual read/parse, so it's important that you have the tools readily available to parse this data for actionable information on a short notice. Your staff should be trained on how to use these tools effectively.

These best practices guidelines are only a starting point, but they give you guidance on how to develop an auditing strategy that will work for your organization.

CHAPTER SUMMARY

Auditing is the process of validating that an environment complies with its design. Basically, auditing helps ensure that your computers are doing what they are supposed to be doing and nothing more. Although the process sounds simple, it takes substantial thought and planning to get to the point of successfully performing an audit. You must clearly define the standards and guidelines for your environment. Then, you must collect and retain the information that provides evidence your environment is operating as designed. Finally, you must develop and execute the procedures that analyze the collected information to decide whether your environment complies with your security policy.

Auditing includes planning to collect information and using tools to collect and organize information for audit analysis. In this chapter, you learned about the planning, the process, and the tools. All that is left is to put it all into practice.

KEY CONCEPTS AND TERMS

Baseline

Microsoft Baseline Security
Analyzer (MBSA)

Microsoft Management Console
(MMC)

Profiling

Security Configuration and
Analysis (SCA)

Security template

Snap-in

CHAPTER 7 ASSESSMENT

1. A baseline is the initial settings in a newly
installed system.

A. True

B. False

2. A baseline, also called a(n) _____, is a collection
of settings at a specific point in time.

3. Which Microsoft tool analyzes a computer's
settings and compares its configuration with a
baseline?

A. SCA

B. MBSA

C. OpenVAS

D. SCT

4. Stored settings that make up a baseline are
stored in which type of files?

A. Baseline configuration

B. Baseline database

C. Security template

D. Security object

5. The Security Configuration and Analysis tool
operates as a snap-in to the _____.

6. Which command-line tool provides the same
scanning capability as SCA?

A. Secedit

B. Mbsacli

C. Scacli

D. Mbsaedit

7. Which of the following products does MBSA *not*
analyze?

A. IIS

B. SQL Server

C. Adobe Acrobat

D. Windows 7

8. MBSA automatically ranks vulnerabilities by
severity.

A. True

B. False

9. Which command-line tool provides the same
scanning capability as MBSA?

A. Secedit

B. Mbsacli

C. Scacli

D. Mbsaedit

10. Which security scanner commonly runs as a
Linux virtual machine?

A. SCA

B. OpenVAS

C. Retina

D. MBSA

11. Which vulnerability scanner discussed in this
chapter makes its source code available?

A. Retina

B. nexpose

C. Nessus

D. OpenVAS

12. Which security scanner runs in a web browser
and doesn't require that you install a product
before scanning?

A. MBSA

B. OpenVAS

C. SCT

D. PSI

13. Which of the following statements best describe the relationship between profiling and auditing?

    A. Auditing is often a part of profiling.
    B. Profiling is often a part of auditing.
    C. Profiling and auditing are interchangeable terms.
    D. If auditing is in place, profiling is not necessary.

14. When designing an audit strategy, you should log access attempts on the _____ number of objects.

15. What is the main purpose of an audit?

    A. To uncover problems
    B. To catch errors
    C. To validate compliance
    D. To standardize configurations

Microsoft Windows Backup and Recovery Tools

AVAILABILITY IS ONE OF THE PROPERTIES, or pillars, of the C-I-A triad of information systems security, along with confidentiality and integrity. Secure information must be available to authorized users when they request it. Ensuring information availability requires planning and preparation to confront issues that threaten to make your information unavailable. Issues include attacks to deny service, degraded performance, and failures or disasters that limit or terminate access to your information. A solid security plan includes both components to avoid situations that threaten information availability and procedures to deal with problems if they do occur.

In this chapter, you'll learn about the basics of creating backup images and using them to restore your information. You'll learn about different scenarios that can result in loss of information and how to recover from different types of loss. Although most people consider the backup the most important component of a recovery plan, you'll learn how important other components really are. When you finish this chapter, you will be better prepared to protect your Windows systems from information loss.

Chapter 8 Topics

This chapter covers the following topics and concepts:

- What Microsoft Windows operating system (OS) and application backup and recovery are
- What workstation, server, network, and cloud backup techniques are
- What Microsoft Windows and application backup and recovery is in the context of business continuity planning and disaster recovery planning
- What the Microsoft Windows File History is
- What the Microsoft Windows Backup and Restore utility is
- What rebuilding systems from bare metal is
- How organizations manage backups with virtual machines
- What best practices for Microsoft Windows backup and recovery are

Chapter 8 Goals

When you complete this chapter, you will be able to:

- Describe Microsoft Windows OS and application backup and recovery techniques
- Compare different options for creating backups
- Incorporate backups and restore operations into a business continuity plan
- Use virtual images to create backups

Microsoft Windows OS and Application Backup and Recovery

Most of your efforts to secure information will focus on the **primary copy** of your information. The primary copy of any piece of information is the copy you use most frequently. You'll spend time and effort ensuring your organization's information is accessible only by authorized users. You'll carefully control what users can do with and to your information. But what happens if the primary copy of any data gets damaged or destroyed? What if a fire, flood, or other disaster destroys the computer where information resides? Or what if malware such as a virus infects, corrupts, or even deletes many of your important documents? How do you recover if existing controls do not protect your data?

The Need for Backups

The answer to all of these issues is to have access to a current **secondary copy** of the information you lost. While that solution may sound simple, it takes some thought and planning to provide a usable alternative. A valid **backup** is a crucial part of an organization's ability to recover from losing data. A backup is a defined collection of copies of files you create in case the primary copies of the files are damaged or destroyed. You can lose data many ways. Not all situations that result in losing data are major disasters. You have already seen a few situations that may cause you to lose data. **FIGURE 8-1** shows some of the reasons you may lose data:

- **Hardware errors**—Hard disks or disk controllers can fail. Hardware failures may occur slowly, introducing errors into your data files over time. Equipment can also be lost or stolen. Hundreds of thousands of laptops are left in airports and taxicabs each year.
- **Software errors**—Software bugs and poorly written software can cause you to lose data you thought was safe.
- **Malicious software**—Many types of malware damage or delete files to alter or destroy data.

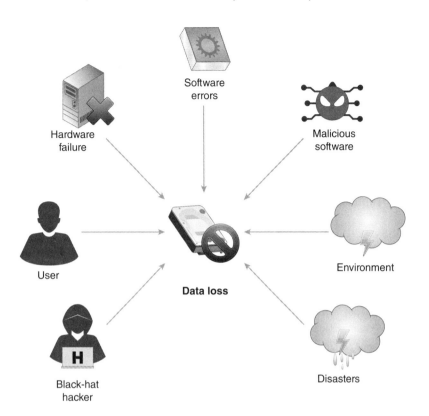

8

Microsoft Windows Backup
and Recovery Tools

- **User actions**—Users can take actions that damage or destroy data. Users can misuse
  application software or OS utilities to cause data loss. Data loss because of user actions
  can be either intentional or accidental. Each type of motivation requires a different type
  of control.
- **Attacks**—Successful attacks on your information systems can cause substantial data
  loss. Many of the controls you implement keep attackers from successfully harming
  your information's security.
- **Environmental issues**—Many issues with the computing environment can cause
  computers to fail and possibly damage data. Air-conditioning system failures can cause
  computers to overheat and possibly result in hardware damage. Fire suppressants and
  sprinkler systems can damage computers as well. Power spikes and fluctuations can
  also cause hardware damage that could result in losing data.
- **Natural disasters**—This is the category most people consider first when discussing
  reasons for backups. Disasters such as fires, floods, tornadoes, and earthquakes can
  cause substantial damage and result in data loss. Any large-scale disaster has the
  potential to damage your data.

When you lose the primary copy of your data, you have two primary choices:

1. Reconstruct the data.
2. Recover the data from a secondary source.

In most cases, reconstructing data is the last resort. Duplicating the work effort required to reconstruct data is often counterproductive, wasteful, and expensive. It also may be difficult to reconstruct if work was done in memory and no other copies exist. Reconstruction does not always supply a full secondary copy when done manually. It is generally faster and easier to recover lost data from a backup system that retains a full secondary copy, or a backup for you. There is one caveat: you must have created a secondary copy of your data prior to the loss for this option to be viable. A scheduled backup is the most common method to create secondary copies of important data to use in the case of primary data loss. A backup doesn't always guarantee that you'll be able to recover all the data you've lost, but it does make recovery a real possibility. You should also consider that backups can also be corrupted, be damaged or incomplete for various reasons.

Technical TIP

To ensure that a backup is more viable, you have many options when it comes to going beyond the backup. Make sure backups are made and then taken to an offsite location that is safe and secure. This can be done manually via tapes or hard drives that are transported from location to location, or snapshots you can send to a cloud provider of the data, thus making a third copy of critical data. You can also have redundant systems configured in an active/active or active/passive configuration to allow for backup of system, and in active/active solutions, backup of data as long as it's configured correctly. The important thing to remember is that when doing backups, disaster recovery planning and business continuity planning, there is always more options you can select from to ensure the safety of data.

WARNING

You should consider only verified backups to be useful. The safest practice is to assume unverified backups are always bad.

The Backup Process

The process to create a backup is fairly simple. You copy the files you want to duplicate to a target location. Ideally, you want to create an effective backup plan that enables the most recovery options; however, it is not so simple and takes time to design. The backup planning process starts with a series of questions to decide how to conduct the actual backup. Common questions include the following:

- Which files or folders will you back up?
- Will you use a static list of files or dynamically identify the items for backup?
- Where will the backed-up files be copied?
- Will you use removable media?
- Does the backup require human intervention?
- How will you label and identify backup media?
- What controls will you use to protect the C-I-A properties of the backup media?
- How frequently will you create a backup?
- What type of backup type/method will you select?

- Will you back up all your data each time, or just what changed since the last backup?
- How many generations of backups will you keep?
- How will you use the backup to recover lost data?
- Where will offsite data be stored, and how will they be retrieved?
- How long will you keep the data?
- What type of data encryption is required?

Backup Media Security

Secure any media that you use for backups. Attackers know that one of the easiest ways to bypass access controls in the operating system is to acquire the media you use to create a backup. If the information on your backup media is not protected, it can provide easy access for attackers. Backups will be targets and should be protected from falling into the wrong hands. Use aggressive physical security controls and even encryption to protect your backup media.

These are just a few of the questions you'll have to answer when deciding how to create a backup. Creating effective backups involves more than just copying files. Once you identify the files and folders you want to back up, you can open a backup utility to create the actual copies.

> **⚠ WARNING**
>
> When using removable media, make sure that you run tests on the media on a scheduled basis to ensure that the media works correctly. For example, you may be doing backups to tape for months only to realize that settings on the backup deck were set incorrectly or the tape media is defective. You may be transporting blank or corrupted tapes back and forth, and it won't be until you need to do a restore from that data that you find out its not working. Running sample tests on a scheduled basis is an important consideration to make. A secondary benefit to doing this is so that your team is also comfortable with conducting restores and understands how to use the systems correctly to do so.

The Restore Process

The real reason for creating any backup is to have the option of restoring if you lose any primary data. A **restore operation** is the process of copying secondary copies of files back to their primary locations. The most common reason to restore files is to replace damaged or missing data.

The restore process involves deciding whether to copy all files and folders from the backup media back to their original locations or only some files and folders. First, identify the files and folders you want to restore. Then, open a restore utility that is compatible with the backup image you created and start the process. There are several important considerations when you choose to restore data from a backup. Answer these three questions to ensure you understand the impact of restoring data to a previous state:

1. How long will it take to restore the selected data?
2. What data will I lose in the restore process?
3. Will I be able to use the data I restore?

All three questions may seem minor, but they have a large impact on how effective your backup policy will be. The first question is one that many IT personnel and users fail to appreciate. Many organizations choose to create complete backup images anytime they create backups. You can be sure you don't miss any files or folders when you back up everything.

The problem with complete backups is that they tend to take longer than backing up only selected files and folders, and they will certainly take longer to restore. Taking longer to create a backup can have other effects as well. If your backups take a long time to complete and it slows down your system to create the backup, you may choose to back up less frequently. That means more time passes, and you make more changes, between backups. The other part of this concern is how long it takes to restore lost data. You must define a target goal for how long it should take to recover from an interruption. Otherwise, it may be difficult to decide on the best recovery option.

Technical TIP

Include estimates of the effort you'll expend to reconstruct data in your restoration plan. After looking at the cost of reconstructing a half day's worth of data, you may find that making more frequent backups saves time and money.

Other Reasons to Restore

The restore process can be used for more than just repairing damage. Sometimes it is beneficial for normal operations to restore a system, or parts of a system, to a previously known state. For example, many organizations that use computers for training use the restore process to reset computers after classes. The ability to restore a computer to a state before students made any changes allows the organization to undo changes students made during a class. You can also use the restore process to undo changes, such as a new software installation, that cause your computer to stop functioning properly.

Most organizations set a **recovery time objective (RTO)** for critical resources. The RTO is the amount of time it should take to recover a resource and bring it back to normal operation. Assume the RTO for a specific server is 3 hours. If a full restore takes 4 hours but you can reenter and verify the lost data in 2 hours, a restore is not the most efficient choice.

The answer to the second question can often lead to many more questions. A backup is a snapshot of a collection of files at the time you created the backup. As long as you make no changes after you create the backup, you can recover all of your data. However, if you make any changes to data files after you create the backup, you risk losing those changes.

The most common reason to restore files is to recover from damaged or lost data. If you restore one or more files from backup media, you will lose any changes made to those files since creating the backup. Waiting longer between backups means you can potentially lose more data if you have to restore files. Carefully consider how you will reconstruct data created or changed since your last backup if you lose primary copies of your data. The common perception that simply restoring the most recent backup will fix everything is not accurate.

The last question addresses data that tend to change very frequently. Most organizations use database management systems to manage large amounts of data. Database files are likely updated frequently and may change during the backup process. Other large files may change while copying during a backup. When a file changes as it is being copied, it may lose its integrity. Most database vendors provide specialized backup utilities for database files to ensure the data maintain its integrity. Get to know your applications and any special requirements for including large files in backup operations. You don't want to find out your backed-up files aren't usable. When it comes to databases, another method to ensure that data is backed up is through replication of data to another entity in real-time, or, in other instances, sent over to a quorum shared by another database server that sits in a cluster. The quorum will help to provide which node is active at the present time. A transaction log will hold state between data in use and if an issue occurs, the secondary node of the cluster can take over and the data are safe in the quorum. Taking one step further into the design, as long as the data in the quorum are spread across an array (such as a RAID array) where disk mirroring or another form of safeguarding is in place, the data can be regenerated in real time if lost. The point is that you have many options that go beyond the basic backup and restore of a system. In today's architected systems, high availability is designed directly into the deployment of critical systems from the onset.

Looking back at the loss of files and how we can restore them from a secondary copy, we should consider the use of restore utilities that can be of assistance. The choice of restore utilities depends on which utility you used to create the backup image. Utilities must be compatible with backups. Beyond basic compatibility, the process depends on the specific options your backup and restore utility provides. In many cases, the restore utility copies everything from the backup media to a location on your hard disk. When you complete a well-planned restore operation, you'll have to take a few additional steps to get running again.

Volume Shadow Copy Service

Microsoft backup utilities make it easy to maintain integrity during backups for applications that support the **Volume Shadow Copy Service (VSS)**. VSS supports utilities and applications in creating snapshots of a running Windows system. Microsoft Backup utility uses VSS to alert applications like Structured Query Language (SQL) Server and Exchange. This allows the backup to take a snapshot of the system. VSS-aware applications stop writing to data files until the snapshot completes. The applications can continue writing but will work with the backup process to ensure blocks that are about to be written are backed up first. In this way, Windows ensures data integrity. For more information about VSS, go to this Microsoft site: https://docs.microsoft.com/en -us/windows/desktop/vss/volume-shadow-copy-service-portal.

Workstation, Server, Network, and Cloud Backup Techniques

Workstation Backups

Workstations store and process some information locally. It is important to ensure all your workstations back up important files. Some organizations overlook workstation backups. This results in data loss when problems arise. Often, locally stored data are an integral piece of organizational data. It is common that a company's security policy will be distributed and give users a method for ensuring they do not lose data, such as backing up their data to a shared drive that only they have access to and is maintained on a server. Other times, data are shared collectively in a group folder, still safe and located on a backed up centrally managed server. Doing this allows users to be a part of making sure they safeguard their own local data. This does not always work as users will often to forget to do this. Or, in some other special cases, they will work and save data on their local systems that needs to be stored locally. For example, software developers often copy programs to their local workstations to make changes. It is not unusual for developers to have several dozen programs in use on their local workstations. When they finish making program changes and testing the changes, they copy their work back to a central repository. What happens if a software developer encounters a problem that results in losing one or more local programs? He or she will lose all the work invested in program changes unless frequent backups for Workstation Domain computers keep current secondary copies of work in progress.

Even if members of your organization do not copy files from a central source to edit locally, backups will protect your workstations from loss. Nearly every workstation user stores local documents, spreadsheets, presentations, custom settings, and other data that would take time to reconstruct. At the very least, backing up workstations will save time if a user loses data.

Starting with Windows 8, Microsoft has expanded the options available for maintaining secondary copies of files. The current main backup solution for Microsoft workstations is **File History**. The File History feature allows users to identify personal files and designate a location to where they will be automatically backed up. Microsoft maintains versions of backed up files and makes it easy to restore one or more files on demand. By default, File History backs up files in your user's home folder. Those are most likely to be the files that frequently change and need protection. You can change the backup settings to protect more or fewer files and folders. **FIGURE 8-2** shows the File History Backup Options window.

Technical TIP

Open the Windows Backup (File History) options on a computer running Windows using these steps:

1. Choose the Windows Start button > Settings (the small gear icon on the left side of the menu).
2. Select Update & Security > Backup.
3. If the toggle box under Automatically back up my files is Off, click it to turn it On.
4. Select More options under Backup files using File History.
5. Scroll down to the bottom of the window and select Restore files from a current backup to browse through backed-up file versions and restore any backed-up version.

Restoring files to previous versions is easy too. You can browse through all backed-up file versions as shown in **FIGURE 8-3**, or look at versions of specific files from the File Explorer context (right-click) menu. **FIGURE 8-4** shows the previous versions for a specific file that are available. You can restore any file that has been backed up to any previous version.

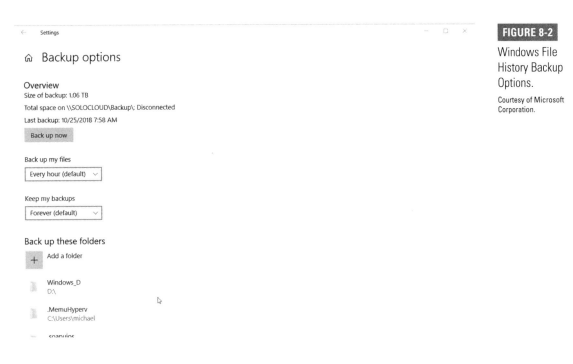

FIGURE 8-2

Windows File History Backup Options.

Courtesy of Microsoft Corporation.

8

Microsoft Windows Backup and Recovery Tools

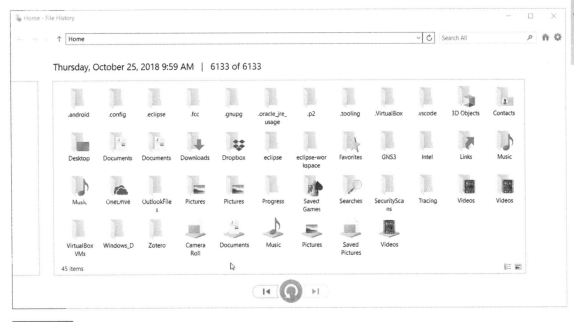

FIGURE 8-3

File History File Versions browser.

Courtesy of Microsoft Corporation.

FIGURE 8-4

Previous versions of a file via File Explorer.

Courtesy of Microsoft Corporation.

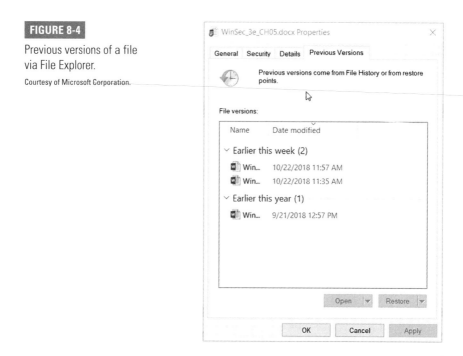

For more specific control over what is backed up and when, Microsoft also includes an updated version of the legacy Backup and Restore utility with Windows. Now called the Backup and Restore (Windows 7) utility, it has been upgraded from its Vista predecessor to make backing up and restoring workstations simpler. With the current version of Windows at version 11, there is no change in the name or usage of the backup systems available with the most current system available.

In order to configure the utility, the Windows Backup and Restore Wizard asks you to provide answers to three main questions to configure your backup scope and schedule. **FIGURE 8-5** shows the Windows Backup and Restore utility in action.

Provide three types of information to describe your backup process. Follow the Backup and Restore Wizard prompts to enter the following:

- **Where Windows will store the backup**—Select a local hard disk, removable media, or network resources. The wizard will display a list of all valid known backup locations.
- **What to back up**—Let Windows select the most important files and folders to back up or select which files and folders to include.

FIGURE 8-5

Windows Backup and
Restore (Windows 7) utility.

Courtesy of Microsoft Corporation.

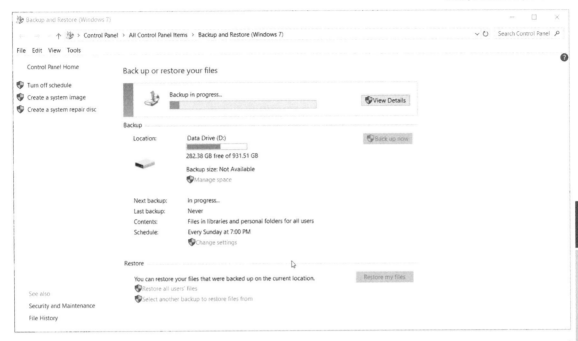

- If Windows selects the files to back up, it will choose data files that are saved in libraries, on the desktop, and in default Windows folders for all user accounts on the computer.
- If the drive you are saving the backup on is formatted using NTFS and has enough disk space, Backup and Restore (Windows 7) will also include a system image of programs, windows, and all drivers and Registry settings in the backup.
- **When to back up**—Select the frequency and time Windows will start the backup. **FIGURE 8-6** shows the options Windows provides to schedule a backup.

That's it—Windows does the rest. Once the Backup and Restore (Windows 7) utility is set up, it creates a backup according to the defined schedule. Of course, you have to ensure that your computer is turned on when your scheduled backup should run. If your computer is turned off, the backup will run at the next scheduled time. You can also back up your selected files at any time by choosing the Back Up Now button and change any settings by selecting the Change Settings link.

Workstation Backups from the PowerShell Command Line

You can also create Windows backups from the PowerShell command line. The wbadmin command provides a way to create Windows backups without using the graphical user interface (GUI). You can find the complete syntax of wbadmin at https://docs.microsoft .com/en-us/windows-server/administration/windows-commands/wbadmin.

FIGURE 8-6

Backup and Restore
(Windows 7).

Courtesy of Microsoft Corporation.

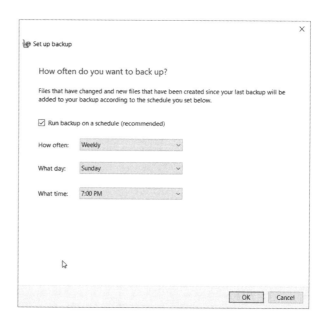

Here is a sample command you can use to create a backup of drive C: and store on drive I:

```
WBADMIN START BACKUP -backupTarget:I: -include:C: -allCritical
-vssFull -quiet
```

Other Workstation Backup Utilities. Microsoft doesn't provide the only software for backing up and restoring Windows workstations. There are many alternatives. If you want to explore other products that provide more control over how you create and manage backups, look at what other vendors offer. **TABLE 8-1** lists a few of the more popular Windows backup programs. Compare the features of the various products and select the one that best fits your requirements.

TABLE 8-1 Commercial Products for Windows Backup and Restore

PRODUCT	WEBSITE
Acronis Backup	https://www.acronis.com/en-us/
EaseUS ToDo Backup	https://www.easeus.com/backup-software/
Macrium Reflect	http://www.macrium.com/
MSP360 (formerly CloudBerry Lab) Backup	https://www.msp360.com/
MiniTool ShadowMaker	https://www.minitool.com/backup/
AOMEI Backupper	https://www.ubackup.com/
Paragon Backup & Recovery	https://www.paragon-software.com/home/brh/

© Jones & Bartlett Learning.

Server Backups

Although it's likely that some of your organization's data are stored and processed on workstations, the majority of data probably reside on servers. Server computers provide many services within an organization, including storing large volumes of data. Servers exist to provide software and data-dependent services to an organization's users. To put things into perspective, **TABLE 8-2** lists just a few common types of servers and the types of data they store and process.

Compensating Controls for Backups

In many cases, you will identify multiple controls that meet a specific goal. A frequent backup schedule is the primary control to protect any organization from data loss. There are other methods to avoid losing data due to errors of failure. These "other" controls are often called **compensating controls**. Compensating controls fulfill the original goal without implementing the primary control. The alternate control compensates for the absence or failure of the primary control.

Many hardware manufacturers provide hardware-based solutions to protect computers from certain types of data loss. For example, a **redundant array of independent disks (RAID)** system if you select the right level can protect computers from disk failure–related data loss. For example, RAID 0 offered no redundancy, therefore no ability to recover data. RAID 1 allows for disk mirroring and RAID 5 for disk striping, both offering a level of redundancy and allowing for the backup of data if a single disk fails. Most RAID systems store extra data and can reconstruct damaged data if a disk fails. While RAID systems can protect systems from more common types of hardware failure, they can't protect organizations from other types of failures, such as fires or floods. In fact, RAID systems themselves are not immune to failure. You still need a good backup strategy.

TABLE 8-2 Types of Windows Servers

SERVER	TYPE OF DATA
Directory Server	A Directory server (Microsoft's Active Directory) manages configuration data for users, groups, and resources in one or more domains
Web server	Configuration and files to support websites and applications
Database server	Database management system configuration data and all managed data in your databases
Application server	Programs and configuration data to support distributed applications
Media server	Audio and video configuration and data to support streaming applications and bulk media storage
Mail server	Server and mailbox data for mail-related functions
File server	Any files and folders stored on central servers

Technical TIP

Install the Windows Server Backup utility on a computer running Windows Server by following these steps:

1. Choose the Windows Start button > Server Manager.
2. Select Manage from the menu bar, then select Add Roles and Features.
3. Choose Next several times to advance to the Select Features window.
4. Check the box next to Windows Server Backup.
5. Choose Next, then Install.
6. After the Windows Server Backup installs, close the Server Manager.

Server Backups from the Command Line

You can also create Windows Server backups from the command line. The wbadmin command is the same one you saw from the previous section on workstation backups. You can find the complete syntax of wbadmin at https://docs .microsoft.com/en-us/windows -server/administration/windows-commands/wbadmin.

Many more types of servers store many different types of data. You can begin to see how many organizations depend on servers and server data. The loss of one server can cause a significant interruption to normal operations. For example, consider the impact of losing an email server. How much of a problem would it be if an organization lost all of its email messages? A good backup and restore strategy becomes increasingly important when considering the impact of losing even a little data. It is crucial to back up each server frequently and manage the backup images efficiently. Make sure your plan includes methods to easily and quickly retrieve the backup images on demand.

Microsoft provides a utility for backing up Windows servers. All Windows Server versions, except for the Core Server installation, include the Windows Server Backup utility. Before the backup utility can be used, it has to be installed on each server that you want to back up. Once the utility is installed, it can be configured to create flexible backups according to your organization's needs.

Once you have installed the Windows Server Backup utility, you can schedule and create backups for your servers. Since Windows servers perform different functions, they often have different backup needs. The Microsoft Windows Server Backup utility addresses many different server backup needs and takes more effort to configure than a simple workstation backup (**FIGURE 8-7**). The basic steps are similar to setting up a workstation backup—but more options are available.

You provide three types of information to describe your backup process. Follow the Backup Wizard prompts to enter the following:

- **What to back up**—Back up an entire server or select which files and folders to include. Microsoft recommends backing up entire servers in most cases.
- **When to back up**—Select the frequency and time Windows will begin the backup process.
- **Where Windows will store the backup**—Select a disk dedicated for backup images, a volume with other files on it, or a shared network folder.

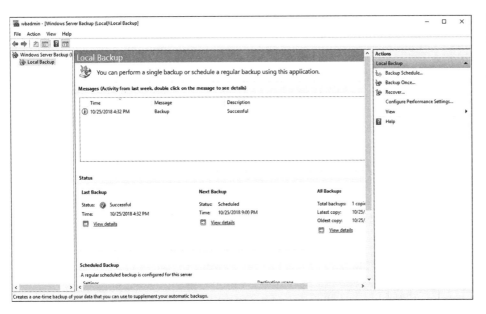

FIGURE 8-7

Windows Server Backup.

Courtesy of Microsoft Corporation.

Once you set up your server backups, Windows handles copying the files and folders you identified to another disk. If you want to copy your backups to removable tape drives, you will have to do that manually. The Windows Server Backup does not support backing up directly to tape drives. You will have to create a scheduled job to copy the backup files from the Server Backup destination to your tape drive.

Technical TIP

You can find detailed instructions for creating and managing Windows Server Backups at https://learn .microsoft.com/en-us/windows-server/administration/windows-commands/windows-server-backup -command-reference.

Technical TIP

Open the Windows Server Backup utility on a computer running Windows Server using these steps:

1. Choose the Windows Start button > Windows Accessories > Windows Server Backup.
2. Select the Backup Schedule link (in the Actions list on the right side of the window) to launch the Backup Schedule Wizard to configure a scheduled backup.

Select the Backup Once link (in the Actions list on the right side of the window) to launch the Backup Once Wizard to configure a one-time backup.

TABLE 8-3 Commercial Windows Server Backup Software	
PRODUCT	**WEBSITE**
NovaBACKUP	https://www.novabackup.com
Acronis Backup	http://www.acronis.com
Veritas Backup Exec	https://www.veritas.com/protection/backup-exec
Arcserve ShadowProtect	https://www.arcserve.com/products/arcserve-shadowprotect
Macrium Reflect	https://www.macrium.com/products/business
BackupAssist	https://www.backupassist.com/

© Jones & Bartlett Learning.

Other Server Backup Utilities. Microsoft doesn't provide the only software for backing up and restoring Windows servers. As with workstation backups, many alternative server backup utilities are available. If you want to explore other products that provide more control over how you create and manage backups, look at what other vendors offer. **TABLE 8-3** lists a few of the more popular Windows Server Backup programs. Compare the features of the various products and select the one that fits your requirements best.

Network Backups

Most backup utilities provide the ability to back up files and folders to a network shared folder or device. This approach has both advantages and disadvantages. Be sure to evaluate the impact to your system before selecting network destinations for any new backup operations. Adding new backups to network destinations without assessing the impact of additional network traffic can seriously degrade your network performance. It can even make your network unusable. Remember that you are establishing backups as controls to support the availability principle, not violate it.

Backing up files and folders to network destinations provides two main benefits:

WARNING

Virtual images make backing up data easy. Both your primary copy and secondary copies may reside on the same physical server. But this can actually reduce your data's security. A catastrophic failure could cause you to lose both copies. If your backup image is not physically located on a separate server, you should plan to archive the backup image on removable media or another server.

1. Files and folders are copied to another computer or device. Copying data to another computer or device protects the backed-up data from damage to the primary computer or storage device. In the past, network backups implied that the backup location was physically separate from the source. In today's environments where virtual machines and cloud computing resources are more common, don't assume backing up to a network destination ensures physical separation. The networked destination may be another virtual device on the same physical server.

2. Local disk space is not used to create backups. The backup process consumes disk space on the destination device and makes it easier to separate disk usage impact from live servers.

Backing up files and folders to network destinations has drawbacks:

1. Backups consume network resources. Backups across a network, just like all network applications, send messages to the remote destination. Backups send a lot of messages across your network. If all of the bandwidth on the network segment between the backup source and backup destination is used, you will experience slower service during the backup. If you do not have sufficient bandwidth to handle the extra traffic, your network services may experience extreme slowdowns, timeouts, and may even crash.

2. Backups across networks will be slower than backups using local disks. The degree to which network backups run more slowly depends on available network bandwidth. Available network bandwidth depends on the speed of your network and what other applications are using your network. It is a good idea to use only backups to network folders connected using fast network segments.

3. Backups to networked shared folders may time out and fail more frequently than local resources. Closely monitor your backup status to detect failed backups. Remember that a failed backup means your data are not protected from loss.

Networked shared folders can provide convenient destinations for both workstation and server backups. Before setting up networked backups, ensure your network can handle them. Monitor network activity to detect any bandwidth problems before they become critical. As you modify scheduled backups, try to stagger backups to avoid saturating your network with multiple backups running simultaneously. Another caveat is that network segments that contain choke points, insufficient bandwidth (like some WAN links), overwhelmed network components and memory buffers all could impact not only your backup but also the network. Causing impact on your network could very well also impact other applications trying to run and other data transfers and jobs that need to take place. Backups are timed and can take long periods of time so if your network is impacted, the backup will continue to run until finished causing even more contention during busy times.

Cloud Backups

Backing up data across the internet to remote cloud servers is another backup option that is very popular in some environments. Data backed up to the cloud are physically separate from your local computer. It provides a high level of protection from any damage to local data. By far, the biggest restrictions for cloud backups is the lack of bandwidth and the distance (network hops) that the data need to be sent in a secure manner. Bandwidth continues to get better over time, but the cloud's biggest restriction is that data need to travel across public links in an encrypted form, which then needs to be decrypted. The challenge is using the public internet, which normally will not have the higher level of performance your private network (internally and externally) will. The internet's architecture virtually guarantees that there will be several segments between your computer and any destination, and many other users are sharing the bandwidth with you.

Your data's confidentiality is a valid concern if you do not encrypt it. Sending data across the internet exposes this information to the outside world. Anyone with a network sniffer between you and the backup destination can intercept your data. Never use an

TABLE 8-4 Internet Backup Software

PRODUCT	WEBSITE
CrashPlan	http://www.crashplan.com/
Carbonite	http://www.carbonite.com/
Backblaze	http://www.backblaze.com/
IDrive	https://www.idrive.com/
Acronis Data Cloud	http://www.acronis.com
Genie9	http://www.genie9.com/
MSP360 (formerly CloudBerry Lab) Backup	https://www.msp360.com/

© Jones & Bartlett Learning.

internet backup product unless using strong connection encryption. This will ensure your data are safe during the transfer process. In addition to confidentiality concerns during transit, carefully consider how the data will be handled by the cloud service provider. If you are paying another company to handle your backup data on its servers, how secure are its servers? Make sure any organization that stores your data has an aggressive security policy. One other consideration is cost, especially when it comes to ingress and egress data transfers. Moving large quantiles of data to a cloud provider may not cost a lot, but taking it back in may cost substantially more. It's very important to read the fine print when considering using a cloud service.

TABLE 8-4 lists a few of the products that specialize in backups to the cloud.

Technical TIP

The online backup market changes rapidly and there are many more providers than those listed in Table 8-4. Visit http://en.wikipedia.org/wiki/Comparison_of_online_backup_services for a more comprehensive and up-to-date list of companies that provide online backup software and services.

Historically, the most common use for cloud backup solutions has been for workstation computers and devices specifically in small or home offices. Cloud backups have always been popular for laptop computers that change locations frequently, but these solutions are becoming popular for server backups as well. Computers and devices can be set up to perform backups at specific times or to continually back up changed files whenever you are connected to the internet. Having current backups available in the cloud for mobile devices is a useful additional layer of protection from damage or theft. As overall internet connection bandwidth increases, cloud backup solutions are becoming more and more common for servers that either don't change locations or may just be virtual images with no specific location.

Microsoft Windows and Application Backup and Recovery in a Business Continuity Setting

Recall that the real value of a backup is not the backup itself, but its ability to play a part in recovering lost data. You must have a recovery plan in place before the backup is of much use. You must have two main types of plans in place to ensure your organization doesn't suffer when the unexpected happens. The first plan is a **disaster recovery plan (DRP)**. Your DRP covers the actions you must take when a disaster strikes to address the damage and return your infrastructure to a point where you can continue operations. The next plan is a **business continuity plan (BCP)** that ensures critical business functions continue in the face of interrupted processes. While these two plans are related and do work together, they each have their own purpose.

Disaster Recovery Plan

A DRP contains the steps to restore an IT infrastructure to a point where an organization can continue operations. If a disaster occurs that causes damage and interrupts your business functions, it is important to return to productive activities as soon as possible. If your organization can't carry out its main business functions, it cannot fulfill its purpose. A solid disaster recovery plan carefully identifies each component of your IT infrastructure that is critical to your primary business functions. Then, the plan states the steps you can take to replace damaged or destroyed components.

Several options are available after serious disasters damage or destroy major IT infrastructure components (**FIGURE 8-8**). Following are a few of the most common options, starting with the most expensive option with the shortest cutover time:

* **Hot site**—A complete copy of an environment at a remote site. Hot sites are kept as current as possible with replicated data, so switching from the original environment to the alternate environment can occur with a minimum of downtime. The site is operational at all times and experiences little to no delay when disaster strikes at the primary site.

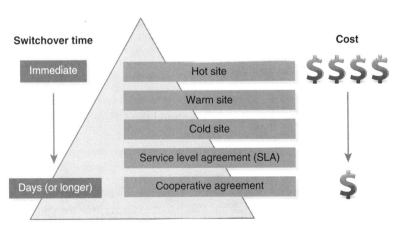

Switchover time — Immediate ... Days (or longer)

Hot site
Warm site
Cold site
Service level agreement (SLA)
Cooperative agreement

Cost — $$$$ ... $

FIGURE 8-8

Disaster recovery options.

© Jones & Bartlett Learning.

- **Warm site**—A complete copy of an environment at a remote site. Warm sites are updated only periodically—normally daily or even weekly. When a disaster occurs, there is a short delay while a switchover team prepares the warm site with the latest data updates. Commonly, you may need to make configuration changes at the warm site, power on needed systems or restore files to key systems in order for business operations to continue. There will be a small delay in getting the secondary site to function as the primary.
- **Cold site**—A site that may have hardware in place, but it will not likely be set up or configured. Cold sites take more time to bring into operation because of the extensive amount of configuration work required for hardware and software. These sites likely need to be configured, brought completely online, tested and validated, and data restored in full. There will be a large delay in getting a cold site to act as primary.

Regardless of which option best suits your organization, the purpose of a disaster recovery plan is to repair or replace damaged IT infrastructure components as quickly as possible to allow the business to continue in operation. If you select hot, warm, or cold, be aware that you may be obligated to provide your customers a specific level of service, and not meeting that level could be very costly, especially if you cost a partner vendor their ability to conduct their business. This comes in the form of a service-level agreement. You may need to think about other DRP considerations as well:

- **Cooperative agreement**—An agreement between two or more organizations to help one another in case a disaster hits one of the parties. The organization that is not affected by the disaster agrees to allow the other organization to use part of its own IT infrastructure capacity to conduct minimal business operations. Usually a specified time limit allows the organization that suffered damage time to rebuild its IT infrastructure.
- **Service level agreement (SLA)**—A contract with a vendor that guarantees replacement hardware or software within a specific amount of time. SLAs normally come with a monetary penalty or other contractual obligation based on whether or not the SLA was kept.

Now that you have selected the appropriate plan options and know what your level of tolerance is to a disaster that your company needs to recovery from, how does a company relay on keep business operations running daily when problems arise but are not at the same level of a declared disaster? You need a BCP that sets the policy and procedures for how to create continuity of operations (COOP).

Business Continuity Plan

When learning about a BCP, it's important to clearly understand the differences when using it or a DRP. The two plans work closely with one another and depend on one another for success. You can summarize the difference between the two plans into two main points:

1. A BCP is the overarching plan or policies and procedures that specify how a business will continue its operations. A DRP, however, is a part of a BCP that explains how the company will recover from a declared disaster.

2. A DRP is more focused on the exact specifics on how a company will restore its ability to function if key systems that are required for the company to function are unable to work.

To summarize, a BCP is proactive and speaks to how a company will continue its operations if any issues arise, where the DRP specifically talks about the steps required to restore key systems impacted by a current disaster event. A comprehensive BCP will state how a DRP will take effect any time there is a disruption to business functions and cover the exact steps that need to be taken to restore it back to service. An example would be a power outage or a water main break that interrupts water flow to your main office. A DRP takes effect when an event causes a major disruption. A major disruption is one where you must intervene and take some action to restore a functional IT infrastructure. A fire or tornado that damages your datacenter would be an example of a disaster.

Where a Restore Fits In

Any time data are lost, at least part of a previous backup will need to be restored. In most cases, this means using a restore utility to extract some, or all, of the files and folders you backed up during the most recent backup operation. The restore procedure is a technical operation. Your DRP will contain the steps you follow to get your organization back up and running. While the restore procedure is an important part of a successful recovery, it is only one part of a solid plan.

Microsoft Windows Backup and Restore Utility

Recovering from data loss can be a fairly straightforward process when you follow a solid plan. If you carefully developed a DRP and BCP, along with detailed procedures for backing up and restoring data, this part should be easy. If you do not have a plan, you'll likely spend extra time figuring out what to do.

The process of restoring is basically the opposite of creating a backup. Of course, you can schedule a backup, but you will probably execute the restore process manually. In nearly every case, you follow these steps:

1. Verify that you have a stable infrastructure. Since you just suffered data loss, be sure that you know why you lost data and that you have addressed the problem. If you have not addressed the problem, you could end up losing more data.
2. Open your restore utility. The utility you choose will depend on the backup utility you used to create your backup images. In short, you have to use a restore utility designed to work with your backup utility.
3. Select the backup image to use and the type of restore (complete or selective) you'll perform.

Once you start the restore process, the restore utility will copy the selected files back to their original locations. The result should be an environment with the damaged or missing data restored. You should be up and running again.

Restoring with the Windows Backup and Restore Utility

Use the Windows Restore utility to restore some, or all, of the files you backed up with the same utility (**FIGURE 8-9**).

You provide three types of information to the restore process. Follow the Backup and Restore Wizard prompts to enter the following:

- **The scope of the restore operation**—Choose one of the following options:
  - Select the Restore My Files button to restore only files that you own.
  - Select the Restore All Users' Files link to restore files for all users.
  - Select the Select Another Backup to Restore Files From link to restore files from a different backup location.
- **What files and folders to restore**—Add individual files and folders you want to restore.
- **Where Windows will place the restored files**—Restore files back to their original location or to another folder.

Technical TIP

You can open the Windows Backup and Restore (Windows 7) utility using these steps:

1. Choose the Windows Start button > Settings.
2. Select Backup > Go to Backup and Restore (Windows 7).

FIGURE 8-9

Windows workstation Backup and Restore (Windows 7).

Courtesy of Microsoft Corporation.

Restoring with the Windows Server Recovery Utility

Several pieces of information you provide describe the recovery process. Follow the Server Recovery Wizard (**FIGURE 8-10**) prompts to enter the following:

- **Where Windows can locate the backup image**—Choose the local server or a remote server.
- **When the backup was created**—Choose the desired date for the backup you want to use.
- **What to recover**—You can recover four different ways. Select one of the following:
  - **Files and folders**—Select individual files and folders to recover.
  - **Volumes**—Select entire volumes to recover.
  - **Applications**—If you chose to back up specific applications, you can select the applications to recover.
  - **System state**—Choose to recover only the system state to recover essential system settings.
- **Where Windows will store the recovered files and folders**—Files and folders can be recovered to their original location or another location. You can also select what Windows does if it encounters duplicate files and whether the recovery operation should recover access control lists (ACLs) along with recovered files and folders.

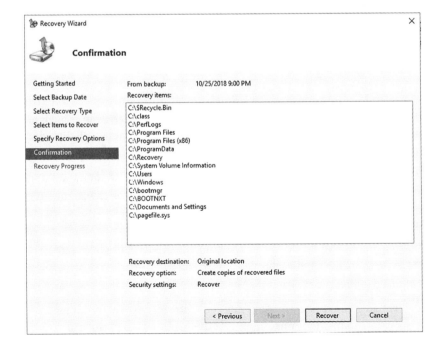

FIGURE 8-10

Windows Server recovery.

Courtesy of Microsoft Corporation.

Technical TIP

You can open the Windows Server Backup utility on a computer running Windows Server using these steps:

1. Choose the Windows Start button > Windows Accessories > Windows Server Backup.
2. Select the Recover link (in the Actions list on the right side of the window) to launch the Server Recovery Wizard.

Rebuilding Systems from Bare Metal

A solid recovery plan will allow you to recover from any interruption. Some interruptions are minor, and others are catastrophic. If a fire destroys your entire datacenter, along with all your computer hardware, you have to replace the hardware first. Once you have the proper hardware in place, you can start the software restore process. The specific steps you take depend on the type of backup you previously created.

Technical TIP

Since the OS, software, or data can't be restored until you have working platform, consider keeping extra hardware or a virtual machine around to swap out in critical situations. Explore the option of acquiring an identical physical copy or virtual image of critical hardware devices. If you suffer hardware failure and you have a spare server or laptop available, you may be able to restore your hardware functionality by just swapping the spare hardware or launching the virtual image for the damaged hardware.

If you backed up only critical files or folders, you'll need to build each computer back to the point where you can restore those critical files. In most cases, those steps will include the following:

- Install the operating system.
  - Be sure to install all patches and service packs to match the predisaster environment.
- Configure the operating system to match the predisaster settings.
- Install utility and application software.
  - Be sure to install all patches and service packs to match the predisaster environment.
- Configure your software to match predisaster settings.
- Restore the critical files you backed up from the most recent backup.

Although backups probably run quickly and are simple, restoring your environment from a catastrophic disaster can be time consuming. Another option is to perform a complete backup of the computer. This includes the operating system and all items you'll need to restore the operating system, all configuration settings, and all applications and data. A complete system backup generally takes a lot longer since you are backing up literally everything. It can also make the process of restoring computers much easier. You need to create a complete system backup that includes all of the OS and physical settings only once. After that, you can either perform full server backups or back up selected volumes or files and folders.

All Microsoft backup utilities provide the option to create a complete system backup that supports restoring to a computer with no operating system installed. Most third-party utilities provide this option as well. A restore that includes the operating system and all configuration settings is called a **bare metal recovery**. The name comes from the fact that you can restore everything from your backup media. All you need is the actual hardware, or the bare metal. If using Microsoft backup utilities, you can create a bare metal recovery backup with the GUI (**FIGURE 8-11**) or the command-line tool.

Technical TIP

You can open the Windows Server Backup utility on a computer running Windows Server using these steps:

1. Choose the Windows Start button > Windows Accessories > Windows Server Backup.

2. Select the Backup Once link (in the Actions list on the right side of the window) to launch the Backup Once Wizard.

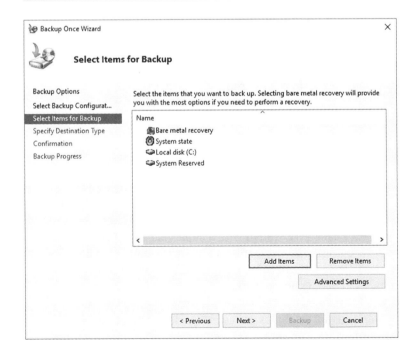

FIGURE 8-11

Creating a backup for a bare metal recovery.

Courtesy of Microsoft Corporation.

Follow these steps to create a one-time complete backup for a bare metal restore:

1. Select Different Options, then choose Next.
2. Select Custom, then choose Next.
3. Choose Add Items.
4. In the Select Items window, select the Bare Metal Recovery checkbox, choose OK, and then, choose Next.
5. Select Local drives to store the backup on a local drive or select Remote Shared Folder to store the backup on a shared network folder, and then, choose Next.
6. Select your desired location to store this special backup from the drop-down list, and then, choose Next.
7. On the Confirmation page, choose Backup.

Since the backup serves as protection from catastrophic failures, you should store it either on a remote shared folder or on an external drive. The external drive should be stored at a different location to ensure a disaster that destroys the primary computer does not destroy the backup as well. The recovery process starts with a stable computer and Windows boot media (DVD or USB device). Follow these steps on the target computer to perform a bare metal restore:

1. Boot from the Windows boot media (ensure any external drives you'll need are connected).
2. In the main window, select Next.
3. In the Install Now window, select the Repair Your Computer link.
4. Load any necessary drivers on the next window, then select Next.
5. Select the Windows Complete Restore link.
6. Select the backup to restore and select Next.
7. Enter any additional settings and select Next.

Windows will install all computer settings and OS using the backup selected. When the backup finishes, you should be able to reboot from your hard disk and log on to your newly restored computer. Unless you routinely create bare metal recovery backups, you will need to execute a normal restore to recover the most recent backup information.

Managing Backups with Virtual Machines

Many organizations have incorporated **virtualization** into their IT infrastructure and for most organizations, a majority of their infrastructure is both virtualized and in the cloud. Virtualization is the ability to run multiple **virtual machines (VMs)** simultaneously on a single physical computer or hardware system with a hypervisor. A VM is a software implementation of a physical computer. Virtualization allows organizations to do more with less physical hardware. T Using virtualization in an IT infrastructure has many benefits, including advantages in managing backups.

Windows Server includes Microsoft's **Hyper-**technology. Hyper-V is a product that supports creating and running virtual machines in newer Windows Server OSs. Hyper-V requires CPU support for virtualization and is optimized for server-based operations.

While Hyper-V has many features and benefits, it supports the ability to create snapshots of a running VM. This ability makes creating a virtual backup image nearly trivial. All you have to do is create VM snapshots anytime you want to create a rollback point. Hyper-V lets you restore a VM back to any snapshot.

Virtualization offers many advantages to single-purpose physical hardware use. Many organizations enjoy increased performance as well as decreased cost of physical hardware. The backup and recovery features alone may make it worthwhile to explore virtualization in your environment.

Hyper-V Alternatives

Hyper-V is not the only virtualization product for Windows. Hyper-V is provided by Microsoft and is tightly integrated with Windows Server, but other products also work well with Windows. If you are new to virtualization, look at these products as well:

- **VMware**—Commercial virtualization products for workstation and server environments: http://www.vmware.com/
- **VirtualBox**—Open-source virtualization software that runs on multiple OSs, including Windows: http://www.virtualbox.org/

Technical TIP

You can get complete details on Microsoft Hyper-V at https://learn.microsoft.com/en-us/virtualization/hyper-v-on-windows/about/.

In fact, virtualization has many more benefits than just convenient ways to roll back. The entire movement toward cloud computing is based on virtualization. Cloud computing is based on running several virtual machines on physical servers that are easily accessible to any internet-connected device. Cloud service providers make it easy to create, resize, and dispose of VMs. This flexibility makes it possible to provision just the right number of virtual servers to meet current application demands. Cloud service providers can maintain the physical servers and allow customers to manage virtual machines for a fee.

Cloud computing continues to grow in popularity and has changed the way organizations conduct business. It is possible to create VMs, then add and remove capability based on current needs. Clouds can also make backing up and restoring easier than with traditional methods. The concepts are the same, however. Every organization, whether based in the cloud or in a traditional datacenter, must evaluate its needs for backup and recovery. Regardless of the techniques used, resilience in the face of disruptions or disasters is crucial to any organization's survival.

Best Practices for Microsoft Windows Backup and Recovery

All too often, backup scheduling occurs as an afterthought—part of the list of items after setting up a new system. The backup should be an integral part of a complete recovery plan. A recovery plan should be in place before you physically install new computers or devices. Planning ahead for recovery protects your organization from unexpected interruptions that may impact critical business functions. Here are some industry best practices that will help keep your Windows environment and all the data it contains available to users:

- Ensure that you know which business functions are critical to your organization. These are the functions you must ensure do not permanently cease due to interruptions or disasters.
- Develop a plan to continue all critical business functions. This business continuity plan should cover all aspects of your organization to ensure your organization can resume operation after an interruption.
- Define recovery time objectives for each critical resource. Identify resources required for the recovery process. You'll need to identify which parts of your recovery plan are sequential and which ones you can work on simultaneously. For example, assume you have eight servers you need to recover. Each server has an RTO of 4 hours. If only one person is working on the recovery plan, it is unlikely all eight servers will be operational within the RTO. You'll likely need more people working to recover the servers.
- Define recovery point objectives so there is a known amount of data that the organization can lose after a disaster recovery event. The RPO will be defined by time and should be discussed and decided what the organization deems acceptable.
- Develop a backup plan for each resource that minimizes the impact on performance while keeping secondary copies of data as up to date as possible. Explore various options, including alternate sites and virtualization.
- Automate as many backup operations as possible. Create logs and reports that make problems with backup operations easy to recognize.
- Verify all backup operations. A secondary copy of data with errors may be no better than damaged primary copy data.
- Document all backup and recovery procedures. Train all primary and backup personnel on all procedures.
- Test all recovery procedures rigorously. Conduct at least one full interruption recovery test each year. A full interruption test is one that actually interrupts normal operation to test the full recovery process. This type of test is the only way to fully test your recovery plan.
- Review your complete recovery plan quarterly (or more frequently) and adjust for any infrastructure changes.
- Implement security controls around your data backups, including encrypting data at rest and in transit, logical access controls, and physical access controls.

These best practices provide a solid foundation for creating a secure recovery plan for your organization's IT assets.

CHAPTER SUMMARY

Availability is one of the three main pillars of security. A secure system ensures information is available to authorized users on demand. That means a secure system is one that is protected from data loss and unexpected interruptions. A solid recovery plan ensures even the most catastrophic disaster interrupts your business process only temporarily. The plan should also specify what the maximum downtime will be so that the company has assurances of its uptime and meets internal and external SLA expectations. To facilitate this, backups of work-stations and servers are an important part of the strategy. By ensuring that you have regular backups made and available for recovery, you can quickly recover data and resume business operations following any disaster.

In this chapter, you learned how to create backups, how to restore those backup images, and how to design a recovery plan. You also learned what questions to ask to develop a recovery plan that fits your organization. Your complete recovery plan will help protect your organization's information and ensure its overall security.

8

Microsoft Windows Backup
and Recovery Tools

KEY CONCEPTS AND TERMS

Backup
Bare metal recovery
Business continuity plan (BCP)
Compensating control
Disaster recovery plan (DRP)

File History
Hyper-V
Primary copy
Recovery time objective (RTO)
Redundant array of independent
   disks (RAID)

Restore operation
Secondary copy
Virtual machine (VM)
Virtualization
Volume Shadow Copy Service
   (VSS)

CHAPTER 8 ASSESSMENT

1. A valid backup is all an organization needs to recover from a disaster.

   A. True
   B. False

2. Which of the following options are valid approaches to recovering from lost data? (Select two.)

   A. Manually reconstruct lost data.
   B. Reinstall the operating system and application software.
   C. Restore from a backup.
   D. Use anti-malware software to heal infections.

3. Which of the following is the focus of data availability?

   A. Backup plan
   B. Backup schedule
   C. Recovery plan
   D. Disaster response plan

4. Using removable media for backups generally _____ data availability, as opposed to using internal disks.

5. Using removable media for backups generally _____ data confidentiality, as opposed to using internal disks.

6. The only valid uses for restoring a backup image are to recover lost data and quickly load programs and files on completely new computers.

   A. True
   B. False

7. Which of the following best describes RTO?

   A. The goal for how much time a recovery effort should take
   B. The maximum time a recovery effort can take
   C. The minimum time a recovery effort should take
   D. The maximum downtime an organization can sustain

8. Which of the following do you *not* need to tell the Microsoft Windows Backup and Restore utility?

   A. What to back up (files, folders, volumes, etc.)
   B. What type of backup (full, incremental, blocks versus files)
   C. Where to store the backup (local disk or shared network folder)
   D. When to back up (date and time, frequency)

9. The wbadmin command-line utility performs the same functions as the Microsoft Windows Backup and Restore utility on Windows workstations.

   A. True
   B. False

10. Only the Microsoft Backup utilities can create valid backup images for Windows computers.

    A. True
    B. False

11. Which type of plan addresses minor interruptions such as a power outage lasting several hours?

    A. RTO
    B. DRP
    C. VSS
    D. BCP

12. Which of the following terms refers to an alternate recovery site that has the basic infrastructure in place but no configured hardware and no software installed?

    A. Warm site
    B. Cold site
    C. Hot site
    D. Initial site

13. A recovery strategy that installs the operating system and all software and data on a completely new physical computer is called a(n) _____.

14. Virtual image snapshots can back up only virtual machines that are not running.

    A. True
    B. False

Microsoft Windows Network Security

MICROSOFT WINDOWS COMPUTERS can be very useful by themselves, but they are far more effective when they are able to communicate with one another. Windows computers that can communicate and exchange information have the ability to assume specific roles that make your organization's computing environment more efficient and effective. Unfortunately, connecting computers also makes accessing your organization's information easier for unauthorized as well as authorized users. That means you have to be diligent to ensure the confidentiality, integrity, and availability of your data.

In this chapter, you'll learn about techniques that many organizations use to ensure that their Windows networks are secure. You'll learn how to connect computers together without risking your organization's information to loss, alteration, or disclosure.

Chapter 9 Topics

This chapter covers the following topics and concepts:

- What network security is
- What the principles of Mirosoft Windows network security are
- What Microsoft Windows security protocols and services are
- How to secure Microsoft Windows environment network services
- How to secure Microsoft Windows wireless networking
- What Microsoft Windows desktop network security is
- What Microsoft Windows server network security is
- What best practices for Microsoft Windows network security are

Chapter 9 Goals

When you complete this chapter, you will be able to:

- Describe goals for securing Microsoft Windows networks
- Secure Microsoft Windows networking services
- Secure Microsoft Windows wireless networks
- Secure Microsoft Windows workstations and servers

Network Security

Today's IT environments include components connected to form a **network**, or multiple networks. A network is a collection of computers and devices joined by connection media. Network components work together to support an organization's business functions. This makes information available for various uses and many users. As networks grow and become more functional, they can become complex to manage. One way to organize components is to use an IT Infrastructure approach to group components into functional areas, or domains. **FIGURE 9-1** shows an IT infrastructure with seven domains. These are the domains you'll commonly encounter as you study IT environments.

In a general network perspective, users typically use their workstations to access other resources that are connected to an organization's **local area network (LAN)**, a **metropolitan area network (MAN)**, or even a **wide area network (WAN)**. **TABLE 9-1** lists each of the basic three network types and their characteristics.

Organizations rely on networked resources more than ever in today's environments. Networks make it possible to share expensive resources. Examples of shared resources are color printers, network storage subsystems, and applications. Networks increase efficiency in critical business functions by supporting faster information transfer and resource sharing. These benefits often result in direct cost reductions and productivity increases. Organizations rely on network resources to maintain cost-efficient operations. Protecting the network-based resources and services directly affects cost and efficiency. Implementing the controls necessary to support your security policy and protect your networks makes your organization more secure and effective.

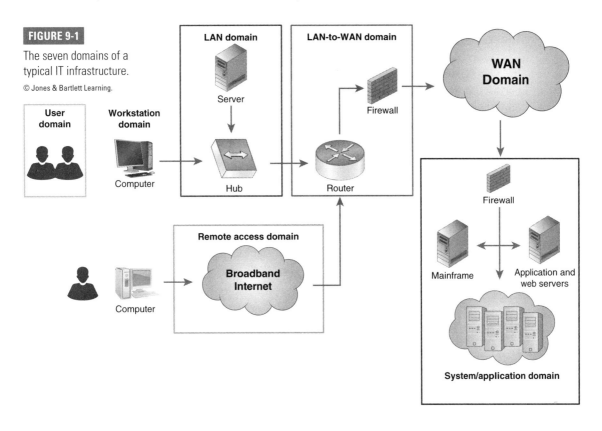

FIGURE 9-1

The seven domains of a typical IT infrastructure.

© Jones & Bartlett Learning.

TABLE 9-1 Network Types

NETWORK TYPE	SIZE	DESCRIPTION
Local area network (LAN)	A LAN covers a small physical area, such as an office or a building.	LANs are common in homes and businesses and make it easy to share resources such as printers and network storage.
Metropolitan area network (MAN)	A MAN connects two or more LANs but does not span an area larger than a city or town.	MANs are useful to connect multiple buildings or groups of buildings spread around an area larger than a few city blocks.
Wide area network (WAN)	WANs connect multiple LANs and WANs and span very large areas, including multiple country coverage.	WANs provide network connections among computers, devices, and other networks that need to communicate across great distances. For example, the internet is a WAN.

© Jones & Bartlett Learning.

Technical TIP

There are other types of networks, and you may see a few more terms used to describe networks. These terms aren't in widespread use, but they do describe specific types of networks. Other types of networks include the following:

1. **Personal area network (PAN)**—A PAN consists of one or more workstations and its network devices, such as printers, network storage systems, and scanners. A PAN refers to the networked devices one person would likely use and normally does not span an area larger than an office or cubicle.

2. **Campus area network (CAN)**—A CAN is larger than a LAN but generally smaller than a MAN. CANs are useful to connect the LANs across multiple buildings that are all in fairly close proximity to one another.

3. **Global area network (GAN)**—A GAN is a newer term for a super-WAN. A GAN is a collection of interconnected LANs, CANs, MANs, and even WANs that span an extremely large area.

Network Security Controls

Network security controls often focus on limiting access to **remote resources**. A **local resource** is any resource attached to a local computer—the same computer to which the user is logged on. A remote resource is any resource attached to another computer on a network that is different from the computer to which the user is logged on. The user's computer and the remote computer must be connected to the same network to provide access to the remote resource. Many of the security controls you'll find to protect network resources are similar to controls found protecting local resources. You'll learn more about how each type of control works in a Microsoft Windows network environment in this chapter. The main types of network security controls include the following:

- Access controls for protected resources, such as printers and shared folders
- Communication controls to limit the spread of malicious software and protect traffic
- Anti-malware software on all computers in the network to detect and eradicate malware
- Recovery plans, including backups, for all computers and devices in the network
- Configuration management software and procedures to control network device configuration changes
- Monitoring tools and other detective controls to help detect and stop suspicious network activity
- Software patch management for all computers and devices in the network

Principles of Microsoft Windows Network Security

A secure Microsoft Windows network allows access on demand to resources for authorized users while denying access for unauthorized users. While the goal is similar to securing a single computer, putting that goal into practice involves more types of controls. Setting up a network exposes all resources in the network to security threats. Securing a Microsoft Windows network requires attention to three main types of vulnerabilities:

- **Physical and logical access**—Locate important computers and devices in physically secure areas and limit access to them. Separate networks logically into smaller segments to control resource access. Logically separating networks is beneficial when you need to keep groups of devices separate. This is common in larger networks.
- **Traffic flow**—Use firewalls and other types of filters to discard unauthorized traffic on a network. Filters should exist at all network boundaries and between segments to control network ingress and egress.
- **Computer and device security**—Ensure each computer and device on the network is prepared to handle any known attack. Any computer or device that does not have proper security controls deployed poses a threat to the entire network.

Securing a Microsoft network involves deploying controls that protect all network components from all known threats. Although that may sound like a large goal, it's manageable when you approach it in a structured manner. The first step in understanding how to secure a network is to explore the most common components of networks.

Common Network Components

The main purpose of any network is to provide users with the ability to access and share remote resources. Networks use three main types of components to meet this goal. These components work together to allow users to share resources and reduce the need for multiple dedicated resources such as printers, file storage systems, and backup devices. The three main types of components in networks include the following:

- **Connection media**—The adapters and wires that connect components together. Not all connection methods use wires. With wireless devices, radio waves transmit data. So, connection media also includes wireless adapters.
- **Networking devices**—Hardware devices that connect other devices and computers using connection media.
- **Server computers and services devices**—Hardware that provides one or more services to users, such as server computers, printers, and network storage devices.

Many physical devices found in networks are actually combinations of several types of components. These components should work together to provide easy access to desired resources and still maintain the security of an organization's information. **FIGURE 9-2** shows common network components.

Connection Media

The purpose of any network is to allow multiple computers or devices to communicate with each other. By definition, networked computers and devices are connected to one another and have the necessary software to communicate. In the past, networked computers and devices were connected using cable. Today's networks contain a mix of cables and wireless connections. While the technical details of network connections are beyond the scope of this discussion, it is important to have a general understanding of a network's components.

Connection media	Networking devices	Servers and services
• Unshielded twisted pair (UTP) • Shielded twisted pair (STP) • Coaxial • Fiber optic • Wireless	• Switch • Router • Gateway • Firewall	• File server • Print server • Data access • Application server • Firewall

There are two options to establish network connections between computers and devices. You either build your own network or pay another organization to allow you to use their network for your purposes, such as a cloud provider. The following sections that cover connection media assume you own the connection media and are installing the hardware necessary to establish network communications. The following network connection media options appear most commonly in LANs, CANs, and MANs but may be used in other networks as well.

Wired Network Connections

Most physical network connections use one or a combination of four basic cabling options, including **coaxial cable**. Each option has its own advantages and disadvantages. If you choose to use physical cables for part or all of your network, you will have to run cables to each device. Running cables between devices takes careful planning. Make sure that when you explore cabling options, you evaluate the cost of installing all of the cables and connection hardware to support both your current and future needs. **TABLE 9-2** lists the four basic cable options, along with the advantages and disadvantages of each one.

Technical TIP

The advent of software-defined networking (SDN) created an easier way to do networking, cloud computing, and virtualization. Software-defined networking is logically based connectivity using resources within a system to provide infrastructure as code (IaC). As SDN becomes more and more prevalent in today's networks, less cabling, connections, and physical hardware will be used, and more logical connectivity will be deployed.

Wireless Network Connections

Wireless connections are popular in today's network environments, where flexibility is an important design factor. Wireless connections allow devices to connect to your network without you physically connecting a cable. This flexibility makes it easy to connect computers, or devices, in situations where running cables is either difficult or not practical

TABLE 9-2 Basic Network Cabling Options

CABLE TYPE	DESCRIPTION	ADVANTAGES AND DISADVANTAGES
Unshielded twisted pair (UTP)	The most common type of network cable, UTP generally consists of two or four pairs of wires. Pairs of wires are twisted around each other to reduce interference with other pairs. The most common types of UTP are Category 5 (Cat 5) UTP for 100 megabits per second (Mbps) networks and Cat 6 for 10 gigabits per second (Gbps) networks.	• Lowest cost • Ease of installation • Susceptibility to interference • Limited transmission speeds and distances
Shielded twisted pair (STP)	Same as UTP, but with foil shielding around each pair and optionally around the entire wire group to protect the cable from external radio and electrical interference.	• Low cost • Ease of installation • Greater resistance to interference than UTP • Same speed limitations as UTP but support for longer run lengths
Coaxial cable	A single copper conductor surrounded with a plastic sheath, then a braided copper shield, and then the external insulation.	• Higher cost • Difficult installation • Strong resistance to interference • Higher speeds and longer run lengths
Fiber-optic cable	A glass core surrounded by several layers of protective materials.	• Highest cost • Ease of running cable • Special tools needed to install end connectors • Immunity to radio and electrical interference • Extremely high speeds and long run lengths

© Jones & Bartlett Learning.

9

for temporary connections. The **Institute of Electrical and Electronics Engineers (IEEE)** defines standards for many aspects of computing and communications. The **IEEE 802.11** defines standards for **wireless local area network (WLAN)** communication **protocols**. A protocol is a set of rules that govern communication.

Seven main protocols are currently in the 802.11 standard. There are also two emerging protocols that will likely play a role in future wireless networks. As with the discussion of wired network connections, the technical details are beyond the scope of this discussion, but it is important to know the basic differences between different wireless protocols. **TABLE 9-3** lists the most common current and emerging wireless protocols.

TABLE 9-3 Common Current and Emerging 802.11 Wireless Standards

PROTOCOL	MAXIMUM TRANSMISSION SPEED	RANGE (FT) INDOOR/ OUTDOOR	FREQUENCY
802.11a	54 Mbps	115/390	5 GHz
802.11b	11 Mbps	125/460	2.4 GHz
802.11g	54 Mbps	125/460	2.4 GHz
802.11n	300 Mbps	230/820	2.4 GHz/5 GHz
802.11ac	1.3 Gbps	115	5 GHz
802.11ad (WiGiG)	6.7 Gbps	30	2.4/5/60 GHz
802.11ah (HaLow)	347 Mbps	3200 (proposed)	900 MHz
802.11ax (HEW)	4 Gbps (proposed)	(Not determined)	2.4 GHz/5 GHz

© Jones & Bartlett Learning.

Generally, hardware that supports protocols with faster speeds and longer range costs more than hardware with slower protocols. Your choice of wireless protocols will likely be based on cost, transmission speed requirements, and other devices that may cause interference in a specific frequency.

Bluetooth is a popular wireless protocol for connecting devices over short distances. The most popular use of Bluetooth is to create PANs of devices that communicate with a computer or device. Headsets, mice, printers, and connections with automation in automobiles are some examples of devices that commonly support the Bluetooth protocol. From a security perspective, it is important to consider Bluetooth support for your computers and devices when you are developing wireless policies and controls. Bluetooth-enabled computers are vulnerable to several types of wireless attacks unless you protect all wireless connections.

⚠ **WARNING**

In all cases, allowing wireless connections access to your network increases the potential for unauthorized users to access network resources. If you choose to implement wireless connections, you must ensure you are using strong access controls and strong wireless encryption. In other words, use Wi-Fi Protected Access (WPA/WPA2). Never use Wired Equivalent Privacy (WEP), which has been shown to be extremely easy to compromise.

Communication Protocol

A communication protocol isn't as complex as the name implies. The technical details of each protocol can be quite complex, but the concept is pretty simple. A protocol is just a set of rules parties use to communicate. You use protocol rules every day. For example, suppose you want to invite a person to attend a meeting. If that person is a close friend, you would use an informal greeting and style of conversation. If, however, the person is an elected official, you would likely use a far more formal greeting and choice of words. You decide how to communicate based on your own protocol rules. You'll learn more about computer communication protocols later in this chapter.

Networking Devices

Once you decide on the types of connections you'll use for your network, you have to decide how your components connect to one another. Only the simplest networks with very few devices have every component connected. With more than just a few devices, this arrangement would make managing your network connections extremely difficult. Networks in today's environments use several types of devices to keep connections manageable. You'll see many different types of devices, but the following two sections discuss the ones you'll most commonly use.

Hub (Legacy Device)

The simplest network device is a **hub**. Hubs used to be popular in smaller networks but have largely disappeared from use. A hub is simply a box with several connectors, or ports, that allows multiple network cables to attach to it. Common hubs had 4, 8, 16, or 32 ports. A hub is simply a hardware repeater. It takes input from any port and repeats the transmission, sending it as output on every port, including the original input port. As networks have become faster and more complex, hub use has all but disappeared.

Switch

The main problem with hubs is that they repeat all network traffic to all ports. This often causes message collisions and a frequent need to resend messages. They also tend to contribute to network congestion since every computer and device receives all network traffic. Networks are designed to handle collisions and congestion but at the cost of high performance. A **switch** can help avoid many collision and congestion issues and actually speed up networks. A switch is a hardware device that forwards input it receives only to the appropriate output port.

For example, if Computer A wants to send a message to Computer B, a switch will send the message from Computer A's port only to Computer B's port. No other computers ever see the message. As an additional benefit, if Computer C wants to send a message to Computer F at the same time Computers A and B are talking, the switch can handle both connections at the same time without causing a collision. Switches are also more secure since the only computers that actually see information exchanged over the network are the computers involved in the transfer. This is more secure than a hub that repeats messages to all connected computers. In the years since 2000, switch prices have fallen to a point that they are about the same cost as the simpler hubs and now are far more popular in networks of all sizes than hubs. **FIGURE 9-3** shows a simple network created using a single switch.

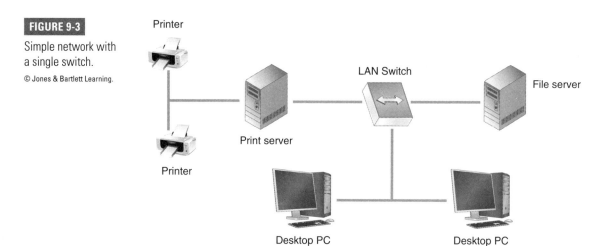

Router

A **router** is another network device that connects two or more separate networks. A router can connect any types of networks as long as they use the same protocols. Routers are more intelligent than switches and actually inspect the address portion of the packets on your network. The router examines the destination address and then forwards the packet to the correct outbound port. Routers can be stand-alone hardware devices or computers with multiple network interfaces running routing software.

Routers also provide an important security capability. You can define rules for each router that tell the router how to filter network traffic. You can restrict which packets are allowed to flow through the network. Routers give the ability to aggressively control how users and applications use the network.

Gateway

A **gateway** is a network device that connects two or more separate networks using different protocols. Networks using different protocols may include wired LANs, wireless LANs, and WANs. A gateway can perform many of the tasks a router performs but also has the ability to translate network packets from one protocol to another. Since it translates messages between protocols, a gateway is much more complex than either a router or a switch.

One of the most common types of gateways is one that connects a LAN to the internet. This type of gateway is often called an **internet gateway**. Gateways are necessary anytime you want to connect two networks that use different protocols. Gateways provide the same filtering capabilities of routers and much more. Gateways analyze more than just the destination address and port of each message. Since the gateway has to translate an entire message from one protocol to another, detailed rules can be set up to filter out inappropriate traffic.

Server Computers and Services Devices

Networks provide easy access to shared resources and shared services. Centralized services make it possible for multiple users to share information and physical resources at a lower cost than duplicating information or purchasing devices for every workstation. Examples of shared resources include the following:

- File storage
- Printer and print services
- Central database and document management systems
- Central authentication services

Network File Server

One common service present in even the earliest networks is the file sharing service. A **file server** is a computer or hardware device that has at least three distinct components:

- One or more connected storage devices
- A network interface
- Software to provide network access to files and folders on the attached storage devices

In the past, most file servers were computers that managed shared folders or file systems. The file server managed connections and supported authorized read/write access to its storage devices by remote users. Computer-based file servers are still in widespread use, but stand-alone hardware devices with internal disk drives are becoming more popular. A file server's main purpose is to provide secure access to its stored data for remote users.

Specialized network storage devices generally come in two flavors: **Network Attached Storage (NAS)** and **Storage Area Network (SAN)**. A NAS is a stand-alone hardware device with its own internal storage media, normally hard disks, and its own operating system. NAS devices are normally connected to the LAN and are visible as mapped remote folders or drives. SANs are often confused with NAS devices, but there are several differences. A SAN can be a single device or a collection of devices. SANs are generally connected to the computers that use them via fiber channel for a very fast data read and write rate. And SAN devices offer block-level I/O, as opposed to file level I/O for NAS devices. Even though SANs are remote devices, they appear to the operating system that uses them as local disk drives.

Network Print Server

A **print server** provides the interface between computers and devices connected to a network and one or more printers connected to the same network. Like file servers, the actual server can be a computer or a stand-alone hardware device. In either case, the print server accepts print jobs from authorized users and processes them. That means the print server may contain the intelligence to store multiple print jobs and provide advanced abilities to manage the printing process. Print servers vary widely in capabilities, but all generally exist to allow multiple remote users to share printers.

Data Storage

Network data storage may sound like the service the file server provides, but the two services are distinct. A file server only stores files. A data storage server organizes data and attempts to make the data more accessible than just a list of files. Data storage software includes database management systems and document management systems. Both types of management software provide efficient, effective centralized access to data and documents for remote users.

Another substantial difference between file servers and data storage products is that data storage products generally provide far greater control over access authorization. File servers can control access to individual folders and files, but data storage software can control access to the contents of files. Database management systems and document management systems often provide their own features to maintain and authorize users and requests. These systems manage large amounts of data and can grant or deny access to individual pieces of information stored inside very large files. The advantage of databases and document management systems is that they can provide fast and efficient access to large amounts of data while maintaining security of the data down to a very specific level.

Application Servers

Application servers are computers that run application programs on behalf of remote users. Instead of having remote users install and run programs, a user can request that an application server run the program and return the results. Using application servers has several advantages:

1. Software does not need to be installed on every user's computer; one license supports all users on one server (or several servers).
2. Updating software is easier; only application servers need to be updated.
3. Programs running on application servers tend to be closer to the database servers that store the data they need to run. Running programs on servers that are close to database servers can make accessing data much faster.
4. Since the database sends less data to the users' computers, more data stays inside an organization's secure network.
5. Server computers generally have the ability to serve many users efficiently, speeding up application programs.

Many of today's application programs rely on distributed design, which means at least part of the application runs on an application server. This application model gets a lot of attention from developers and attackers alike. Be sure to secure application servers along with the other components of your network.

Firewalls

A firewall is a common network component. It filters network traffic to block suspicious packets or messages. A firewall has the capability to examine network traffic and compares it with predefined rules. Firewall rules tell the firewall software whether to forward or deny traffic based on different characteristics found in the traffic itself. Some common ways to filter traffic using a firewall is based on source/destination IP address, destination port, or the communication protocol being used. After matching traffic to its rules, a firewall should drop or reject any network messages that are unauthorized or suspicious, so much of a firewall's effectiveness is based on its rules.

Firewalls run as software on computer, or as stand-alone devices. Either way, the firewall needs at least two network adapters to separate incoming traffic from outgoing traffic. Routers and gateways often include firewall functionality and the ability to filter traffic before forwarding it.

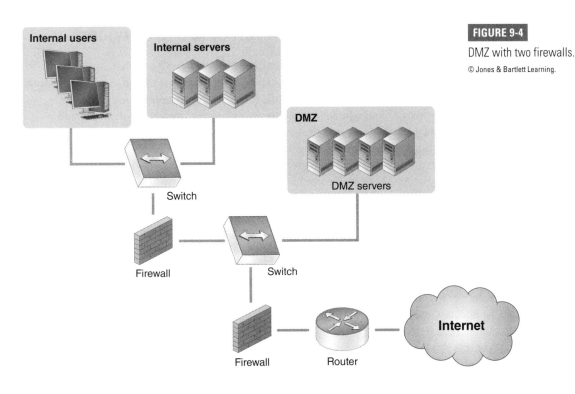

FIGURE 9-4

DMZ with two firewalls.

© Jones & Bartlett Learning.

One very useful application of firewalls is to separate your organization's secure networks from its insecure networks. This is most useful when you want to separate your internet access point from the secure network. Many organizations want to expose some services to the internet while maintaining separation from the internal network. Firewalls make this scenario possible. Many organizations use two firewalls to create an untrusted network that internet users can access and a trusted network for secure resources. The two networks are connected but separated by a firewall.

A company's untrusted network is called a **demilitarized zone (DMZ)**. The DMZ is a convenient place for web servers, File Transfer Protocol (FTP) servers, or any servers you want unauthorized users to access without being able to get into your trusted network. FIGURE 9-4 shows a DMZ with two firewalls.

Many firewalls provide the ability to translate an external IP address into an internally mapped IP address. The firewall stores a table that allows the software to translate the IP address for incoming and outgoing traffic. This feature, called **network address translation (NAT)**, hides the true IP address of internal computers from outside nodes. External nodes see only a generic IP address. The firewall receives traffic from the external IP address and changes the destination IP address to route the message to the correct internal IP address.

The main principle of Microsoft Windows network security is to ensure you enforce the C-I-A triad properties, confidentiality, integrity, and availability, for your information. Design the controls for the network media, traffic flow, and network computers and devices to ensure a secure environment and information.

Microsoft Windows Security Protocols and Services

Every computer or device connected to a network is called a **node**. Nodes communicate with one another by agreeing on a set of communication rules called a protocol. A communication protocol sets the rules for how nodes construct, send, receive, and interpret messages. Each protocol serves a specific purpose and has its own structure for constructing and addressing messages. In fact, several protocols are necessary to transport a message from one application to an application running on a remote computer. The physical media has one way of handling data, the network addressing software uses a different protocol, and applications use yet another set of rules to communicate.

Most discussions of network protocols include a discussion of the **Open Systems Interconnection (OSI) Reference Model**. The OSI Reference Model is a generic description for how computers use multiple layers of protocol rules to communicate across a network. The OSI Reference Model defines seven different layers of communication rules. You'll also likely encounter another popular reference model, the Transmission Control Protocol/Internet Protocol (TCP/IP) Reference Model, when discussing network protocols. The **TCP/IP Reference Model** defines four different layers of communication rules. Both models are useful to describe how protocols work and how to implement them in network communications. **FIGURE 9-5** shows the TCP/IP Reference Model and the OSI Reference Model.

Protocols provide the ability for applications to exchange information with other applications on other computers. For example, most web browser applications communicate with a web server application using the **Hypertext Transfer Protocol (HTTP)**. Web browsers can use other protocols, but HTTP is the most common protocol for regular webpages. HTTP also has a more secure variation known as Hypertext Transfer Protocol Secure (HTTPS). The web browser passes the message to the networking software layer. That layer handles the details of breaking the message into smaller packets suitable for networks, addressing the target machine, and routing the request across the network to ensure it arrives.

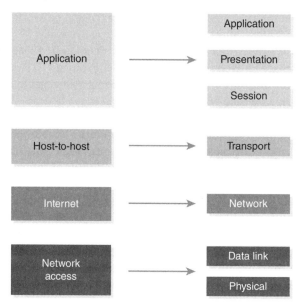

FIGURE 9-5

TCP/IP and OSI Reference Models.

© Jones & Bartlett Learning.

A common networking protocol is **TCP/IP**. TCP/IP is actually a combination of two separate protocols, but they work together in so many environments that they are often referenced as a single protocol.

Finally, the networking software passes the messages off to the software that physically controls the hardware that sends the data using physical media. This is the software and hardware that create the radio transmission for wireless networks or electrical signals for Ethernet.

It is important to know the protocols your systems and applications use. You can change many protocol settings to make your systems more secure. You'll want to learn more eventually about the specific protocol settings to use in hardening systems. For now, you should be aware of the most common protocols and the ones that relate most directly to security. **TABLE 9-4** shows a list of common protocols and how each one relates to your environment's security.

TABLE 9-4 Common Network Communication Protocols

PROTOCOL	DESCRIPTION	SECURITY NOTES
Telnet	Legacy protocol used for connecting terminals to servers. Sends text to and from the server. Historically used for remote administration accessing command-line utilities.	Telnet sends all information, including usernames and passwords, in readable text. Telnet should always be considered insecure and should not be used.
Secure Shell (SSH)	Similar to Telnet, except messages are encrypted. Useful for secure remote system administration using command-line utilities.	Older versions, such as 1.X, contain documented vulnerabilities. Newer versions are secure for most uses.
HTTP (Hypertext Transfer Protocol)	Used for most web browser/web server communication.	All data are sent in the clear. HTTP is not appropriate for confidential data.
HTTPS (Hypertext Transfer Protocol Secure)	Secure HTTP. Useful for exchanging confidential information between web browsers and web servers.	HTTPS uses SSL/TLS to provide encryption services. Ensure your web server is using SSL version 3.X or TLS.
SSL/TLS (Secure Sockets Layer/Transport Layer Security)	SSL is the predecessor of TLS. Both protocols provide encryption for Application Layer protocols, such as HTTPS.	TLS is the most secure. Do not use versions 1.X or 2.X of SSL. Use only SSL 3.X or TLS unless your application does not support newer versions.
TCP/IP (Transmission Control Protocol/Internet Protocol)	The most common protocol pair for internet communication.	TCP/IP is a frequent target for attackers since it is used in so many applications. Use helper protocols, such as TLS, to secure TCP/IP communications and filters to detect malicious traffic.

9

Microsoft Windows
Network Security

(Continues)

TABLE 9-4 Common Network Communication Protocols   (*Continued*)

PROTOCOL	DESCRIPTION	SECURITY NOTES
UDP (User Datagram Protocol)	Another common protocol used in place of IP when persistent connections are not necessary or desirable.	Use the same precautions as TCP/IP. Use UDP with other protocols and filters.
IPSec (Internet Protocol Security)	A protocol suite used to secure IP communication by encrypting each IP packet.	IPSec secures any messages that use IP to communicate. IPSec is transparent to applications that use it.
IKEv2 (Internet Key Exchange)	Tunneling protocol developed by Microsoft and Cisco.	When paired with IPSec, or other protocol that provides authentication, IKEv2 is a very secure and capable VPN.
PPTP (Point-to-Point Tunneling Protocol)	One of three common protocols used for virtual private networks (VPNs).	PPTP relies on PPP's encryption and authentication features to provide a VPN for applications that use TCP.
Layer 2 Tunneling Protocol (L2TP)	Another common protocol used for VPNs.	L2TP operates at a lower level than PPTP and must rely on a higher-level protocol, such as IPSec, to provide encryption. L2TP relies on UDP to transport messages.
SSTP (Secure Socket Tunneling Protocol)	New VPN protocol that uses SSL/TLS to encrypt HTTP traffic in a tunnel.	SSTP overcomes limitations that PPTP and L2TP messages have with firewalls and NAT devices. SSTP has no conflicts with NAT.
WEP (Wired Equivalent Privacy)	Older protocol for securing wireless network traffic.	WEP is a legacy protocol to encrypt wireless network traffic. It is better than nothing but not sufficient to secure confidential information. Not recommended for use.
WPA (Wi-Fi Protected Access)	WPA and WPA2 are more secure protocols than WEP with stronger encryption for wireless network traffic.	The latest versions of WPA, WPA2, and WPA3 are based on Advanced Encryption Standard (AES) and support several modes for varying needs of encryption security.
Kerberos	Protocol network nodes can use it to authenticate themselves to one another using an insecure network.	Windows uses Kerberos as a default authentication protocol.

© Jones & Bartlett Learning.

Layered Protocols in Real Life

The idea of layered protocols sounds complex. It really reflects what happens in human-to-human communication. Layers and translations are used in subtle ways every time you talk with a different person. Here's an example that demonstrates the obvious need for multiple layers.

Consider how delegates communicate in the United Nations (**FIGURE 9-6**). Assume the U.S. delegate wants to send a written note to the delegates of China, Russia, and Italy. In this example, the protocol rule in place requires all written messages to be presented in French. Here is how the message travels through the United Nations:

1. The U.S. delegate writes a message in English, then hands the message to a translator—the delegate layer passes the message to the translator layer.
2. The translator translates the message into French, then hands it to an aide to take to the mailroom—the translator layer passes the message to the aide layer.
3. The aide makes three copies of the message, addresses each copy and places the messages in the U.S. outbox in the mailroom—the aide layer duplicates and passes the messages to the mailroom clerk layer.
4. The mailroom clerk picks up the messages from the U.S. outbox and places them in the appropriate inboxes for China, Russia, and Italy—the mailroom clerk handles the physical transfer.
5. An aide for each country, China, Russia, and Italy, picks up the message and delivers it to the translator—the aide layer collects a message from the mailroom and passes it to the translator layer.
6. The translator translates the message from French into the country's national language and gives it to the delegate—the translator layer translates the message and passes it to the delegate layer.
7. The delegate for each country reads the message and takes appropriate action.

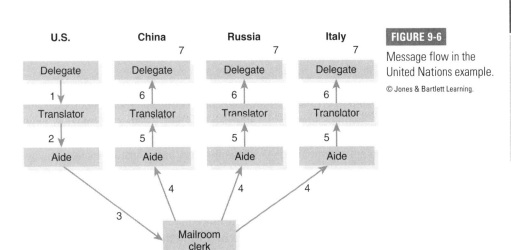

FIGURE 9-6

Message flow in the United Nations example.

© Jones & Bartlett Learning.

Windows uses protocols to communicate with other nodes across a network. This allows a program running on one computer to communicate with a program on another computer. It is common that the program on at least one end of a communication channel is a **Windows service**. A Windows service is a long-running program that performs a specific set of functions, such as a firewall, database server, or a web server. Services generally run without requiring user intervention and commonly run on server computers. Most services that provide network-related functions monitor one or more **ports**. A port is a numeric identifier that programs use to classify network messages.

Technical TIP

Most web traffic is directed to port 80 or port 443 on a server computer. When a server receives a web-related message, it redirects the message to the service that monitors port 80 for unencrypted traffic and port 443 for SSL/TLS encrypted traffic. Most likely, any service that monitors port 80 or port 443 is a web server.

Securing Microsoft Windows Environment Network Services

Securing services is an important step in securing Windows computers. Services are often powerful programs that can be dangerous if an attacker takes control. Since services are just programs, they can contain programming errors and vulnerabilities. While there are many specific configuration strategies to secure each type of service, three high-level strategies will keep all your services more secure: keeping all service software up to date, limiting the permissions granted to service user accounts, and removing unneeded services.

Service Updates

Before enabling any service, develop a plan for keeping the service up to date. Service programs generally run for long periods waiting for requests. The services commonly monitor communication ports for requests and respond anytime they receive messages. Attackers know which services are in widespread use, and they also know how to find out if you are running any services of interest. Whenever attackers uncover new vulnerabilities, they generally share the information with other potential attackers and start looking for vulnerable systems.

Once a new vulnerability surfaces, it is important to mitigate it as soon as possible. You can mitigate many vulnerabilities using compensating controls. The best way to address a vulnerability is to remove it. Many updates to service software do just that. Keep current on the latest releases available for any services you run. Keeping Windows updated with the latest service packs will keep many services up to date but will not address any non-Microsoft services you run. If you run any non-Microsoft services, such as the Apache web server or an Oracle database, you'll need to consult their websites for update information. Keeping your services up to date will help maintain your environment's security.

Service Accounts

Windows defines rights and permissions based on user accounts. Windows runs every program as a specific user. That means even services run as a user. By default, many services run as a local admin account. If an attacker can exploit a vulnerability and compromise a service, it is possible the attacker could assume the identity of the user running the service. For this reason, it is important to run each service as a user that possesses the minimum privileges necessary to perform the service's functions.

FYI

Microsoft continually introduces features with each new version to make the operating system more secure. Windows Server 2008 R2 included the new managed service accounts (MSA) feature. While this made managing service accounts easier, it didn't solve all of the issues. MSAs did provide automatic password management and instance name registration. However, the accounts could not be shared across multiple servers. Windows Server 2012 introduced group managed service accounts (gMSA). These accounts extend the earlier capabilities. Windows Server 2012 computers can share gMSAs and even use them for scheduled tasks. Administrators can also use the new gMSAs for more common software services, such as Microsoft Exchange or Microsoft SQL Server.

Carefully review the user account used for each service. You can see which user Windows uses for each service in the Services Microsoft Management Console (MMC) snap-in. You can use these steps to access the Service Properties:

1. Choose the Windows Start button, then select Administrative Tools > Services.
2. Select a service, right-click to open the context menu, and then, select Properties.
3. Choose the Log On tab to view or change the user account Windows uses to run the service.

⚠ WARNING

Avoid using a domain admin account for any service. If a domain admin account is used, an attacker can jeopardize an entire network by compromising a service running on your least secure computer.

Instead of using default accounts for services, create one or more user accounts that limit what services can do. Here are guidelines for creating secure accounts for services:

- Create a new account, with leading underscores in the name, which makes it easier to identify service accounts.
- Use strong passwords.
- Revoke all logon rights for local and remote logons.
- Set the Password Never Expires property.
- Set the User Cannot Change Password property.
- Remove the user from all default groups.
- Assign the minimum privileges necessary to run services.

These guidelines will help create user accounts that are safer for services. Any service compromise will have less impact than a service using a local or domain admin account. Be sure to test the new accounts extensively. Be sure to grant sufficient permission to the user for the service to perform all the necessary tasks.

Necessary Services

The best way to secure a specific service is to disable or even remove it. If the service isn't running, it isn't providing any functionality. If a service is not needed on a computer, stop it from running. It is important to disable unused services. Since a service monitors one or more communications ports, each service is a potential point of attack. Start only the necessary services.

For Windows Server computers, enable only the role(s) you need the computer to perform. Windows will not install services that do not fit a specific role. For example, if you don't need a web server running on a computer, don't enable the web server role. A server that doesn't have Internet Information Services (IIS) installed is immune to IIS vulnerabilities. For both Windows client and server computers, review all of the services in the Services MMC snap-in. Ensure that you need each running service.

If a service is not needed, you can take several steps:

> ⚠️ **WARNING**
>
> If you do not turn on the security features of your wireless internet devices, you may be the victim of Wi-Fi jacking. This occurs when attackers walk or drive through business areas and neighborhoods and identify unprotected wireless LANs from the street using a laptop or a handheld computer. When they find an unprotected network, they can hijack that wireless connection to download illegal materials, send spam, etc. They can also use their connection to the wireless network to hack into other computers on the LAN to steal information and identities.

- **Stop it**—Stop a service in the Services snap-in. Change its Startup Type to Manual to disable the service from starting automatically when the system boots.
- **Disable it**—Change the Startup Type to Disabled to tell Windows not to start a service.
- **Remove it**—If an unneeded service is installed on a computer, remove the software for the service. The procedure to remove a service depends on the type of service.

FIGURE 9-7 shows the startup options in the Services MMC snap-in.

Regardless of your mitigation actions, take the time to review all of the services your computers run. Ensure each running service is necessary for that computer to accomplish its goals. Stop any unnecessary services. Each service you stop removes another potential attack point from your environment.

Securing Microsoft Windows Wireless Networking

Securing your wireless network is a crucial step in securing your overall Windows environment. Allowing unsecured wireless access to your Windows network can provide easy access for attackers and undermine your efforts to secure your environment. Wireless access makes it easier for anyone to connect to your network even from outside your physical environment. An attacker armed with a notebook computer and a wireless card can access an unsecured wireless network from as much as several hundred feet away from the access point. You can't rely on any physical security measures to protect your wireless networks as you can with wired connections.

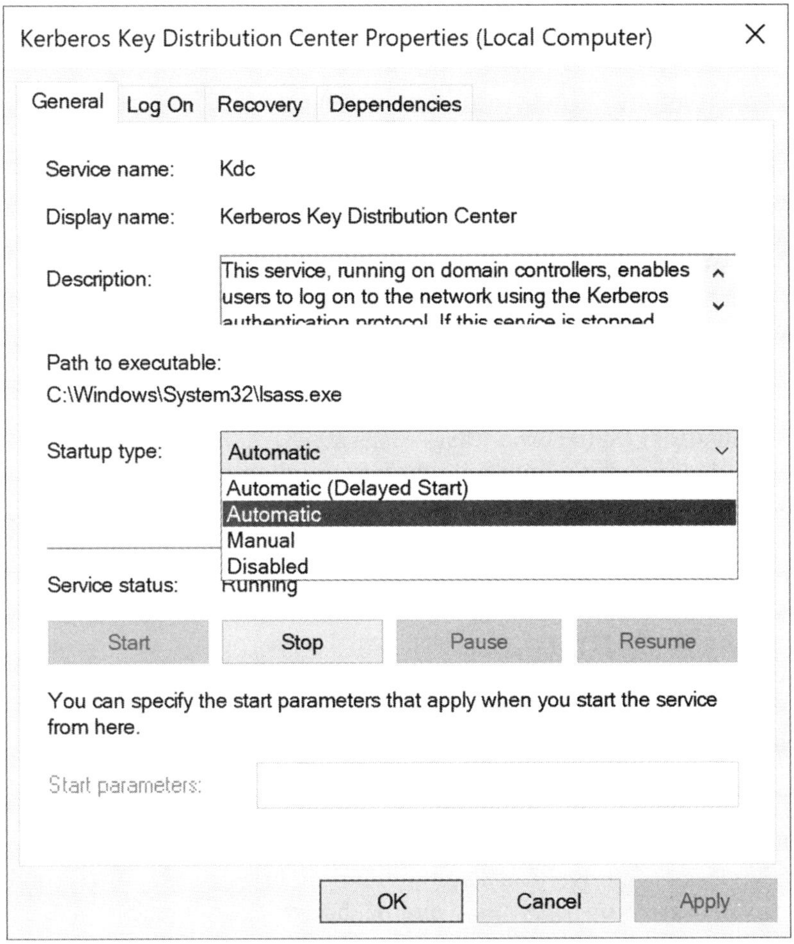

FIGURE 9-7

Windows services startup options.

Courtesy of Microsoft Corporation.

In the past, only computers used to access networks. Once networks became more popular and computing devices started getting smaller, mobile devices began emerging, and users wanted to use them to access internal networks. These laptops, tablets, and now even smartphones have become common in most organizations and require newer, more aggressive security controls. Today, the transformation to the next generation of network access is underway. The Internet of Things (IoT) has most recently become one of the most challenging security concerns. IoT refers to the rapidly growing number of smart devices that connect to networks. Both homes and businesses are connecting cameras, security devices, climate control, and many other types of devices to its network. Each of these devices present a potential vulnerability and entry point for an attacker to access an internal network. Applying solid security practices to every IoT device is necessary to keep networks secure.

You can take several steps to secure wireless networks. The actual steps you take to enable each of the following suggestions depend on your wireless hardware manufacturer. However, all current wireless devices provide the ability to make your wireless network more secure. For specific instructions for your hardware, consult the hardware manufacturer's website or user guide. Follow these guidelines to make any wireless network more secure:

- **Use WPA or WPA2 encryption**—Do not use WEP unless your wireless access point does not support WPA/WPA2. Security professionals have demonstrated they can compromise WEP in a matter of minutes. WPA/WPA2 is the only secure protocol you should consider for confidential information available on a wireless network. If support is available, use WPA3 for the highest level of security and encryption.
- **Use Media Access Control (MAC) address filtering**—Most wireless access points allow you to define valid MAC addresses. If you enable MAC address filtering, only valid MAC addresses can connect to the wireless network. MAC address filtering does make administration more difficult and attackers can spoof MAC addresses, but adding layers of controls makes the environment safer.
- **Disable Service Set Identifier (SSID) broadcast**—Many attackers scan for potential victim networks by collecting information for all networks broadcasting (**SSIDs**). Turning off the SSID broadcast doesn't make your network more secure, but it does make it less visible to casual scanners.
- **Limit outside eavesdropping**—Each wireless access point has an effective transmission range. You can move the devices away from external walls to make it harder to use a signal outside your physical environment. Locate your wireless devices as far away from external walls as possible while still providing ample coverage for your organization's users.
- **Physically separate wireless networks by purpose**—Many organizations deploy at least two wireless networks. One wireless network is secure and requires each new device and user to register with an administrator before getting access. This wireless network would likely provide access to the organization's internal network. Another wireless network uses fewer controls and makes it easy for guests to connect. This second wireless network would likely connect only to an internet bridge. This approach makes it easy to give guests internet access without exposing your organization's network.

Limiting access to wireless networks makes your environment far more difficult for attackers to compromise. Wireless security is only one layer in your overall security plan, but it is an important one.

Microsoft Windows Workstation Network Security

Windows desktop computers operate in the Workstation Domain in the IT infrastructure and generally operate as clients in network communications. That means desktop computers generally initiate communication by sending requests to servers in another domain. The main areas of focus with respect to desktop network security should be user authentication and authorization, malicious software protection, and outbound traffic validation.

User Authorization and Authentication

Users can do only what you allow them to do. One of the best ways to keep attackers away from your network is to keep them away from your workstations. In addition to physical controls to limit unauthorized access to workstations, it is important to aggressively protect workstations from unauthorized logons. This means deploying a user account policy that makes it difficult for an attacker to log on as an authorized user. Here are some guidelines to protect your workstations from unauthorized access:

- Train all users on how to create strong passwords and protect user account credentials.
- Require unique user accounts with strong passwords for each user.
- Use the principle of least privilege to grant minimal rights and permissions to users.
- Audit failed access attempts.
- Audit all logons for privileged accounts.
- Enable account lockout after five failed logon attempts.
- Explore alternate authentication methods. For more privileged users or workstations, consider multifactor authentication.
- Remove or disable unused user accounts.
- Disable remote access.
- Require password rotation periodically.
- Be sure to remove user access immediately following termination of employment.
- Enable screen lockouts after a short amount of inactivity.

Malicious Software Protection

A popular attack vector for central servers is to compromise a trusted workstation using malicious software. A workstation is often easier to compromise than a server due to the relative lack of attention to security controls. Workstations are frequent targets for attacks. Don't forget to consider all workstations that will access your organization's environment. This includes remote workstations. Remote workstations can be very difficult to manage, but you cannot overlook the security risks associated with any workstation.

You should require all workstations have anti-malware software installed before you allow them to connect to your environment. This includes antivirus and anti-spyware software. Ensure the software and the software's signature databases are up to date. You can use Group Policy to enforce this requirement. You should also create a schedule to scan workstations for malicious software. Just because the software is present doesn't mean the computer is clean. It is important to proactively scan workstations at least weekly along with active anti-malware shield software to maintain as clean an environment as possible for your workstations.

Outbound Traffic Filtering

Despite your best efforts, it is possible that one or more of your workstations may be compromised. One popular attack when targeting workstations is to place malicious software on a workstation that creates a flood of messages. Since the workstations inside your network are trusted nodes, your network will accept the traffic. Several attacks will send a large volume of network messages that end up flooding the network and making it unusable for legitimate traffic. Attacks of this type are called **denial of service (DoS) attacks**. Successful DoS attacks makes information unavailable to authorized users since the network is too saturated to respond. If the attack coordinates with other compromised workstations, it is called a **distributed denial of service (DDoS) attack**.

You can protect your network from many DoS and DDoS attacks by configuring each workstation's firewall to filter outbound traffic. Most DoS and DDoS attacks create traffic that a firewall can easily recognize and refuse to pass onto the network. Although your workstation has still been compromised, the attack is not effective if the traffic doesn't make it to the network. Make sure all workstations have active and up-to-date firewall rules that filter incoming and outgoing traffic for known suspicious packets.

Microsoft Windows Server Network Security

Windows servers provide various types of services for enterprises. In many cases, servers either directly or indirectly enable enterprise applications to access shared data to support business functions. While compromising a workstation may open a door into an organization's secure network, compromising a server will likely allow an attacker to get even closer to sensitive or confidential data.

Although each layer of security is important to the overall security of your organization's data, you should view server security controls as even more crucial. The controls you place on server computers will only act as obstacles for attackers that have already found ways to defeat outer layers of controls. It is likely any attacker who has made it this far is sophisticated and skilled. You must carefully design, deploy, and monitor controls for servers in your network to increase the likelihood that you'll stop an attack before it compromises the data you're trying to protect.

Authentication and Authorization

All three of the C-I-A triad properties of data security depend on the positive identification of an authorized user. Your servers inside your organization's secure network should require specific user accounts to use any service. You may allow anonymous users or shared user accounts to access some resources, such as generic webpages or public file downloads, but these servers should reside in the DMZ and not in your secure network.

Inside the secure network, you should authenticate all computers and users before processing resource access requests. Windows uses Kerberos by default to provide a secure method to establish two-way authentication. This level of authentication assurance provides protection from eavesdropping or certain types of replay attacks. A replay attack is one where an attacker intercepts authentication messages. Unless the attacker is working with a protected network, it is possible to replay the authentication messages and log on again. It is similar to your web browser storing your password to a website. But in this case, the attacker is storing someone else's password. Kerberos gives both sides of a network conversation the assurance that the other party is who he or she claims to be.

Carefully examine each server's role to ensure that no unnecessary services are running. For the services you are running, make sure you have defined access control lists (ACLs) for all authorized users and all protected resources. Apply the principle of least privilege for all users. Use Group Policy Objects (GPOs) as much as possible to standardize security settings.

Malicious Software Protection

Servers are vulnerable to malware just like workstations. You must install antivirus and anti-spyware software on each Windows server on your network. As with workstations, be sure to update both the software and signature databases frequently. Check for updated software and signature databases daily for server computers.

Use Group Policy to enforce this requirement on servers as well as for workstations. You should also create a schedule to scan each server for malicious software. Your scan schedule depends on the services and data on any server, but weekly scans should be the minimum frequency. Scheduled scans, along with active anti-malware software, will help you to maintain as clean an environment as possible for your servers.

Network Traffic Filtering

Firewalls protect services running on servers by filtering out suspicious traffic that attackers could use to compromise servers. The success of your firewall depends on its rules and location. Stand-alone firewalls can be used to filter traffic before it reaches a server or you can implement firewalls on your servers.

> ⚠️ **WARNING**
>
> Be careful about logging firewall traffic. Your log file can become quite large if you don't monitor and clear it out periodically. Log only the events you really need and carefully monitor the size of your log files. Consider using a secure information event manager (SIEM) to monitor your firewall logs and traffic such as Splunk or Solar-Winds SIEM. An SIEM will alert you to possible compromises of your network.

Either option has advantages and disadvantages. Stand-alone firewalls relieve some of the workload from your servers. The firewall device processes firewall rules and forwards only approved traffic. The server never sees traffic that does not match your firewall rules. The disadvantages of stand-alone firewalls include additional administrative workload, since stand-alone firewalls are separate devices and an additional hardware cost.

Firewalls that are integrated with servers have advantages and disadvantages. First, Microsoft's firewall uses the familiar MMC interface for administration. You can also use GPOs to enforce standard rules across multiple servers. Microsoft's firewall also comes with Windows Server operating systems and does not require an additional license or hardware purchase. The main disadvantage is that an embedded firewall adds to the server's workload. The server must examine all network traffic to apply its filtering rules. Another disadvantage is that since a firewall is a program, it can have vulnerabilities that attackers may be able to exploit. An attacker who compromises a server firewall may be able to gain access to protected resources on that server.

Regardless of the type of firewall, set up rules to allow only valid traffic for the specific server functions you define. Deny, and potentially log, all other traffic.

Internal Network and Cloud Security

In addition to securing workstations and servers, you should examine the network itself and any external cloud-based services your users interact with. For example, most of today's modern network environments have been expanded with the use of some form of cloud technology. Even with very secure workstations and servers, most networks have multiple devices that not only connect to them but make the networks work. And as more and more organizations integrate cloud-based services into their normal operation, the scope of the organization grows to include the cloud service providers. The most common example of this expanded scope comes in the form of hybrid cloud environments where each company has some on-premises technology connected up to cloud technologies in a private or public cloud. With complexity comes challenges with security so it's imperative to understand when moving to a cloud environment that security reviews are taken even more seriously and all steps are taken to validate a strong security posture.

IPv4 versus IPv6

Using IPv6, as opposed to the more common IPv4 protocol, provides many security benefits. IPv6 was designed for security and has several built-in security features. Although some IPv6 features can be used in IPv4 now, such as end-to-end encryption using IPSec, these features are retrofitted into IPv4. The same features are native in IPv6 and will likely end up being used more because of the fact that they are integrated features that do not require additional software installation or administration.

IPv6 is much newer and not as well understood as IPv4. IPv6 presents a steeper learning curve to manage, and organizations may find that some legacy applications or hardware do not support it. Most current operating systems support dual-stack IP networking, in that they will support both IPv4 and IPv6 concurrently. This may be a good interim option for organizations that must evaluate whether all software and hardware will support IPv6. A dual-stack approach allows the organization the ability to enjoy the benefits of IPv6, including end-to-end encryption and more secure name resolution, without having to immediately retire components that do not support it.

Cloud Computing

Internal organizational networks don't provide the clear trust boundaries anymore. Before the proliferation of cloud computing, it was easy to define the network perimeter for any network. But today, cloud applications such as Microsoft Office 365 or Salesforce.com are integral parts of an organization's operations. It is important that all security considerations and reviews include cloud service providers as well.

For example, you must ensure that your cloud service provider supports the level of anti-malware that you require in your own internal network. Likewise, your cloud service provider should at least match your recovery goals. And with respect to practicing the principle of least privilege, cloud service providers should provide enough user accounts to define access to the level of granularity you need to manage your users. In short, your cloud service provider should meet or exceed the security requirements you use for your internal network.

If you determine that your cloud service provider does not meet your minimum-security requirements, making changes to meet those requirements may result in agreement changes. Changes may cost you more in-service fees. That's why it is always better to validate security requirements during the negotiation phase before you sign up for cloud service provider services. Always review your cloud service provider's **Service Level Agreement (SLA)** and know what each one promises.

When it comes to anti-malware, the cloud has bolstered up the protection of systems with utilities that allow your resources to be secure both on premises and in the public or private cloud. For example, with Microsoft Azure cloud solutions, you can set up your Windows server systems and run Microsoft Defender for Cloud to add layers of protection to ensure adherence to policy, compliance and security of your infrastructure.

FIGURE 9-8 shows the Microsoft Defender for Cloud Tool.

Microsoft Defender for Cloud allows you to secure your cloud resources with relative ease. Microsoft Defender for Cloud is Microsoft's flagship cloud-based security posture management system that allows for workload protection. It allows you to not only secure what is in your cloud subscription, but also any systems you have on-premises, across clouds, and in multi-cloud scenarios like with Amazon AWS or Google GCP. As long as it's compatible, Defender for Cloud can add security functions and help manage security across platforms. The focus areas of Microsoft Defender for Cloud are allowing for a security score from consistent assessments of your security posture, tracking capabilities that allow for in depth reporting, the ability to use workload automation, the use of workbooks to allow for security posture review, and recommendations that will allow you to take action on threats. All of this combined adds to your defense in depth structure.

A service such as Microsoft Defender for Cloud can provide proactive tools to keep your systems secure. Using a workbook you can find systems at risk for exploitation. The workbook will allow you to review CVE data and from there provide recommendations. One of the biggest attacks of the past year or so has been with the Log4j vulnerability that literally impacted a wide array of systems worldwide back in the beginning of 2021. The Apache Log4j vulnerability originally surfaced as a simple dormant threat; however, it was

FIGURE 9-8

Workbooks for the Log4j vulnerability.

Courtesy of Microsoft Corporation.

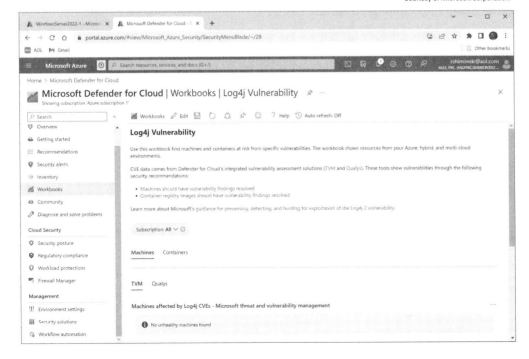

officially exposed and exploited in 2021, and any system running Apache was at risk. The threat revolved around Apache's logging facility and, when exploited, could lead to remote code execution exploitation. The challenge with Log4j is that this particular threat was found across most Apache deployments and very commonly used. This made this threat incredibly problematic since most web systems had to be "touched" to patch them or shut them down until a fix could be put in place. Another major concern with this threat is that older systems that could not be patched required OS, application, and system vendors to create a patch, and most did not want to create patches for out-of-date systems. Therefore it required end users (i.e., companies, personal users) to consider and decide if they wanted to upgrade systems that they had not planned on upgrading. Another consideration is that the systems that had to be upgraded forced the upgrade of the applications running on them. It's still a known issue so there needs to be continued validation that this (or any other) exploit does not still exist on your current systems. To show how the cloud can help to alleviate these types of problems, the workbooks for Microsoft Defender for Cloud will search the CVE database and provide guidance and alert on systems that need repair.

In regards to least privilege, the cloud provides a suite of tools allowing for least privilege use. In other chapters of this book, the concept of least privilege are covered to explain how to ensure that a Windows desktop such as Windows 11 or a server platform such as Windows Server 2022 can be secured. Another level is the cloud platform that the virtual machines run on which also needs to be secured. With Azure Access Control IAM (Identity Access Management) solutions, you can provide another level of access control to your cloud properties.

FIGURE 9-9 shows the Microsoft Access Control IAM tool.

To configure least privilege, you simply need to understand what role you want to set up for a user or group of users and use a predefined role or you can create a new customized role. By doing this, you can allow for those who manage servers and systems to do so with specific permissions. The actions taken can also be logged and monitored as well as alerted on.

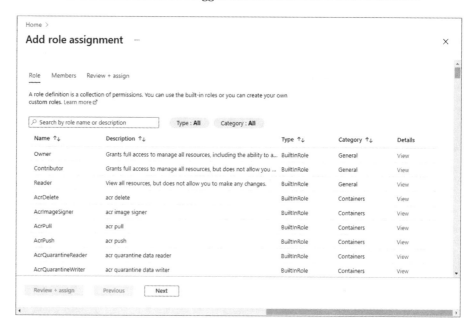

FIGURE 9-9

Configuring Access Control with IAM.

Courtesy of Microsoft Corporation.

FIGURE 9-10

Creating Security Alert Queries.

Courtesy of Microsoft Corporation.

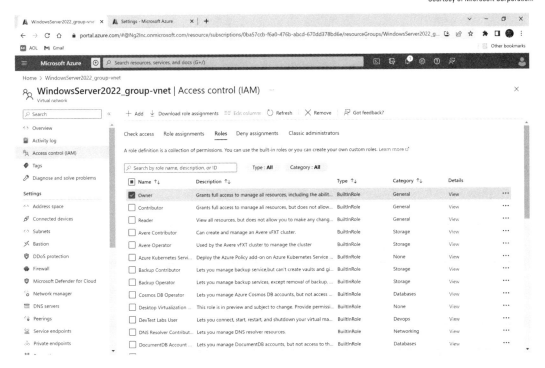

A good way to ensure that your administrators, cloud engineers, and even your cloud provider is meeting your expectations is to perform event logging and performing audits. By configuring security alerts in the Azure Resource Graph Explorer within Microsoft Defender for Cloud, you can create queries for alerting. You can find within the explorer a way to customize your security alert needs to your specific needs.

FIGURE 9-10 shows the Azure Resource Graph Explorer tool.

Another way to help build a strong security posture is to be able to query alerts across your cloud subscription to allow for complex policy processing and verifying governance. You can assess the impact of applying policies across your cloud subscription quickly and easily removing the manual efforts to do so in order to verify your cloud resources are secure. Ensuring governance and compliance to security policy at scale across cloud and on-premises systems in your enterprise can allow you to report more easily on what you need to address in your risk register.

Lastly when it comes to cloud resources, the ability to set a security policy for compliance across your environment (both cloud and multi-cloud) is invaluable. With the Security Policy function within Microsoft Defender for Cloud, you can address your infrastructures compliance to policy using the Azure Security Benchmark, but also others, including PCI DSS. Similar to how we applied security policies to individual systems, you can see here how using cloud tools will allow you to address the entire environment with enterprise-level tools.

FIGURE 9-11 shows the Security Policy settings.

9

Microsoft Windows
Network Security

Setting a Security Policy.

Courtesy of Microsoft Corporation.

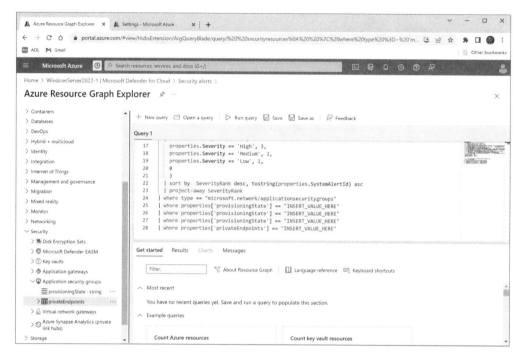

Best Practices for Microsoft Windows Network Security

Securing a Windows network is an ongoing endeavor. Although the process never really ends, you can reach a level of assurance that your network is secure from most threats. It is important to continually monitor controls to ensure they are as effective as expected. Here are some best practices that will help you get started securing your network and provide a good set of guidelines for ensuring your network stays secure:

- Identify sensitive data.
- Protect sensitive data at rest using encryption.
- Establish unique domain user accounts for each user.
- Enforce strong passwords for all user accounts.
- Create new user accounts with limited rights and permission for services.
    - Do not allow any services to run as a domain admin user.
- Use Kerberos for secure authentication.
- Install firewalls to create a DMZ.
    - Place all internet-facing servers—web servers and other publicly accessible servers—in the DMZ.
    - Use encrypted communication for all traffic flowing through the DMZ and the trusted network.

- Use encryption for all communication involving sensitive data.
- Establish firewall rules.
  - Deny all suspicious traffic.
  - Allow only approved traffic for servers.
  - Filter inbound and outbound traffic for servers and workstations for malicious messages.
  - If your firewall supports it, automatically terminate connections with sources generating DoS traffic to mitigate DoS attacks in process.
- Install anti-malware software on all computers and establish frequent update schedules and scans.
  - Update software and signature databases daily.
  - Perform quick scans daily.
  - Perform complete scans at least weekly.
- Use WPA, WPA2, or WPA3 for all secure wireless networks. Do not use WEP.
- Disable SSID broadcast for secure wireless networks.
- Do not enable wireless or mobile broadband cards while connected to your organization's internal network. Always disable your wireless adapter before connecting a laptop to the wired network.
- Do not allow visitors to roam around your facilities using wireless LANs. Many access points can be physically reset to insecure factory default settings by pressing a reset switch on the box.
- Avoid connecting to public networks. When you connect to an open wireless network, you should have no expectation of privacy or security.
- If you have to use an open wireless connection, do not visit websites that require usernames, passwords, or account numbers, such as online banking. Use an encrypted connection or a virtual private network.
- Install a separate wireless access point connected only to the internet for guests.
- Disable or uninstall any services that you do not need.

These best practices provide a solid foundation for establishing and maintaining a secure Windows network.

CHAPTER SUMMARY

Securing a Windows network means securing all of the components. You learned about the different components that make up a Windows network. You learned about workstations, servers, devices, and software. You also learned about the process to secure each type of component. While securing a Windows network takes planning and effort to be successful, it is possible.

Once you know your network and what each component does, you're ready to start planning for the most effective security controls. No control set is best for every organization. The controls that work best for your network will maximize the C-I-A triad properties for your data and still support your business functions.

KEY CONCEPTS AND TERMS

Application server
Coaxial cable
Demilitarized zone (DMZ)
Denial of service (DoS) attack
Distributed denial of service
  (DDoS) attack
File server
Gateway
Hub
Hypertext Transfer Protocol
  (HTTP)
IEEE 802.11
Institute of Electrical and
  Electronics Engineers (IEEE)

Internet gateway
Local area network (LAN)
Local resource
Metropolitan area network
  (MAN)
Network
Network address translation
  (NAT)
Network Attached Storage (NAS)
Node
Open Systems Interconnection
  (OSI) Reference Model
Port
Print server

Protocol
Remote resource
Router
Service Level Agreement (SLA)
Service Set Identifier (SSID)
Storage Area Network (SAN)
Switch
TCP/IP Reference Model
Transmission Control Protocol/
  Internet Protocol (TCP/IP)
Wide area network (WAN)
Windows service
Wireless local area network
  (WLAN)

CHAPTER 9 ASSESSMENT

1. A(n) _____ is a network that generally spans several city blocks.

2. A local resource is any resource connected to the local LAN.

   A. True
   B. False

3. Which of the following network devices connects networks that use different protocols?

   A. Switch
   B. Hub
   C. Gateway
   D. Router

4. _____ cabling provides very good protection from interference but is difficult to install.

5. Even the newest wireless protocols are slower than using high-quality physical cable.

   A. True
   B. False

6. Which LAN device commonly has the ability to filter packets and deny traffic based on the destination address?

   A. Router
   B. Gateway
   C. Hub
   D. Switch

7. A(n) _____ is an untrusted network that contains internet-facing servers and is separated from your trusted network by at least one firewall.

8. Which network device feature provides the ability to hide internal network node addresses?

   A. DMZ
   B. NAT
   C. STP
   D. OSI

9. Which network layer reference model includes four layers to describe how computers use multiple layers of protocol rules to communicate across a network?

   A. IEEE
   B. IPSec
   C. UDP
   D. TCP/IP

10. Which of the following actions is *not* an effective way to secure Windows services that you do not use?

    A. Stop it
    B. Disable it
    C. Block it
    D. Remove it

11. You should disable the _____ broadcast to make wireless networks harder to discover.

    A. SSID
    B. NAT
    C. MAC
    D. WPA

12. A successful DoS attack violates which property of the C-I-A triad?

    A. Availability
    B. Integrity
    C. Consistency
    D. Confidentiality

13. Where must sensitive data appear encrypted to ensure its confidentiality? (Select two.)

    A. While in use in the workstation
    B. During transmission over the network
    C. As it is stored on disk
    D. In memory

14. Which authentication protocol does Windows Server use as a default?

    A. NTLM
    B. Kerberos
    C. WPA
    D. NAT

15. What can some firewalls do to attempt to stop a DoS attack in progress?

    A. Alert an attack responder
    B. Log all traffic coming from the source of the attack
    C. Terminate any connections with the source of the attack
    D. Reset all connections

Microsoft Windows Security Administration

THE SECURITY OF AN ORGANIZATION'S INFORMATION is a direct result of the quality of its security policy. The security policy states the importance of security and defines a secure environment. Once a solid security policy is defined, it must be put into practice. Administering the components of a security policy means creating and deploying controls that ensure compliance with the policy.

In this chapter, you'll learn how to ensure that your organization meets your security policy's goals. You'll learn about the responsibilities of a security administrator and the tasks needed to go from a policy to usable controls. You'll also learn how important it is to constantly review and measure performance to ensure that you maintain the most secure environment possible.

Chapter 10 Topics

This chapter covers the following topics and concepts:

- What security administration is
- How to maintain the C-I-A triad in the Microsoft Windows operating system (OS) world
- What Microsoft Windows OS security administration is
- How to ensure due diligence and regulatory compliance
- What the need for security policies, standards, procedures, and guidelines is
- What best practices for Microsoft Windows OS security administration are

Chapter 10 Goals

When you complete this chapter, you will be able to:

- Describe Microsoft Windows OS security administration
- Maintain the C-I-A triad in the Microsoft Windows OS
- Ensure due diligence and regulatory compliance
- Understand the need for security policies, standards, procedures, and guidelines

Security Administration Overview

Security administration is the process of putting security controls into effect within the IT infrastructure. Security administrators configure and maintain all of the computers and devices to uphold your security policy. While many of a security administrator's tasks center on Windows server and workstation computers, other devices also require attention. As a security administrator, you'll be responsible for ensuring that the following hardware components are secure:

* Windows servers
* Windows workstations
* Mobile devices
* Network connection media
* Network connection devices (hubs, switches, routers, gateways, and firewalls)
* Wireless access points
* Printers
* Shared storage devices
* Scanners
* Any other network devices

The responsibilities of security administration extend far beyond managing hardware. The following are examples of additional items security administrators must ensure are up to date and configured to be as secure as possible:

* User accounts
* Authentication methods and credentials
* Windows OSs
* Application software
* Anti-malware software and signature databases
* Other supporting drivers and software
* Software tools and utilities
* Group Policy
* Active Directory (AD)
* Backup schedules
* Recovery plans
* Maintenance plans

Security administration is the process that puts security controls in place.

The Security Administration Cycle

The security administration process is not a straight-line process that is completed and finished. Security administration is a cycle. The Deming cycle is one common method that describes the phases that you will encounter in security administration. The **Deming cycle** was made popular by Dr. W. Edwards Deming. It explains standardized quality control. The Deming cycle is also known as the **Plan-Do-Check-Act (PDCA)** process:

- **Plan**—Establish objectives and the processes to meet a goal. In security administration, the stated goal is one aspect of a security policy. A specification document will be created during the planning activity. It details how to measure your results to determine if you've met your goal.
- **Do**—Implement the process you planned in the previous step.
- **Check**—Measure the effectiveness of the new process and compare the results against the expected results from the plan.
- **Act**—Analyze the differences between expected results and measured results. Determine the cause of any differences and proceed to the Plan process to develop a plan to improve the performance.

FIGURE 10-1 shows the PDCA cycle.

Security administration is a quality process. Several basic concepts help keep activities in perspective. First, quality is a continuous process, not a single goal. There is always room for improvement in any IT infrastructure. It is your responsibility as a security administrator to constantly follow the PDCA cycle. Following the cycle ensures that your environment maintains the highest level of security possible.

Second, a proactive plan for security is less expensive than a minimal plan relying on detective controls. Manufacturers know that reducing defects in their processes saves more money than using inspections to catch the defective items. Prevention is always better than a cure. The same concept in security means it is better to implement preventive controls than to rely on detective controls to throw an alert when something bad happens. In reality, both types of controls are needed. Search for a control that denies an undesired action. If controls stop an attack before damage occurs, you'll spend less time hunting through audit logs trying to figure out what happened.

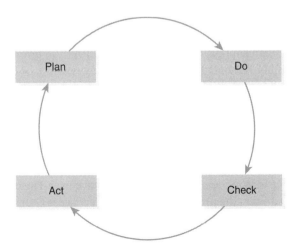

FIGURE 10-1

Plan-Do-Check-Act cycle.
© Jones & Bartlett Learning.

Security Administration Tasks

The security administration process includes any tasks that directly support an organization's security policy. The security administrator's role includes tasks to keep a Windows environment secure. **TABLE 10-1** lists some of the more prominent tasks of a security administrator.

The tasks in Table 10-1 do not represent all of the responsibilities of a security administrator. The tasks listed tend to be common examples across organizations. Each organization will have a slightly different list of tasks its security administrators carry out to maintain a secure environment.

Partial Security Is No Security

Failure to ensure any of the three C-I-A triad properties is failure to protect your data. For example, assume you are the security administrator for a group of physicians. You manage a small Windows network. The network runs software to process and store medical and billing records for the medical practice. You store all of the medical records in an encrypted database. You restrict access to medical data to a limited number of user accounts. You allow only authorized clients to access the network using encrypted connections. Your database stores record-based access control lists (ACLs) that allow only specific access for viewing and changing data. You create a backup of the entire database daily to protect from data loss.

Your use of encryption, user accounts, and ACLs enforces data integrity and confidentiality. However, you find that there is no plan to replace the computer hardware for the database server if it fails. You find that ordering a replacement server would take at least 24 hours to arrive and another 6 hours to prepare for use. Your medical data would be unavailable during that time. Since you have not protected the availability property of your data, the information isn't really secure.

Maintaining the C-I-A Triad in the Microsoft Windows OS World

Every security control deployed should directly address a security policy goal. Each goal in the security policy should support one or more of the C-I-A triad properties—confidentiality, integrity, and availability. As controls are developed and deployed, be sure to protect all three properties for data at multiple layers. Any unaddressed security property leaves your data vulnerable to attack.

Maintaining Confidentiality

Protecting data confidentiality means keeping it safe from unauthorized access. All object access decisions made in Windows depend on the effective user. The effective user is the user account that is running the process requesting object access. Any decision to grant or deny access to an object depends on the discretionary access control list (DACL) that exists for the object and effective user. Ensuring that you know the identity of the user running any

TASK	DESCRIPTION
TABLE 10-1 Common Security Administrator Tasks	
Provide input for acceptable use policies (AUPs)	AUPs provide users with a documented statement of actions that are acceptable and unacceptable. AUPs provide guidance for aspects of computer use, such as email, internet, personal use of business computers, and standard of care when handling business information. Developing AUPs gives planners the ability to state security goals, define controls, and decide on consequences for noncompliance.
Enforce password controls	Password controls are some of the most common and visible controls because they affect every user. A user's password is one of the first targets for many attackers.
Enforce user access Control	Security administrators are often responsible for ensuring the principle of least privilege is maintained in regards to limiting user access to company systems and resources.
Enforce physical security standards	Physical security is an important layer to secure all components in the IT infrastructure. Components that store or transmit sensitive data should have stronger physical controls. For example, the database servers that store an organization's most critical and confidential data should be located in a room with a controlled environment and very limited physical access. Any access provided should be credentialed, monitored, and auditable.
Deploy controls to meet encryption requirements	Enforce encryption for data at rest and when sensitive data are transmitted across the network. Appropriate controls depend on data sensitivity and its destination. For example, most, if not all, data should be encrypted when the information is transferred to clients over the internet. Data transferred between two trusted servers both in a secure datacenter, however, may not need encryption. Strong encryption methods with recommended ciphers should be used.
Implement backup policies	Develop schedules and procedures to ensure all IT infrastructure components are backed up with current data, tested, and recoverable. Waiting too long between backups may mean available backups aren't very useful for recovery. Ensure that your organization understands and defines its recovery time objective (RTO) and recovery point objective (RPO).
Keep software up to date	Ensure all OS and application software has as many necessary patches applied as possible without affecting the environment's ability to perform business functions.
Ensure anti-malware controls are current and in force	Enforce requirements to ensure anti-malware software is in place on all computers and is kept up to date.
Monitor log files	Identify log files and regularly review each file for unauthorized activity. Know what you're looking for and have a plan of action if unauthorized activity is located. Ensure log files are also secure and unalterable.
Monitor system and network performance	Monitor system performance measurements for critical computers and network devices for unusual activity. Have plans in place to react to any identified unusual data or traffic patterns.
Revoke user access	It's very important to remove user access immediately upon dismissal to prevent disgruntled employees from initially damaging company systems.

process is crucial to protecting integrity and confidentiality. With respect to user identity and authorization, you can use the same types of controls to enforce confidentiality that you used to enforce integrity.

Confidentiality extends the scope of protecting data to ensure that no unauthorized user can view data. Many OSs and applications use encryption as a primary confidentiality control. Encrypting data and then providing decryption keys only to authorized users enforces confidentiality for data either at rest or in transit. **TABLE 10-2** lists some controls that help maintain data confidentiality.

TABLE 10-2 Security Controls that Protect Data Confidentiality

CONTROL	DESCRIPTION
Data Labeling	The first step in protecting confidentiality is properly identifying sensitive data. This is commonly done through some type of data labeling that identifies files, servers, databases, etc. that contain sensitive data.
Encryption	Encrypting any data scrambles the information in such a way that it is unreadable. Anyone who possesses a valid decryption key can unscramble that data back to its original form. By distributing decryption keys to authorized users only, you can use encryption to enforce data confidentiality. You can employ encryption at different levels, including disk, volume, folder, file, or application-level data object.
Password policies	Documented password policies serve as a basis for user training. Password settings in Group Policy make it easy to enforce password policies across your entire Windows environment.
Object DACLs	Extend DACLs used to protect integrity to include restrictions on users authorized to read or access objects, not just modify them.
Active Directory (AD)	Active Directory (AD) provides a central repository for security policy settings along with the ability to easily deploy settings to many target locations. AD is an important part of an effective security administration plan.
Physical access controls	If you employ Windows Encrypting File System (EFS), an attacker can boot from alternate media and cause you to lose data. If the attacker can boot and reset passwords, users will be unable to decrypt data that were encrypted before the password reset. Physical access controls will protect you from this type of attack.
Anti-malware protection	Malware can substantially modify or delete data. Successful attacks can render all or part of your data unavailable for use.
OS and application software updates	Many attacks target known OS and software vulnerabilities. Apply all available software patches to remove as many vulnerabilities as possible.
DLP Software	This is software that is specifically designed to identify sensitive data based on its format and prevent that information from leaving company systems.

Maintaining Integrity

Protecting integrity is crucial to maintaining trust in your data's accuracy. Your main goal is to ensure no unauthorized user can change data. Changing data includes modifying or deleting data. The majority of the controls you'll deploy to protect integrity focus on user identification, authentication, and authorization. Windows provides you with the tools to positively identify a unique user and determine what that user can do. The three main types of integrity concerns include the following:

* **User identification**—The first step in granting or denying actions is to identify the user attempting an action. Users are identified in Windows through a user account. Organizations using AD can define users. AD uses the same account when accessing different resources, avoiding a logon each time.
* **User authentication**—Authentication is proving to Windows that you are who you say you are. The most common type of authentication is providing a password when you log on. You can choose to use other methods with, or instead of, passwords. You can make it harder for attackers to log on using someone else's user account by requiring a security token, smart card, or even a biometric input. Doing so allows you to implement two-factor or multifactor authentication (MFA), which today will provide you with the most secure authentication environment possible. You can use any method that provides assurance that a user is authentic.
* **User authorization**—Once you know who a user is, you can determine what that user can do. Windows grants rights to users that dictate what they can do. You can also define DACLs for individual objects to allow or deny users, or groups of users, different types of access to the object. AD and Group Policy Objects (GPOs) make this process manageable across a network of any size.

When considering the integrity property of data security, make sure to deploy controls addressing each of the areas of concern listed in **TABLE 10-3**.

Maintaining Availability

Availability can often be the trickiest of the three security properties to protect. The unforeseen issues must be uncovered to establish the best controls. Ensuring data availability requires controls that address both daily operation and unusual situations. Four main types of concerns affect data availability. All four types of issues must be addressed to ensure that data are available when needed. The four main types of availability concerns are as follows:

* **Attacks**—Denial of service (DoS) and distributed denial of service (DDoS) attacks specifically target your network's ability to provide data and system access. If the network or server is too busy to service authorized users' requests, your data are not available. Other types of attacks move, modify, or destroy data and can affect availability.
* **Performance**—All computing and networking environments tend to suffer performance loss over time. Increased resource load, low speed disks, lack of memory or buffers, out-of-date configuration settings, unneeded installations, and malware are examples of why computers get slower. Network devices and their connectivity can suffer similar performance constraints, including processing, memory buffer, and overutilized bandwidth. Monitor system and network performance and fix any performance problems. This ensures that your environment does not become slow. Slow environments limit access to data that users need to do their jobs.

TABLE 10-3 Security Controls That Protect Data Integrity

CONTROL	DESCRIPTION
Password policies	Documented password policies serve as a basis for user training. Password settings in Group Policy make it easy to enforce password policies across your entire Windows environment.
Object DACLs	Each object DACL defines specific access permissions for users. Since Windows stores DACLs in AD, the settings can be globally administered and deployed (within an AD domain or forest). DACLs protect integrity by restricting permissions to write or modify object data to authorized users.
Active Directory (AD)	Active Directory provides a central repository for security policy settings along with the ability to easily deploy settings to many target locations. AD is an important part of an effective security administration plan.
Physical access controls	Persistent attackers can defeat the best access controls. One tactic is to boot a computer from alternate boot media and load a different operating system. The attacker can then use tools to directly access files and folders without going through Windows and its controls. Since an attacker needs to physically access a computer to insert alternate boot media, physical access controls can limit an attacker's ability to carry out such attacks.
Message/file authentication	You can use a **message digest** to detect unauthorized modifications to messages or files. A message digest is a shortened unique string of digits that represent a file or message. You can use one of several popular hashing algorithms to create a message digest. The recipient uses the same hashing algorithm to create a message digest of the received message. If the two digests are identical, the message has not been modified.
Anti-malware protection	Malware can substantially modify or delete data. Successful attacks can render all or part of your data unavailable for use.
Operating system and application software updates	Many attacks target known operating system and software vulnerabilities. Apply all available software patches to remove as many vulnerabilities as possible.
Digital Signatures	This should not be confused with the signatures used to sign contracts digitally. In this context a digital signature is a specific use of a cryptographic key to prove that the person sending a message is who they claim to be (authentication).
Audit Logs	Logs files are a good way to keep record of who made changes to a particular file/document.

© Jones & Bartlett Learning.

- **Interruptions or disasters**—Short-duration interruptions, such as a power outage or a network service interruption, can prevent your users from accessing data. Disasters, such as fires or floods, can cause data loss and interruptions lasting longer than minutes or hours. You need to plan for both types of availability problems. Make sure your systems are resilient, redundant, highly available, and can recover from interruptions quickly or not be affected by them at all.

- **Other security controls**—Controls protecting data integrity or confidentiality can violate availability. For example, you can choose to disable access to your database for all users outside your organization's local area network (LAN). This control can help protect the data's integrity and confidentiality. However, it makes your data unavailable to users in remote locations. Always search for controls that balance all three security properties. The best way to uncover the side effects of controls is to check each one thoroughly in a test environment. Ensure that new or changed controls allow users to do their jobs.

When you consider the availability property of data security, be sure to deploy controls that address each of the four areas of concern in the preceding list. The goal is to ensure your data are always available to authorized users when needed, and never available to unauthorized users. **TABLE 10-4** lists some controls that help maintain data availability.

Consider the controls you'll need to ensure authorized users can access data, regardless of any other influences. Other controls, interruptions, disasters, and attacks can reduce users' ability to access data. Your job is to ensure the data are available.

Microsoft Windows OS Security Administration

Once controls are planned to maximize the C-I-A triad properties, you can implement them. The steps to implement each control depend upon the type and goal. Security administrators most commonly implement technical controls. Personnel from other departments typically implement administrative and physical controls. You implement most technical controls by installing software, updating software, or modifying settings. In this section, you'll learn about the most common tools security administrators use to create objects and change security settings.

FYI

Microsoft provides a wealth of information on how to secure its OSs. For more information on how to secure Windows Server 2008 R2, visit https://learn.microsoft.com/en-us/previous-versions/windows/it-pro/windows-server-2008-R2-and-2008/dd548350(v=ws.10)?redirectedfrom=MSDN. For more information on how to secure newer versions of Windows Server, visit https://learn.microsoft.com/en-us/windows-server/security/security-and-assurance.

TABLE 10-4 Security Controls That Protect Data Availability

CONTROL	DESCRIPTION
Firewall, intrusion detection system (IDS), intrusion prevention system (IPS)	A firewall can block traffic that matches specific rules. In many cases, firewall rules are based on IP address and port numbers. An IDS can analyze traffic and detect a potential intrusion based on traffic patterns. An IPS can not only detect an intrusion but also change firewall rules in real time to prevent further damage from an attack.
System and network performance monitors	Windows workstation and server versions include the Windows Performance Monitor (PerfMon) toolset. PerfMon provides a rich collection of monitors, alerts, logging options, and reports to create baselines and real-time samples of your Windows systems' performance. Several third-party vendors also provide tools to make it easy to monitor network traffic and recognize problems. You can also download and use Microsoft Network Monitor (NetMon) tool to conduct performance tests on your network, connectivity from hosts, and perform packet analysis.
Backup and recovery plan	Use the Windows backup utilities to create frequent backups and know how they fit into your complete business continuity plan (BCP) and disaster recovery plan (DRP).
Security control testing	Test all new controls and changes to existing controls before deploying them to a live environment. More restrictive controls may limit availability as they increase integrity and confidentiality protection. Virtual machines are useful when testing any configuration and software changes.
Anti-malware protection	Malware can substantially modify or delete data. Successful attacks can render all or part of your data unavailable for use. Controlling this type of threat overlaps with protecting data integrity.
Resource redundancy	When you have a critical resource like a web server, database etc., it's a best practice to have backups of that resource so that if one or more of those resources is made unavailable, then the business can still operate.

© Jones & Bartlett Learning.

Technical TIP

You can open the Windows Defender Firewall with Advanced Security MMC snap-in using these steps:

1. Choose the Windows Start button > Windows Administrative Tools.
2. Select Windows Defender Firewall with Advanced Security.

Firewall Administration

You can maintain Windows Firewall settings in the Windows Firewall with Advanced Security Microsoft Management Console (MMC) snap-in. This new utility combines Windows Firewall settings with Internet Protocol Security (IPSec) settings. You can manage both groups of settings using a single utility.

FIGURE 10-2 shows the Windows Defender Firewall with Advanced Security MMC snap-in.

The Windows Defender Firewall with Advanced Security snap-in allows you to maintain four main types of information:

- **Inbound rules**—Rules to filter inbound network traffic using program, port, predefined, or custom criteria.
- **Outbound rules**—Rules to filter outbound network traffic. The available criteria are the same as for inbound rules.
- **Connection security rules**—IPSec rules for establishing connections between computers.
- **Monitoring**—Access to firewall performance information for firewall rule analysis.

Performance Monitor

The **FIGURE 10-3** shows the Windows Performance Monitor, which enables you to view real-time performance data or data from a log file. The Performance Monitor can identify potential problems threatening data availability. Data Collector Sets can configure and collect performance data based on specifications for analysis and reporting. You can view detailed information about hardware resources and system resources that the OS and

FIGURE 10-2

Windows Defender Firewall with Advanced Security MMC snap-in.

Courtesy of Microsoft Corporation.

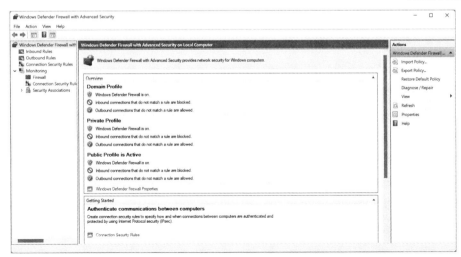

10

Microsoft Windows
Security Administration

FIGURE 10-3

Windows Performance Monitor.

Courtesy of Microsoft Corporation.

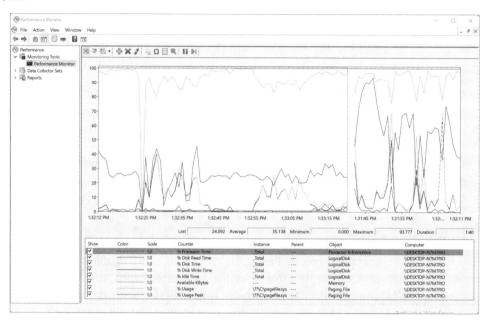

You can open the Windows Performance Monitor using these steps:

1. Choose the Windows Start button > Windows Administrative Tools.
2. Select Performance Monitor.

running programs use. You can also start and stop services, stop processes, and analyze process locking activity.

Figure 10-4 shows the Windows Network Monitor.

Backup Administration

A valid backup is a crucial part of an organization's ability to recover from losing data. One of the most visible recurring tasks you will have as a security administrator is to create frequent backups of your organization's data. You can use either Microsoft backup utilities or third-party programs. Either way, you should frequently create fresh backup copies of the data your organization cannot afford to lose.

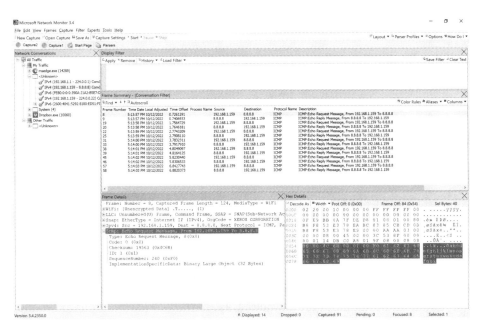

FIGURE 10-4

Windows Network Monitor.

Courtesy of Microsoft Corporation.

Technical TIP

To focus on the network performance and get an in-depth look at the packets that traverse a network, what they contain, and the clues they provide to network performance, you can use the Windows Network Monitor. This packet capture and analysis tool that once came standard in older versions of the Windows Operating System is now its own freestanding application that can be installed and used on Windows systems. Once installed, it can be used to help troubleshoot performance, but it can also be used to show you unencrypted traffic and what it contains. For example, if you run this tool and try to log into a website using clear text passwords without any encryption, the tool will capture that username and password in transit and expose it to whomever may have access to the tool's dashboard.

You can open the Network Monitor using these steps:

1. Download the Network Monitor tool on to your workstation by going to https://www.microsoft .com/en-us/download/details.aspx?id=983b941d-06cb-4658-b7f6-3088333d062f.

2. Once downloaded, run the installer and take all of the defaults provided. You can install Typical, Custom, or Full. Use Typical if you are new to using the tool.

3. Once installed, on the desktop you will find the Network Monitor icon. Click it to run and Network Monitor will open as seen in **FIGURE 10-4**.

4. In the open dialog box, select New Capture and click Start to begin the packet capture. You can click on Stop to end the capture. You will see the captured packets in the associated window panes in the dialog box.

Technical TIP

As we begin to talk more in depth about backup administration, another solution to ensuring high performance and resilience is to use replication. Having real-time data replication and synchronization between hosts in an active/active design architecture allows you to have peace of mind that if you lose a system and the data it contains, it will be highly available in another data center on a snapshot virtual machine (VM) that can takeover with a copy of the replicated data synchronized in real time. Although this is more reliable, it is also the most costly to reproduce.

Windows Workstation Backups

Microsoft has included an updated Backup and Restore utility starting with Windows 7. The utility has been upgraded from its Vista predecessor to make backing up and restoring Windows workstations simple. Even though we are using the most current version of Windows, which is version 11, the Windows 7 backup utility is still being used in this most current distribution of the OS. To use it, navigate to the tool and open it. The Windows Backup and Restore Wizard asks you to provide answers to three main questions to initially configure your backup scope and schedule. **FIGURE 10-5** shows the Windows Backup and Restore utility in action.

Technical TIP

Open the Windows Backup and Restore utility on a computer running Windows 7 using these steps:

1. Choose the Windows Start button > Settings (the little gear icon on the left side of the menu).
2. Navigate to Control Panel.
3. Select System and Security > Update & Security.
4. Select Backup > Go to Backup and Restore (Windows 7).

Technical TIP

Open the Windows Server Backup utility on a computer running Windows Server using these steps:

1. Choose the Windows Start button > Windows Accessories > Windows Server Backup.
2. Select the Backup Schedule link to launch the Backup Schedule Wizard. This allows you to configure a scheduled backup.

You can also select the Backup Once link to launch the Backup Once Wizard to configure a one-time backup.

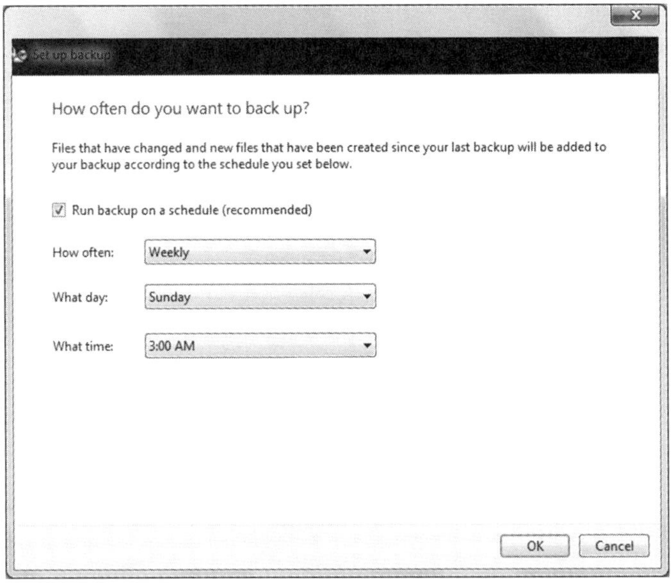

FIGURE 10-5

Windows Backup and Restore for Windows 7.

Courtesy of Microsoft Corporation.

Windows Server Backups

The Microsoft Windows Server Backup utility must be installed on computers running the Windows Server OS. Once installed, you can use it to schedule and create backups for your servers. Since Windows servers perform different functions, they often have different backup needs. The Microsoft Windows Server Backup utility addresses the many different server backup needs (**FIGURE 10-6**). It may take a little more effort to configure than a simple workstation backup. The basic steps are similar to setting up a workstation backup—you just have more options available to you.

OS Service Pack Administration

Microsoft developed the Microsoft Baseline Security Analyzer (MBSA) utility. This utility evaluates computers in accord with Microsoft security recommendations. MBSA checks to ensure the OS and current Microsoft software are up to date. The latest version of MBSA, version 2.3, supports Windows Server 2008 R2, Windows Server 2012, Windows 7, and Windows 8, as well as several previous Windows versions. Notice that MBSA does not support the latest versions of Windows, most currently Windows Server 2022. The MBSA utility is a legacy security utility but does still have some value. While it will not find some of the latest vulnerabilities, it does provide a general level of confidence that basic security concerns have been addressed. MBSA can still be one of the tools in your security toolbox. You can find MBSA version 2.3 at https://www.techspot.com/downloads/3886-microsoft-baseline-security -analyzer.html.

Windows Server Backup.

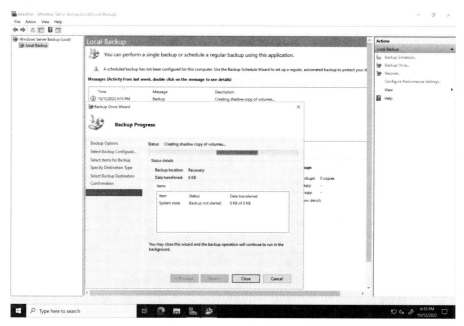

MBSA GUI.

Follow these steps to use the MBSA graphical user interface (GUI) (**FIGURE 10-7**) to scan your computer for vulnerabilities:

1. Open MBSA. Choose the Windows Start button > Microsoft Baseline Security Analyzer.
2. Select the desired operation mode:
   a. Select Scan a Computer to scan a single computer.
   b. Select Scan Multiple Computers to scan more than one computer in a single session.
   c. Select View Existing Security Scan Reports to view the results of previous scans.
3. If you choose to scan one or more computers, enter the computer/domain name or IP address(es):
   a. For single computer scans, enter either a computer name or an IP address.
   b. For multiple computer scans, enter a domain name or a range of IP addresses.
4. Select the checkboxes next to the desired scanning options. In many cases, leaving all options checked provides the most extensive analysis.
5. Choose Start Scan to begin the scanning process.
6. Whether you selected the scan option or selected an existing security scan report, MBSA presents the scan results in a user-friendly report. Each report issue includes a description of what was scanned, details of the result, and in many cases, descriptive information on how to resolve the issue.
7. Choose OK to close the report viewer and return to the MBSA main window.

Group Policy Administration

You can define GPOs at the local level or in AD. Defining GPOs in AD gives you the ability to centralize security rules and control how Windows applies each rule. You create AD GPOs on a domain controller, and Windows automatically replicates the GPOs to other domain controllers. This feature reduces the workload of administrators. Using Group Policy in AD relieves the need to define security rules on multiple computers one at a time.

AD GPOs are created on the domain controller using the Group Policy Management Console (GPMC) (**FIGURE 10-8**). Although there are multiple ways to create GPOs, the most common method is to create GPOs under the desired domain in the GPMC. Once a new AD GPO is created, link it with an entity to activate it.

Follow these steps to open the GPMC on a Windows Server domain controller:

1. Choose the Windows Start button.
2. Select Windows Administrative Tools > Group Policy Management.

Follow these steps to open the GPMC using another method:

1. Launch a Windows PowerShell window.
2. Type gpmc.msc at the prompt.
3. Press the Enter key.

Technical TIP

Here's how to display and edit any object's DACL:

First, open the object's Properties dialog box. Use any one of these procedures:

1. Right-click the object, and then select Properties.

2. Select the object, press SHIFT+F10, and then select Properties.

3. Hold the ALT key and double-click the object.

In the Properties dialog box, select the Security tab.

FIGURE 10-8

Group Policy
Management Console.

Courtesy of Microsoft
Corporation.

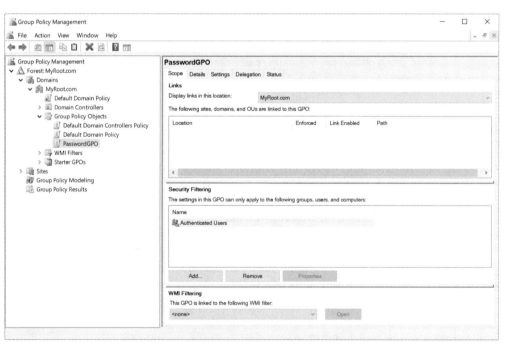

DACL Administration

Windows uses an object's DACL to determine if it should grant access a subject has requested. Any object you want to protect must have a DACL for Windows to control access to the object. Objects without a DACL defined are accessible by any subject—any process, any user. An object's DACL is a collection of individual ACLs and can be modified in the object's Properties dialog box (**FIGURE 10-9**).

FIGURE 10-9

Object Properties Security
dialog box.

Courtesy of Microsoft Corporation.

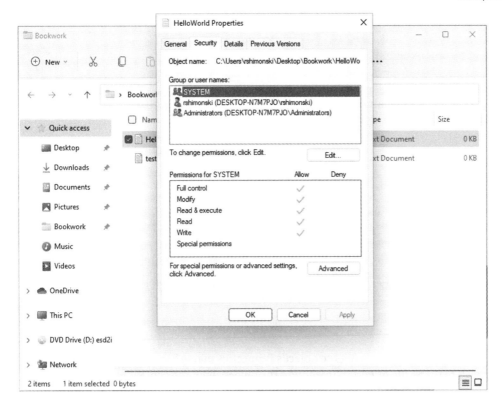

The Security page of the object Properties dialog box allows you to view and modify the security permissions for the selected object. On the Security page, the Group or User Names area lists the users and groups for which each access control entry (ACE) is defined. Recall that each entry in an ACL is an ACE. The Permissions for Users area shows the current permissions for the selected user or group.

The Advanced page provides access to individual object permissions, as opposed to predefined groups of permissions in the general Security page (**FIGURE 10-10**). The Advanced page lists each individual permission for the selected user or group.

Encryption Administration

Windows supports three main methods to encrypt stored data: Encrypting File System (EFS), BitLocker, and BitLocker To Go. Other methods are available within applications. Additional solutions are available from other vendors. Consider your encryption needs and evaluate each method based on its specific capabilities. The best choice of encryption methods is the one that best meets your needs. If you choose one of the default Windows encryption methods, all you have to do is enable your selected encryption option.

FIGURE 10-10

DACL advanced security settings.

Courtesy of Microsoft Corporation.

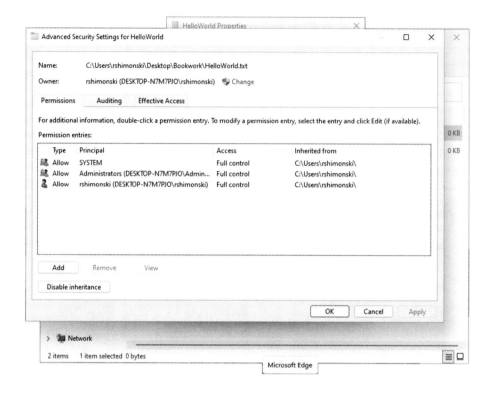

Enabling EFS

You enable EFS for objects using the object's Properties dialog box. Open Windows Explorer and navigate to the file or folder. To encrypt the object, open the context menu by right-clicking the object, and then select Properties. From the Properties dialog box, choose the Advanced button. In the Advanced Attributes dialog box, select the Encrypt Contents To Secure Data checkbox, choose OK, then choose OK again to close the Properties dialog box. The object is now stored as an encrypted object. No further action from the user is necessary. **FIGURE 10-11** shows the Properties and Advanced Attributes dialog boxes.

Enabling BitLocker or BitLocker To Go

Enabling BitLocker or BitLocker To Go is just as easy as EFS. The main difference between the two is that BitLocker To Go encrypts removable media. To enable either BitLocker version, open Windows Explorer and navigate to Computer. Open the context menu of the selected volume by right-clicking on the desired volume, and select Turn On BitLocker or Turn On BitLocker To Go. **FIGURE 10-12** shows the BitLocker option on the object's context menu.

Alternatively, you can launch the BitLocker management tool to view and manage BitLocker for all volumes. Open the Windows Control Panel, select System and Security, and select BitLocker Drive Encryption. The BitLocker management tool displays all volumes, along with an option to turn BitLocker on or off for each volume. **FIGURE 10-13** shows the BitLocker management tool.

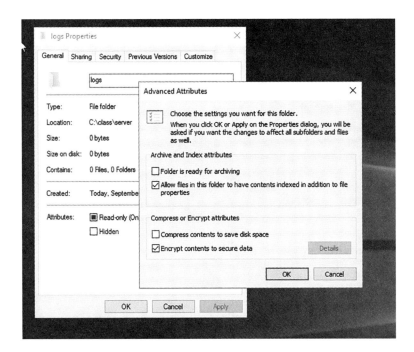

FIGURE 10-11

Object Properties—Advanced Attributes.

Courtesy of Microsoft Corporation.

FIGURE 10-12

Enabling BitLocker.

Courtesy of Microsoft Corporation.

After enabling BitLocker, Windows asks you to pick an authentication method and to determine where to save a recovery key. Once you provide the required information, Windows handles the rest and encrypts your data when you store it on the disk.

10

Microsoft Windows Security Administration

BitLocker management tool.
Courtesy of Microsoft Corporation.

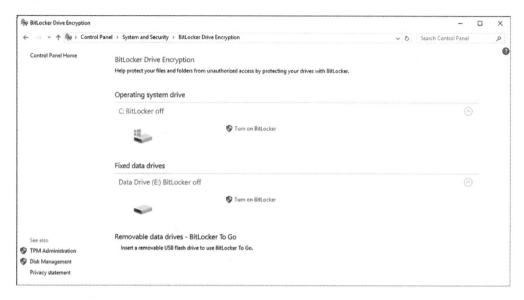

Anti-Malware Software Administration

The key to keeping computers malware free is to identify all known malware on each computer, remove it, and diligently keep the computers from getting infected with new malware. The most important step in the process is making the commitment to pursue a malware-free environment. There are many anti-malware software options, and your specific scan, update, and removal procedures will depend on your software.

The following steps are key to staying malware free:

- Require antivirus and anti-spyware software for every computer before you allow it to connect to your network.
- Ensure that all anti-malware software is current and all data are up to date.
- Scan each computer at least weekly to search for malware.
- Ensure anti-malware shield software runs on every computer that connects to your network.
- Modify user permissions so that they cannot turn off any of your anti-malware solutions or uninstall them.
- Be sure to include a software solution for safe browsing, this is important to prevent people from browsing to insecure websites that may infect their machines with malware.
- Use an email solution that scans email attachments for potential malware.

Ensuring Due Diligence and Regulatory Compliance

Compliance is more than just checking items off a list. It is a dynamic process. It ensures the items in each domain of your IT infrastructure meet or exceed your security goals.

This should include all legal, regulatory, and standard requirements. Conditions change in any organization. The status of how well you are meeting your goals can change as well. Make all decisions related to security controls to satisfy your security policy. Be sure to meet any other relevant compliance requirements. For example, the Health Insurance Portability and Accountability Act (HIPAA) and Health Information Technology for Economic and Clinical Health Act (HITECH) place requirements on handling health and medical information. The Gramm-Leach-Bliley Act (GLBA) and Sarbanes-Oxley Act (SOX) place requirements on financial information. Many states place additional requirements on personally identifiable information. Ensuring compliance to your security policy keeps security-related actions headed in the right direction.

The move toward cloud-based applications and components leads to more noncompliance exposure. In the past, the European Union's **General Data Protection Regulation (GDPR)** has added more requirements on how organizations collect and use individual's personal data. In the United States, the state of California has enacted the **California Consumer Privacy Act (CCPA)** of 2018 that bears some similarities to GDPR. In both cases, organizations must provide controls to limit what personal data are collected and how they are stored, used, and disposed.

It is important to implement compliance requirements to minimize the impact on **business drivers**. Business drivers are the components (including people), information, and conditions that support business objectives. Any negative impact on business drivers may have a negative impact on your organization's ability to satisfy business objectives. Carefully research the impact to business drivers before you implement any compliance controls.

Remember that compliance requirements dictate how your organization conducts its activities. Whether the compliance requirement comes from legislation, regulation, industry requirements, or even your organization's standards, the result is the focus. In most cases, your organization can control activities multiple ways to ensure compliance. Always consider alternative controls to achieve the end result compliance requires. You'll likely find that some controls are less costly and less intrusive than others. Don't just accept the first control that does the job. Many times, alternate controls are just as good but intrude less on your organization's activities.

Due Diligence

Paying attention to compliance can reduce liability in direct and indirect ways. You can think of it in terms of additional insurance. In the context of information security, the term **due diligence** means the ongoing attention and care an organization places on security and compliance. You can reduce your exposure to third-party liability by investing resources into establishing and maintaining compliance. Demonstrating aggressive compliance activities can reduce the liability potential if security incidents result in damages. In short, being compliant looks good in court.

You can follow the PDCA cycle to demonstrate due diligence. PDCA directs your activities to continuously evaluate your security position and make any changes necessary to better meet your security policy. As long as your policy contains all necessary compliance requirements, documenting your PDCA activities will provide substantial evidence of due diligence.

Cloud-Based Compliance

As more and more workloads move off premises and into the cloud, it is important to consider the security aspects revolving around compliance. The risks to your environment can be increased simply by connecting your network to a cloud environment. For example, if you have a well-defined security posture in place for your internal network and a hardened DMZ in place protecting ingress and egress points in and out, once you connect to a cloud environment that entire network increases the risks of ingress and egress. It also adds a large amount of complexity especially if you are using multiple cloud vendors in a multi-cloud architecture.

For example, by connecting to a cloud providers network, you will want to put a domain controller in the cloud environment for a few reasons: first, to ensure that you have performance gains by allowing Windows systems the closest domain controller it can find, but secondly, to ensure that if you lose connectivity to an on premises domain controller, the one in the cloud serves as a backup. The complexity adds risks but also benefits. When it comes to due diligence and compliance, you may want to ensure that you place a read-only copy of the domain controller in place to make it more security and perhaps comply with your internal security policies. This is but one example of a real-world use case where security risks are increased and compliance becomes even more important to consider and enforce. To enforce compliance, you can benefit from using tools focused on risk, compliance and audit.

Microsoft has developed a risk assessment portal and tools specifically to address cloud-based application risks. You can find these tools in the Microsoft Service Trust Portal which can be accessed by going to https://servicetrust.microsoft.com/. This assessment program and associated tools incorporate the requirements of multiple standards and regulations, including ISO 27001, ISO 27018, NIST, HIPAA, and GDPR. The portal helps users of Microsoft cloud-based services, such as Office 365 and Azure, assess and evaluate their organization's level of compliance with a range of standards and regulations. **FIGURE 10-14** shows a sample screenshot of the Microsoft Purview Compliance Manager (from within the Azure Portal). You can learn more about the Microsoft Purview Compliance Manager at https://learn.microsoft.com/en-us/microsoft-365/compliance/compliance-manager?view=o365-worldwide.

Microsoft Purview's solutions provide cloud governance of data by providing a single pane of glass view into a structure unified governance service, which provides for end-to-end data lineage. You can create data maps and data landscapes, classify data as sensitive, run reports, gather metrics, and allow for a single solution for compliance. You can learn more about Purview by reviewing https://www.microsoft.com/en-us/security/business/services/compliance-program-microsoft-cloud and https://learn.microsoft.com/en-us/compliance.

The Need for Security Policies, Standards, Procedures, and Guidelines

Security doesn't just happen. It's not a single event. Security, or more precisely, the pursuit of security, is an ongoing process. As Bruce Schneier, internationally renowned security

FIGURE 10-14

Microsoft Purview Compliance Manager.

Courtesy of Microsoft Corporation.

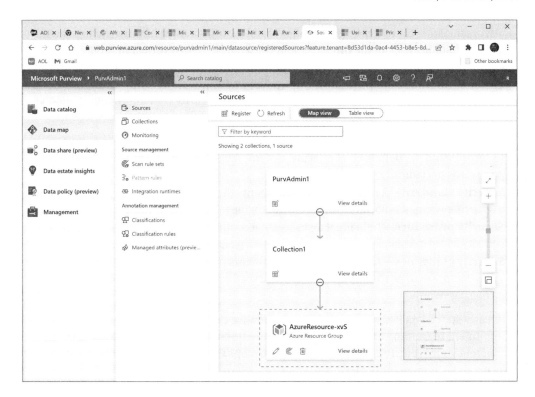

technologist, said, "Security is a process, not a product." It is a process of continually working to reach your organization's security goals. Every organization is different, and security goals likewise differ among organizations. The process of reaching security goals is a continual process that requires specific direction.

Any organization's success at satisfying security goals depends on three main elements. A weakness in any of the three elements makes it more difficult to comply with your organization's security requirements. These three elements are the following:

- **Clearly stated security goals**—You must have a clear security goals document that the organization's upper management fully endorses. A lack of clear goals means you don't really know what you're trying to do, how you're doing it, and when you're done. A lack of upper management support means you'll likely encounter resistance when you try to implement any new controls. In fact, trying to fulfill the responsibilities of a security practitioner in an organization without upper management's support is difficult at best.
- **Documented plans**—A plan is a series of steps designed to achieve a goal. You should have a plan for each security goal. Each plan may have additional guidance documents that provide more details to meet security goals.

- **Communication with stakeholders**—A stakeholder is anyone who has an interest in, or is affected by, some activity. Documented plans are worthless if no one who is doing security work knows about them. A common point of failure in security administration is a lack of direction. In many cases, a lack of direction comes from just not knowing what plans have already been made.

An organization that desires to implement solid security in the IT infrastructure should commit to fulfilling each of the three elements of security. Follow the list in order. Start with stating security goals that are appropriate for the organization's culture and compliance requirements. Next, develop any additional guidance documents. A solid security plan will include several types of guidance documents. Good security training should stress the importance of compliance and cover the important parts of these guidance documents:

- **Security policy**—A high-level statement that defines an organization's commitment to security and the definition of a secure system, such as the importance of changing passwords periodically
- **Security standard**—A collection of requirements the users must meet, typically within a specific system or environment, such as changing a Windows password every 6 months
- **Security procedure**—Individual tasks users accomplish to comply with one or more security standards, such as the steps to change a password
- **Security guidelines**—A collection of best practices or suggestions that helps users comply with procedures and standards, such as suggestions on how to create strong passwords

Clearly stated goals, complete plans and guidance documents, and a strong commitment to training and communication can dramatically increase the success rate of meeting your security goals. Following these steps will put you well on your way to a secure environment.

Best Practices for Microsoft Windows OS Security Administration

Effective Windows security administration ensures your organization has all the technical controls in place to support its security goals. It takes more than just technical controls to meet all security goals, but security administrators mainly focus on deploying and maintaining technical security controls.

Here is a list of Windows security administration best practices that will help you deploy and maintain the controls to support your security policy. Change the list to suit your organization, but pay attention to the suggestions—they can help you avoid wasting time and resources:

- Clearly state security goals in your security policy.
- Include all compliance requirements for applicable legislation, regulation, and vendor standards in your security policy.
- Use the PDCA method for all security administration activities.
- Communicate with all stakeholders—share as much information as possible.

- Strive for simplicity in all controls and systems—complexity invites failures.
- Search for controls that have little impact on users. Users tend to bypass controls that they find intrusive or difficult.
- Coordinate AUPs with technical controls.
- Automate as much as possible—use scheduled jobs whenever possible.
- Use AD GPOs for as many security settings as possible.
- Coordinate physical controls with technical controls.
- Never allow a computer that doesn't have current anti-malware controls in place to connect to your network. This rule applies to all computers—even laptops owned by distinguished guests. Enforce the rule or be prepared to put your malware removal plan into action.
- Develop a plan to monitor system and network performance and follow it.
- Ensure the OS and all software are up to date for all computers.
- Periodically examine log files for suspicious behavior.
- Stay current on emerging attacks and trends and update your controls appropriately.
- Fully test your recovery plans at least annually, or more often, if possible. You'll never really know how your recovery plan works until you actually execute each of the steps.
- Define DACLs when necessary and modify or remove them when user account roles change.

CHAPTER SUMMARY

Windows security administration is as much a business process as a security endeavor. While getting the right technical controls in place is the ultimate goal for the security administrator, it is only one part of the process. Substantial analysis and planning precedes deploying any control. After deployment, you should conduct an ongoing effort to ensure that the right controls are in place and working well. Implementing the quality concept of continuous improvement can make you more effective as a security administrator. Take the time to learn and implement the PDCA method in your security activities. It will be well worth the investment and will make your organization's environment more secure.

KEY CONCEPTS AND TERMS

Business driver
California Consumer Privacy Act (CCPA)
Compliance
Deming cycle

Due diligence
General Data Protection Regulation (GDPR)
Intrusion detection system (IDS)

Intrusion prevention system (IPS)
Message digest
Plan-Do-Check-Act (PDCA)
Security administration

CHAPTER 10 ASSESSMENT

1. Security administration is the process of developing an organization's security policy.

   A. True
   B. False

2. What is the most important feature of PDCA?

   A. PDCA was developed for security administration.
   B. PDCA is a Microsoft standard.
   C. PDCA repeats and does not end.
   D. PDCA was developed by Dr. Deming.

3. Which of the following activities would a security administrator be *least* likely to do?

   A. Monitor log files.
   B. Deliver AUP training.
   C. Keep software up to date.
   D. Enforce physical security controls.

4. If time to recover exceeds the recovery goal, which property of security have you violated?

   A. Availability
   B. Integrity
   C. Confidentiality
   D. Consistency

5. Which of the following devices or software programs can detect intrusions? (Select two.)

   A. Firewall
   B. IDS
   C. IPS
   D. NAT

6. A valid backup is an integral part of your _____ and _____.

7. Protecting both integrity and confidentiality depends largely on knowing a user's identity.

   A. True
   B. False

8. A DACL is used primarily to enforce which security properties? (Select two.)

   A. Integrity
   B. Consistency
   C. Confidentiality
   D. Availability

9. You can use the _____ tool to ensure your Microsoft operating system is up to date and has all patches and service packs installed.

10. Active Directory requires that you create multiple GPOs, one for each computer.

   A. True
   B. False

11. Which of the following terms is best described as a collection of requirements users must meet, typically within a specific system or environment?

   A. Security policy
   B. Security standard
   C. Security procedure
   D. Security guideline

12. Which type of Windows component would you use to define which users can create files in a folder?

   A. DACL
   B. NAT
   C. User right
   D. IPSec rule

13. Which tool would you use to edit the setting that disables user-installed desktop gadgets for all users?

   A. Local Group Policy Editor
   B. MBSA
   C. GPMC
   D. Performance Monitor

14. Microsoft provides a command-line utility for creating backups on Windows server and workstation OSs.

   A. True
   B. False

PART III

Microsoft Windows Operating System and Application Security Trends and Directions

Hardening the Microsoft Windows Operating System

IN THIS CHAPTER, you'll learn how to apply what you've studied to make a computer running a Microsoft Windows operating system more secure. You'll find out where you should focus your efforts for the most effective use of resources. You'll also learn how to ensure each computer is as secure as possible. You'll also learn how important a documented and repeatable process is when making computers more secure.

Chapter 11 Topics

This chapter covers the following topics and concepts:

- What the hardening process and mindset are
- How to harden Microsoft Windows operating system authentication
- How to harden the network infrastructure
- How to secure directory information and operations
- How to harden Microsoft Windows operating system administration
- How to harden Microsoft servers and client computers
- How to harden data access and controls
- How to harden communications and remote access
- How to harden public key infrastructure (PKI)
- How to harden Microsoft Azure Cloud Platform
- What user security training and awareness is
- What the best practices are for hardening Microsoft Windows operating system and applications

Chapter 11 Goals

When you complete this chapter, you will be able to:

- Describe the Windows operating system hardening process
- Harden all aspects of Windows computers and network environments
- Provide security training and awareness

Understanding the Hardening Process and Mind-set

Software vendors of all types, including operating system vendors, encounter a basic dilemma when deciding on default installation options. One school of thought is to install the most features possible to showcase what the product can do. This approach is the one that vendors generally select because it promotes the richness of their product's features. The other approach is to only install the bare minimum of features to avoid increasing the product's vulnerability to attack. Many vendors, however, end up showcasing more features. This raises the risk of making their product more vulnerable. The software a computer runs that is vulnerable to attack is called the attack surface. The primary goal in securing Windows computers is to reduce the attack surface. While you can't ever reduce the risk of attack to zero, you can employ controls to make your computers more secure.

The reduction of an attack surface in a software environment requires that you start with understanding how at risk you may be through discovery. You can use many of the tools mentioned in the book thus far to conduct an assessment of vulnerabilities and exploits. Once you understand what your inventory is, you can then identify the actual risks by assigning risk categories through assessment and identification. You can add these risks to a risk register so you can open and close each one via a documented process that can be tracked. Once you have started the hardening process and therefore reduced risk as well as the attack surface, you can continue on iteratively by continuing to test, remediate through the risk register, and monitor for new changes. For example, you upgrade your desktop or server operating system, add services, functions or roles, third-party tools, additional software or even hotfixes, all of these re-engage the iterative process through discovery and monitoring and force a new test, identification, and then hardening process. Remember that this process never ends throughout the product lifecycle and should become a regular process conducted by your security team.

Strategies to Secure Windows Computers

When considering how to harden your Windows systems, you have two main strategies to choose from to reduce a computer's attack surface. First, disable or remove programs that contain vulnerabilities. This strategy is the most secure method. For example, suppose you are concerned about vulnerabilities in the Microsoft Internet Information Services (IIS) web server. This web server is running on your computer and is named WebServ01. You could disable IIS on WebServ01 or remove it entirely. An attacker can't compromise a program that isn't present or running on a computer. Unfortunately, WebServ01 is an important service for your organization. It is a web server for your e-commerce application. Since you can't disable or remove IIS, you'll have to use another strategy. A quick way to deploy this strategy especially when using virtualization is to create a base system image with the minimal amount of resources needed and authorized in your environment. From there, you can add roles or other services as needed by the project demands, such as adding IIS for a web server. This way, you start with a hardened system and then just add what you need. You can then run a vulnerability scanner on the finished system to perform a quality assurance check and ensure that no vulnerabilities still exist.

The second main strategy to reduce the attack surface is to establish controls on running programs to mitigate any known vulnerabilities. This method is always more difficult and less complete. It is also more time consuming than just disabling unneeded programs or services. Despite this, it is necessary when running a program that contains vulnerabilities. One example of this is to use a web application firewall (WAF). This is a security control that is used to protect web applications against potential attacks like cross site scripting, SQL injection, and more. Since many companies have web applications that serve a business function, disabling or removing it would not be practical; therefore, it's good to introduce security controls like a WAF to limit your risk.

In this chapter, you'll learn the steps to reduce the operating system attack surface of your computers. The process of making configuration changes and deploying controls to reduce the attack surface is called **hardening**.

Hardening Windows computers is not a single activity—it is an ongoing process. When installing Windows, choose the installation options for programs and services you absolutely need. Then, harden each computer as soon as you complete the installation process.

Technical TIP

Always consider disabling or removing programs or services that you don't really need. You shouldn't install programs if you don't need them. You'll find that if you disable or remove unneeded components, the hardening process is easier. You end up with a more secure computer. Always explore which programs or services you actually need before researching controls.

Install Only What You Need

The workstation versions of the Windows operating system installation procedures follow a standard process. You can't easily change which programs the process installs. If you are installing or using older legacy systems such as Windows 7, Windows 8, Windows 10, or upgrading to the newly released Windows 11, you'll have to complete the install process and then remove any unwanted components. When you install a Windows Server operating system, you have the ability to select which programs to install. The easiest way to customize a server is to define one or more **roles** for the computer. A role is a predefined set of services, programs, and configuration settings that enables a computer to fulfill specific requirements. The available roles depend on the edition of Windows you are installing. Microsoft offers multiple editions of each of its server operating systems. Each edition can support different types of roles.

Windows Server 2016, Windows 2019 AND Windows 2022 Editions and Roles

Recall that Microsoft offers the following editions of Windows Server 2008 R2:

- **Essentials**—Cost-effective, entry-level server for small businesses
- **Standard**—Supports more features than Essentials edition for medium-sized businesses
- **Datacenter**—Optimized for large-scale deployment using virtualization on small and large servers

⚠ **WARNING**

Before installing Windows Server, ensure you have the correct edition to support the roles you'll need. For more information on the limitations on role support for each edition, go to https://learn.microsoft.com/en-us /windows-server/get-started /editions-comparison-windows -server-2016?tabs=full-comparison for Windows Server 2016; https://learn .microsoft.com/en-us/windows -server/get-started/editions-comparison -windows-server-2019?tabs=full -comparison for Windows Server 2019; and https://learn.microsoft.com/en-us /windows-server/get-started/editions -comparison-windows-server -2022?tabs=full-comparison for Windows Server 2022. This will allow you to fully understand each version and the specific functions, roles and services each edition will provide.

TABLE 11-1 lists the 17 Windows Server 2016 roles and which editions support each role.

Microsoft also provides another installation option that makes it easier to exclude programs you don't need. The **server core installation** option provides a minimal Windows Server environment that includes only programs necessary for the roles you select. A server core installation doesn't even include a Windows graphical user interface (GUI). You use a command-line interface to interact with the operating system. Since Microsoft limits the programs a server core installation installs, your choice of roles is limited. **TABLE 11-2** lists the roles from which you can choose for a server core installation of Windows Server 2016.

Taking the time to select the right role for each Windows Server installation is the first step in hardening your Windows servers.

Windows Server 2019 Editions and Roles

Recall that Microsoft offers the following editions of Windows Server 2019:

* **Essentials**—Cost-effective, entry-level server for small businesses
* **Standard**—Supports more features than Essentials edition for medium-sized businesses
* **Datacenter**—Designed for large-scale deployment on servers that support extensive virtualization

TABLE 11-3 lists the Windows Server 2019 roles and which editions support each role.

Windows Server 2019 supports server core installations as well. The Windows Server core installation is essentially

TABLE 11-1 Windows Server 2016 Standard Installation Roles and Editions

ROLE	ESSENTIALS	STANDARD	DATACENTER
Active Directory Certificate Services	Yes (installed by default)	Yes	Yes
Active Directory Domain Services	Yes (installed by default)	Yes	Yes
Active Directory Federation Services	No	Yes	Yes
Active Directory Lightweight Directory Services	Yes	Yes	Yes
Active Directory Rights Management Services	Yes	Yes	Yes
Application Server	Yes	Yes	Yes
DHCP Server	Yes	Yes	Yes
DNS Server	Yes (installed by default)	Yes	Yes
Fax Server	Yes	Yes	Yes

File and Storage Services	Yes (installed by default)	Yes	Yes
Hyper-V	No	Yes	Yes
Network Controller	No	No	Yes
Network Policy and Access Services	Yes (installed by default)	Yes	Yes
Print and Document Services	Yes	Yes	Yes
Remote Desktop Services	Yes (installed by default)	Partial	Yes
Web Services (IIS)	Yes (installed by default)	Yes	Yes
Windows Deployment Services	Yes	Yes	Yes
Windows Server Update Services (WSUS)	No	Yes	Yes

© Jones & Bartlett Learning.

TABLE 11-2 Windows Server 2016 Core Installation Roles and Editions

ROLE (CORE INSTALL)	INSTALLED BY DEFAULT?
Active Directory Certificate Services	No
Active Directory Domain Services	No
Active Directory Federation Services	No
Active Directory Lightweight Directory Services	No
Active Directory Rights Management Services	No
Device Health Attestation	No
DHCP Server	No
DNS Server	No
File and Storage Services	Yes
Host Guardian Service	No
Hyper-V	No
Print and Document Services	No
Remote Access	No
Remote Desktop Services	No
Volume Activation Services	No
Web Server (IIS)	No
Windows Server Essentials Experience	No
Windows Server Update Services	No

© Jones & Bartlett Learning.

TABLE 11-3 Windows Server 2019 Standard Installation Roles and Editions

ROLE	ESSENTIALS	STANDARD	DATACENTER
Active Directory Certificate Services	Yes	Yes	Yes
Active Directory Domain Services	Installed by default, only a single domain controller is allowed	Yes	Yes
Active Directory Federation Services	Yes	Yes	Yes
Active Directory Lightweight Directory Services	No	Yes	Yes
Active Directory Rights Management Services	Yes	Yes	Yes
Device Health Attestation	Yes	Yes	Yes
DHCP Server	Yes	Yes	Yes
DNS Server	Installed by default	Yes	Yes
Fax Server	Yes	Yes	Yes
File and Storage Services	Yes	Yes	Yes
Host Guardian Service	No	Yes	Yes
Hyper-V	No	Yes	Yes
Multipoint Services	Yes	Yes	Yes
Network Controller	Yes	Yes	Yes
Network Policy and Access Services	Yes	Yes, when installed with Desktop Experience	Yes, when installed with Desktop Experience
Print and Document Services	Yes	Yes	Yes
Remote Access	No	Yes	Yes
Remote Desktop Services	No	Yes	Yes
Volume Activation Services	Yes	Yes	Yes
Web Services (IIS)	Installed by default	Yes	Yes
Windows Deployment Services	Yes	Yes	Yes
Windows Server Essentials Experience	No	Yes	Yes
Windows Server Update Services	Yes	Yes	Yes

© Jones & Bartlett Learning.

a Windows Server installation without any GUI components. Due to the lack of a GUI, it has a smaller footprint and offers a smaller attack surface. Windows Server core installations work well in datacenters where command-line interaction or remote web-based administration are sufficient. In fact, in every Windows Server release since Windows Server 2012, you can switch between a full server and server core installation without having to reinstall the entire operating system. Windows Server 2019 offers server core installation options for the Standard and Datacenter editions.

Windows Server 2022 Editions and Roles

Recall that Microsoft offers the following editions of Windows Server 2022:

- **Standard**—Supports more features than Essentials edition for medium-sized businesses
- **Datacenter**—Designed for large-scale deployment on servers that support extensive virtualization
- **Datacenter: Azure Edition**—Designed for large-scale deployment on servers that support extensive virtualization

TABLE 11-4 lists the Windows Server 2022 roles and which editions support each role. Windows Server 2022 supports server core installations as well. The Windows Server core installation is essentially a Windows Server installation without any GUI components.

TABLE 11-4 Windows Server 2022 Standard Installation Roles and Editions

ROLE	STANDARD	DATACENTER	DATACENTER: AZURE EDITION
Active Directory Certificate Services	Yes	Yes	Yes
Active Directory Domain Services	Yes	Yes	Yes
Active Directory Federation Services	Yes	Yes	Yes
Active Directory Lightweight Directory Services	Yes	Yes	Yes
Active Directory Rights Management Services	Yes	Yes	Yes
Device Health Attestation	Yes	Yes	Yes
DHCP Server	Yes	Yes	Yes
DNS Server	Yes	Yes	Yes
Fax Server	Yes	Yes	Yes
File and Storage Services	Yes	Yes	Yes
Host Guardian Service	No	Yes	Yes
Hyper-V	Yes	Yes; including shielded virtual machines	Yes; including shielded virtual machines
Multipoint Services	Yes	Yes	Yes

(Continues)

TABLE 11-4 Windows Server 2022 Standard Installation Roles and Editions   *(continued)*

ROLE	STANDARD	DATACENTER	DATACENTER: AZURE EDITION
Network Controller	No	Yes	Yes
Network Policy and Access Services	Yes, when installed with Desktop Experience	Yes, when installed with Desktop Experience	Yes, when installed with Desktop Experience
Print and Document Services	Yes	Yes	Yes
Remote Access	Yes	Yes	Yes
Remote Desktop Services	Yes	Yes	Yes
Volume Activation Services	Yes	Yes	Yes
Web Services (IIS)	Yes	Yes	Yes
Windows Deployment Services	Yes	Yes	Yes
Windows Server Update Services	Yes	Yes	Yes

© Jones & Bartlett Learning.

Due to the lack of GUI, it has a smaller footprint and offers a smaller attack surface. Windows Server core installations work well in datacenters where command-line interaction or remote web-based administration are sufficient. In fact, in every Windows Server release since Windows Server 2012, you can switch between a full server and server core installation without having to reinstall the entire operating system. Windows Server 2022 offers server core installation options for the Standard and Datacenter editions.

Security Compliance Toolkit

Microsoft provides a set of tools to help manage Windows security baselines. According to Microsoft, the **Security Compliance Toolkit (SCT)** "… allows enterprise security administrators to download, analyze, test, edit, and store Microsoft-recommended security configuration baselines for Windows and other Microsoft products." The SCT provides guidance to administrators that makes it easier to ensure policies adhere to policy best practices.

SCT is not installed with the operating system but must be downloaded from Microsoft's website. You can get the SCT at https://www.microsoft.com/en-us/download/details.aspx?id=55319. Once you navigate to the download website, click the Download button. The action will display a list of files that you can download. You can choose from the following files:

- **LGPO.zip**—The Local Group Policy Object tool
- **Office-2016-baseline.zip**—Baseline recommended policy settings for Office 2016
- **PolicyAnalyzer.zip**—The policy analyzer tool to compare sets of GPOs and analyze their differences.

- **Windows 10 Version xxxx (multiple available versions) Security Baseline.zip**—
  Separate baseline recommended policy settings for Windows 10 versions 1507, 1511,
  1607, 1703, 1709, and 1803
- **Windows 10 Version 1809 and Windows Server 2019 Security Baseline.zip**—
  Baseline recommended policy settings for Windows 10 Version 1809 and Windows
  Server 2019
- **Windows Server 2012 R2 Security Baseline.zip**—Baseline recommended policy
  settings for Windows Server 2012 R2 (and Windows Server 2016)
- **Windows 11 Security Baseline.zip**—Baseline recommended policy settings for
  Windows 11
- **Windows Server 2022 Security Baseline.zip**—Baseline recommended policy settings
  for Windows Server 2022

Technical TIP

After downloading the SCT, review all of the available baselines as there are others included
for products such as Microsoft 365 and the Edge web browser.

After you download the files that match the versions for Windows you have installed,
extract each of the zip files into a folder of your choice. The baseline zip files contain
Microsoft recommended configuration settings for specific versions of Windows. You'll find
documentation, policy examples, and Microsoft Excel spreadsheets that list all of the group
policy settings, along with Microsoft's recommendations.

The supplied baseline information contains so many recommendations. The SCT include
two tools to help manage the baseline input, along with managing your own GPOs. The
LGPO tool helps to automate managing your local GPOs. The LGPO tool is a command-line
utility that you can run from a Windows PowerShell. For example, suppose you want to
view the contents of a local computer's Registry.pol file. This file is a binary file that contains
a registry-defined policy. By default, you can find this file at C:\Windows\System32
\GroupPolicy\Machine\Registry.pol (assuming that Windows is installed in C:\Windows).
You can't view this file directly since it is a binary file, but you can use LGPO to see what it
contains. The command lgpo /parse /m C:\Windows\System32\GroupPolicy\Machine
\Registry.pol will show what the Registry.pol file contains. (This command assumes that
the directory where you extracted LGPO.exe is your current directory.)

The other utility available in SCT is the policy analyzer tool. The policy analyzer tool
displays GPOs and compares selected GPO values. This makes it easy to compare the
Microsoft supplied baseline GPOs with your own. You can even use the policy analyzer
to create your own baseline GPOs and use those to quickly see if any computers in your
organization have changed their settings to violate your security policy.

After you extract the policy analyzer zip archive you downloaded, change your working
directory to the location where you extracted PolicyAnalyzer.exe. Then, you can launch the
policy analyzer by running PolicyAnalyzer.exe. The first time you run the policy analyzer,
the window is blank. Try loading the Registry.pol file. Click Add, then File -> Add Computer

Configuration (registry.pol). Navigate to C:\Windows\System32\GroupPolicy\Machine and select Registry.pol. Click Import, then close the Policy File Importer window. Select Local policy (at the top of the window) and the registry entry you just imported, then click View / Compare. The policy analyzer shows all of the settings in selected GPOs and will highlight any differences. **FIGURE 11-1** shows the Policy Analyzer selection window, and **FIGURE 11-2** shows the Policy Viewer (the result of the policy comparison).

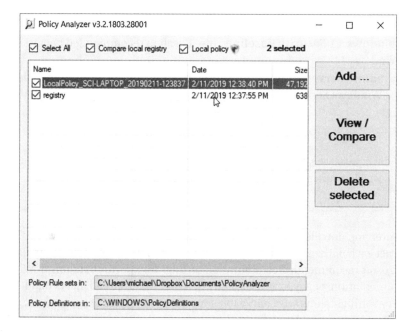

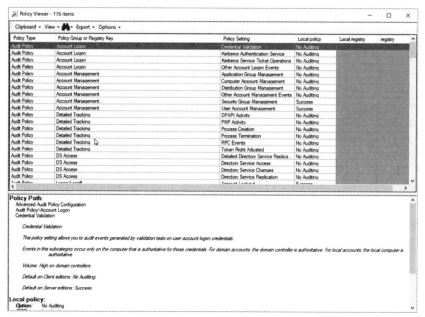

Manually Disabling and Removing Programs and Services

Before proceeding, back up the Windows Registry. It is a good idea to back up the Windows Registry before making any changes. Some of the changes you make to Windows can cause unexpected results. A Windows Registry backup may help you research problems and restore settings. In addition, make changes on a test computer whenever possible. Making changes on test computers gives you the ability to test the results of those changes before they impact your production environment.

Technical TIP

You can create a Windows Registry backup by following these steps:

1. Choose the Windows Start button > Run.
2. Type **regedit.exe** in the text box.
3. Select File > Export from the menu.
4. Enter the desired filename for the Registry backup and choose Save.

The next step is to evaluate each computer. Identify remaining programs and services that you don't need. If you carefully select the roles for each server computer, you shouldn't have to remove or disable many programs. Since workstation versions of Windows do not provide the option to install the operating system based on roles, you'll likely find several programs and services installed you don't need. For example, it is a good idea to disable the Remote Registry service. This service allows remote users to modify their Windows Registry. Once you identify any unneeded programs or services, either disable or remove them.

The most permanent and secure option is to remove unneeded programs. Make sure you know what a program is before you remove it. Don't just remove a program because you don't know what it is. If you don't recognize a program, try searching for the program name using an internet search. You'll likely find information that will help you decide whether or not to remove the program. You can remove unneeded programs using the Control Panel -> Programs and Features utility. You can also use the Add or Remove Programs app to manage applications. Removing a program makes it impossible for an attacker to use that program to compromise a computer. **FIGURE 11-3** shows the Programs and Features utility for Windows 11.

Many programs in the Windows operating system run as services. Services are programs that run in the background and help other programs to run. For example, the DHCP Client service is a program that you don't see on your display, but it provides the important service of requesting an IP address for your computer. You'll find many services running on servers as well as workstations. The Windows Services maintenance utility allows you to start, stop, and change the settings for services defined for a computer. An alternative to removing or uninstalling a program that runs as a service is to disable it. When a Windows computer boots, the operating system reads the list of services and starts the services with a Startup type value of Automatic. Windows will also start services with a Startup type value of

Uninstalling a program in Windows 11 using the Programs and Features utility.

Courtesy of Microsoft Corporation.

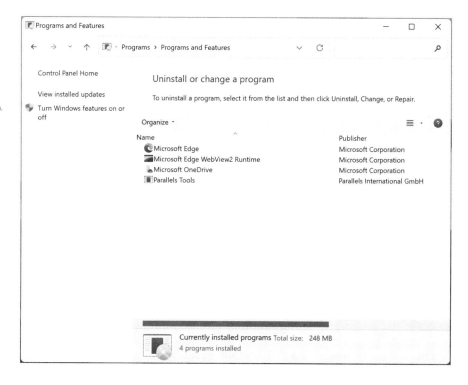

Automatic (delayed start) as well once all of the Automatic services have started. You can change the Startup type to Disabled for any services you want to prevent Windows from starting. Although it is possible to manually start a service by running the program, disabling a service reduces the probability an attacker can use it to compromise a computer.

FIGURE 11-4 shows the Windows Services Maintenance utility.

FIGURE 11-5 shows the Windows Services Properties dialog box.

After you've identified unneeded programs and services and have either removed or disabled them, you can address remaining vulnerabilities. To continue the hardening process, learn about common vulnerabilities in running programs and deploy controls to secure your computers from those vulnerabilities.

Technical TIP

Open the Programs, then the Programs and Features utility on a computer running Windows 11 or Windows Server 2022 using these steps:

1. Choose the Windows Start button > Control Panel. For Windows 11, you can search for Control Panel for quick access.

2. Select Programs and Features.

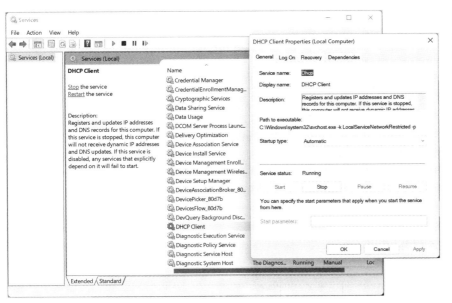

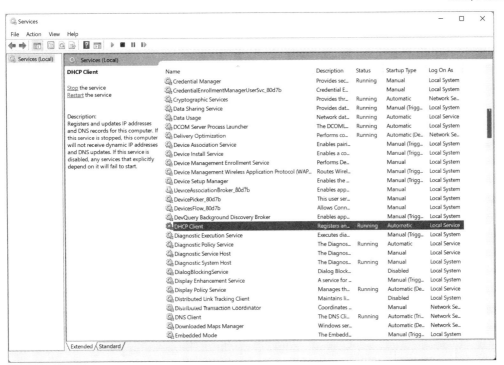

Hardening Microsoft Windows Operating System Authentication

The next step in hardening your Windows operating systems is to address authentication weaknesses. Current operating system versions, regardless of vendor, tend to be more secure and provide more features. If all of the computers in your environment are running the latest version of Windows, then you should disallow older authentication methods. For example, computers that run Windows 2000 or later support NTLMv2 authentication. Earlier versions of Windows only support the older NTLM protocol. If all your computers are running Windows 2000 or later, you can disable support for NTLM.

Technical TIP

Launch and use the Windows Services console on a computer running Windows 11 or Windows Server 2022 using these steps:

1. Choose the Windows Start button > Windows Administrative Tools.

    a. On Windows 11, choose the Windows Start button > All Apps > Windows Tools > Services. You can also search for Services to find the console quickly.

2. Select Services.

3. To edit the properties of any service, select the service, open the context menu by right-clicking on the service, then select Properties.

Remove or disable any unused or inactive user accounts defined for each computer, both locally and in Active Directory (AD). Unused user accounts provide additional targets for attackers. The most dangerous user for any Windows computer is Administrator. This user has elevated permissions and exists on every Windows computer. Attackers know that accessing the Administrator account allows them many ways to compromise a computer. Unfortunately, you can't delete the Administrator account. But you can disable it. The best way to protect your administrative rights from attackers is to follow these steps:

1. Create new accounts that will become the new Administrator users.
2. Assign the necessary Administrator rights to the new users, or to a group object. Test each of the new Administrator accounts to ensure they possess the necessary rights and permissions.
3. Disable the default Administrator account.

Following these steps will make it more difficult for attackers to escalate their privileges to include administrative rights. They have to guess which users now have administrative rights. Many automated attacks target the default Administrator user, so if you have disabled that user, such attacks will fail. Once you have disabled the Administrator user, remove other users, such as Guest, that you do not need. As with the Administrator user, attackers know that many Windows operating systems have default users no one took the time to remove. They'll try to use these accounts to compromise your computers. In the event that you are going to use any of these default accounts, be sure to change it from the default password asap.

The next step in hardening Windows authentication is to establish and enforce strong account policies. The Microsoft Security Compliance Toolkit provides many policy recommendations and makes it easy to compare recommendations with the setting you have in place. Create or edit Group Policy to modify settings for the following policies:

- **Password policy**—Settings for password age, length, complexity, storage, and history. The goal for passwords is to require users to change passwords frequently, but not too frequently. If you force users to change passwords too often and make them too complex, users will likely just write down passwords and keep them close to their workstations. A good rule of thumb is to set the maximum password age to 60 days, enable password complexity, and require that passwords be at least eight characters in length. Users will have to change their passwords every 60 days and create passwords that contain upper and lowercase characters as well as digits or special symbols.

- **Account policy**—Settings for account lockout duration, threshold, and reset count. Use these settings to make it more difficult for automated tools to use brute-force attacks to guess passwords. A good rule of thumb is to use an account lockout threshold of five to lock a user account after five failed logon attempts. You could set the duration and reset count to 15 to force a user to wait 15 minutes after five failed logons. After 15 minutes, the user could try to log on and have five more attempts before either successfully logging on or being locked out again.

- **Kerberos policy**—Settings for logon restrictions and ticket lifetimes. These settings tell Windows how long Kerberos tickets should be allowed to live and whether the Kerberos servers should authenticate users on every request. The default ticket lifetime is 10 hours. This default works well unless your environment routinely supports users who work for more than 10 hours at a time. The Kerberos lifetime should be a little longer than a user's workday.

Ensuring you only have the accounts you need, both at the local computer level and in AD, can reduce your exposure to attack. Reviewing, and if needed, strengthening the password policies will harden your Windows authentication and make it harder for attackers to compromise your Windows computers.

Hardening the Network Infrastructure

Once you've reduced the ability for unauthorized users to log on to your Windows computers, the next step is to harden other access methods. Computers communicate with other devices and computers on a network by sending messages to a destination port address. The combination of a protocol, a host name or address, and a port number identifies the intended target location for a message. For example, assume a Transport Control Protocol (TCP) message travels to www.myserver.com at port 80. Port 80 is the commonly used port for web traffic. It is likely that there is a web server on the server at the address www.myserver.com. If this server is a web server, then you would want to accept TCP traffic on port 80. If you didn't accept the traffic, your web server would never receive any web requests and essentially wouldn't be able to do its job.

Identify all of the network server and client services that require access to ports. In the previous example, you know that the web server needs port 80 to be open. If other services are running on the same computer, investigate which ports each service needs. Once you know what your computer needs to operate, modify your firewall settings to open those ports. Depending on which ports you need, you may find that they're already open. Close all other ports. If a specific server computer does not run a web server, it generally doesn't need port 80 open. The SCT tools and baselines help you define firewall rules that correspond to server roles and services required to support those roles. You can customize your firewall rules to fine-tune your network infrastructure security for Windows server computers. You should also be sure to use the more secure version of any protocols that are required. For example, HTTPS is preferred to HTTP, SFTP is preferred to regular FTP and so on.

In legacy versions of Windows, you would make firewall changes directly in the Windows Firewall maintenance utility. Starting with Windows 7 and Windows Server 2008, you now can maintain firewall rules in two different ways. One way is to use the Windows Firewall with the Advanced Security maintenance utility. Alternatively, you can use the Local Group Policy Editor to manage firewall settings. Using Group Policy to manage your firewall makes maintenance easier. Create one or more Group Policy Objects (GPOs) for firewall settings in AD and apply them to groups of computers without having to edit each one. **FIGURES 11-6** and **11-7** show the Windows Defender Firewall with Advanced Security and editing firewall settings in the Group Policy Management Editor.

FIGURE 11-6

Windows Defender Firewall
with Advanced Security.

Courtesy of Microsoft Corporation.

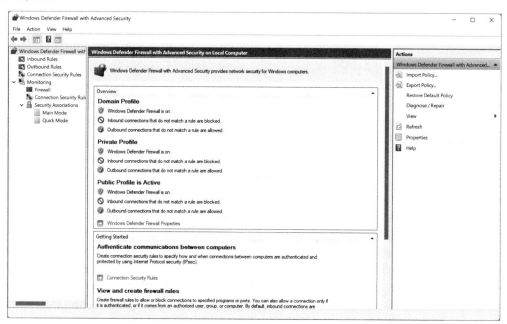

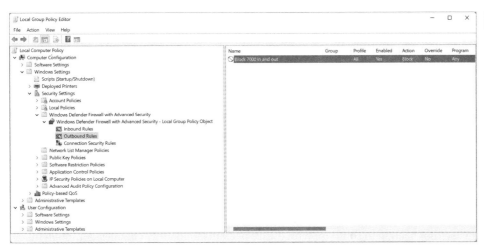

FIGURE 11-7

Group Policy
Management
Editor—Windows
Defender Firewall
with Advanced
Security.

Courtesy of Microsoft
Corporation.

Regardless of the method you use to edit firewall settings, close all ports and disallow all connections except for those ports and applications you need. Fewer entry points to your computers make them more secure.

Securing Directory Information and Operations

AD is a valuable feature of Microsoft Windows for IT operations. AD centralizes many maintenance tasks and makes it easy to standardize security settings. It also is a valuable target for attackers because it stores so much useful information. Since AD is a target for attackers, it should also be a target for your hardening efforts.

Begin by recognizing the value of compromising AD. Limit the number of administrators with access to AD. Ensure that administrators managing AD do so using separate Administrator user accounts. Administrators should have one account for AD administration and at least one other account for other administration tasks. Isolating privileged user accounts makes the accounts harder to compromise. You can create an AD security group with necessary privileges for this purpose. To add additional AD administration restrictions, require that AD administrators do their AD work only from dedicated terminal servers instead of their workstations. This requirement reduces the potential of malware infections on workstation computers to infect AD or allow AD compromise.

Periodically change the **Directory Service Restore Mode (DSRM)** password. And immediately change it from the default password after installation. This password is what you use to log on to a domain controller (DC) that has been booted into DSRM mode to create an offline copy of AD. This capability would allow an attacker to copy all your AD information. Protect the DSRM password for each DC and change it at least every 6 months.

Other steps you can take to harden AD include ensuring all DCs are physically secure. Locate your DCs in a datacenter or other location with limited access. Configure your DCs to audit important activities and use Internet Protocol Security (IPSec) between all servers. IPSec may be a little difficult to use for client connections, but setting it up for use between servers doesn't take a lot of effort. IPSec will help ensure that your AD remains secure.

Hardening Microsoft Windows OS Administration

Hardening the Windows operating system (OS) administration involves protecting the Administrator user accounts and ensuring computers are up to date. You've already learned that disabling the built-in Windows Administrator account is a recommended step. After you create other user accounts with Administrator privileges, disable the default Administrator account and use the new accounts for all administrative tasks. Enable strong passwords and set Administrator passwords to expire on a regular basis. These settings will help keep your Administrator user accounts secure.

Since a common administrative activity is to evaluate and change security settings, it is very helpful to create and maintain baselines. Baselines are copies of files and settings you can use for comparison or to restore if necessary. Create a full backup of each system both before and after hardening. The post-hardening backup will be your initial secure baseline. You can use that backup to compare with future backups to identify changes. Although full backups contain all files and folders, it may be beneficial to create individual backups of policies each time you change them. The Group Policy Management Console (GPMC) gives you the ability to back up and restore GPOs. The GPMC also allows you to manage backups of all GPOs. **FIGURE 11-8** shows the Backup GPO option in the GPMC.

Another critical component of hardening operating system administration is ensuring all Windows systems are updated to the latest patch. Ensure that Windows Update is configured to automatically download and install the latest updates from Microsoft.

FIGURE 11-9 shows the Windows Update window.

FIGURE 11-10 shows the Windows Update Advanced options.

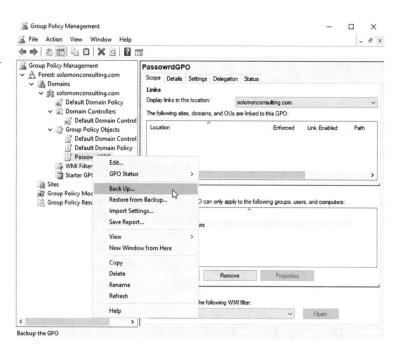

FIGURE 11-8

Group Policy Management Console— Backup GPO.

Courtesy of Microsoft Corporation.

FIGURE 11-9

Windows Update.

Courtesy of Microsoft Corporation.

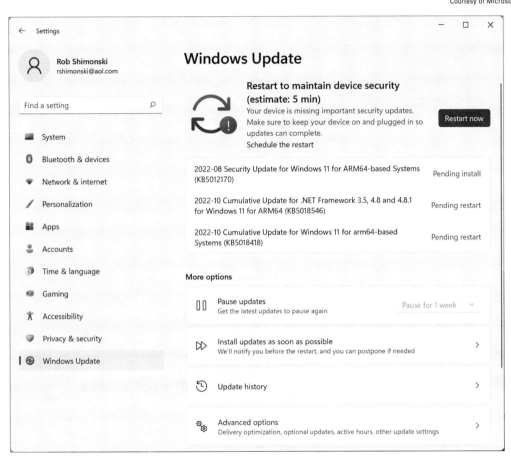

Change the Windows Updates settings in Windows 11 and Windows Server 2022 using these steps:

1. Choose the Windows Start button > Settings.
2. Select Update & Security.
3. Select Windows Update. From this window, you can change Windows Update settings, manually check for available updates, or view update history.

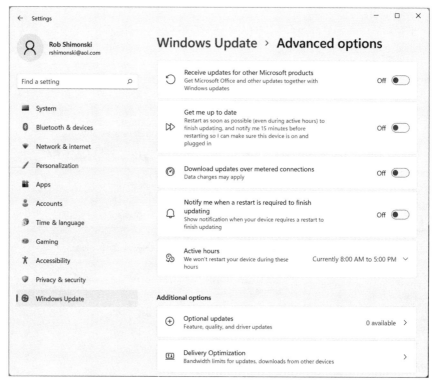

Hardening Microsoft Servers and Client Computers

Don't neglect any computer that is attached to your network. You should harden both servers and workstation computers. Any compromised computer that is connected to your network is a threat to the entire network. Microsoft makes the process of hardening server computers easier with the SCT. You can implement many of the hardening recommendations just by implementing recommendations in the SCT. Unlike earlier versions of Windows, workstation computers are integrated into the SCT recommendations. This means you don't need to manually harden your workstations. Although Windows workstation installations are more secure by default than in the past, you'll need to take extra steps to ensure that they are as secure as possible.

Hardening Server Computers

Server computers exist on your network to provide one or more specific services. You have two main areas to address when hardening servers. First, ensure that your server computers don't do anything they're not supposed to do, such as run extra services that aren't needed. If a server should provide database services only, then it probably shouldn't have IIS installed as well. Second, harden the services they are supposed to provide. Start off by installing only the roles you need for any particular server to fulfill its purpose.

One of the first steps to take after installing any new server is to use the SCT tools. The SCT tools help identify many of the unneeded services and open ports. Run SCT to disable any roles or services you don't need and then review the remaining services in the Windows Services window. Disable any services that are still running but you don't need.

After running SCT and disabling additional services, it is a good idea to scan each server using a port scanner to identify any open ports you may have missed. Use the **nmap** utility or any other port-scanning software to identify open ports. Your open port scan shouldn't find any unexpected open ports. If it does locate any ports that are open, find out what service is using them and decide whether to close the ports or add them to your approved open ports list. You should know how every open port is being used.

To make it harder for unauthorized users to connect to your server computers, enable IPSec for all server-to-server connections. IPSec will require that any computer that attempts to connect to your server be authorized to connect. Using IPSec and removing or disabling unnecessary user accounts will make it more difficult for attackers to compromise your server computers.

Once you've taken these steps to harden your servers, focus on the services that are still running. Every server will have some services running and some ports open. The second main phase of hardening servers is to focus on these components.

Technical TIP

Get more information on the free nmap utility at http://nmap.org/. The utility can be downloaded from this site and installed on any computer. Before you use nmap to scan any computer, ensure you have permission in writing from the computer and network owner to perform the scan. Port scanning can cause substantial network activity and even trigger intrusion alarms. You don't want to cause someone to treat your scan as a hostile attack. Make sure all stakeholders know what you're planning to do, when you're planning to do it, and that you have permission to do it.

Nmap offers many command options, but here are a few simple ones that will provide a list of open ports:

nmap -vA 192.168.1.128

The previous command scans for any open ports on 192.168.1.128 and also attempts to detect the operating system running on the computer at that Internet Protocol (IP) address.

nmap -vsT 192.168.1.128

The previous command scans and attempts to connect to any open ports on the computer at 192.168.1.128. Using the "-vsT" option is slower than the "-vA" scan but also provides more complete information on services that are running and monitoring open ports.

For even more command options, go to the nmap website for additional details and complete documentation. Nmap can help you identify any vulnerability on your computers.

Hardening Workstation Computers

While many of the strategies for hardening computers apply to all computers, some are especially important for workstations. In general, workstation computers act as clients, not servers. When hardening workstation computers, one of the main goals is to ensure the computer maintains a clean identity and doesn't attempt to violate your security policy.

One of the more common issues with workstation computers is malware. Since workstations tend to connect to many internet resources and run many software programs, they run into malware frequently. Removing malware is often far more difficult than preventing it. Ensure that every workstation computer has up-to-date anti-malware software installed and that its database of known malware is up to date as well.

In addition to ensuring workstations are protected from malware, it is important to mitigate as many other vulnerabilities as possible. Most workstation installations add many unneeded programs and services. And no single program effectively analyzes a workstation's role and recommends changes to make it more secure. Review all running services and programs and disable the ones you don't need. Likewise, review the Windows Firewall settings to only allow network traffic for the services and applications your workstations really need.

> ⚠ **WARNING**
>
> Securing workstations requires control. You can exert control over workstations your organization owns or directly manages. Group Policy makes it possible to effectively manage and enforce nearly all security settings for your organization's workstations. Remote users pose a more difficult challenge. It is very difficult to exert any control over workstations your organization doesn't own or manage. You should provide a separate access path for internal versus external workstations. Isolate external workstations and restrict what resources they can access.

Hardening Data Access and Controls

The key to deploying the best Windows access controls is to first develop a clear idea of what you are attempting to control. In general, minimize the number of user accounts on all computers and carefully control access to accounts with Administrator rights. Access to data and resources is based on identity. You have to implement secure identity management before you can trust your access controls. As you've already learned, having fewer user accounts and using strong passwords make your systems more secure. But just limiting user account access is only part of the solution.

Once you identify the data and resources you need to control, use Windows Group Policy to establish access control lists (ACLs) that limit access to specifically defined users and groups. The easiest way to implement access control in a large environment is to use AD and global groups for as many ACLs as possible. Avoid allowing anonymous or guest user accounts to access any sensitive data.

To protect data at rest, either use Windows Encrypting File System (EFS) for folders that contain sensitive data or Windows BitLocker to encrypt entire volumes. Regardless of the option you choose, ensure any backups encrypt your data as well.

Hardening Communications and Remote Access

Remote connections can present additional security challenges. You need the ability to evaluate several attributes of a connection request's source before granting access to your network. Define different access profiles based on your policies to meet the needs of different types of network users. **Network access control (NAC)** is a solution that defines and implements a policy that describes the requirements to access your network. NAC defines the rules a connecting node must meet to establish a secure connection with your network. It also allows you to proactively interrogate nodes that request a connection to your network to ensure they don't pose a risk. Use NAC to classify connecting nodes based on the level of compliance with your access rules. NAC allows you to evaluate node attributes such as the following:

- Anti-malware protection
- Firewall status and configuration
- Operating system version and patch level
- Node role and identity
- Custom attributes for enterprise configuration

NAC solutions enable you to exert control over which nodes can connect to your networks and what rights you'll grant to them once they connect. NAC provides a formal method to establish relationships with several types of security controls and helps you minimize threats from malware, increase LAN-to-WAN availability, and provide proof of compliance through NAC-related auditing data. NAC is a method of controlling network access that several vendor products support. **TABLE 11-5** lists some vendors that provide NAC software.

TABLE 11-5 NAC Software Products

PRODUCT	WEBSITE
PacketFence (Open source)	http://www.packetfence.org/en/home.html
Sophos Network Access Control	http://www.sophos.com/en-us/your-needs/features/nac.aspx
Broadcom Symantec Endpoint Protection	http://www.symantec.com/endpoint-protection
Checkpoint Advanced Endpoint Protection	https://www.checkpoint.com/harmony/advanced-endpoint -protection/
Cisco Network Access Control	https://www.cisco.com/site/us/en/products/security/identity -services-engine/index.html
Aerohive A3	https://www.aerohive.com/products/a3/

© Jones & Bartlett Learning.

You can choose from many products to implement NAC. NAC software alone won't secure your networks, but it gives you the ability to define and enforce policies that can get you closer to your security goals.

Authentication Servers

Once remote computers are authorized to connect, you'll need to authenticate the remote user as well. You have many ways to authenticate remote users, but three main approaches are common. The first two, RADIUS and TACACS+, rely on centralized authentication databases and servers to handle all remote users. Either of these approaches works well when there are a large number of remote users or you need to manage remote users from a central location. The third option is to use a virtual private network (VPN).

RADIUS

Remote Authentication Dial In User Service (RADIUS) is a network protocol that supports remote connections by centralizing the management tasks for authentication, authorization, and accounting for computers to connect and access a network. RADIUS is a popular protocol that many network software and devices support and is often used by internet service providers (ISPs) and large enterprises to manage access to their networks.

RADIUS is a client/server protocol that runs in the Application Layer—Layer 7 in the Open Systems Interconnection (OSI) Reference Model or Layer 4 in the TCP/IP Reference Model—and uses the User Datagram Protocol (UDP) to transport authentication and control information. Servers with RADIUS support that control access for remote users, and devices communicate with the RADIUS server to authenticate devices and users before granting access. In addition to just granting access and authorizing actions, RADIUS records network services used for accounting.

TACACS+

Terminal Access Controller Access-Control System Plus (TACACS+) is another network protocol. TACACS+ was developed by Cisco. TACACS+ has roots back to an earlier protocol, TACACS, but is an entirely different protocol. TACACS+ provides access control for remote networked computing devices using one or more centralized servers. TACACS+ is similar to RADIUS in that it provides authentication, authorization, and accounting services, but TACACS+ separates the authentication and authorization information. TACACS+ also uses the TCP protocol for more reliability.

One difference between RADIUS and TACACS+ is important to security. RADIUS only encrypts the password when sending an access request packet to the server. TACACS+ encrypts the entire packet. That makes it a little harder to sniff data from a TACACS+ packet.

VPNs and Encryption

VPNs are one of the most popular methods to establish remote connections. A VPN appears to your software as a regular network connection. It is actually a virtual connection, also called a tunnel, which uses a regular WAN connection of many hops but looks like a direct connection to your software. Most VPNs offer the option to encrypt traffic using different modes to meet different needs.

Technical TIP

Most people associate VPNs with encrypted traffic. Although most VPNs include encrypting all of the traffic transported through the VPN tunnel, encryption is an option and not a part of the VPN itself. The private part of VPN really refers to private addressing, not data privacy.

The concept of **tunneling** is central to most VPNs. Tunneling allows applications to use any protocol to communicate with servers and services without having to worry about addressing privacy concerns. Applications can even use protocols that aren't compatible with your WAN. Here's how tunneling works:

1. Your application sends a message to a remote address using its Application Layer protocol.
2. The target address your application used directs the message to the tunnel interface. The tunnel interface places each of the packets from the Application Layer inside another packet using an **encapsulating protocol**. This encapsulating protocol handles tunnel addressing and encryption issues.
3. The tunnel packet interface then passes the packets to the layers that handle the WAN interface for physical transfer.
4. On the receiving end, the packets go from the WAN to the remote tunnel interface where the packets are decrypted and assembled back into Application Layer packets and then passed up to the remote Application Layer.

This arrangement provides excellent flexibility and security. Depending on your VPN solution, you can choose from several encapsulating protocols, including:

- **OpenVPN**—An open source VPN protocol used on a variety of operating systems. Although generally slower than other protocols, OpenVPN enjoys wide acceptance and is generally considered one of the most secure VPN protocols.
- **IPSec**—A protocol suite designed to secure IP traffic using authentication and encryption for each packet.
- **Layer 2 Forwarding Protocol (L2FP)**—A tunneling protocol developed by Cisco Systems to establish VPNs over the internet. L2FP does not provide encryption— it relies on other protocols for encryption.
- **Point-to-Point Tunneling Protocol (PPTP)**—A protocol used to implement VPNs using a control channel over TCP and a Generic Routing Encapsulation (GRE) tunnel for data. PPTP does not provide encryption.
- **Layer 2 Tunneling Protocol (L2TP)**—A tunneling protocol used to implement a VPN. L2TP is a newer protocol that traces its ancestry to L2FP and PPTP. Like its predecessors, L2TP does not provide encryption itself.

- **Secure Socket Tunneling Protocol (SSTP)**—SSTP is fully integrated with the Windows operating system. It was developed by Microsoft and provides an easy to use VPN when communicating with other Windows computers. SSTP operates over SSL/TLS and provides an easy way to use a VPN even through a firewall that may block other VPN traffic. SSTP also supports Linux and Berkeley Software Distribution (BSD) clients, and mobile device operating systems can connect using third-party clients.
- **Internet Key Exchange Version 2 (IKEv2)**—Like SSTP, IKEv2 is a protocol developed jointly by Microsoft and Cisco. IKEv2 only provides tunneling services and is often paired with other protocols, such as IPSec, to provide authentication and encryption.

The VPN you select depends on several factors. Some VPN solutions are vendor specific and rely on one type of hardware. Other types of VPNs are operating system specific. For example, SSTP is only available for the Windows operating system. SSTP is Microsoft's attempt to provide a solution that works on any networking hardware. SSTP uses a Secure Sockets Layer (SSL) to transport Point-to-Point Protocol (PPP) or L2TP traffic. Using SSL removes many of the firewall and NAT issues some other protocols encounter.

Regardless of the remote authentication method you choose to use, ensure that you configure each server and client to establish connections only using your preferred method.

Hardening PKI

One method of hardening authentication is by using digital certificates. Certificates can increase the security of IPSec, SSL connections, and web server authentication. Implementing such an approach requires a method of creating, distributing, and maintaining certificates. A common approach is to implement a PKI, a term that refers to the hardware, software, policies, and procedures to manage all aspects of digital certificates. PKI has the reputation of making environments more secure, but this is only true if your PKI components are secure.

The most important component of securing PKI is to ensure all computers that participate are hardened. This is especially true for the Certificate Authority (CA) servers. In addition to hardening CAs like other servers, ensure your CAs are physically secure and only accessible by authorized administrators. Ensure that you back up the CA keys and store them in a safe location. You'll need these to recover certificate access after restoring from some types of disasters.

Use GPOs to distribute root CA certificates. Using GPOs gives you the ability to control and automate the certificate distribution. To ensure you can track down unauthorized certificate actions, enable auditing for all CA and certificate events. You will probably need to increase the maximum audit log file to store log entries for more than a few days for heavily utilized servers.

Hardening the Microsoft Azure Cloud Platform

One of the most important aspects of hardening is now focused on cloud computing, cloud platforms, and cloud providers. For example, when you move your workloads into the cloud, you will need to consider hardening of the exact same things you learned about

FIGURE 11-11

Azure Cloud Security
Services.

Courtesy of Microsoft Corporation.

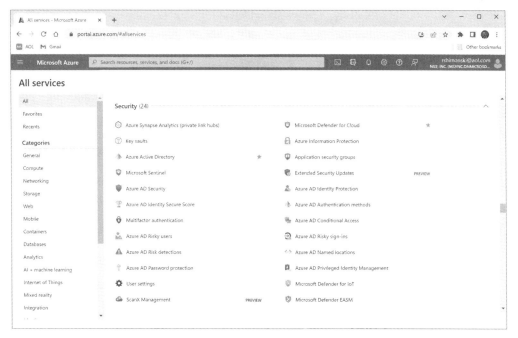

earlier. For example, you set up a hosted VM with public internet access in the cloud.
If you are using an IaaS (Infrastructure as a Service) solution, you would be responsible
for making sure that your services on the public facing system were shut off, secured,
or hardened. Since this chapter already covered how to harden Windows hosts systems,
this section will focus on how to further harden your systems and increase your security
posture leveraging Windows Azure Cloud solutions and services. In **FIGURE 11-11**, you
can see the many service offerings to help secure your cloud infrastructure and protect
your workloads.

An important consideration to make is which one of these services to use to harden
the systems and when they should be used. **TABLE 11-6** lists some of the most common
ones you would use and how to use them to harden your environment and reduce
vulnerability.

The overall security posture of your cloud architecture will depend on how you deploy
services and functions such as those listed here or the many others that are available. This
is specific to Azure cloud. Many other third-party toolsets are available in the commonly
used cloud marketplaces to add even more security services to your cloud deployment.
When hardening your cloud architecture, remember to first consider the hardening of
your base infrastructure, which is your servers and systems running in the cloud. Normally
this would be limited to IaaS, since in most PaaS (Platform as a Service) there is less for
a customer to be concerned about and in a SaaS (Software as a Service), even less. However

TABLE 11-6 Azure Cloud Security Services

SERVICE	FUNCTION
Microsoft Defender for Cloud	Microsoft Defender for Cloud is a cloud-based solution that provides additional protection for cloud security posture management (CSPM) and cloud workload protection (CWP). It is used to find vulnerabilities, weaknesses, and problem areas in your cloud infrastructure as well as if you are also configured to connect to on premises workloads. https://learn.microsoft.com /en-us/azure/defender-for-cloud/defender-for-cloud-introduction?wt .mc_id=defenderforcloud_inproduct_portal_external
Multifactor Authentication (MFA)	Harden access to your multi-cloud and hybrid cloud environments with multifactor authentication (MFA). MFA allows you to not only use passwords for authentication, but also multifactor solutions such as text or an authenticator app. https://learn.microsoft.com/en -us/azure/defender-for-cloud/multi-factor-authentication-enforcement
Microsoft Sentinel	Microsoft Sentinel allows you to use Microsoft Defender for Cloud with connectors for streaming security alerts. This would typically be done to allow for immediate alerting of compromised systems that exhibit problematic behaviors. When a threat is detected, alerts can be ingested into Sentinel, and the alerts can be managed in a single dashboard where you can configure actions. This is a common practice in cloud-based systems to send to tools such as this or others like a Security Information and Event Management (SIEM) or a Security Orchestration Automated Response (SOAR). https://learn.microsoft.com/en-us/azure/defender -for-cloud/export-to-siem
Application Security Groups	Application security groups (ASGs) allow you to further harden an application's security posture by allowing for VM grouping by policy so restrictions can be set for application groups. ASGs allow you to configure IP address restrictions, advanced rule sets and other criteria to help enforce rules based on a security policy. https://learn.microsoft.com/en-us/azure/virtual-network/application -security-groups
Key Vaults	To further harden your cloud assets, Azure Key Vault allows you to store and keep secrets such as passwords, certificates, API keys and more. https://learn.microsoft.com/en-us/azure/key -vault/general/basic-concepts

© Jones & Bartlett Learning.

in a shared responsibility model, the customer is always responsible for security in most aspects; therefore, you must consider it as a risk. In IaaS, remember to follow the lessons learned in this chapter to harden your compute-level virtualized resources on host VMs and then use the Azure portal and other Microsoft services to further harden, secure, and test your security posture for the cloud platform itself.

User Security Training and Awareness

One of the most important aspects of hardening any computer is how the computers are used. Although malicious attackers are a threat to computer security, so are authorized users. Many security incidents result from poorly trained, forgetful, or stubborn authorized users. In some environments, users view security as a barrier and stubbornly refuse to abide by the security policy. Security awareness training is crucial from a person's first exposure to your environment.

Each new employee, contractor, or visitor should go through security awareness training that corresponds to his or her level of system access. Employees generally have the greatest privileges in any organization's information systems and should be required to undergo the most comprehensive security training. Contractors or other temporary personnel have less access than employees. Visitors often have even less access. You should design security training for each group of users, based on their access and responsibilities. Part of internal personnel training should include procedures for granting access to visitors. Security awareness programs are always good ideas, and they also may be mandatory. If your organization must comply with the European Union General Data Protection Regulation (GDPR), Sarbanes–Oxley, Payment Card Industry-Digital Signature Standard (PCI-DSS Act), Health Insurance Portability and Accountability (HIPAA), or the Federal Information Security Management Act (FISMA), you must implement a security awareness program. **TABLE 11-7** lists different groups of users and suggested security training requirements.

Regardless of the type of user, anyone who connects to your computer systems should encounter frequent reminders of the importance of security. Use any of these formats to remind users of the importance of security:

- Physical posters and banners in conspicuous locations, such as in break rooms and cafeterias, and around printers, fax machines, or shredders
- Email newsletters, social media contact, and security policy updates
- Periodic website reminders
- Social media messages
- Daily or weekly tip programs
- Contests with security themes
- Security events on specific dates, such as November 30, International Computer Security Awareness Day
- Lunch-and-learn meetings about topics of interest to employees personally—such as identity theft or cyberbullying—as well as topics of interest to your organization
- Visible modeling of good security behaviors by your organization's leaders

TABLE 11-7 User Types and Suggested Security Training

USER TYPE	DESCRIPTION	SECURITY TRAINING
Employee	Person employed by an organization with permanent responsibilities and access to certain information system resources	Employees receive mandatory security policy training with signed acceptance of acceptable use policies (AUPs), completion of information system access security training prior to receipt of access credentials, and mandatory recurrent security awareness and policy update training. Properly trained employees should be able to recognize security breaches and know what to do about them.
Contractor	Temporary worker with limited temporary access to information resources related to assigned responsibilities	Contractors receive mandatory pre-engagement security policy training with signed acceptance of AUPs, completion of information system access security training that relates to assigned responsibilities prior to receipt of access credentials, and mandatory recurrent security awareness and policy update training. Properly trained contractors should be able to recognize security breaches and know whom to notify if a breach occurs.
Visitor/guest	Transient user with very limited access to information system resources	Visitors/guests agree to comply with AUPs.

© Jones & Bartlett Learning.

Best Practices for Hardening Microsoft Windows OS and Applications

Many resources are available to you for hardening Windows computers. Some resources focus on a few high-level suggestions while others go into detailed lists of suggestions. To make your job of securing Windows computers easier, here is a list of best practices for securing different types of computers. These best practices may not all apply to every one of your computers. They do provide a solid starting point that will result in a far higher level of security than taking no action at all. The key to hardening your Windows computers is to reduce each computer's attack surface to the absolute minimum while still allowing the computer to fulfill its purpose.

Here are the best practices for hardening Windows operating systems:

- Install only the Server Core option when you don't need extra functionality (i.e., GUI).
- Select the minimum number of roles when installing Windows Server.
- Use SCT immediately after installing the operating system for any Windows computer, specifically for computers that participate in an organization's network.
- Update each computer with the latest operating system patches.
- Configure each computer for automatic Windows updates.
- Install and run Microsoft Baseline Security Analyzer (MBSA) and at least one other Windows security vulnerability scanner.

- Create one or more user accounts with Administrator rights.
- Disable the Administrator and Guest user accounts.
- Determine which services are needed and disable all unneeded services.
- Close all ports not required by services or applications.
- Create GPOs for all security settings, including firewall rules.
- Use AD to distribute all configuration changes using GPOs.
- Create a backup of each GPO.
- Scan all computers for open ports and known vulnerabilities.
- Limit physical access to all critical servers.
- Create an initial baseline backup.
- Change the AD DSRM password periodically, at least every 6 months.
- Install anti-malware software on each computer.
- Ensure all anti-malware software and data are current.
- Use NAC software or devices to control remote computer connections.
- Use remote authentication methods to authorize remote computers and users.
- Require secure VPNs to access internal network resources.
- Use IPSec with digital certificates to authenticate computer-to-computer connections in the datacenter.
- Require security awareness training prior to issuing access credentials.
- Require periodic recurrent security awareness training to retain access credentials.
- Provide continuing security awareness through different means.

CHAPTER SUMMARY

Hardening is the process of making computers more secure. The process involves identifying vulnerabilities and implementing compensating controls. In this chapter, you read about some of the most important steps to make your Windows computers more secure. You learned how to install servers to be more secure and how to make both servers and workstations more secure after installation. Following the best practices at the end of this chapter will help you keep your Windows environment secure and difficult for attackers to compromise.

KEY CONCEPTS AND TERMS

Directory Service Restore Mode (DSRM)	Network access control (NAC)	Security Compliance Toolkit (SCT)
Encapsulating protocol	Nmap	Server core installation
Hardening	Role	Tunneling

CHAPTER 11 ASSESSMENT

1. The term *attack surface* refers to all of the software a computer runs that is vulnerable to attack.

    A. True
    B. False

2. The best way to secure an unneeded service is to disable it.

    A. True
    B. False

3. The process of making configuration changes and deploying controls to reduce the attack surface is called _____.

4. Which Windows Server feature allows you to specify which services you want to include during the operating system installation?

    A. Edition
    B. Role
    C. GPO
    D. Configuration

5. Which Windows Server installation option includes only a minimal environment to just run selected services?

    A. Server core
    B. Foundation
    C. Standard
    D. Runtime

6. Which Microsoft tool guides administrators and creates policies based on least privilege to reduce the attack surface of a Windows server after installation?

    A. GPO
    B. MBSA
    C. SCT
    D. NMAP

7. You can use GPOs to deploy Windows Firewall rules.

    A. True
    B. False

8. Which of the following actions is the best action to take to secure an unneeded service?

    A. Close the port.
    B. Disable the service.
    C. Delete the service from Services.
    D. Create a GPO restriction for the service.

9. You should disable the _____ user account to make it harder for attackers to access the default escalated-privilege account.

10. AD makes securing many computers in a network more complex.

    A. True
    B. False

11. The _____ tool is a handy open source tool to scan computers for open ports.

12. Which term describes software that defines and implements a policy that describes the requirements to access your network?

    A. SCW
    B. VPN
    C. GPO
    D. NAC

13. VPNs increase security of remote connection by guaranteeing all traffic is encrypted.

    A. True
    B. False

14. Which Microsoft VPN protocol makes it easy to use VPNs even through firewalls?

    A. L2TP
    B. SSTP
    C. TLS
    D. TCP

15. _____ refers to the hardware, software, policies, and procedures to manage all aspects of digital certificates.

Microsoft Application Security

O NCE YOUR OPERATING SYSTEM IS SECURE, you can focus on securing the software that runs in the operating system. Operating system software is different from application software. Regardless of how secure your operating system is, one vulnerable application can put your organization's data at risk. This chapter will teach you about the most popular Microsoft applications. You will also find out how to make each one more secure to protect your organization's data.

Chapter 12 Topics

This chapter covers the following topics and concepts:

- What the principles of Microsoft application security are
- How to secure key Microsoft client applications
- How to secure key Microsoft server applications
- What you can learn from case studies in Microsoft application security
- What best practices for securing Microsoft Windows applications are

Chapter 12 Goals

When you complete this chapter, you will be able to:

- Describe the principles of Microsoft application security
- Secure Microsoft client applications
- Secure Microsoft server applications
- Apply lessons learned from application security case studies

Principles of Microsoft Application Security

Application security covers all activities related to securing **application software** throughout its product lifecycle. Application software is any computer software that allows users to perform specific tasks. Examples of these tasks are sending and receiving email, browsing the web, creating a document or spreadsheet, or entering orders for materials. Ensuring application software security includes ensuring security during design, development, testing, deployment, maintenance, and retirement. All too often, organizations view application security as a deployment issue. Security must begin earlier in the design and development process. In this chapter, you'll study how to harden software after it has been completed or acquired by your organization. The most common strategy is to make sure that security is baked-in to your SDLC in the planning phase. This way the security process is considered in every step of the process.

A secure application is one that protects each of the three C-I-A properties of data security at all times. The three C-I-A properties are confidentiality, integrity, and availability. Check that your software, whether developed in-house or licensed, makes the data it manages available to authorized users on demand while denying access to unauthorized users. This chapter applies to any application software running on a server or client computer. Your applications provide access to data. They must also make certain that only authorized users can view or modify data based on your organization's specific security restrictions. In short, application security is all about ensuring that your applications add at least one more layer of controls between users and your data.

Common Application Software Attacks

Understanding the basic principles of securing applications starts with understanding how attackers damage applications. Hackers have many ways to harm applications. Several approaches are more common and deserve the most attention. The more common types of attacks include the following:

- **Injection**—This is the most common attack in modern day. Including SQL injection, which has accounted for a majority of known exploits for years, injection attacks are widely used to exploit vulnerable systems. Because of unsanitized user input, an attack is able to get back-end information to include table data, credentials, and more.
- **Malformed input**—This is one of the most common types of attack. Computer criminals provide input to an application that is designed to cause results the developers did not intend. They use malformed input to crash programs, disclose or modify data, or hijack connections.
- **Privilege escalation**—This adds more authority to the current session than the process should possess. There are several methods to escalate privileges, and all compromise the access control lists (ACLs) you have in place to limit data and resource access.
- **Denial of service (DoS)**—DoS attacks focus on either making the application or network slow enough that it can't respond to user requests in a timely manner or crashing the application. Either way, users can't get to the data they need. The amplified

version of this attack where multiple systems conduct a DoS in unison is called a distributed denial of service or DDoS attack.

- **Identity spoofing**—This means assuming the identity of another user. **Spoofing** means masquerading as another person or process. In most cases, the other user is one who possesses more privileges, and this greater access allows an attacker to get into more data and resources. In some cases, hackers use identity spoofing just to hide their own identities—not to escalate privileges.
- **Direct file or resource access**—This refers to exploiting holes in access controls that allow a user to directly access files or other resources. If your application allows direct object access, users may be able to bypass normal access controls.
- **Extra-application data access**—This means accessing your application's data outside the application. This could be from the operating system or from another program, or by just taking or copying backup media.
- **Malicious File Upload**—This is an attack method where the attacker attempts to upload malicious scripts/files by changing the file extension to make it appear to be a legitimate file.

Each of these attacks is preventable. Some of the controls to stop attacks, such as processing malformed input, depend on the application's design. You can implement additional controls to stop other attacks. Just as operating systems need to be hardened to be as secure as possible, it is just as important to follow steps to harden each application you run on any computer.

Technical TIP

Many options are available to harden applications. One resource is the Open Web Application Security Project (OWASP). OWASP is a not-for-profit organization that focuses on improving application security. It offers many valuable resources related to application security. You can find many informational videos, the latest Top 10 Web Application Security Risks list, and many other resources to help organizations secure applications of all types. Although primarily focused on web applications, information on this site applies to all application security topics. The OWASP webpage is located at http://www.owasp.org. For a detailed list of many of the current or modern attacks in use review https://owasp.org/www-community/attacks/.

Hardening Applications

Hardening applications generally follows several steps. The specific actions differ from application to application, but the overall strategy remains the same. Here are the general steps to hardening applications:

- Install the application using only the options and features you plan to use.
- After installing the application, remove any default user accounts and sample data, along with any unneeded files and features.

- Configure the application according to the principle of least privilege.
- Ensure your application has all of the latest available security patches applied.
- Test your security to ensure your security posture. You can run a vulnerability scan or test as well as penetration testing to ensure that you have closed all known holes in the applications security configuration. If any issues are found, fix and iterate the testing process.
- Monitor application performance to verify that your application adheres to security policy.
- Ensure all user supplied input is filtered and ran with only the permissions necessary to achieve its function.

Keep general guidelines in mind and follow the recommendations for each type of application software. You'll end up with a far more secure environment than when you started.

Securing Key Microsoft Client Applications

Many applications tend to run as either client or server components. Clients generally initiate connections and request services from servers. Servers generally listen for incoming connection and respond to requests. Your approach to securing each type of application software will be different based on the systems role and services offered. Client applications are often targets because many workstations, laptops, and mobile devices are not aggressively hardened. With so many personal computers that are insecure and contain client applications, common applications are attractive to attackers who want to compromise an organization's data. This leaves your organization open to a multitude of client-side attacks. If an attacker can compromise a client application that an organization uses to access a server application, that hacker is one step closer to your data. In this section, you'll learn about how to secure, or harden, several of the most popular Microsoft client applications.

Technical TIP

When considering client-side attacks, review the OWASP commonly exploited client-side vulnerabilities located at https://owasp.org/www-project-top-10-client-side-security-risks/. One of the most commonly used pieces of software and equally exploited on the client (and server) side is the web browser. OWASPS top 10 includes Not Using Standard Browser Security Controls as a prominent client-side attack vector and should be a focus of every security analyst looking to ensure a high level of application security is implemented in their organizations. Commonly seen vulnerabilities are misconfiguration, lack of patching, and exploiting known bugs in the browser code.

Web Browser

Arguably, the most popular and frequently used client application is the web browser. A web browser allows a user to access content from web servers across a network.

In most cases, users access resources and applications using the internet. Web browsers are attractive targets because they are the primary client of web applications. A compromised web browser can make it easy for an attacker to access stored server connections by means of stored credentials. Hackers can even compromise your organization's data without attacking the web browser directory but by intercepting the information your web browser sends to the web server.

Web browsers are attractive targets for several types of attacks:

- **Infect with malware**—Several default web browser settings allow web browsers to run helper programs, such as JavaScript or Flash, to enhance the user experience. Although many such extensions are useful, attackers can provide substitute programs that are actually malware.
- **Intercept communication**—Authorized users can access sensitive organizational data, often using a web browser. Any device or computer that sits between the client and the server sees all traffic passing back and forth between the two. An attacker who places a proxy server between a web browser and a web server can see and collect all of the traffic, including sensitive data that are intended only for the authorized user. This type of attack is often called a **man-in-the-middle attack**.
- **Harvest stored data**—Some versions of web browsers have vulnerabilities that allow webpages to collect information stored on the client computer. This information includes usernames, passwords, account numbers, and local copies of sensitive data. This stored information can appear in cookies, application files, and settings. Criminals can look for this type of information and tell your web browser to send it to malicious locations.

These are just a few of the many types of web browser attacks. You can, however, harden each web browser to resist attacks. Some of the hardening suggestions may reduce the web browser's flexibility and functionality, but it will be more secure. Change settings in any web browser by opening the settings or options page. Most of the following suggestions apply to all web browsers, but the actions in the following table are specifically oriented toward Microsoft Edge. **TABLE 12-1** lists steps to secure a web browser.

> **NOTE**
>
> After over 20 years of use, Microsoft's Internet Explorer (IE) web browser was officially retired on June 15, 2022. Because IE is officially retired (and disabled for use), there is no worry about older versions causing issues in an enterprise unless it exists on legacy systems air gapped on your segmented network.

Technical TIP

Access the Internet Options dialog box by using either of these procedures:

1. Inside Microsoft Edge, select Settings (the little gear symbol) within the options menu denoted by three horizontal dots. You can also find this gear icon to the right of the "Search the Web" field at the top of the browser; however, this will lead to the page settings so do not use it accidently to get to the browser options.
2. From Windows, launch Control Panel, and then select Internet Options.

TABLE 12-1 Securing a Web Browser

ACTION	DESCRIPTION
Set the security level of the Internet zone to High from the Security tab.	Setting the security zone to High in IE automatically enables many features that block most known vulnerabilities. Setting the security zone to High will also likely reduce the web browser's functionality. For Edge, the default is medium; therefore, setting it to high is the first step in hardening your browser for use.
Add specific sites you trust as Trusted Sites from the Security tab.	When you are visiting sites defined as trusted, IE relaxes the restrictions placed on general internet sites. This setting allows more helper programs to execute, such as Flash and JavaScript components.
Change the cookie settings from the Privacy tab. On the Advanced dialog box, select to prompt for first-party and third-party cookies.	This setting will alert you any time a website attempts to access any cookies. This requires user interaction each time a website wants to access a cookie. It gives you the chance to deny cookie access. You can also add any sites from which you want to accept all cookies to the list of allowed sites. You won't be prompted for cookie access from the listed sites. You can also select the Delete Browsing History on Exit checkbox on the General tab to have IE delete all cookies and other browsing history each time you exit IE.
Uncheck Enable Third-Party Browser Extensions from the Advanced tab.	This setting limits the potential of browser helpers from disclosing private data.
Check Always Show Encoded Addresses from the Advanced tab.	This setting makes it harder to spoof internet addresses.
Uncheck Play Sounds in Web Pages from the Advanced tab.	This setting prevents an attacker from infecting your computer using a sound file.
Use the most secure transport protocols.	To ensure the proper level of transport encryption is used, it is recommended to disable SSL and weaker forms of TLS and opt to use TLS versions 1.2 or higher.
Set your browser to auto update.	In order to make sure your browser stays up to date with the latest security patches, enable auto update on all of your workstation's browsers.

© Jones & Bartlett Learning.

FIGURE 12-1 shows the Internet Properties dialog box, Security tab for Microsoft Edge. Here you can ensure that the browser is hardened for use. You can select the Security level for this zone lever and per zone, adjust the security level. For this example, the Internet zone (the least trusted) is changed from Medium (default) to High.

Internet Properties dialog box:

Internet Properties ? ✕

General Security Privacy Content Connections Programs Advanced

Select a zone to view or change security settings.

Internet | Local intranet | Trusted sites | Restricted sites

Internet
This zone is for Internet websites, except those listed in trusted and restricted zones.

Sites

Security level for this zone

Allowed levels for this zone: Medium to High

High
- Appropriate for websites that might have harmful content
- Maximum safeguards
- Less secure features are disabled

Custom level...   Default level

Reset all zones to default level

OK   Cancel   Apply

FIGURE 12-1A shows the Internet Properties dialog box, Advanced tab box for Microsoft Edge. Here we can configure more secure methods of communication by using only TLS 1.2 or higher.

Lastly, you can configure your Microsoft Edge browser to be more secure per use when you use the InPrivate browsing option. Because tracking cookies can be placed on your system to track your steps and watch your browsing habits, you can open the browser up in a secure format to allow it to not accept cookies, store information, and download into history. To use this method, open the browser and select the three horizontal dots, then select New InPrivate window. **FIGURE 12-1B** shows the Microsoft Edge browser used InPrivate mode.

Many more settings are available, but the settings in Table 12-1 and the other tips we shared will help to establish a good baseline and harden your web browser as well as limit the damage an attacker can do using your web browser.

FIGURE 12-1A

FIGURE 12-1A

Internet Properties dialog
box, Advanced tab,
in Microsoft Edge.

Courtesy of Microsoft Corporation.

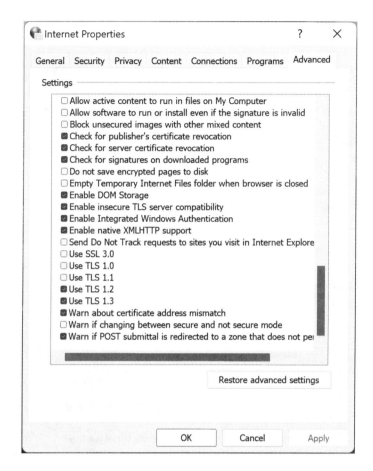

FIGURE 12-1B

Microsoft Edge InPrivate
browser window.

Courtesy of Microsoft Corporation.

Email Client

Email clients are another popular type of client software. Most of today's email clients connect to a mail server and either display or download email messages. One of the most popular email clients is Microsoft Office Outlook. As with web browsers, there are other popular email clients.

Generally, the key to hardening email clients is to limit any malicious code that may be attached to email messages. Next, take steps to ensure email message privacy. The first step requires additional software. You should already have anti-malware software installed on each computer. Select anti-malware software that integrates with your email client. Many current anti-malware software packages work with email clients to scan all incoming and outgoing messages for malware. It is important to scan incoming messages to detect any malware before it infects your computer. It is also important to scan outgoing messages to ensure your computer is not sending malware to other destinations.

The second step to securing an email client is to safeguard message privacy. Require the use of Secure Sockets Layer/Transport Layer Security (SSL/TLS) when connecting to your mail server to make certain that all message exchanges are encrypted. This option will work only if your mail server supports it and is properly configured to handle encrypted connections. The main drawback is that once your message reaches your mail server, the message is decrypted and sent on its way. Alternatively, you can encrypt each message to guarantee your message stays encrypted all the way from your email client to the recipient's email client. As with the discussion on the web browser, it is recommended to only use TLS version 1.2 or higher.

Unfortunately, there is no automatic method to encrypt email messages for generic recipients. Microsoft Office Outlook includes Secure/Multipurpose Internet Mail Extensions (S/MIME) encryption as long as the recipient has your public key. Several add-on products work with most email clients to encrypt messages as well. For example, OpenPGP, GPG, and S/MIME are all examples of email message encryption methods. Before using any of the methods or software, confirm that the recipient of your email message uses the same method. Additionally, his or her email client must be capable of receiving and decrypting the message. Since you have to take special steps for each recipient to whom you send email, encrypting email messages is not used extensively for sending messages to large groups of people. It does work very well in situations where you know you'll be sending several private messages to the same person or a small group of people.

> **Technical TIP**
>
> Some attacks on your computer are intended to turn your computer into a **zombie**. A zombie may also be called a bot. It is a computer that follows the instructions sent from another computer. Attackers often use zombies to send spam or malware to all the email addresses in a zombie's address book. Outbound malware scanning will catch many of these attacks.

Most general hardening recommendations are appropriate for other email clients. The following specific recommendations apply directly to Microsoft Office Outlook. **TABLE 12-2** lists steps to make your email client more secure.

TABLE 12-2 Securing an Email Client

ACTION	DESCRIPTION
Install anti-malware software that integrates with your email client.	Integrated anti-malware software should scan each incoming and outgoing message. Have a plan to keep all anti-malware software and data up to date.
Enable the junk filter function.	Configure your email client to filter suspicious messages and put them in a junk messages folder. Keep them separate from your regular messages.
If your mail server supports secure connections, force your email client to use only secure connections when retrieving or sending email.	Although this setting will encrypt all email messages between your email client and the mail server, messages that travel beyond your mail server will be transmitted in the clear.
Do not preview messages.	Many attackers embed malicious code in images or other email content. Train users to never open an email message from an unknown source. Since many types of malware send email messages using the sender's address book, users shouldn't open any attachments they aren't expecting.
Change the default mail format to plaintext.	Plaintext does not contain embedded commands that could result in malware infections. HTML messages are much more visually appealing but more dangerous as well.
Use an Encrypting File System (EFS) or BitLocker to encrypt the folder or drive that contains your email data files and attachments.	Keeping your email messages and attachment folders encrypted makes it harder for attackers to access the contents of your email messages without encountering operating system access controls.
If you need to exchange private email messages with a number of recipients, either use Microsoft's email encryption or acquire additional software to use another solution.	Ensure both sides of the email exchange use the same encryption method. Also, each recipient must have the sender's public key. In most cases, this is accomplished by first sending a digitally signed message to the recipient. The recipient receives the message and adds the public key to the address book. The recipient can now receive and decrypt encrypted messages from the sender.

© Jones & Bartlett Learning.

Even if you install and use the most advanced layers of protection for email clients, most successful attacks depend on the user. One important step in securing email is to properly secure the email users. That means you'll need to provide sufficient security awareness training to all users. Many attacks, such as phishing or ransomware attacks, start with an email message that looks enticing enough for a user to follow a bad link. The ultimate success of securing email is to stop users from carrying out actions that result in attack success.

Productivity Software

Most workstations and even mobile devices have some type of productivity software installed. Productivity software is any software enabling users to accomplish general work more efficiently. Productivity software may be installed as several separate programs or as a collection, or suite, of software. Common productivity software programs include the following, along with Microsoft's product for each solution:

- **Word processing**—Microsoft Word
- **Spreadsheet**—Microsoft Excel
- **Lightweight database**—Microsoft Access
- **Presentation**—Microsoft PowerPoint
- **Project scheduling/management**—Microsoft Project
- **Publishing**—Microsoft Publisher

12

Microsoft Application
Security

Technical TIP

The most commonly used productivity suites used today exist as platforms in the cloud. For example, Microsoft 365 (formerly Office 365 or O365) is the cloud solution for users and businesses to access premium office applications such as Outlook, Word, Excel, PowerPoint, Publisher, and Access as well as leverage secure cloud services including Teams, Exchange, OneDrive, SharePoint, Intune, and Azure Information Protection. Because of this ability, it will be easier for those who use it to keep it secure since the backend exists in the Microsoft cloud and security becomes a shared responsibility. As more and more connections move to the cloud, less "on-site" hardening of lightweight client applications installed on the OS remains an issue.

Productivity software packages are also targets for attackers, especially the more popular programs. The main goals for compromising productivity software are malware infection and private data disclosure. Many types of malware infect computers when users open infected files. Infected documents, spreadsheets, presentations, and databases can exploit vulnerabilities in your productivity software and launch malware that infects your computer. Many successful attacks still introduce malware to computers using productivity software document types that appear to be harmless.

The standard file extensions also identify potential content types to attackers. If a criminal is looking for private data that are likely stored in an Access database, any files with the extension .accdb are good candidates. **TABLE 12-3** lists the general steps to help secure your productivity software.

File Transfer Software

One of the earliest uses of networks was to transfer files from one computer to another. Users still transfer files routinely between computers, sometimes over large distances. Every file download or upload is a file transfer. Unfortunately, the protocols most

TABLE 12-3 Securing Productivity Software

ACTION	DESCRIPTION
Install anti-malware software that integrates with your productivity software.	Integrated anti-malware software should scan each file before opening it. Make sure you have a plan to keep all anti-malware software and data up to date.
Use EFS or BitLocker to encrypt the folder or drive that contains your productivity software documents and databases.	Keeping your document folders encrypted makes it harder for attackers to access the contents of your documents without encountering operating system access controls.
Never open a file unless you trust the source.	Many malware infections depend on a user opening an infected file.
Ensure your productivity software has the latest security patches installed.	New vulnerabilities are discovered daily. Unpatched software is at risk.
Disable macros by default and only run them when necessary	Many productivity software solutions like Word or Excel allow for macros, which are software scripts written in Microsoft VBA language. These scripts are usually used for automation but can also be used by hackers as a form of malware. To be safe, you should disable macros by default and train users not to run macros that they themselves have not written.

© Jones & Bartlett Learning.

commonly used to transfer files send the contents of each file in the clear, which means unencrypted. The reason for sending data in the clear is that it is much faster than encrypting the data first. However, security is a greater concern than efficiency for private data. Do not use standard file transfer methods for any files that contain private data. Use a secure transfer method.

The most common method of transferring files across a network is the **File Transfer Protocol (FTP)**. FTP uses the Transmission Control Protocol/Internet Protocol (TCP/IP) suite to decompose a file into small messages and send the file to a recipient where the file is reassembled. The process is solid but insecure. As security has become more and more important, additional methods have been introduced, including FTP over a Secure Shell (SSH) and Secure FTP (SFTP). Virtual private networks (VPNs) are also a good choice for transferring files. Use unencrypted FTP within a secure VPN to achieve very good privacy.

Regardless of the specific choice you use, both ends of the network connection must agree on the methods. The main point of securing file transfer software is to ensure all files that contain private data are transferred using some type of encryption.

 WARNING

In modern times, attempt to never use an unsecured protocol such as FTP over any medium. Always use the secure versions of older IPv4 protocols such as FTP, Telnet, and others, if at all.

AppLocker

Microsoft includes a feature in Windows that allows you to restrict program execution using Group Policy. This feature, called AppLocker, is included with Windows Server and Enterprise editions of Windows workstation versions. AppLocker provides the ability to whitelist applications, telling the operating system which applications are OK to run. Prior to AppLocker, Microsoft provided basic software restriction capabilities through the Software Restriction Policies (SRP) in previous Windows versions. SRP are still in newer Windows versions but is harder to use in a larger enterprise than AppLocker. Define rules using Group Policy to restrict which applications computers can run using these types of rules:

- **Path rules**—SRP and AppLocker allow you to define specific paths from which users can execute applications. Any application located in paths not approved by these Windows features cannot run. Unless you carefully restrict users from common installation folders, they can just copy new applications into a common folder and essentially bypass the path rule restriction.
- **Hash rules**—SRP and AppLocker allow you to create a cryptographic hash for each executable to distribute to workstation computers. Windows validates that the executable program matches the approved hash value each time you run a program. This type of rule is more secure than a path rule, but it requires that you update the hash value each time you distribute a program update.
- **Publisher rules**—AppLocker makes application security easier than SRP by introducing a new type of rule. Publisher rules use digital signatures provided by application publishers. Use these signatures with additional criteria, such as minimum version to define allowable applications. For example, you could allow Microsoft Word to run on a workstation only if it has a valid publisher certificate and is at least version 12.0. Although AppLocker publisher rules are slightly similar to SRP certificate rules, AppLocker has added a lot of features and made defining rules much easier.

Besides the additional features AppLocker provides with Publisher Rules, AppLocker makes it easy to define rules for any number of users employing Group Policy.

Technical TIP

Access AppLocker settings in the Group Policy Management Console (GPMC) on Windows Server 2008 R2 by following these steps:

1. Choose Start > Administrative Tools > Group Policy Management.
2. Select a Group Policy Object (GPO) or create a new GPO.
3. Open the context menu for the selected GPO and select Edit.
4. Expand Computer Configuration\Policies\Windows Settings\Security Settings\ Application Control Policies\AppLocker.

Securing Key Microsoft Server Applications

Server applications are designed to listen for requests and provide some service as a response. They commonly run in the background on server computers, listen to one or more defined ports, and process requests on behalf of clients. Server applications often interact with centralized data and will likely have access to private data. All three properties in the C-I-A triad are of concern in server applications. A secure application is available to respond to client requests and enforces the integrity and confidentiality of the data it manages. Several types of server applications are common in organizations, and each has its own specific security concerns.

One of the most useful features of Windows Server is the definition of server roles. When you select a server role, Windows installs only the services you'll likely need to fill that role. The first step in securing any server software is to secure the server computer. One of the best ways to secure a server computer is to limit the roles you install. Install only roles that are necessary for each server to fulfill its purpose.

Web Server

A web server is a software program that monitors a specific port, normally port 80 or 443, for web requests and provides content for a web client. Web servers support many types of requests and apply various protocols to respond to requests. The two most common protocols that web servers use for normal web traffic are the Hypertext Transfer Protocol (HTTP) and **Hypertext Transfer Protocol Secure (HTTPS)**. The web server receives a message from the inbound port in the form of a request that includes a **uniform resource locator (URL)**. The URL contains information for the web server to know how to handle the request.

For example, suppose you are running a web server at the address www.Microsoft ApplicationSecurityChapter12.com. Your web server may receive a URL that looks like this: http://www.MicrosoftApplicationSecurityChapter12.com/scripts/wsisa.dll /WService=catlookup?isbn=076372677X

TABLE 12-4 describes the individual parts of a URL.

TABLE 12-4 Individual Parts of a URL	
DESCRIPTION	**VALUE**
Protocol	*http*—The protocol the web server will use for this exchange
Separator	*://*—Standards separator between the protocol and the host name or address
Host name or address	*www.MicrosoftApplicationSecurityChapter12.com*—The name or IP address where the web server is running
Web server command	*Scripts/wsisa.dll/WService=catlookup?isbn=076372677X*—The rest of the URL contains information the web server uses to interpret the client's request. In this case, the web server would attempt to execute wsisa.dll in the scripts folder.

The web server receives the message and evaluates the web server command. The web server command tells the web server what to do. If your web server executes a command without taking any precautions, any anonymous user can tell it to do many malicious things, such as return private data, delete files, or shut down the server. Any of these actions would violate the server's security.

Since you don't want any web server blindly executing commands, you need to restrict what the web server accepts and what it can do. Make a web server more secure by following a few simple strategies. **TABLE 12-5** lists some of the main strategies for securing any web server.

The strategies in Table 12-5 represent a few of the tasks necessary to fully secure a web server. Since web servers are often exposed to the internet and provide an interface into your network, they are attractive targets. Make sure you spend the time securing each web server you deploy.

12

Microsoft Application Security

TABLE 12-5 Strategies to Secure a Web Server

STRATEGY	DESCRIPTION
Disable unused protocols/services.	Web servers can support many more protocols than HTTP and HTTPS. Each protocol gives attackers additional methods to compromise a server. If you don't need a particular protocol, such as FTP, disable it in the web server configuration and ensure the corresponding service is disabled as well.
Remove samples, help, and administration scripts.	Some web servers install additional components you don't need on a production server and may be vulnerable to attacks.
Disable scripts for types you don't need.	Web servers recognize many different types of file extensions and will attempt to interpret scripts and programs it receives. Hackers use this knowledge to send attack scripts to exploit vulnerabilities.
Deny directory traversal and listing.	Stop web clients from sending paths or commands that access resources outside the web server path. Also, don't let anyone see a directory listing of directories on your server. Criminals use information to plan more attacks.
Enable auditing of failed logon attempts and failed resource requests.	Auditing can provide information to identify attacks or reconnaissance on your web server.
Put all web content on a disk drive that is separate from the operating system or any private data.	Separating web server files from system files and private data reduces the damage an attacker can do if your web server is compromised.
Require secure connections for any private data exchange.	SSL/TLS connections encrypt traffic between the web server and the web browser, keeping messages private.
Use operating system access controls to limit access for web users.	Operating system access controls can limit the objects any user can access, including web users.

(continues)

TABLE 12-5 Strategies to Secure a Web Server	*(continued)*
STRATEGY	**DESCRIPTION**
Disable any web server authentication methods your application does not need.	Some web server authentication methods, such as digest authentication, are vulnerable and should not be used.
Remove any unused encryption ciphers.	Many web servers install several encryption ciphers to support as many types of encryption as possible. Remove any ciphers that are weaker than your minimum requirements. This stops clients from negotiating a weaker encryption algorithm with the web server.
Modify your default error messages.	Sometimes web servers can return sensitive information via their error messages that can help attackers in performing an attack. Be sure to modify your error messages to return very general information that can't be used by an attacker to better understand your server's vulnerabilities.

© Jones & Bartlett Learning.

Microsoft's web server, Internet Information Services (IIS), has long been a familiar component in Windows environments. The latest version of IIS that ships with Windows Server represents Microsoft's most secure web server to date. Microsoft learned many lessons from previous versions of IIS and made the latest version secure from the beginning. If you take the time to install IIS with only the options you need, it doesn't require much additional work to create a secure web server.

The starting point for installing IIS is a computer with Windows Server installed. Install IIS to a standard Windows server or a Windows Core Server installation. You'll learn about adding IIS to a standard server in this chapter. You install IIS by adding an additional role to the server.

Technical TIP

You can add a role to a Windows Server 2008 R2 server and above from the Server Manager window. Follow these steps to add a new role to a server in Windows Server 2022:

1. From the Windows desktop, choose Start > Server Manager.
2. Select Manage > Add Roles and Features.
3. Select Next three times to see the roles you can add to the current server.
4. Check the Web Server (IIS) box and choose Next several times, then Install.

FIGURE 12-2 shows the Add Roles Wizard windows for adding the Web Server (IIS) role to Windows Server 2022.

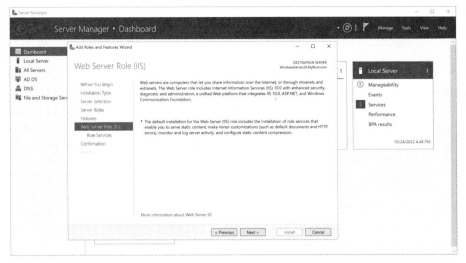

FIGURE 12-2

Add Roles Wizard for adding Web Server (IIS) role to Windows Server 2022.

Courtesy of Microsoft Corporation.

Notice in Figure 12-2 that Windows provides several resources to help you add IIS to your server. Read through an overview of the role services included with IIS. These services allow you to pick and choose just the services your web server needs to run your websites and applications. This saves you the time and effort of having to disable unneeded services after installation. Microsoft also provides detailed checklists to help you install IIS with the features and security you want. After reviewing the help and documentation, proceed to the role services selection window.

FIGURE 12-3 shows the Select Role Services window for adding the Web Server (IIS) role to Windows Server 2022.

Windows lets you select the services your web server will need before it installs anything. This is the step that can make your web server lean and secure. Carefully review each selection before checking any box. Once you have all of the desired services selected,

FIGURE 12-3

Select Role Services for adding Web Server (IIS) role to Windows Server 2022.

Courtesy of Microsoft Corporation.

continue installing IIS. Although IIS installs in a fairly secure state, you should still review the server and the web server software to ensure the highest level of security possible.

Email Server

Another common server you'll find in many organizations is an email server. Microsoft's email server is Microsoft Exchange Server. An email server provides mail services to clients. Clients connect to the email server and either receive email messages from the server or send email messages to the server. One connection could include both operations. Clients can either download messages to read locally or read messages directly from the email server. If you allow it, each client can choose between remote or local message storage.

When considering email server security, cover all three properties of the C-I-A triad. Your email server must be available. One of the most frustrating situations for users to encounter is an email server that is unavailable. Email is such an integral part of daily tasks that access to it is expected. Your email server must also ensure private messages are private and no message changes in transit. While the confidentiality and integrity properties are important for some messages, the overhead generally doesn't warrant securing all messages.

It is important to secure all email that is stored on your email server. Your email server may store messages for short periods of time or for months, or even years. Double-check that both your email server software and the operating system protect email message data using file, folder, or drive encryption. Since many people rely on the practice of storing email messages on the email server, have a solid disaster recovery plan (DRP) and business continuity plan (BCP). These plans protect your email in case of data loss.

Unlike IIS, Exchange Server is a separate commercial product. Once you purchase a license, you can acquire and install Exchange Server on your Windows Server computer. During installation, you specify many of the characteristics to secure your email server. Exchange Server allows you to select from several roles that define whether the server will store messages, provide client access to messages, transport messages to other email servers, or even perform a combination of roles. The specific role your email server plays tells the installation process how to configure the software for the most functionality and highest security.

An email server must deal with several vulnerabilities to support secure email exchange. When securing an email server, address these issues:

- **Limit operating system logons and administrator rights**—Only a limited number of user accounts should have administrator access to the email server computers.
- **Enforce strong email user authentication**—Require strong authentication for all email clients.
- **Use encrypted connections for all communication between Exchange servers**—This is the default behavior.
- **Enable only the protocols your email clients require**—Post Office Protocol version 3 (POP3) and Internet Message Access Protocol 4 (IMAP4) are older protocols and are disabled by default. Enable them if necessary, but Exchange allows these connections only if they are encrypted.

- **Patch all Exchange Server instances**—Frequently check for security updates and install them to all your Exchange servers.
- **Use anti-malware software on each server**—Windows Defender is just one option that is available.
- **Encrypt folders or drives that store email messages**—Use EFS or BitLocker.
- **Plan for high availability**—Develop a solid BCP and DRP that ensure maximum uptime.

Email servers are frequent participants in spreading malware. Good anti-malware software, along with strong access controls, can reduce the potential for your email server spreading malware. Requiring encryption of all connections will greatly increase the overall security of messages exchanged within your organization. Remember that messages that travel outside your organization are not encrypted by default. It is the responsibility of the email clients to agree and encrypt messages. Microsoft Exchange Server goes a long way toward ensuring your email messages are as secure as possible.

Database Server

Nearly every application needs some type of stored data on which to operate. Some applications use their own internal data storage techniques. The majority of applications use separate database management products to store data. Application developers write application software that interfaces with one or more databases to maintain the data each application needs. Today's databases are getting larger. It is not uncommon to see database sizes in excess of many terabytes. As applications rely on database management systems more and more to provide access to data, organizations are isolating databases on separate servers. These specially configured database servers are efficient platforms for applications and attractive targets for attackers.

Database management systems routinely store application data for rapid and secure retrieval on demand. Databases can store private and public data. They handle each type of data differently. Separating all of an organization's data to a database server gives the organization greater control over how to secure those data. Securing a database, like securing any other server software, depends on a secure operating system first. After the basic security needs of the underlying platform have been addressed, databases can help ensure the confidentiality, integrity, and availability of stored data.

Current database management systems have several options and strategies to provide maximum availability. Take frequent backups, archive transactions logs, or implement data replication. Most current database products also provide configuration options that are specific to high availability. One configuration option is using failover clustering to protect from hardware failure. Regardless of the options you choose, research your database management system's capabilities and deploy the configuration that fits your budget and provides the greatest availability.

The ability of a database management system to provide confidentiality and integrity depends on the quality of the authentication, access controls, and query preprocessing. First, use strong authentication for all database queries. In the database world, a **query** is any statement that accesses data. A query can read, write, create, or delete data. Each query requests access to data on behalf of a specific user or process. Enforce unique user accounts and strong authentication. Legacy database applications often allowed generic user accounts that multiple users shared. While this practice is acceptable for public data, it is not acceptable for databases that contain sensitive data. Do not allow this practice for databases that contain sensitive data. Each user should have a unique account. Unique user accounts make it possible to grant access privileges to specific users and audit activity more precisely. Just as with hardening the operating system, require the strongest authentication method your clients support.

The next security property is confidentiality. Database management systems use encryption to support confidentiality. To make database access as secure as possible, enforce encrypted connections any time you transfer private data. You can enforce this using VPNs or individual connection encryption. Make sure no private data are transmitting in the clear.

Databases also use encryption to store data. Data at rest have several different encryption options. This list of options includes the following:

 WARNING

If your organization deploys a distributed application, make sure all connections from the client to the database are encrypted. Many applications force secure connections just from the client to the web server. While this strategy protects data transmitted across the internet, data are decrypted and transmitted in the clear from the web server to the application servers and database servers. Encrypt all connections.

- **EFS or BitLocker**—Although encrypting a file, folder, or volume does store data in an encrypted format, most database administrators prefer more granular control over what gets encrypted. Encrypting data at the operating system level may lead to far more data being encrypted than what an organization needs.
- **Transparent Data Encryption (TDE)**—Current database management systems generally offer an option to encrypt either selected database objects or even an entire database. TDE encrypts all data without requiring any user or application action.
- **Application encryption**—The most fine-grained control is for the application to decide what data to store encrypted and carry out the encryption process directly. This last option provides the most control over encrypted data but at the cost of substantial software development effort.

The last major security property that database management systems protect is data integrity. Although database vendors go to great lengths to ensure internal data integrity, integrity in a security context has a slightly different meaning. To support both confidentiality and integrity, database management systems make certain that no unauthorized user can view or modify data. To enforce these two properties, the database management system must know the identity of the user who submitted the query. Positive identification and authentication provide a trusted user account. The next step is to authorize a user to carry out a data operation. Most of the commercial database management systems support the **Structured Query Language (SQL)** to access data in a database. SQL defines a security model that grants or revokes access privileges to specific pieces of data. The database management system evaluates each field, or column of data, based on the permissions defined for the current user.

SQL security is quite good. The problem is that it can be cumbersome to manage. SQL security is based on users, and granting data access to anonymous users can allow anyone to access your data. As long as you have unique user accounts, you can secure data in your database at a very detailed level. Doing so requires substantial effort in verifying that all permissions are current and accurate.

One common problem arises with storing secure data in a database. Most database products interpret SQL queries at run time. In other words, the query statement isn't evaluated until it is time to execute the statement. Many attackers have learned how to trick the database query processor into doing more than intended. It is possible to add SQL statements to input data, and if an attacker is crafty and careful, he or she can make a database server respond to nearly any command. Adding SQL statements to data for the purpose of sending commands to a database management system is called **SQL injection**.

The best defense against an SQL injection attack is to validate all input before sending it to the SQL query processor. Have your client application validate each input field to ensure it meets your input standards, but make your server validate input as well. Recall that man-in-the-middle attacks sometimes use proxy servers. They also use these servers in injection attacks. If an attacker can intercept network traffic, he or she can also modify the traffic. That means a computer criminal can modify any data that already passed validation on the client. For that reason, never trust data from a client—always validate all input on the server. By validating all input, your database server can detect and remove illegal input such as injected SQL statements.

Keeping all these points in mind, here are the general steps to securing a database server:

- **Secure the operating system**—Always start with a secure operating platform.
- **Install the latest patches**—Check that you have the latest security patches and develop a plan to acquire and install all released patches.
- **Require strong authentication**—Require authentication of all users before processing a query and force the strongest authentication method your clients can support.
- **Use separate user accounts for database administration**—These are separate system administrators, database administrators, and database user accounts.
- **Install only necessary components**—Do not install database services or components you don't need. Review the installation process and remove unneeded components.
- **Remove or disable default users**—Most database management systems install default user accounts. Attackers know which default users exist in most databases. Remove or disable all of these default accounts.
- **Use auditing**—Enable auditing for failed logon attempts and possibly access to critical data. Be aware that auditing any data access can create a large number of log entries.
- **Change default ports**—Never use the default ports to access database services. Attackers know these default ports. Select alternate ports for all database accesses.
- **Revoke any developer access to production environments**—Developers should have access only to development and testing environments.
- **Encrypt private data**—Select an encryption method that secures private data.
- **Develop and maintain plans for business continuity and disaster recovery**—Plan for disruptions and know how to minimize your downtime.
- **Validate all input**—Never evaluate a database query without validating the query first to ensure that no extra data are in the query.

- **Monitor performance**—Monitor how well the database is executing queries and be prepared to respond if performance degrades.
- **Use database redundancy**—To ensure availability of your database for internal and external use, be sure to have multiple copies of your production database available.

Let Microsoft Handle Your Database and Cloud Computing Needs

Microsoft offers another option for organizations that use Microsoft SQL Server. Microsoft Azure provides SQL Server database services, along with a comprehensive set of cloud-based services as a subscription. Your database and applications no longer reside in your environment but reside and are managed in Microsoft's cloud environment. The advantages to this approach are that Microsoft handles all of the patching, high availability, and basic security tasks for you. You can find more information on Microsoft Azure at https://azure.microsoft.com/en-us/.

These steps will help you create a database environment that supports your data's security. You can choose to build in an IaaS, PaaS, or other type of environment that allows the support of and creation of databases in a cloud environment.

Enterprise Resource Planning Software

Enterprise Resource Planning (ERP) software is an integrated collection of software programs. It manages many aspects of a business, including finances, human resources, assets, and business processes. ERP software generally serves to unite different users and organizational units by sharing and combining data. ERP software provides centralized data storage and functional software capabilities that streamline business processes.

The security concern of ERP software is that a large portion of an organization's data is centralized. Most, if not all, of the users in the organization access the ERP software as part of their normal business function. That means many users have access to the application and the database. Each software vendor provides specific recommendations for its product, but many strategies to secure ERP software are common among vendors. Follow these guidelines to secure any ERP software application:

- **Create unique user accounts**—Securing shared data depends on uniquely identifying users. Don't allow users to share accounts.
- **Enforce strong authentication**—Since data security depends on user- or group-based authorization, choose the strongest authentication type your application allows.
- **Restrict access to application components**—Use application security options to restrict function access by user or group.
- **Develop ERP acceptable use policy (AUP)**—Develop AUPs for the ERP software. Train all users on current AUPs.
- **Secure workstations**—Follow recommendations for securing any workstation that accesses your ERP application.

- **Require encrypted connections**—Require secure VPN or other encrypted connection to access the ERP application.

Line of Business Software

ERP applications address mostly generic business needs. Some organizations have specific business processes that are unique to their market or organization. Many organizations either develop or acquire specialized application software to help them conduct business. Software applications that are specific to a particular process in an organization are called line of business (LOB) software. For example, LOB software can include any of these applications:

- Enterprise project management
- Workflow control
- Service technician tracking and scheduling

LOB software isn't necessarily unique to an organization, but it isn't needed by all organizations. The security concerns are the same ones as with ERP applications. The workforce depends on the application's operation and the data's security. The application must be available, responsive, and dependable. Follow the same recommendations as in the ERP application section, and you'll have a secure LOB application.

Cloud-Based Software

Most of the application software you have seen so far are on-premises applications. That means they are installed on your computers. Traditionally, that's the way organizations used applications. You purchase a license for software or write it yourself, and then install and use that software in your organization. That model has already changed. While on-premises software still exists and is in use, more and more enterprise software is cloud-based. Microsoft is a leader in providing cloud-based services to meet enterprise and individual user needs. Microsoft's three leading cloud-based products are Microsoft 365, Microsoft Azure, and Microsoft OneDrive. Each of these software offerings target different users but provide services that are all based on Microsoft's cloud architecture.

When it comes to securing cloud-based applications, many of the issues are the same as the on-premises issues you've already seen. Even when you use cloud-based software, you should review the options and settings and configure the software to run the way you need it to run. Don't assume that cloud-based software is secure by default. It isn't. You still have to harden software, regardless of where it runs.

Case Studies in Microsoft Application Security

When learning new concepts, it often helps to see examples. The best examples are real-life examples. Microsoft makes it easy to read about how real organizations have deployed Microsoft products in ways that have resulted in more secure and effective operations.

The Microsoft case study resource is located at https://azure.microsoft.com/en-us/case-studies/. While the initial case studies presented focus on Microsoft Azure, you can search for case studies from a specific industry, for a specific Microsoft product, or that implemented a specific Microsoft solution. You can find case studies that cover nearly every type of business environment. Try searching for a case study for an organization that is similar to yours. You'll likely find some innovative ideas. Learning how others solved problems often saves the time of building a solution from scratch.

Best Practices for Securing Microsoft Windows Applications

A little research on securing applications will yield many resources. You can find tutorials, how-to guides, and complete reference works with detailed instructions to follow. While there are many details necessary to make your applications as secure as possible, several general guidelines will address the most important security needs.

Although each application and each organization are different, they all share common strategies to establish good security controls and foil attackers. The following recommendations come from practical experience with many organizations and applications. They are the strategies that produce the best results. These best practices will help you establish a solid foundation for securing your applications:

- Harden the operating system first.
- Install only the services necessary.
- Use server roles when possible.
- Use Security Compliance Toolkit (SCT) to ensure you are adhering to Microsoft baseline best practices.
- Remove or disable unneeded services.
- Remove or disable unused user accounts.
- Remove extra application components.
- Open only the minimum required ports at the firewall.
- Define unique user accounts.
- Use strong authentication.
- Use encrypted connections for all communication.
- Encrypt files, folders, or volumes that contain private data.
- Develop and maintain a BCP and DRP.
- Disable any unneeded server features.
- Ensure every computer has up-to-date anti-malware software and data.
- Never open any content or files from untrusted sources.
- Validate all input received at the server.
- Audit failed logon and access attempts.
- Conduct penetration tests to discover vulnerabilities.

These best practices apply to most server applications and ensure you are protecting your data at the server level.

CHAPTER SUMMARY

Securing applications is an integral part of an overall security plan. The most secure environment is not very secure if the servers aren't hardened as well. Attackers know that servers store an organization's valuable data and the programs that manipulate those data. Your servers will be targets, regardless of where they may physically reside. Your clients will be targets too. In many cases, attackers will attempt to compromise clients to get to your servers. Have a plan for foiling assaults at both the client and server levels. That plan should start with hardening your applications to make them as secure as possible.

In this chapter, you learned how to secure several types of application software. You found out how to secure both client and server applications and why each one is important. You also reviewed best practices that will provide a solid foundation for a secure application environment.

KEY CONCEPTS AND TERMS

Application software

Enterprise Resource Planning (ERP)

File Transfer Protocol (FTP)

Hypertext Transfer Protocol Secure (HTTPS)

Man-in-the-middle attack

Privilege escalation

Query

Spoofing

SQL injection

Structured Query Language (SQL)

Transparent Data Encryption (TDE)

Uniform resource locator (URL)

Zombie

CHAPTER 12 ASSESSMENT

1. The main focus when securing application software is confidentiality.

   A. True
   B. False

2. Which type of application attack attempts to add more authority to the current process?

   A. Privilege spoofing
   B. Identity escalation
   C. Privilege escalation
   D. Identity spoofing

3. Which of the following is the best first step in securing application software?

   A. Install all of the latest patches.
   B. Harden the operating system.

   C. Configure application software using least privilege.
   D. Perform penetration tests to evaluate vulnerabilities.

4. A(n) _____ is an attractive target because it is the primary client of web applications.

5. Why does JavaScript pose potential security risks?

   A. JavaScript can contain malware and run on the client.
   B. JavaScript can contain malware and run on the server.
   C. JavaScript requires that you divulge sensitive authentication details.
   D. JavaScript is outdated and generally used by older web applications.

6. Enabling secure connections ensures email messages are encrypted between sender and recipient.

   A. True
   B. False

7. Which of the following is a simple step to make email clients more secure?

   A. Use EFS/BitLocker to store email messages on the server.
   B. Install third-party message encryption.
   C. Turn off message preview.
   D. Remove email clients and use server-based email access.

8. Which of the following steps can increase the security of all application software?

   A. Install anti-malware software.
   B. Use whole disk encryption on client workstations.
   C. Run SCT on workstations.
   D. Require SSL/TLS for connections to a web server.

9. You use Windows server roles to configure each Windows server computer to perform only one task.

   A. True
   B. False

10. A URL can contain commands the web server will execute.

   A. True
   B. False

11. How do you install IIS on a Windows Server computer?

   A. Purchase IIS and install it.
   B. Download IIS for free and install it.
   C. Add the Web Server (IIS) role to a server.
   D. Install IIS from the Windows install DVD.

12. A(n) _____ is any statement that accesses data in a database.

13. _____ encrypts all data in a database without requiring user or application action.

14. SQL injection attacks are possible only against popular Microsoft SQL Server databases.

   A. True
   B. False

15. Is requiring secure connections between your web server and your application server worth the overhead and administrative effort?

   A. No, because both the web server and application server are inside your secure network.
   B. Yes, because your web server is in the demilitarized zone (DMZ) and is internet-facing.
   C. No, because secure connections between high-volume servers can dramatically slow down both servers.
   D. Yes, because your application server is in the DMZ and is internet-facing.

Microsoft Windows Incident Handling and Management

DESPITE THE BEST EFFORTS to secure a computing environment, no organization is completely safe. Sooner or later you will encounter a security policy violation. It may be a minor violation such as a user attempting to log on too many times after forgetting a password. Or it could be a major incident such as an attacker destroying your organization's primary database. Either way, learn how to react. When you discover a security violation, you have only one proper response—to follow your plan.

Map out your response to security violations before any occur. In this chapter, you'll find out how to plan for the inevitable actions that result in security violations. You'll learn how to recognize violations and how to develop a plan for handling each one. You'll study up on the Microsoft tools available to collect information and manage a response process. Some violations are more severe and may result in law enforcement involvement or litigation. In this chapter, you will also learn the right ways to collect and protect evidence that is admissible in court.

Chapter 13 Topics

This chapter covers the following topics and concepts:

- How to handle security incidents involving Microsoft Windows operating system (OS) and applications
- How to formulate an incident response plan
- How to handle incident response
- What incident handling and management tools are available for Microsoft Windows and applications
- How to investigate Microsoft Windows and applications incidents
- How to acquire and manage incident evidence
- What the best practices are for handling Microsoft Windows OS and applications incidents and investigations

Chapter 13 Goals

When you complete this chapter, you will be able to:

- Describe Microsoft Windows OS security incidents
- Use available tools to handle and manage security incidents
- Investigate incidents, including acquiring and managing evidence

Understanding and Handling Security Incidents Involving Microsoft Windows OS and Applications

A security policy is a description of how an organization defines a secure computing environment. It is a collection of rules and guidelines that define appropriate and inappropriate behavior. Once an organization deploys controls to govern behavior, it's helpful to devise a method to measure how effective the controls are. All activity in a computing environment is made up of individual events. An **event** is any observable occurrence within a computer or network. An event could be a user logging on, an application server connecting to a database server, an authentication server rejecting a password, or an antivirus scanner reporting a suspected virus. Any event that results in a violation of your security policy, or poses an imminent threat to your security policy, is an **incident**.

The first step in responding to an incident is to recognize that an incident has occurred. Many incidents go unnoticed because no one is looking for them. It's common to review OS and application software log files after a major incident, such as data loss or a system failure. In some cases, there is evidence of smaller incidents leading up to the big event. Many organizations lack the procedures to identify incidents early. Like any persistent problem, identifying incidents in a timely fashion can help contain any damage and prevent further damage.

The adage, "An ounce of prevention is worth a pound of cure," applies to incidents. The best way to avoid handling incidents is to prevent them. Securing computers and network devices is better than dealing with security incidents. The only exception is when the cost of the controls is more than the loss you would incur if an incident did happen. Microsoft has a lot to say about handling incidents for Windows environments and recommends pursuing prevention first. According to Microsoft's recommendations, these strategies can help any organization minimize the number and impact of security incidents:

- Develop, maintain, and enforce a clear security policy that management supports and promotes. A security policy defines incidents and behaviors that lead to incidents.
- Conduct routine vulnerability assessments to discover vulnerabilities that could lead to incidents.
- Ensure all computers and network devices have the latest available patches installed.
- Train all computer system users on acceptable and unacceptable behavior. Establish frequent and visible security awareness reminders. Use both physical and virtual methods to notify and remind users.
- Enforce strong passwords throughout your environment.

- Frequently monitor network traffic, system performance, and all available log files to identify any incidents or unusual events. The first logs you'd likely analyze would be logs from your intrusion detection system or intrusion prevention system.
- Ensure you have a solid business continuity plan (BCP) and disaster recovery plan (DRP) that you test at least annually. A serious incident will likely require that you enact one or both of these plans.
- Create a **computer security incident response team (CSIRT)**. The CSIRT is a team organized to respond to incidents.

All of the suggestions in the previous list are really just elements of good security. These are things you should be doing already to maintain a secure environment. The last suggestion, create a CSIRT, is specific to handling incidents. This is the team of people who will respond to any incidents. There are six separate steps to handling incidents. Understanding and following all six steps will help your CSIRT with incident handling and help to avoid an expanding incident. **TABLE 13-1** lists the six steps for handling incidents.

TABLE 13-1 Six Steps to Handling Incidents

STEP	DESCRIPTION
Preparation	In this step, you create and train the CSIRT; develop plans for handling incidents; assign roles and responsibilities; and assemble any supplies, hardware, and software you'll need. In short, most of your time is spent in this step, so you'll be ready to respond when an incident occurs. The CSIRT can prepare by running tests and drills.
Identification	This step is usually post activation of a CSIRT and when the team members start handling an incident. When you suspect that an incident has occurred, validate it, then identify the type and, if possible, the source. You may respond differently to a website defacement than to a compromised database encryption key.
Containment	Once you have identified the type of incident, the next step is to contain the damage the incident has caused or is causing. Incidents often are not single events but processes that can continue to cause damage. It is important to take action to limit the amount of damage to as small a scope as possible. This may require removing an affected computer from your network or other actions to keep the damage from spreading. Note that taking action may also mean not doing anything. In some instances, you may need to monitor an APT and not alert the intruder you are aware of an issue. At some point, the team will need to contain as required.
Eradication	Once the damage is contained, remove the vulnerability that allowed the incident to occur. This may involve configuration changes, software updates, or physical modifications. Eradicating an incident includes deploying any new or modified controls to ensure the incident does not happen again.
Recovery	The recovery step includes the actions necessary to return any affected systems to an operational state. Recovery actions will likely be driven by your BCP and DRP.
Lessons learned	One of the characteristics of a good team in any endeavor is that they continually learn and improve. The step that will improve long-term security is to document the lessons learned. The team should review their performance in handling the incident and make any changes necessary to the response plan to make the next response even better.

> **Technical TIP**
>
> Remember that when conducting incident handling responses, a CSIRT must understand legal aspects as well so that chain of custody is maintained. For example, when containing an incident and gathering evidence, very specific processes need to be followed so that evidence may be entered into a court of law and not be discarded for improper handling.

The most important aspect of properly handling incidents is preparing to do it right. Once you understand what it takes to respond well to security incidents and have your CSIRT in place, you are ready to begin developing your response plan.

Real-Life Incidents

Security incidents can be disruptive to any organization. They end up costing a lot of money and time. The following are three examples of historical incidents that caused substantial damage to different organizations. Learn from these incidents. Take every opportunity to avoid being the next example:

- Marriott Starwood hotels had 500 million guest information records, including passport numbers and some payment card details, stolen between 2014 and September 2018— https://www.vox.com/the-goods/2018/11/30/18119770/marriott-hotels -starwood-hack.
- T-Mobile had an insecure application programming interface (API) that allowed hackers to extract two million customers' account data, including billing information, in August 2018—https://www.pcworld.com/article/3300160/security/t-mobile-data -hack-faq.html.
- Quora suffered a breach in 2018 that resulted in 100 million user names, passwords, and other personal information to be leaked—https://www.pcworld.com/article/3325199/ symantec /quora-data-breach-faq-100-million-hacked-users.html.

If you doubt the impact one security incident can have on an organization, visit the websites above and look at the stock prices for each organization after each incident. To help understand that this is a chronic issue that will only continue to take place and become even more difficult to stop, let's look at newer large-scale attacks. The two most recent wide scale incidents that have taken place are on Uber and Roblox. Uber is well known for the "taxi-like" service model allowing riders to call up and use pick up and drop off car services accounting for millions of customers. Roblox is a large-scale gaming site with a large grouping of players (many of whom are kids) online. Both represent very different group characteristics; however, what they both have in common is that they are considered "services" and collect and contain your private and sensitive information. If their databases are breached, it could spell disaster for customers worldwide.

- In July 2022, three prominent gaming sites—Roblox, Neopets, and Bandai Namco—were hit by data breaches within 3 weeks of each other. Roblox had a large number of player data stolen, exposing up to 69 million players. A breach took place where an attacker was able to gain unauthorized access to internal systems. https://www.cshub.com/attacks /articles/data-breaches-on-gaming-sites-are-becoming-more-common.

- Uber's October 2022 security compromise was the second largest compromise in the company's history and was conducted by an 18 year old with breached credentials, MFA fatigue, and social engineering. The attacker gained internal network access to a Slack server. https://www.bleepingcomputer.com/news/security/what-the-uber-hack-can-teach-us -about-navigating-it-security/.

> **Technical TIP**
>
> Responding to incidents goes far beyond the scope of Microsoft computers. You can find more information about handling computer security incidents at https://nvlpubs.nist.gov/nistpubs/ specialpublications/nist.sp.800-61r2.pdf. This resource provides good discussion of the standard incident response process. Find more information on Microsoft's recommendations for handling incidents on the Microsoft website. You can find Microsoft articles and blog posts at https://learn .microsoft.com/en-us/compliance/assurance/assurance-incident-management. You can find a good overview discussion of Microsoft's approach to responding to incidents at https://learn.microsoft.com /en-us/security/compass/incident-response-process.

13

Microsoft Windows Incident
Handling and Management

Formulating an Incident Response Plan

The only way to respond to incidents in a predictable manner is to follow a well-documented and well-tested plan. Your strategy for responding to incidents should be one that applies to many different types of incidents. Continually improve this plan. A solid incident response plan (IRP) standardizes the CSIRT's actions and makes each incident response predictable and repeatable.

Formulate Checklists

One of the best ways to formulate an IRP is by building comprehensive checklists. Checklists are good for helping prepare as well as conduct a response in an organized fashion. What is the benefit of a good checklist? Trying to respond to incidents without a plan is like piloting an airplane without any checklists. Even pilots of small aircraft use several checklists for each flight. Just a few used by pilots of small aircraft include preflight, engine start, post-engine start, taxi, run-up, pre-takeoff, and post-takeoff.

Those are the checklists just to get into the air! Since most aircraft incidents and accidents are caused by poor planning, it makes sense to plan well. Checklists are important to pilots because it is easier to follow a well-documented checklist when things are hectic than it is to remember every important detail. Pilots also carry checklists for emergencies, such as an engine out or fire in the cockpit. At those times, they won't want to try to figure out what to do. Those are the times to react efficiently and calmly. As we look at a security incident and trying to prepare checklists for an emergency response, consider Microsoft's online checklists as a great starting point for building your own! On Microsoft's main site, you can use prebuilt checklists to help your Security Operations Center (SOC) respond to cybersecurity incidents. Go to https://learn.microsoft.com/en-us/security/compass /incident-response-planning. One of the first items you will see on this checklist is to conduct a tabletop exercise (which is a precursor to a drill) which helps to build muscle memory to responding to incidents. This is a great preparation and training tool that will allow you to build readiness into your plans.

Plan for Anything That Could Cause Loss or Damage

The first step in properly responding to a security incident is to prepare. By the time an incident occurs, it is too late to get organized. The preparation step includes building the CSIRT and developing a response plan. Preparing also includes assembling any supplies, software, and hardware your team will need to respond to an incident.

Your organization should invest in the resources needed to develop checklists and complete plans to address the results of each likely incident. It will require substantial effort to plan for every likely incident, but focusing on those that could cause loss or damage will be worthwhile. Many CSIRTs discover existing vulnerabilities while developing response plans. You may find problems you can address just by planning for incidents. The greatest reason for preparing for incident response is that your team can decide on the best course of action for each incident when there is time to really think through the alternatives. You probably won't have much time to consider alternatives during an incident. A plan increases the possibility your team can contain the damage and prevent further problems.

When developing your plan, consider every type of incident that can cause unacceptable damage. One way to develop a complete incident response plan is to think of as many potential incidents as possible and rank them by probability of occurrence and severity of impact if that incident does occur. You can use known incidents that have taken place in the past as a good baseline to start from. You should develop a comprehensive incident response plan only after developing a risk management plan. The risk management process includes a risk analysis phase, which provides the list of identified risks, ranked by probability of

---

Technical TIP

To develop a good balance between being overly prepared and underprepared is difficult. You cannot plan for every known issue that could take place. An attempt to plan for every incident will be met with futility because every day there is a new cybersecurity development, threat, change to an environment, and bug-causing exploit creating vulnerabilities in your environment. The best way to build a CSIRT, be as ready as possible, and be successful at handling any incident that takes place is to have good detection methods in place so that you can "assess" issues as they present themselves. Having a good team who is training on how to analyze these assessments and respond to them as needed is better than training for every known issue because a team trained to analyze and assess will be able to handle older known issues but also new unknown issues in the same way and both successfully. Train your team to analyze and assess. Train them to follow well-documented procedures, but if an incident definition is presented that doesn't map to a very specific plan, the team lead can help to determine how to address the incident as its occurring in real time.

occurrence and severity. The process of developing a risk management plan better prepares any organization to handle risks that are realized, including computer security incidents. The most important incidents are those that are most likely to occur and would have the greatest impact on your organization. Those are the incidents to prioritize if your budget doesn't allow developing a plan for all possible and identified incidents.

Build the CSIRT

The first step is to identify and assemble the CSIRT members. A good plan includes input from all team members. Have your initial team in place before you begin developing the plan. The CSIRT is the group that mobilizes to respond when incidents occur. The team should contain all of the members who will authorize, conduct, and communicate every incident response activity. A good way to ensure you have the right team members is to define the roles your CSIRT must fulfill. **TABLE 13-2** lists the CSIRT roles.

The first team members to assign to your CSIRT are the management representative and the CSIRT leader. These assignments originate with the team's sponsor. The sponsor is a member of your organization's management who has the authority to create and fund a CSIRT. The management representative can be the team's sponsor or another member of management. Once the team has management support and a lead, you can start to fill the other roles on the team.

After the initial team is in place, begin planning. Depending on the team's existing knowledge of security incident response, you may need to provide some training on the subject. The idea is to give team members enough of a foundation in incident response that they are prepared to develop your initial plan.

Plan for Communication

Before you start to develop checklists for each specific type of incident, take the time to plan the framework. Your CSIRT should handle all incidents in the same way. The severity of incidents will change some of the team's responses. However, the overall manner in which the team responds should be consistent across incidents. You achieve consistent behavior by developing a response framework. One crucial part of your response framework is your plan for communication. A simple plan for communicating CSIRT actions can reduce overall tension during an incident and may contribute to a successful incident resolution.

Your plan for CSIRT communication should include sections for each of the following topics:

- **Contacts and hierarchy**—Include a list of every internal and external stakeholder in your information system environment. Identify areas of interest for each one. This list should also include media contacts. Store this information in a database or spreadsheet to make it easy to query and sort. Storing areas of interest can cut down on the number of people in the communication chain when efficient communication is important. For example, assume the CSIRT is responding to a Microsoft update that causes remote client computers to crash. Remote users are very interested in this incident, but database administrators are not as interested. On the other hand, an incident resulting from corrupted data in the central application database would be of interest to database administrators and remote users. Also include in this section any hierarchy of indirect communication if you use multiple points of contact to distribute information.

TABLE 13-2 CSIRT Roles

ROLE	DESCRIPTION
Team lead	Leader of the CSIRT and the primary point of contact for all CSIRT issues.
Incident lead	Member of the CSIRT assigned to lead activities for a specific incident. Medium and large organizations may routinely need to respond to multiple incidents simultaneously.
IT liaison	Point of contact for communicating with the IT department. Even though there will likely be IT department members on the CSIRT, having a single point of contact makes communicating easier. Primary responsibilities include communicating CSIRT activities to IT and keeping everyone aware of how incident response actions might impact IT operations. The IT liaison also helps identify the IT expertise and resources needed to respond to incidents.
Legal representative	Generally an attorney who specializes in law related to security incidents. The legal representative advises the CSIRT on incident-handling methods that minimize the organization's legal liabilities. The legal representative will also communicate with law enforcement as needed and address evidence-handling procedures to maintain admissibility.
Public relations representative	Person responsible for communicating with the media and customers regarding incident-related events. The main goal for this role is to protect the organization's reputation.
Management	Person with ability to authorize team activities. Without solid support from management, the CSIRT will not have the authority or resources to be successful.
Subject matter experts (SMEs)	As the name implies, SMEs are experts in at least one area. For example, your team may need a network security SME, a malware SME, and an application security SME. One person may fill multiple roles. SMEs may be full team members, or you may just consult with them as needed, especially during the planning phases.
Computer forensic specialist	Each incident response team needs someone who is proficient in gathering and preserving digital evidence during the investigation. This is particularly important for any incidents that will be going to court.
Data privacy specialist	In the case of incidents that affect personally identifiable information (PII), it's valuable to have a data privacy specialist who can advise you on notification requirements related to the data breach.

© Jones & Bartlett Learning.

- **Responsibilities**—Descriptions of CSIRT communication responsibilities include press releases, incident notifications, updates, and resolution notification. This section assigns the responsibility for each type of communication to avoid finger pointing.
- **Frequency expectations**—This section states the expected frequency of communication based on incident severity and type. Critical incidents require updates at least every 15–30 minutes while minor incidents may only warrant daily updates. The incident's severity in the initial notification lets stakeholders know when to expect an update. Consider your audience as well when determining update frequency. You'll likely keep management more up to date than the press.
- **Methods**—This section informs stakeholders of how the CSIRT will communicate with them. Avoid frustration by ensuring everyone knows where to find messages that relate to incidents. Options include email, website status pages, social media methods, and physical signs or banners. This section also includes plans for secondary communications in the case of severe incidents. A fully prepared CSIRT would likely have radios to communicate when all other methods fail.

Technical TIP

Exabeam publishes a good overview of incident response planning. You can find the overview, along with templates and examples at https://www.exabeam.com/incident-response/incident-response-plan/.

Technical TIP

Be creative and responsive when communicating CSIRT activities. Most important, know your audience. If your organization is largely made up of tech-savvy employees, you may find that sending tweets is a very effective strategy to release status updates that don't contain any confidential or sensitive content.

Plan Security

When an incident occurs, the CSIRT responds to it in the manner prescribed in the incident response plan. In other words, the team follows the plan. Make sure your team has access to the plan. Ensure the team can retrieve the most current version of the plan regardless of the circumstances. Have multiple copies available in different formats stored in different locations. An incident that corrupts the document management system could make life difficult for your CSIRT if the response plan is stored in the corrupt system. Part of your plan should ensure that the plan is available when needed.

A comprehensive plan will likely contain proprietary information. This information should only be available to authorized users. Likewise, only authorized users should be able to make changes to the plan. Unauthorized changes to the response plan could result in incorrect steps, making an incident worse. The best way to guarantee your response plan is available, confidential, and trustworthy is to consider the plan private and essential data. Then, pursue controls to ensure the confidentiality, integrity, and availability (C-I-A) properties of data security that you've learned about.

Revision Procedures

Regardless of the effort invested to create your initial plan, you'll encounter situations that require changes to it. You may have left some incidents or procedures out of the initial plan. You may also have discovered better methods for handling incidents. In any case, include a formal procedure to change the plan. In general, the whole team or an appointed group of team members should review any changes. They should then either approve or deny them. As long as you review all change requests and fully document any changes approved for the plan, you can continually make your plan better.

Also include formal periodic reviews in the plan. The entire team should review the response strategy at least annually. This periodic checkup ensures changes to the plan or changes to your environment haven't weakened the team's ability to respond to an incident.

Plan Testing

The final step in the recurring cycle of incident response planning is to test the plan. Regardless of how good your plan looks on paper, you won't know how well it works until you try it out. This is why tabletops and drills are important to your preparation!

Simulated incidents test the plan and train your team. These simulations can be informal walk-throughs where team members talk through plan steps or more realistic simulations where the team responds with realistic actions. The more realistic simulations better train team members and reveal any plan weaknesses. Test your response as often as you can to ensure you're ready when a real incident occurs.

In addition to testing your plan, it's important to plan for investing in training for your security staff. It's good to have good processes and security tools, but your staff need to be trained on how to effectively use these tools to perform a security investigation and resolve the incident effectively. You should work with upper management to determine a budget and plan out training for your staff throughout the year.

Handling Incident Response

You learned earlier in this chapter that there are six steps to responding to a security incident. These steps are not purely linear and can be iterative. You may repeat some steps several times while responding to incidents. Each step is important because it isolates a specific area of concentration that you must address to respond well to any incident.

For simple incidents, several steps may be combined or are trivial. Regardless of an incident's simplicity, however, each step is important. A solid incident response plan ensures a CSIRT will address each step for all types of incidents.

Preparation

The first step in a proper incident response is to prepare for the incident. In other words, get ready for incidents before they occur. Taking the time to prepare to respond to an incident after it occurs likely will worsen the incident's effects. Being prepared greatly increases the probability that you can respond to an incident in a positive, professional manner. If you have a comprehensive response plan, a complete and trained CSIRT, and all of the supplies the team will need, you should be ready to handle incidents.

Identification

The main purpose of the identification step is to decide the next course of action. The first question is whether an incident has occurred at all. Many incidents go unnoticed while other events that are harmless are reported as incidents. Identifying incidents starts with a complete definition of what an incident is. In your plan, include procedures to identify incidents your security policy defines. Some events such as defacing a website are obvious incidents for any organization. Other events such as an attempt to use an incorrect password five times may or may not be an incident. Each organization's security policy should contain enough details to decide whether any event is an incident.

Once you decide to implement a formal incident response plan, create a method to report suspected incidents and publicize the proper reporting steps. You could publish an incident reporting form on an intranet page, use an emailed form, or hard-copy forms. In some organizations, the help desk is the primary point of contact for incidents. Help desk personnel would likely be the ones to determine whether to refer an event to the CSIRT. When this is the case, the CSIRT should have a help desk representative as a member. The procedure you decide to use should be standard for your organization and should contain enough information to determine the next step. **FIGURE 13-1** shows a sample incident reporting form.

General Information

Name: _____   Date & Time detected: _____
Title: _____   Location: _____
Phone: _____   Email: _____

Type of Incident

__ Unauthorized access   Failed access attempt   __ Scan
__ Unauthorized use (AUP)   __ Malware   __ denial of service (DoS)
__ Hardware/Software failure __ Infrastructure failure   __ Other: _____

Details

How did you detect the incident?_____
_____
_____

Additional information:
_____
_____
_____

FIGURE 13-1

Sample incident reporting form.

© Jones & Bartlett Learning.

NOTE

Your end-user security training should encourage users to report any activity that could be an incident. For example, you want to know about social engineering attacks that do not succeed as well as those that do. Keeping data on all attack attempts helps identify trends and attack patterns.

Once you have an incident reporting form available for your users, train the person who might report a violation on the proper reporting procedures. The initial part of incident reporting training is to help users identify, analyze, and assess potential incidents. First, teach users how to find out if any scheduled maintenance (change management) or known issues are causing the events. If no known issues are present, users should report a potential incident if any of the following events occur:

- A password has been changed without taking any action.
- They are asked for their password or other private information by someone who does not have a need to know. This includes requests that users change their password to one an outside party supplies.
- They notice email responses to messages they did not send, messages in their Sent Messages mailbox they didn't send, or an increase in spam.
- Their web browser home page changes, or they can't close pop-up ads.
- They notice changes in the way their desktop appears when they log on.
- They can't connect to servers or webpages they need to complete tasks.
- Noticeable increases in disk activity, network activity, or wait time to complete any task occur.
- New files or folders appear that they haven't seen before.
- Files on their system are being encrypted without them doing so.

Once users suspect that an incident has occurred, they should save their work, leave all applications open, and notify the CSIRT using the published notification procedure. Users should leave the computer in its current state rather than shut it down or reboot. However, it's a good practice to disconnect the machine from Wi-Fi or unplug the network cable. This prevents the potential malware from spreading, receiving new instructions from a command and control server, or performing data exfiltration while still preserving all of the digital evidence. The CSIRT will likely want to see what the computer is doing before making any changes to its configuration.

Once the CSIRT receives the suspected incident report, it is assigned to a team member. That team member becomes the incident lead. The incident lead reviews the information and begins an investigation. The first step is to determine whether the report contains information about an incident or some other event. This is where you will rely on the technical expertise of your team members. If the incident lead validates the incident, the next activity is to determine the incident's attributes. Three main attributes of an incident direct subsequent action:

- **Classification**—What type of incident is this? An incident's classification tells the CSIRT what actions to take. **TABLE 13-3** lists common suggested incident classifications.
- **Scope**—How many computers or users does this incident affect, and how long has the issue existed? Knowing the incident scope helps the CSIRT determine if it needs more resources and how to handle communication. The most important activity for this is to identify patient zero, which is the first machine that was infected. Once you have

TABLE 13-3 Incident Classifications

CLASSIFICATION	DESCRIPTION
Unauthorized access of a privileged account	An unauthorized user has gained access to a privileged account, either by an unauthorized logon or a privilege escalation.
Unauthorized access of a limited account	An unauthorized user has gained access to a limited account, either by an unauthorized logon or a privilege escalation.
Failed attempt to access any account	An attempt to log on or change user accounts has failed.
Unauthorized scan of one or more systems, or even users, as in social engineering queries	A port scan has targeted one or more computers or devices to collect information about the computers or devices. In the case of social engineering attacks, calling multiple users with the same request could be a process to identify potential victims.
AUP violation	A user action violates AUPs, including both accidental and malicious actions.
DoS attack	An attack has resulted in a reduction or total DoS.
Malware infection	Malware infection has occurred.
Hardware or software failure	A computer, device, or software error or failure not related to malicious activity has occurred.
Infrastructure failure	Any failure of supporting services and utilities, including power; heating, ventilation, and air conditioning (HVAC); and communications, has occurred.

© Jones & Bartlett Learning.

identified patient zero, then you can track the spread of compromise across your network to identify all infected/compromised machines.

- **Severity**—How bad is this incident? Setting the severity level helps the CSIRT and management allocate resources efficiently. More severe incidents get higher priority, and more resources as needed. **TABLE 13-4** lists suggested incident severity levels.

Applicable IOCs—IOC stands for indicator of compromise; once you have determined that you have an incident it's important to use threat intelligence and other methods to identify any applicable IOCs. This will be very valuable for identifying infected machines and updating your security controls to block/remove malware.

This step may also include notifying other parties, including law enforcement, of certain types of incidents. If your investigation produces evidence of illegal material, such as copyrighted material or child pornography, the law requires you to report it to the proper authorities. In such situations, the CSIRT legal representative will provide the direction for the proper course of action. You can find a great reporting tool for reporting such issues at https://us-cert.cisa.gov/forms/report.

TABLE 13-4 Incident Severity Levels

SEVERITY	DESCRIPTION	RESPONSE EFFORT
Severe	Potential long-term negative effects on an organization's reputation or the ability to conduct critical operations. One or more critical systems have been compromised. An example would be discovering that an intruder extracted a large number of credit card numbers from your customer database.	Invoke the DRP.
High	Compromise of one or more noncritical systems or a verified threat of an imminent attack, such as the theft of a laptop that contained only sales presentation information.	Expend substantial effort for an extended period of time.
Moderate	Verified threat of a future security incident, such as identifying infection of malware that triggers on a certain date and time.	Expend a moderate amount of effort for a limited amount of time.
Low	Indication of a potential future security incident, such as a port scan or multiple telephone calls from a person asking users to disclose information.	Expend minimal effort.

© Jones & Bartlett Learning.

 NOTE

Effective April, 2017, the U.S. Computer Emergency Readiness Team (US-CERT) put into place requirements for federal agencies to submit incident notifications to the National Cybersecurity and Communication Integration Center (NCCIC). See the US-CERT Federal Incident Notification Guidelines website for more information: https://www.cisa.gov/uscert/incident-notification-guidelines. While this document covers requirements for federal agencies, nonfederal organizations may fall under other regulations that require incident reporting, including U.S. Securities and Exchange Commission (SEC) requirements, Health Insurance Portability and Accountability Act (HIPAA), or General Data Protection Regulation (GDPR).

Containment

The classification, scope, and severity attributes of an incident direct the containment activities. The main purpose of containment is to keep the incident's scope from expanding. The specific steps you follow to contain an incident vary from one incident to another. The SMEs who participated in developing your incident response plan would have provided the technical details to contain each type of incident.

Steps you take to contain the damage an incident causes depend on several factors. Once you understand the current incident's nature, the steps necessary to contain the incident should become clear. However, the steps will only be clear if your response plan includes steps to deal with the current incident. There is no substitute for having a comprehensive incident response plan that includes input from SMEs in several areas. The SMEs you use to help develop your incident response plan or carry out investigations don't have to be CSIRT members. The CSIRT has the flexibility to use the best available resources for each investigation. The steps you take to contain incident damage may include some of the following actions:

- Disable networking services.
- Physically detach the computer or device from the network and disable wireless adapters.
- Logically separate the affected computers or devices into a separate subnet. Ensure the subnet cannot communicate with another subnet by conducting air-gapping.
- Turn off the computer or device.
- Terminate one or more programs or services.
- Remove software from the computer or device.
- Restore the computer or device to a previous state.
- Initiate appropriate communications to let interested parties know an incident's status.

> ⚠ **WARNING**
>
> Only trained CSIRT members should conduct containment tasks to ensure that the threat (incident) is understood prior to taking action. For example, if there is an APT, advanced detection methods, threat hunting, or other processes that need to take place during an incident, terminating, shutting down, or removing things may not be the correct path to take. This will be further explained in threat hunting.

Regardless of the option your SMEs select, the most import consideration in the containment step is to keep the incident damage scope from expanding. Consider any incident to be like an infectious disease. Setting up a quarantine area can help keep the disease from spreading and making healthy people (computers) sick.

Eradication

Containment stops the incident damage from expanding. This allows you to remove the vulnerability that allowed the incident to occur in the first place. The steps you take will depend entirely on the incident's nature and the course of action your SMEs recommend. In general, pursue the least intrusive course of action that will completely remove any vulnerability to prevent further incidents. Note that the eradication step doesn't remove the incident's effects—it just removes the vulnerabilities that allowed the incident.

Depending on the nature of the incident, the eradication step can include any of the following actions:

- Modifying firewall rules to close one or more ports or block Internet Protocol (IP) addresses
- Update your security controls with relevant IOCs
- Installing operating system or application software patches or updated software
- Removing malware
- Providing targeted user training
- Removing or detaching hardware devices or device drivers
- Restricting remote access to deny offending computers
- Replacing or repairing failed hardware
- Changing user login credentials and enabling two-factor authentication
- Firing a disgruntled employee and terminating his or her account access

IT SMEs working with trained security analysts can provide the best course of action to eradicate each type of incident.

Recovery

The final technical step is to return the affected computers or devices to a fully operational state. That means to restore the hardware, OS, software, and data to a state that is usable in your environment and no longer able to create more issues when brought back online or into production. The incident's severity and nature will direct the team's actions during this step. Minor incidents may require no recovery. For example, suppose your web server encountered a series of unauthorized scans from a specific range of IP addresses. During the eradication step, you could add rules to your firewall to block any traffic from the range of IP addresses that initiated the scan. Unless complicating circumstances arise, you wouldn't need to take any further recovery steps. The recovery step is unnecessary in this situation.

While some incidents require no restore activity, others require austere measures. Suppose your incident investigation revealed that a critical server contains a rootkit. Further investigation reveals that the rootkit exists on several recent backups. In most cases, you'll have to rebuild the server from bare metal. From there, you'd identify the usable parts of your backups to extract the latest data possible. Sometimes, restoring a compromised system isn't as easy as just restoring a backup.

Technical TIP

What are complicating circumstances? Suppose the range of IP addresses showed that the unauthorized scans originated from within your largest business partner's network. Blocking those IP addresses would also restrict your ability to conduct business. You'd have to work with your customer's IT department, or hopefully their CSIRT, to find out whether they have a malware infestation or someone who is doing bad things.

Technical TIP

To get more information on current incidents, visit the following websites:

- The Computer Emergency Response Team: http://www.cert.org/
- The Veris Community Database (VCDB): http://veriscommunity.net/vcdb.html
- The Repository of Industrial Security Incidents requires a membership fee: http://www.securityincidents.org/

Lessons Learned

Regardless of the effort required to respond to an incident, formally review the incident and all team actions. Larger incidents should be reviewed by the whole team. Analyze what went well and what didn't work so well. Use the information you uncover after each incident to improve the plan. Review incidents as soon after the actual events as possible. Memory fades and takes valuable insight with it. The lessons learned can keep you from repeating mistakes and help you avoid making new mistakes.

It is also a good idea to learn from other organizations' mistakes and successes as well. Be on the lookout for any stories about security incidents and how organizations handled them. You can learn a lot from how others handle the same issues you encounter.

Advanced Incident Handling Techniques

When conducting a response to an incident (incident response), a CSIRT may conduct incident handling. We just learned a lot about what a typical CSIRT may be trained and prepared to do. Along the way while we discussed these techniques, it was mentioned that there will be cases where you would not follow the plan exactly as prescribed. Most times incident response is just that, "a response" to an incident. Incident handling is just that, "handling of a developing incident." Both are reactive in nature and cause teams to form around something that is or has taken place. If security measures, your security posture, reduced attack surface, known attack vector, and hardened systems can still fall victim to exploit, responding to and handling incidents is after that fact. A method of allowing for "proactive" handling of incidents is called threat hunting.

> **NOTE**
>
> While more and more systems are becoming automated and using AI/ML technology, the system still needs to be tuned to ensure that false positives, true negatives, anomalies, and so on are accounted for to ensure smooth responses. Also, there needs to be a thorough process of updating these system to make sure that they too do not fall to victimization and exploit.

Another method of handling issues is to remove much of the manual nature of the CSIRT and put actions back into technical systems. This can be done with tools like a Security Information and Event Management (SIEM) tool in conjunction with a **Security Orchestration, Automation, and Response (SOAR)** tool. Both provide value in event management but also in the "handling" of the events (or incidents) that are identified in an orchestrated fashion. As we look at the future of tool based automation, we can also look at the future of how artificial intelligence (AI) systems and machine learning (ML) will help play a role in threat detection, identification, classification, response, and handling. While technical automation allows for less manual efforts, there is still a need for the maintaining of said systems and helping to manage them as part of the response effort whether it be proactive or reactive.

Threat Hunting

As we just learned, reactive responses to incidents include incident response and incident handling. What if security teams could proactively respond to an incident? This methodology is called "threat hunting," and many techniques, processes and tools surround this method. Threat hunting should be used with incident response and incident handling and not replace it. Incident response will account for many of the issues that are brought to light reactively. Issues take place, and the CSIRT will respond to it, handle the incident, and follow normal processes. However, incidents will take place that will not be detected but need to be found. This is where the foundations of threat hunting takes place, to help augment the current CSIRT process and strategy. For example, most APTs are dormant. They are activated and running in your network and unknown. When your team conduct threat hunting, they seek out these incidents proactively to identify them.

The tools used for threat hunting include an organizations SIEM; however, teams hunt by using other tools, applications like endpoint detection and response (EDR), system logs, firewall logs, and much more. Threat hunters can mine data, run complex queries on data, and search for anomalies. Different type of hunts can take place, either structured or unstructured. Structured hunts are based on attack indicators. By using a system like the MITRE Adversary Tactics Techniques and Common Knowledge (ATT&CK) framework, a hunter can find indicator of attack (IoA) as well as TTPs. Tactics, techniques, and procedures (TTPs) used in conjunction with IoA's allow a framework to map together issues that should be considered and proactively eradicate them. Go to MITRE to learn about the framework at https://attack.mitre.org. Unstructured hunts can be set forth by a trigger. A trigger can be an indicator of compromise (IoC) and can help guide where to look, how to address potential issues or incidents, and what steps to take next.

Threat hunting when it comes to Microsoft systems is handled by tools and techniques similar to the ones just discussed but with minor differences. First, at Microsoft the team responsible for handling threat hunting is named DART, or Microsoft Detection and Response Team. DART's mission is to help customers in responding to security incidents. Proactive and reactive investigative services from DART include threat hunting functionality. Microsoft calls it looking beyond the known for the unknown so that it can help find signs of advanced implants and anomalous behavior and provide a recovery process post incident: https://www.microsoft.com/en-us/security/blog/2022/09/08/part-1-the-art-and-science-of-threat-hunting/. To review Microsoft's most current blog entries on DART, incident handling and threat hunting, visit https://www.microsoft.com/en-us/security/blog/microsoft-detection-and-response-team-dart-blog-series/.

To use current Microsoft tools to proactively seek out and conduct structured or unstructured hunts, you can use Microsoft Defender and, in the cloud, Microsoft Sentinel. You can proactively hunt for threats with advanced hunting in Microsoft 365 Defender by visiting https://learn.microsoft.com/en-us/microsoft-365/security/defender/advanced-hunting-overview?view=o365-worldwide. This article can show you how to use a tool like Defender to proactively seek out possible issues that are not event triggered or detected. You can look at any tool's logs to help to parse, query, and find anomalies, so following threat hunting basic logic, start to look for things that seem out of place and research them to see what could be taking place outside of what known issues exist. Things to consider can be memory resident apps that seem to take up a lot of memory over what they normally would use, for example a svchost.exe that seems out of place and anomalous. Another example can be parsing audit logs for entries that are legitimate but seem to take place out of known patterns, like an administrator logging in in the middle of the night every Friday and mapping that to an exfiltration of data that doesn't seem to make sense. Hunting threats helps to proactively identify problems with not just Microsoft systems, but all systems in your organization.

Automated Incident Handling

As mentioned, you should not remove or replace your CSIRT or not have an incident response or incident handling plan in place in lieu of using automation. You should not remove any part of your plan. When you implement tools like a SIEM and SOAR, you simply add to your security posture by creating more functionality around a response effort.

Automating incident response and incident handling procedures can help to speed up the reaction to issues or speed up the delivery of the response.

Another method of handling issues is to remove much of the manual nature of the CSIRT and put actions back into technical systems. This can be done with tools like a SIEM tool in conjunction with a SOAR tool. Both provide value in event management but also in the "handling" of the events (or incidents) that are identified in an orchestrated fashion.

SOAR allows you to automate and orchestrate responses to security incidents, incident response, and incidents handling. It does this by using your SIEM and other toolsets like User and Entity Behavior Analytics (UEBA) to create playbooks for a response. This is what is meant by the orchestration of a response based on predefined actions mapped out in playbooks.

Threat modeling and threat detection are also very important parts of incident identification and response. This too can be automated; however, there are concerns around a fully automated system, especially a self-learning (AI/ML) one that also conducts an automated response. Until systems are more mature, fully automated systems can be compromised themselves or miss issues entirely. Learn more at www.infosecurity-magazine .com/opinions/ai-automated-response-dangerous/.

Incident Handling and Management Tools for Microsoft Windows and Applications

Managing incidents using the techniques you have learned in this chapter requires you to collect and deal with a substantial amount of information. Improve your team's performance and make the entire process smoother by identifying and acquiring the right tools to help run the process. Two basic types of tools can aid in your work. The first type helps manage the CSIRT's activities and gather information about the incident response process. The second type collects information about the incident itself. You'll learn about several tools of both types in this section.

> **Technical TIP**
>
> The European Network and Information Security Agency (ENISA) website has a document dedicated to incident-handling management. This document is a great reference for researching many of the tools available to support your CSIRT. You can find the ENISA document at https://www.enisa.europa.eu /topics/trainings-for-cybersecurity-specialists/online-training-material/documents/2016-resources /incident_handling_management-toolset.

CSIRT process management tools help team members collect and organize information about managing incidents. These tools assist the CSIRT with the normal, day-to-day responsibilities of managing the information flow and status of current and historical incidents. These CSIRT responsibilities include the following:

- Tracking incidents
- Reporting on incidents
- Archiving incident reports
- Communicating incident information

TABLE 13-5 Incident Process Management Tools

PRODUCT	WEBSITE
D3 SOAR	http://www.d3security.com/
Microsoft Sentinel	https://learn.microsoft.com/en-us/azure/sentinel/automation
Palo Alto Cortex XSOAR	https://www.paloaltonetworks.com/cortex/cortex-xsoar
Sumo Logic Cloud SOAR	https://www.sumologic.com/solutions/cloud-soar/
PagerDuty	https://www.pagerduty.com/
Rsam Incident Management	http://www.rsam.com/
xMatters	https://www.xmatters.com/
OpsGenie	https://www.opsgenie.com/
IBM Security QRadar	https://www.ibm.com/products/qradar-soar

© Jones & Bartlett Learning.

You can find a growing number of software packages specifically designed to help CSIRTs manage the process of incident response. In the past, most of the process of handling incidents was manual. New software tools are emerging that attempt to automate some of the tasks required to respond to incidents. As already covered, these tools are collectively called SOAR tools. They help CSIRT teams coordinate information from multiple sources, automate initial Incident Response (IR) tasks, and organize the steps to effectively respond to incidents. **TABLE 13-5** lists some incident process management tools.

Investigating Microsoft Windows and Applications Incidents

The second type of tool helps CSIRT members collect technical information to support incident investigation and resolution. These tools enable forensic investigators to collect evidence of incident activity to discover what happened, why it happened, how to stop it from happening again, and whether any legal action can be taken against the incident source. These toolsets often provide the ability to discover traces of past activity in memory, stored on disks, or in log files. CSIRT members who are trained to use investigation software can be valuable resources for your team. In many cases, the difference between a successful incident resolution and an unknown loss is the quality of the incident investigation.

Explore the various tools and any training that is available for them. Select the set that fits your CSIRT activities. **TABLE 13-6** lists some incident data collection and management tools.

 NOTE

In addition to the tools listed in Table 13-5, many project management software products contain the basic tools to help manage incident response activities. View each incident as a project, and manage it using industry standard project management standards. To learn more about managing projects, go to the Project Management Institute: http://www.pmi.org.

TABLE 13-6 Incident Data Collection and Management Tools	
PRODUCT	**WEBSITE**
SANS Investigative Forensic Toolkit (SIFT)	https://www.sans.org/tools/sift-workstation/
PlainSight Open Source Computer Forensics	http://www.plainsight.info/
The Sleuth Kit	http://www.sleuthkit.org/
F-Response	http://www.f-response.com/
EnCase Enterprise Platform	http://www.guidancesoftware.com/

© Jones & Bartlett Learning.

The tools you choose will help find evidence of incident activity. The information will only be useful if it supports your investigation's goals. Arbitrarily searching for evidence will likely result in collecting too much data and possibly missing evidence you will need. Before beginning any investigation activities, review your CSIRT's goals for an investigation. Although each organization should develop its own specific goals to direct activities, most incident investigations strive to answer the following questions:

- **What happened?**—Gather as much information about the incident as possible.
- **Who did it?**—Discover as much information as possible about the source of the attack.
- **When did it happen?**—Collect information on when the incident started and when it stopped.
- **Where did the incident originate and where was its target?**—Discover the source's location and the target of the attack.
- **Why did the attacker attack this system?**—Discover the attack's purpose and goal.
- **How did it happen?**—Attempt to understand how the attacker compromised your security controls and accessed your system.

Incident response tools make investigation activities easier, but they cannot take the place of clear goals. Your incident response plan directs all of the activities involved in an investigation, and your investigative tools provide the capability to satisfy your investigation's goals.

Acquiring and Managing Incident Evidence

One of an investigation's goals is to discover evidence that answers the who, what, when, where, why, and how questions you learned about in the previous section. The evidence you collect will further the discovery of facts. The same evidence could provide the proof necessary to result in a legal finding in your favor.

Treat every investigation as if it will end up in court. When you begin a new investigation, you don't know how it will be resolved. Any investigation can end up as an internal matter.

Alternatively, it could end up in civil or criminal court. Ensure that any evidence you collect will be useful in court if that's where you end up.

Your investigation should produce evidence of an incident and possibly support action against an attacker. The evidence you will collect consists of files and their contents left behind after an incident. The existence of some files, such as pictures or executable files, can provide evidence of an incident. In other cases, the contents of files, such as log files, provide the necessary proof. Recognizing and identifying hardware, software, and data you can use is the first step in the evidence collection process.

Types of Evidence

The two types of evidence you'll collect during an incident investigation are **real evidence** and **documentary evidence**. Real evidence is any physical object that you can bring into court. You can touch, hold, and directly observe real evidence. The real evidence you collect during an incident investigation could include computers and other hardware. If your incident involves criminal activity, real evidence may contain fingerprints that can be used in court.

The more common type of evidence you'll collect is documentary evidence. Documentary evidence is any written evidence, such as printed reports or data in log files. Unlike real evidence, documentary evidence cannot stand on its own. Documentary evidence must be authenticated. Much of the evidence you are likely to use in proving a case will be in files, such as log files, database files, and incident-specific files and reports, that provide information indicating what occurred. Because anyone can create a data file or report with desired contents, you must prove that the evidence was collected appropriately and the data it contains prove a fact.

> **⚠ WARNING**
>
> Anytime you introduce documentary evidence, introduce the original document, not a copy. This rule is called the best evidence rule. The purpose of this rule is to protect evidence from being modified inappropriately. If the original document is required, there is less opportunity for a modification to occur during a copy operation. When you testify, you'll have to convince the judge and jury that what you bring into court is the original document.

The majority of activities during your investigation will involve using utilities and tools to explore the contents of the computer and storage media. All files and file contents that support your case will be considered documentary evidence. This is where you'll find most of the evidence for your investigation.

Chain of Custody

All evidence you present in court must exist in the same condition as it did when you collected it. Each device, computer, and operating system has specific procedures for preserving data. Evidence cannot change at all once you collect it; it must be in pristine condition. The court will require you to prove that the evidence did not change during the investigation. You'll have to provide your own proof that all collected evidence exists without changes as it did when your team collected it. The documentation that supplies details of every move and access of evidence is called the **chain of custody**. The chain starts when you collect any piece of evidence. **FIGURE 13-2** shows a sample chain of custody log.

FIGURE 13-2

Sample chain of custody log.

LINE	ITEM	DATE	TIME	WHO	DESCRIPTION
1	Hard disk drive, ser # AB3655798	5/15/10	10:15 AM EDT	M. Solomon	Seized hard drive from ABC Mfg owned computer # 11753 (K. Rudolph)
2	Hard disk drive, ser # AB3655798	5/15/10	10:45 AM EDT	M. Solomon	Transported HDD to evidence locker in main office
3	Hard disk drive, ser # AB3655798	5/16/10	7:30 AM EDT	M. Solomon	Removed HDD to create analysis copy
4	Hard disk drive, ser # AB3655798	5/16/10	9:15 AM EDT	M. Solomon	Returned HDD to evidence locker

© Jones & Bartlett Learning.

The chain of custody must be complete and without gaps. You demonstrate this by providing the evidence log that shows every access to evidence, from collection to appearance in court. A complete chain of custody log also includes procedures that describe each step. For example, an entry might read "checked out hard disk drive serial number XN629H to create a primary analysis image." Also include a description of what "creating a primary analysis image" means. The defense will examine the chain of custody documents, looking for any gaps or inconsistencies. Any issue with the chain of custody has the real potential of causing the court to throw out the evidence in question. Once that happens, the evidence you have collected becomes useless, and your credibility will probably be questioned.

Since you don't know if you'll have to present evidence in court, collect all evidence during an incident investigation as if you will take it to court. If you carefully preserve the chain of custody and do not go to court after all, you just have well-documented evidence. This type of information is great for analyzing incidents for the lessons learned step of incident response. If you are sloppy in the way you collect evidence and then end up going to court, your sloppiness will likely result in having your evidence rejected by the court. Without the evidence you need to prove your case, you may not be able to prevail. Always treat each investigation as if it will end up in court.

Evidence Collection Rules

It is important that you know the rules surrounding evidence collection and handling before starting any investigation. Each state and local jurisdiction may impose slightly different rules, so familiarize yourself with local laws and policies. In addition, different rules govern different types of evidence. For example, analyzing a database that contains confidential personal medical information will have more stringent requirements than a database containing a parts inventory. Medical data falls under federal HIPAA regulations. Ask questions before engaging in evidence collection. Making incorrect assumptions when collecting evidence will likely get it thrown out of court.

A good place to start learning about local laws concerning collecting evidence is by developing a relationship with your local law enforcement agents. Call your local agency and ask for the computer forensics unit. Meet with them and take the time to learn how they approach investigations. Often, law enforcement officers will provide guidance and help you comply with their investigative requirements. Learning from them will save both of you substantial time and effort when an event occurs that requires law enforcement involvement.

Spend time with your organization's legal representatives. Start with your CSIRT's legal representative. He or she can provide valuable input that will guide your investigative efforts as well. The goal is to ensure your processes comply with any statutes, regulations, and policies before an investigation starts.

Best Practices for Handling Microsoft Windows OS and Applications Incidents and Investigations

Handling incidents and investigations is an important discipline within security management. If incidents are handled efficiently, the information system environment can benefit from the experience. To handle incidents professionally, it is crucial that the process of responding to incidents and conducting investigations be carefully thought out and planned. The quality of your organization's response to incidents directly relates to the quality of its planning.

Although all organizations have different structures and needs, many goals and general procedures in the incident response process are standard. Organizations have collectively kept the practices that work and discarded the ones that have not. Here is a general list of best practices for handling incidents and investigations:

- Harden OS and software to avoid incidents.
- Assess computers periodically to expose vulnerabilities, potentially including penetration testing.
- Validate BCPs and DRPs.
- Get full management support for a CSIRT.
- Create a CSIRT.
- Conduct a risk assessment to identify potential incidents that require attention first.
- Develop an incident response plan around the six steps to handling incidents.
- Create an incident reporting form and procedures.
- Distribute and publicize the incident reporting form and procedures.
- Test the incident response plan before attackers do.
- Identify and acquire incident management software.
- Identify and acquire incident investigation software.
- Train key CSIRT members on proper evidence collection and handling.

These best practices are the starting point for your incident response plan. Begin with these guidelines and develop a complete plan that works for your organization to conduct effective and efficient incident response activities.

CHAPTER SUMMARY

Handling incidents well helps keep your organization from losing to the attackers. A solid incident response plan is one that continually improves while directing effective efforts. Taking the time to assemble the right CSIRT members and develop a comprehensive incident response plan results in a more secure system. A solid incident response plan allows the CSIRT to follow a prescribed path instead of making up the next step on the fly. Incidents generally result in less damage and are resolved more quickly. The thoughtful process of developing the incident response plan may even highlight existing vulnerabilities that should be addressed before an incident occurs.

Creating a CSIRT and developing a comprehensive incident response plan makes the statement that your organization values security and can even increase your brand value. A functional CSIRT not only makes a statement by its existence but also makes a difference by ensuring a high quality of security. The CSIRT assures your users and customers that your environment's security is a priority and will be maintained regardless of the prevailing circumstances.

KEY CONCEPTS AND TERMS

Chain of custody	Documentary evidence	Real evidence
Computer security incident response team (CSIRT)	Event	Security Orchestration, Automation Response (SOAR)
	Incident	

CHAPTER 13 ASSESSMENT

1. To ensure a secure computing environment, investigate each reported event.

A. True
B. False

2. Many incidents go unreported because they are never recognized.

A. True
B. False

3. Which of the following is the best description of the CSIRT's initial responsibility for incidents?

A. Recognize incidents.
B. Validate that an incident has occurred.

C. Initiate the incident investigation.
D. Contain the incident damage.

4. The _____ step of handling incidents should always occur before an incident happens.

5. Which incident-handling step might include disconnecting a computer from the network?

A. Identification
B. Eradication
C. Containment
D. Recovery

6. The _____ step to handling incidents is the most important step to continuously improving your incident response plan.

7. IT investigators (SMEs) are all CSIRT team members.

A. True
B. False

8. Which incident classification would apply to a situation where you find that your user account is locked due to too many logon tries using an incorrect password?

A. Unauthorized access of a limited account
B. AUP violation
C. Failed attempt to access any account
D. Unauthorized scan of one or more systems

9. Which incident security level would be appropriate after discovering that several of your workstations are infected with worms that will launch a coordinated DoS attack against your web servers in 12 hours?

A. Severe
B. High
C. Moderate
D. Low

10. Which incident-handling step might include scanning a computer for malware?

A. Identification
B. Containment
C. Eradication
D. Recovery

11. Which incident-handling step might include removing a virus from a computer?

A. Identification
B. Containment
C. Eradication
D. Recovery

12. The contents of log files are which type of evidence?

A. Real evidence
B. Documentary evidence
C. Testimonial evidence
D. Demonstrative evidence

13. The documentation that provides details of every move and access of evidence is called the _____.

14. You should treat every incident as if it might end up in court.

A. True
B. False

15. Any small change to evidence data may render that evidence unusable in your case.

A. True
B. False

Microsoft Windows and the Security Life Cycle

N THIS CHAPTER, you'll learn about securing applications by creating or changing the application code. You'll also study the software development process. You'll learn as well to develop secure applications. And you'll examine the importance of formal testing, validation, and the configuration management process. Finally, you'll be able to apply what you've learned to your own development environments and start making the application software you write more secure from the very start.

Chapter 14 Topics

This chapter covers the following topics and concepts:

- What system life cycle phases are
- What agile software development is
- How to manage Microsoft Windows operating system (OS) and application software security
- How to develop secure Microsoft Windows OS and application software
- How to implement, evaluate, and test Microsoft Windows OS and application software security
- How to maintain the security of Microsoft Windows OS and application software
- What Microsoft Windows OS and application software revision, change management, and end-of-life phaseout are
- What the best practices for Microsoft Windows and application software development security investigations are

Chapter 14 Goals

When you complete this chapter, you will be able to:

- Describe system life cycle phases
- Explain how agile software development differs from traditional software development
- Manage the existing Microsoft OS and application software security
- Implement, evaluate, and test Microsoft OS and application software
- Describe how to manage the process of secure software development

Understanding Traditional System Life Cycle Phases

In the early 1960s, application software developers realized the software development process needed some structure. Computers were becoming more numerous, and the need for programmers was growing. The capabilities of hardware and software expanded. In turn, software development projects began to grow in scope. Organizations that owned computers demanded more functionality from their large investments. The increased demand for functionality required more sophisticated applications. Software developers began to collaborate to create systems of software that were made up of numerous programs that worked together.

Software development began to look like an engineering process. It needed a model to help coordinate all of the individual pieces and people involved. One emerged that is still in use in various forms today: the **System Development Life Cycle (SDLC)**. This model is also known as the Software Development Life Cycle. The software version of the SDLC is focused primarily on software where the system version is a more holistic view of overall architecture. The SDLC is a formal model for creating and modifying software or systems. Although the SDLC has commonly been implemented as a waterfall approach in the past, many of today's organizations implement the SDLC using agile scrum, spiral, or other methods. Regardless of the approach used, the SDLC breaks down the software or system development process into a number of phases with the goal of standardizing and simplifying development management. In the next section, system and software will be used interchangeably. **FIGURE 14-1** shows a 10-phase SDLC model; however, many software development organizations combine several of these phases to create a simplified model with only five to seven phases.

The SDLC uses industry best practices to guide software system development activities. Software development activities have the characteristics of projects. Software projects have specific start and end dates. They also have specific **deliverables**. A deliverable is an object created as a result of project activities. Using the wealth of best practices from project management for software development projects is a good fit. Project management

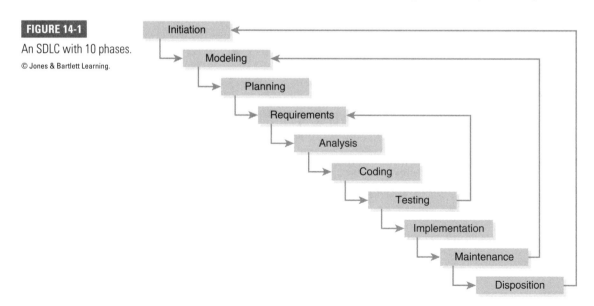

FIGURE 14-1

An SDLC with 10 phases.

© Jones & Bartlett Learning.

techniques help standardize the software development process. These techniques make it easier to identify problems and fix them.

The SDLC provides both control and visibility of the tasks throughout the development project. It can also increase the probability of success. The SDLC encourages the development processes to be repeated in a predictable fashion. The SDLC has been around for quite a while in different forms. It has matured and changed with system architectures, but the overriding themes have remained the same. Throughout the years, the SDLC has also had other names:

- The application development life cycle model
- The classic life cycle model
- The linear sequential model
- The waterfall method

The most important concept in SDLC is **decomposition**, or breaking down a software development project into distinct phases. From a security perspective, this practice provides specific points in time. These points in time allow you to validate or test the product to ensure it meets requirements. You can never start testing too early. The earlier you validate that your deliverables satisfy the requirements for the phase you are in, the more secure the final product will be. The SDLC phases mark different activities along the development process. The 10-phase SDLC defines the following phases:

1. **Initiation**—This phase is where you scope and submit the initial project to management for approval and funding. If management agrees, the process is formally authorized and the process moves to the next phase.
2. **System/Information Engineering and Modeling**—Here you collect information about your environment and the environment's requirements. The idea is that you document everything your computing environment has and any specific requirements or restrictions. For example, if your proposed software system requires Microsoft IIS web server and none of your servers has IIS installed, document this information. You'll need either to change the web server requirement or install IIS. You don't have to make decisions yet, but you'll need these facts for later phases when making decisions. This information will provide a baseline of what your environment currently does and what must be changed to support the new or modified application.
3. **Planning**—You develop your project management plan in this phase. The processes include resource requirements and scheduling. The deliverables of the planning phase direct the remainder of the software project.
4. **Software Requirement Analysis**—You'll document what the software must do in this phase. This includes both functionality and security requirements. Study the business needs that the software will meet. List them in terms of business functions.
5. **System Analysis and Design**—Once you know details about your environment and what the software must do, begin the process of designing software that will fulfill business requirements. The deliverable of this phase is a complete design document that describes the software. You haven't written any software yet—you have just described it. Your descriptions can be formal, such as using Unified Modeling Language (UML), or informal using your own standards. The important point is that the development team clearly understands what it needs to write. This is also the last chance to ensure your project is

still on track before coding begins. If any design documents do not satisfy the requirements from the previous phase or do not fit with your environmental requirements,
address those before continuing.

6. **Code Generation**—This phase is not the starting point. By this stage of the SDLC, most
   big decisions have already been made. Ensure that all code generated during this phase
   meets the design criteria from the previous phase. The code you generate in this phase
   should operate correctly.

7. **Formal Testing**—This phase is the first formal mention of testing. However, you should
   have been validating that each phase's deliverables meet the requirements of the previous
   phase's deliverables. Thorough validation can save a lot of wasted programming effort.

8. **Implementation**—The implementation phase represents the point in the project
   where the customer accepts the software product and the software moves into a production environment.

9. **Maintenance**—This is typically the last phase. It is the step after implementation. Once in
   the maintenance phase, there are really only two main reasons to modify the application.
   One reason to modify the application is an enhancement request. The only other reason to
   modify the application is to fix a bug. In either of these situations, the correct approach is
   to return to Step 1 and go through the whole process again. However, you don't start from
   scratch. This time, you have all of the deliverables from the previous phases. You simply
   start with a description of what you want to change, and then go through each phase until
   you end up with modified code. By ensuring that even code fixes meet the application's
   design goals, you avoid many of the situations where a fix breaks something else. It takes a
   little longer, but you save time and money by not chasing as many bugs later.

10. **Disposition**—This phase represents the activities related to retiring a software
    product and cleansing any hardware of sensitive data. In nearly all cases, plan to
    either archive application data or transfer it to another system. The disposition phase
    addresses all of the activities that reverse the actions in the implementation phase. By
    the end of this phase, you have completely removed all of your sensitive data from any
    hardware or devices that may be sold or recycled.

The SDLC formalizes the development process. This process also keeps you from
jumping ahead and writing code that doesn't satisfy requirements. Don't make the mistake
of allowing your team to start the project by writing code. You will almost always end up
either ditching or rewriting at least parts of software you develop without planning. Some
development approaches rely on prototyping at the beginning of projects. Even in these
cases, though, you should have already put plans in place for ensuring any code is secure.
Any time your software has to interact with other system components, carefully decide
how it should operate. That requires time to make decisions before writing code.

Keep two important points in mind when following the SDLC. One, precede the code
generation phase with several iterations of modeling and design. Two, validate each phase's
deliverables. By the time you reach the code generation phase, make certain you have
substantial documentation on the software's purpose, requirements, and design. It should be
fairly easy to validate whether or not software written in this phase satisfies the system design.

Each phase has defined deliverables. A phase in the SDLC ends when the project team has
accepted the deliverables for that stage. Deliverables are up to standard when they satisfy all of
the goals, including security goals. Each phase generally culminates with a meeting of the project

team to review the phase's deliverables. When the team agrees that the deliverables are valid, the phase ends and the project moves to the next step. Phase validation and testing should identify any areas in your project where you have deviated from the prior phase's deliverables. Make sure that the deliverables for each phase satisfy all preceding deliverables. Testing at every phase ensures that your team will quickly spot any variances from the stated design. Early detection of problems allows you to fix the problems with the minimum cost and disruption to the project.

Agile Software Development

Traditional software development management is still based largely on some variation of the waterfall method. During the 1990s, some organizations began to realize that the software industry was changing in different ways. Increasing demands to develop more complex software more efficiently led to new methods of managing software development. Instead of managing large projects with long delivery schedules, many organizations looked for ways to be more responsive. They wanted to be able to develop their software in smaller pieces. This move toward smaller development cycles eventually became known as the **agile development** method.

Agile loosely describes a method of developing software that is based on small project iterations, or **sprints**, instead of long project schedules. Organizations that use the agile method produce smaller deliverables more frequently and can evaluate a large project in terms of its individual pieces as they are completed. Sprints are generally 1–4 weeks in duration. That means there is some deliverable once or more each month. This focus on frequent delivery makes it possible to see and use pieces of a large software product as it matures over time.

The first organized meeting of agile enthusiasts was in 2001. Several organizations that were exploring this new type of software development sent representatives to a meeting in Snowbird, Utah, to collaborate and exchange ideas. The attendees created the foundational document of the agile movement—the "Manifesto for Agile Software Development." It is a concise document that reflects its writers' affection for simple methods. Here is the Manifesto for Agile Software Development in its entirety:

We are uncovering better ways of developing software by doing it and helping others do it. Through this work we have come to value:

- Individuals and interactions over processes and tools
- Working software over comprehensive documentation
- Customer collaboration over contract negotiation
- Responding to change over following a plan

That is, while there is value in the items on the right, we value the items on the left more.

FIGURE 14-2 shows the basic idea behind the agile method. Unlike the waterfall method, agile is designed to be iterative throughout the development process. Each time around the cycle is a single sprint. It takes many sprints to create a complete software project. Each sprint ends at a specific point in time and should have some deliverable. A deliverable should be something, such as working software, that the team can demonstrate. The focus on working software helps to focus the team on results.

Agile is a growing technique of managing software development projects. It tends to perform well in organizations that encourage ongoing communication and value short development cycles. It is important to begin developing software with security in

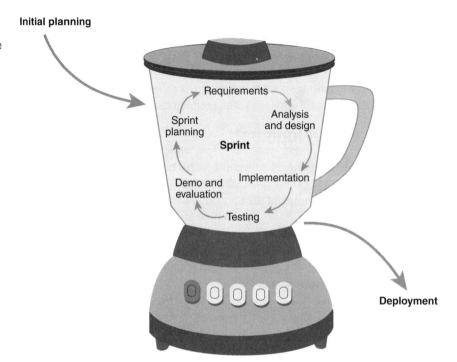

FIGURE 14-2

The agile software development method.

© Jones & Bartlett Learning.

Initial planning

Requirements

Sprint planning

Analysis and design

Sprint

Implementation

Demo and evaluation

Testing

Deployment

NOTE

You can find more information on the Manifesto for Agile Software Development and the agile method in general at http://agilemanifesto.org/. Another good starting point to learn about agile is http://www .agile-process.org/.

mind from the very beginning. Agile methods encourage developers to plan for security and then test for security at the end of each sprint. Developing secure software can become an integral part of the overall development effort, that is, if the organization values and encourages security. Regardless of the development method an organization uses, attention to security is more important than any method.

DevOps

DevOps is a newer growing technique of managing software development projects. It tends to perform well in in environments where continuous development of software requires oversight but not so much that it stops the ability for developers to continue to work on making great systems. DevOps (splits up Development and Operations and then merges the two) takes two very different groups and gets them to work together as seen in **FIGURE 14-3**. Developed in 2009 by Patrick Debois and a group of development leaders trying to find a better way to produce and release code, DevOps is now a force to be reckoned with. It is popular because of the problem that is addressed: how do we deploy code in the life cycle that allows us to continuously create while continuously making changes that are not impactful to consumers? Since operations teams inherently do not want any change in their environments to reduce risk of outage, developers needs to find a way to make changes that were not impactful (or less impactful).

This is done with a pipeline mentality. In DevOps, there is a CI/CD pipeline, and this stands for continuous integration (CI) and continuous delivery (CD). Note, CD also can stand for continuous deployment. Continuously integrating change to production code as needed during the build phase allows software developers to make needed change without having to stop their work. Continuous delivery (or deployment) of these changes to build allows the build to continue to grow and change as products (or services) need to grow and change. Instead of having a major release update that is large and cumbersome, or a large outage of a system to perform a major update, minor updates are pushed in a nonstop fashion.

To safely do this, the second half of DevOps work within the life cycle to ensure that safety, security, accountability in work, and reliability are considered. To reduce risk, these constant change pipeline is checked by quality assurance (QA) and monitored by an SRE team. SRE, or Site Reliability Engineering, allows for the handling of incidents, problem changes, or issues that arise. By creating feedback loops and ensuring that the organizations culture has moved to embrace and support this mindset, DevOps has revolutionized the ability of vendors to release updated software with little to no impact in a cost-effective and time-efficient manner.

> **NOTE**
>
> A form of DevOps is focused on security, called DevSecOps. You can find more information on the DevOps, DevSecOps, and Agile methods in general at https://tech.gsa.gov/guides/understanding _differences_agile_devsecops/.

FIGURE 14-3

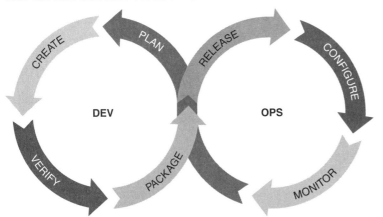

Managing Microsoft Windows OS and Application Software Security

A security representative participating in the development process is your key to managing software security. One benefit of a model like the SDLC or agile method is the group nature of the model process. If you formally implement a development model, you should have required phase pass-off meetings every time your project is ready to move from one stage to another. The frequency of this phase pass-off depends on how you scope your projects. You have many different ways to scope software development projects. **TABLE 14-1** lists several common approaches to software project scope.

In most SDLC environments, the best choice is to create a project for a group of related software programs. This balances the advantages and disadvantages of other approaches. This approach also makes it easy to include maintenance modifications after you have

TABLE 14-1 Common Approaches to Setting Software Project Scope

APPROACH	ADVANTAGES	DISADVANTAGES
Create one project to develop a complete software application.	• Single project • Ultimate visibility	• Difficult to sift through tasks to find related work • Difficult to move to another phase until all components are ready • Very difficult to manage a large number of related components
Create a new project for each individual program.	• Ultimate flexibility • Easy to move from one phase to the next	• Difficult to define interproject dependencies • Difficult to maintain status reporting among multiple projects
Create a project for a group of related software programs.	• A balance of flexibility and visibility • Easy to manage groups of related programs together	• Must maintain interproject dependencies • Some projects may have to wait for dependent projects before moving to a new phase
Use the agile method for each project.	• Flexibility to focus on rapid results • Dynamic team environment that changes as the product matures • Easier to detect and address emerging issues	• Challenging to schedule limited resources • Aggressive production schedules may not suit all organizations • Requires more sophisticated team leadership

© Jones & Bartlett Learning.

implemented your software product. Of course, the first three choices are for SDLC environments. Choosing agile is another choice many organizations make.

Once you decide how you will scope projects, include a security component in every phase. Incorporating security in the earliest phases of software development increases the application's security and decreases the cost of adding safeguards. In fact, many development organizations have one or more security specialists on the development team to ensure such concerns are met. All too often, organizations add security features late in the development cycle. Waiting too late in the design or development process may cause problems that could force a partial redesign. Include security requirements from the very beginning.

Another way to ensure your applications include security concerns early in the development process is to pursue security training for developers. Security classes are available that specifically target software developers. It makes sense to find good training for your analysts and developers to help them learn how to write more secure programs.

Along with ensuring your software developers are fully trained to write secure code, make sure your development environment and tools don't get in the way. Many of the latest development environments integrate tools with secure libraries to empower developers to write more sound applications. One of the most popular development environments for Windows applications is Microsoft Visual Studio. Visual Studio supports developers working in a wide variety of languages developing applications for Android, iOS, web, and cloud environments. Visual Studio includes many features and tools for developing secure applications:

- **Code analyzer**—Identifies many coding errors
- **Application verifier**—Identifies stability, compatibility, and security issues
- **Compiler option**—Helps prevent buffer overflows
- **Secure libraries**—Are used in applications
- **Security exceptions**—Are used in debugging

Visual Studio is available as a fully featured, comprehensive Integrated Development Environment (IDE), or as a free open source general-purpose IDE named Visual Studio Code. Visual Studio Code boasts thousands of plugins that allow it to support nearly every programming language, and it runs on all popular OSs. You can find out more about Visual Studio and Visual Studio Code at https://visualstudio.microsoft.com/.

Each time programs move from one phase to the next, conduct a security review. It is also a good time to perform a risk analysis. The review should cover the programs that have changed to ensure no new vulnerabilities have been introduced into your software. Start your security reviews with the very first phase. Microsoft has formalized the inclusion of security activities into the classic SDLC. To punctuate the need for integrating security into all phases of the development life cycle, Microsoft developed the **Security Development Lifecycle (SDL)**. According to Microsoft, the SDL "is a security assurance process that is focused on software development." The company based the SDL on three core concepts that support secure development: education, continuous improvement, and accountability. The SDL groups security-related activities into seven phases. The SDL's phases correspond to phases in the SDLC. **FIGURE 14-4** shows the phases and activities of the SDL.

FIGURE 14-4

The Microsoft Security Development Lifecycle (SDL)—simplified.

© Jones & Bartlett Learning.

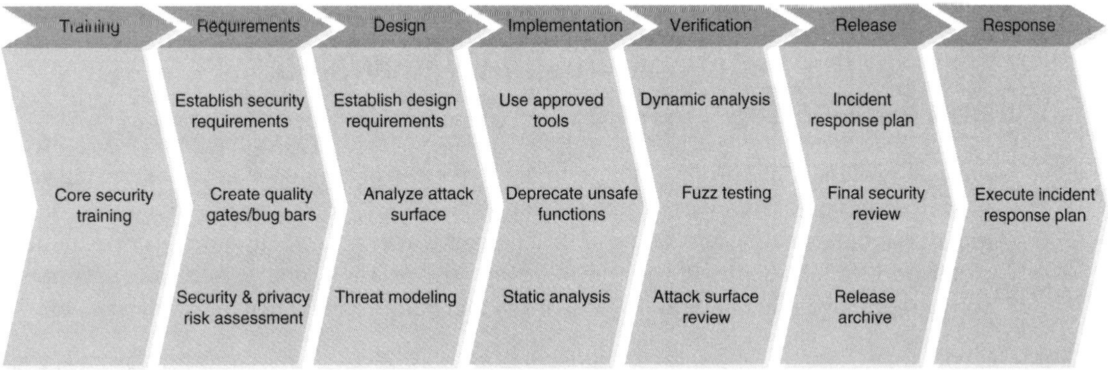

Training	Requirements	Design	Implementation	Verification	Release	Response
	Establish security requirements	Establish design requirements	Use approved tools	Dynamic analysis	Incident response plan	
Core security training	Create quality gates/bug bars	Analyze attack surface	Deprecate unsafe functions	Fuzz testing	Final security review	Execute incident response plan
	Security & privacy risk assessment	Threat modeling	Static analysis	Attack surface review	Release archive	

The Microsoft SDL defines the following phases of development activities:

- **Training**—Ensure all developers are fully trained on security development topics before engaging in any software application development activities. Training all developers on secure development techniques is crucial to creating secure applications.
- **Requirements**—This phase corresponds to the SDLC Software Requirements Analysis phase. During this phase, the development team establishes security requirements as well as creates quality gates and conducts security and privacy risk assessments.
- **Design**—This SDL phase corresponds to the SDLC System Analysis and Design phase. SDL activities include establishing design requirements, analyzing the application's attack surface, and modeling threats to the application.
- **Implementation**—This SDL phase corresponds to the Code Generation SDLC phase. During code generation, SDL activities include using approved tools, deprecating unsafe functions, and performing static code analysis to ensure new or modified code is secure.
- **Verification**—This SDL phase corresponds to the Formal Testing SDLC phase. Formal testing focuses on evaluating functionality, while verification activities include dynamic code analysis, fuzz testing, and attack surface reviews.
- **Release**—This SDL phase corresponds to the Implementation SDLC phase. Once you implement application changes, you can create or update the incident response plan and conduct a final security review.
- **Response**—This phase comes into play when an incident occurs. The response phase corresponds to executing your incident response plan.

The Microsoft SDL extends the classic SDLC and complements standard development activities with a security-related focus. It provides managers with a prescribed method to ensure that the software development process pays appropriate attention to security matters. The three core concepts ensure that developers are well educated, always improving the development process, and accountable for the code they write.

Technical TIP

Find more information on the Microsoft SDL by visiting the SDL webpage at: https://www.microsoft.com/en-us/securityengineering/sdl.

Developing Secure Microsoft Windows OS and Application Software

As an IT professional, you should be soundly convinced of the importance of securing your organization's data. You've seen many techniques to limit access to critical resources and make your data more secure. Some of the controls you've read about directly correspond to software vulnerabilities. If your development organization could create more secure software, you wouldn't have to invest quite so much time and money to compensate for software vulnerabilities. From one perspective, secure software is its own control. So, how do you get started putting the SDLC and SDL models into action? How do you make it all result in more secure code?

A framework developed by a consortium of organizations can help you design a development process that works in real organizations. The **Building Security in Maturity Model (BSIMM)** is the result of a study of large organizations that develop software with a specific focus on security. The organizations studied include Microsoft, Adobe, Google, Bank of America, Intel, Sallie Mae, Nokia, and Capital One. The BSIMM reveals how 120 large organizations use developer training, tool selection, and conducting the right activities to develop secure applications. This study wasn't based on theory, but rather it reported on real situations in today's environments.

The BSIMM defines 116 unique activities, along with the frequency each activity was observed during the study. While that sounds like a lot of work for a development group that is just starting to look at security, the BSIMM makes it clear. The BSIMM also organizes the 116 activities into a framework, called the **Software Security Framework (SSF)**, that groups 12 practices into four domains. **FIGURE 14-5** shows the SSF's components.

The SSF's four domains organize activities into related practices. These domains address the high-level concerns throughout the development life cycle. Here are the SSF domains, along with the BSIMM's definition of each one:

- **Governance**—"Those practices that help organize, manage, and measure a software security initiative. Staff development is also a central governance practice."
- **Intelligence**—"Practices that result in collections of corporate knowledge used in carrying out software security activities throughout the organization. Collections include both proactive security guidance and organizational threat modeling."
- **Secure Software Development Lifecycle (SSDL) Touchpoints**—"Practices associated with analysis and assurance of particular software development artifacts and processes. All software security methodologies include these practices." The Touchpoints provide

Governance	Intelligence	SSDL touchpoints	Deployment
Strategy and metrics	Attack models	Architecture analysis	Penetration testing
Compliance and policy	Security features and design	Code review	Software environment
Training	Standards and requirements	Security testing	Configuration management and vulnerability management

FIGURE 14-5

The Software Security Framework (SSF).

© Jones & Bartlett Learning.

direct correlations with activities in the SDLC. The activity groups in this domain include Architectural Analysis, Code Review, and Security Testing.

- **Deployment**—"Practices that interface with traditional network security and software maintenance organizations. Software configuration, maintenance, and other environment issues have direct impact on software security."

FYI

You may be thinking that the BSIMM looks like just another model. At a high level, it is. But the BSIMM is a direct result of observing development behavior that works and produces secure results. That is not to say that the participating organizations produce perfect software. These organizations have simply identified activities that decrease the number of software defects they produce. And the BSIMM translates directly into defined activities that you can put into practice in your organization. You don't have to figure out how to implement a model's theoretical steps.

Technical TIP

For more information on BSIMM and SSF, visit their website at https://www.bsimm.com/framework.html.

The SSF makes it easy to identify and organize activities in which you should engage throughout the software development process. If you want to simplify the process of developing secure software even further, it all boils down to four areas of focus:

- **Provide training in secure development**—Untrained developers lack the understanding, skills, and motivation to expend extra effort to incorporate security into their code. That may sound harsh, but it is true. While software developers are generally savvy enough to get the training they need on their own, your organization will fall short of its secure software development goals if you ignore the need to provide comprehensive security training for your developers.
- **Include security from the beginning**—Don't wait for coding to begin to include security concerns. Security goals should be part of the initial requirements and subsequent design of any software.
- **Use secure programming techniques**—Here's where the training pays off. Since you know what attackers are looking for and what they can use to compromise an application, don't give it to them. Write applications in a way that is not vulnerable to known tactics.
- **Test for vulnerabilities**—Part of the formal testing activities should include testing for security vulnerabilities. This should include manual testing from developers, secure code reviews and automated testing tools like fuzzers, static analysis tools, and dynamic analysis tools.

Each language has its own set of known vulnerabilities and techniques to avoid them. Learn how to write solid, secure code in your languages of choice. While languages often suffer from different vulnerabilities, a few common programming errors lead to insecure code. If you can't implement a complete secure application development initiative immediately, you can at least alert developers to avoid a few common pitfalls for code they write. Here are a few of the most common application vulnerabilities:

- **Lack of input validation**—Attackers know that developers often don't validate data that come from user input. They use this known issue to launch buffer overflows, injection attacks, and other attacks that rely on a lack of input checking. To avoid this in your applications, confirm that every piece of data you receive is valid before you use it in any way. That means you should check the length of the data as well as the content for any characters that the software might interpret as commands.

- **Information leakage through poor error handling**—One of the early phases of any attack is reconnaissance. Attackers poke around to get information about your application and internal infrastructure. Error messages can be a problem. You want your error messages to provide enough information to understand what has happened but not enough to divulge internal details of your application or environment. Consider using coded error messages instead of explicit details.

- **Sloppy authentication or encryption**—Some applications store authentication credentials or encryption keys either in the application code or in easily accessed files. If attackers find these pieces of information, neither the authentication nor the encryption offers much data security. Carefully design how you'll protect authentication credentials and encryption keys. Another issue is if weak encryption ciphers are used, are found, and can be exploited. An example of this is older versions of TLS or using SSL.

- **Remote system access or code execution**—Some applications allow users to access the server's file system or run commands on the server. While the intention is to restrict what users can do, many software applications lack the controls to ensure users aren't abusing this feature. Carefully validate any commands from users that will result in server access of any type.

- **Dynamic code execution**—Developers write many applications, and especially database applications, so that some code is dynamically generated before it is executed. This feature is an efficient way to handle complex database queries where you don't know all of the query components until the user provides some input. Dynamic code is also helpful when code execution depends on data at run time. Using dynamic code also can make it easy for attackers to alter the intended commands and run malicious code dynamically. A secure application limits the use of dynamic code and aggressively validates any input to ensure it doesn't contain malicious data or instructions.

- **Failure to remove comments in code**—While this is a fairly simple issue to fix, sometimes developers will leave comments in their code that can be published on the front end. These comments can be found by people inspecting the source code of a webpage and reveal information that can be used to hack into the application.

These vulnerabilities are just a few of the opportunities application developers have to make code more securely. There is no substitute for good developer security training. Make sure to raise awareness of your developers on application vulnerabilities and encourage developers to write secure code. One of the advantages of structured development approaches, such as the SDLC you learned about earlier, is that it helps developers create more secure code. Structured development processes provide a framework to aid the entire development process. Developers have a structure that helps them write code from specifications, testers work with developers to test applications for functionality and security, and operations plays a part in the process by deploying code that passes testing. Each participant plays a part in providing secure software to users.

Implementing, Evaluating, and Testing Microsoft Windows OS and Application Software Security

WARNING

Don't think that once you fix a security vulnerability it stays fixed forever. It is not uncommon to see vulnerabilities you previously fixed get reintroduced into your code. Once you identify a particular vulnerability, always test future code for the presence of that vulnerability. This is also known as regression testing.

Once you complete the code generation phase of any software project, you will have a reasonable level of confidence that the software meets your security and functional requirements. However, any program changes may have unexpected side effects when interacting with other programs. The purpose of formal testing is to evaluate how well your application meets overall performance, functionality, and security goals. Once your development group approves a set of application changes for testing, then the testing group applies any changed programs to its separate environment and carries out test scenarios.

Every goal from the original specification should have at least one corresponding testing scenario. The testing scenario evaluates whether the application satisfies the goal. Every time you identify a vulnerability in your application, include a scenario in your testing package that assesses whether or not a vulnerability exists. Your testing activities can be both manual and automated. Manual code reviews and functionality testing can be valuable for finding obvious flaws, but automated software analyzers or testing tools allow you to test for far more vulnerabilities in a short amount of time. Numerous companies produce quality application testing and evaluation tools. Here is a list of a few companies that produce products to help you test your applications:

- **Microsoft Visual Studio Test Professional**—https://visualstudio.microsoft .com/vs /test-professional/
- **NDM Technologies Fortify**—https://www.ndm.net/sast/hp-fortify
- **IBM Security AppScan Source**—https://www.ibm.com/security/application -security/appscan
- **Eggplant Digital Automation Intelligence Suite**—https://eggplant.io/dai
- **uTest**—http://www.utest.com/
- **Inflectra SpiraTest**—http://inflectra.com/SpiraTest/Default.aspx#0

An ideal world features at least three environments: development, testing, and production. First, your code must pass all of the required tests in the testing environment. Then, it is ready to release to your production environment. This is the purpose of the implementation phase of the SDLC. Copying programs from your testing environment to the production environment may not seem difficult, but it can cause issues if not handled properly. The best way to handle implementation is to create a copy of a production environment. Then, have your testing group test the implementation process in that environment. Passing an implementation test means you should have no problems when you implement the real code in the real production environment.

One additional common security control for the software development environment is to employ separation of duties. Since software developers can write software that accesses sensitive data, they have the ability to compromise your data's security. One way to protect your production data from a malicious developer is to not allow any developers to have access to production. Developers write code and can place their software in the testing environment. When testing is complete, another role must have access to move software from testing into production.

So, what can happen from just copying code to production? A lot. Today's applications tend to be large, integrated systems that depend on many small modules of code. If even one doesn't work properly, the whole system could encounter problems. This brief list includes some of the problems you might encounter if you implement faulty code in a production environment:

- **Inconsistent code and schema changes**—Many of today's applications depend on database management systems to access their data. Database management systems use formal declarations, called **schemas**, to describe databases. When you change the way a table or column in a database is defined, you change the database's schema. Programs rely on the database schema to access data and know how to use it. If you implement programs that expect a new schema to a production environment that still has an old schema, your programs may encounter problems. Depending on the language and the database product you use, your programs could either return errors or crash.
- **Inconsistent interfaces with other programs**—Programs generally work with other programs. To do that, each program has to know how to invoke other programs and what kind of data to exchange with them. If you change a program's data requirements but neglect to change other programs that expect to exchange data with that first program, they will likely not be able to operate together any longer. Those problems will probably cause errors or program crashes.
- **Faulty installation procedure**—Due to local environmental differences, your production environment may be slightly different from your testing environment. Any subtle differences, such as folder locations, file permissions, or even defined printers, could cause your programs to behave in an unexpected manner.

You may encounter many more potential issues when implementing programs and application changes. It is important to isolate as many issues as possible during your formal testing. However, you won't identify every problem during testing. Some problems depend on the production environment. You won't see these issues until your application is up and running in production. For this reason, it is necessary to test and evaluate any application changes after implementation.

After installing changes to your application, have your production team execute controlled evaluation scripts that validate the new software functions as prescribed.

> ⚠ **WARNING**
>
> Use extreme caution when testing code in production. The exposure to error is very high, and the practice should be avoided. You don't want to run a test that may slow the system down or cause it to crash. Be restrictive about whom you allow to run tests in a production environment (if you even allow it at all) and which tests you run. A much better approach is to run tests in nonproduction environments that are copies of production environments. Avoid running any unnecessary tests or evaluations in your production environment.

These tests also ensure that the software doesn't do what it isn't supposed to do. Once you are comfortable with the code's functionality, test its security level. One of the best ways to test for security vulnerabilities in code that is in production is a penetration test. You should be conducting penetration tests periodically anyway, so this point in the implementation phase is an effective place to do it. Schedule a penetration test soon after you install any application changes. The test will validate that your changes are secure and that no new vulnerabilities exist in your software.

Maintaining the Security of Microsoft Windows OS and Application Software

In this chapter, you've found out how to develop secure software. To make sure you have the most secure environment to develop secure software, combine all of these topics. Your development environment and tools need to be up to date just like the rest of your application software. Likewise, ensure the OSs on all of your software development computers have the latest security patches. Take the time to treat your development environment computers like production computers, and make sure they are hardened and current.

Once you have confidence that your development environment is secure, provide the same level of assurance to your customers. Just as you expect to receive timely OS and application software updates to address any newly discovered vulnerabilities, so do your clients. It doesn't matter whether the recipients of the software you develop are internal customers or external customers. Your goal is to provide them with secure software, including periodic updates. Prioritize your software development to address any vulnerability discovered in your application software. Don't take any shortcuts, but make every attempt to release security patches that address known vulnerabilities as quickly as possible.

Maintaining a software application often requires making difficult decisions. It would be nice to deliver every request in the order it was received. Realistically, you'll run into times when you have to fast track software modifications. Your customers may need a critical new feature. Alternatively, you may have to address a newly discovered vulnerability or management may simply require you to implement a specific service or function as a priority. Or your organization may require you to suspend or postpone scheduled maintenance software development to address other critical projects. Although it is tempting to treat fast track projects differently than regular development, try not to bypass your development controls to speed up the process. Extreme cases calling for speedy fixes are inevitable. So when they crop up, make sure you document what you did and have a plan to reconcile the production change with testing as soon as possible. The secure development process you adopt isn't there to slow you down—it's there to protect you from making common mistakes. Don't proceed without these protections simply to try to increase the speed with which you deploy maintenance patches.

Releasing patches every few days can make your customers' system administrators scramble to validate and test each patch before they apply it. While not all organizations test new patches in isolated environments, some do. Those that do test patches before applying them to their production environments can get overwhelmed with frequent patches. Further, applying patches generally requires some type of a privileged user account. Frequent updates or patches mean more opportunities for problems during the installation process and more potential for attackers to compromise your environment during installation.

Also, check that all maintenance procedures protect your data's security. For example, if a security patch or feature upgrade requires data conversion, one approach is to export the data to an external file and import the file into a new or modified database table. This strategy will expose the data while the program stores the data on disk. You could store the data in an encrypted folder to protect it from other users, but the disk still resides, at least temporarily, outside of the database and its internal access controls. Take care that you don't expose any data during maintenance procedures. Keep the data secure at all times.

Microsoft Windows OS and Application Software Revision, Change Management, and End-of-Life Phaseout

Developing software is basically the process of creating a collection of useful programs. Unlike other engineering disciplines, software development isn't quite like building physical objects. Software development is far more flexible than building physical objects and generally far less constrained. Software development is as much an art as it is a science. The truth is, software is easy to change. Sometimes, it's too easy. And not only is it easy to change, but controlling those changes in a group environment can be difficult.

When you develop software in a group that is uncontrolled and undirected, imagination can easily turn into a nightmare. That's where models and control methodologies come into play. Although the SDLC and the SDL provide solid frameworks for organizing software development efforts, they still have some issues. Many software development organizations that adhere to the SDLC or the SDL find three main areas of difficulty in producing software products.

Software Development Areas of Difficulty

The first issue is Phase Identification. As simple as it may sound, knowing where you are in the SDLC or SDL flow is not always obvious. The reason behind the difficulty is that different parts of a software application may be at different phases at any point in time. For example, the modifications to an accounting report may be ready for testing while a program changed to fix tax calculation bugs is ready to be released to production. To make matters worse, the new bug found in the general ledger posting programs hasn't been fixed and requires more work.

With so many programs in different development phases, how do you define and communicate which versions of programs are in a specific phase? In other words, how do you know what programs you have at any time in any phase? As the number of developers and the number of programs increase, the problem can get progressively worse.

The second issue, Phase Transition, can also be confusing. Making the transition from one phase to the next often is more complex than it first appears. You need to get answers to several questions each time you move from one phase to another. These questions include the following:

* Which programs are ready to move to the next phase?
* Has the development team documented and approved the phase transition?
* Is the receiving phase prepared to receive the migrated objects?
* What is the residual impact to the receiving phase of migrating objects?

The last of the common issues with software development is activity coordination. It is important that all changes to objects and phase configurations are communicated to all interested parties and agreed to by all necessary parties. Make sure objects aren't copied to a new place without prior notice or approval. Document every change and provide a method to undo changes if needed.

Software Control

Regardless of the specific software development method you use, refer to these common needs for control throughout the development process:

* **Baseline identification**—It is important for any software project to be able to identify which version, or collection of object versions, of an application exist in any defined collection, or configuration. For example, you need to know which versions of the program are currently in production, which versions are being tested, and what your developers are currently modifying.
* **Control of changes**—Since it is almost guaranteed that you will change some of your software, either to address problems or enhance the functionality, you need to control how you change those items. Change control includes the ability to enforce rules that govern how you change items, who can change them, and when you can change them.
* **Communication**—Another common need in any business endeavor is communication. Since software applications are composed of programs and other components that must work together, it is crucial that all interested parties are in the loop throughout the change process. Good communication when using any model is essential to ensure your software satisfies its intended requirements.
* **Repeatable process**—Doing anything well once is good, but doing it well over and over again increases product quality and reduces costs. Software control provides the ability to learn from what you didn't do well last time, implements controls to keep the bad stuff from happening again, and helps you do a better job next time. In short, good software control impacts your bottom line by minimizing loss.

Software Configuration Management

The traditional **software configuration management (SCM)** process is a collection of best practices for handling changes in software projects. It is up to each organization to implement tools and techniques that identify both the functional and physical attributes of software at various points in time, and then perform systematic control of changes. This application of SCM allows you to maintain software integrity and traceability throughout the SDLC and proactively manage all your software assets. The SCM process defines the need to trace changes and the ability to verify that the final delivered software has all of the planned enhancements that are supposed to be included in the release. SCM identifies four procedures, also called activities, that must be defined for each software project to ensure a sound SCM process:

- **Configuration identification**—The process of identifying the attributes that define every aspect of a configuration item. A configuration item is a product that has an end-user purpose. In the context of software development, configuration items commonly include files and schema definitions. The files in a software product can include program code, documentation, configuration files, and data files. A structured collection, or collection of specific item versions, is called a baseline, or configuration. A baseline allows the definition of a snapshot of a configuration and enables change control.

- **Configuration control**—Configuration control is a set of processes and approval stages required to change a configuration item's attributes and to re-baseline them. Any changes to item versions can only occur by following defined procedures. Item version changes include adding and removing items, modifying item versions, and modifying item attributes. The **Configuration Control Board (CCB)** plays a central role in the configuration control process. It can have many or few members and is responsible for making decisions about changes to the system definition during the course of the development life cycle.

- **Configuration auditing**—Configuration auditing is the process of confirming that all system components that should be in a given baseline are present. It is how management ensures that a software project is on track and building what is actually required. As long as a software product complies with all requirements in the current baseline, and all requirements in previous baselines, the product is valid. The process of conducting an audit can be straightforward or very complex, depending on the specific requirements. At the highest level, configuration auditing checks the current software product to ensure it satisfies the baseline requirements. More in-depth validation may be required to ensure any changes since the previous baseline have not invalidated other functionality. In short, the software must still satisfy all requirements. Configuration auditing also ensures that a project satisfies all requirements. Ensuring that changes meet requirements is backward-looking validation. Ensuring all requirements have been satisfied is forward-looking validation. Configuration auditing checks that the baseline scope of work has been fully satisfied without violating existing requirements.

- **Configuration status accounting**—Configuration status accounting is the ability to record and report on the configuration baselines associated with each configuration item at any moment in time. Basically, it is a snapshot of a configuration. It ensures that a complete and accessible record of the changes to a software system and reasons for such changes are available. The objective in configuration status accounting is to record item attributes, as well as why changes are made, when changes are made, and who made the changes. Configuration status accounting is often a reporting function that pulls the required information out of data stores created and managed by the configuration control tools in the SCM system.

TABLE 14-2 Common SCM Tools

PRODUCT	WEBSITE	CLASSIFICATION
Microsoft Azure DevOps Server	https://azure.microsoft.com/en -us/products/devops/server/	SCM
IBM Rational ClearCase	https://www.ibm.com/products/rational -clearcase	SCM
Apache Subversion	https://subversion.apache.org/	VCS
Git	https://git-scm.com/	VCS
Mercurial SCM	https://www.mercurial-scm.org/wiki/Download	SCM
Roundtable Total Software Management System (TSMS)	https://roundtable-software.com/	SCM

© Jones & Bartlett Learning.

SCM is far more than just version control. Version control systems keep track of all changes made to a file over time. Each change creates a new version of the file. Keeping track of changes you have made to files is important both to research a history of changes and also to have the ability to revert back to a previous specific version of a file. SCM includes version control, but also adds build management, promotion management when promoting software from one configuration to another, and unit of work management. Each SCM toolset provides different capabilities, but they all help control the software development process. **TABLE 14-2** lists some common SCM tools. Each tool's classification is either SCM or Version Control System (VCS).

Best Practices for Microsoft Windows and Application Software Development Security Investigations

Creating and maintaining secure applications is the topic of many books and articles. It has emerged as an important concern for software developers. Numerous models and frameworks tell you how to write cleaner, more secure code. One of the main reasons the BSIMM model is so valuable is that it reports on what works in the area of secure application development. When considering any new procedure or technology, it is wise to learn from those who have already used it. Learn from other people's mistakes and adopt strategies that worked. Plan well and you can enjoy a more productive software development environment. The following best practices for developing secure Windows applications represent what many organizations have learned:

- Incorporate security early and often.
- Adopt a software development model to help define your organization's development activities and flow.
- Define activities for each phase in your model.

- Ensure all developers are trained to develop secure applications. Look for developer training from:
  - **SANS**—http://www.sans.org
  - **SEI**—http://www.sei.cmu.edu/
  - **OWASP**—https://www.owasp.org
- Validate your software product at the end of every phase.
- Create separate software projects for each related group of programs or program changes.
- Do not begin a software development project by writing code—plan and design first.
- Keep the three SDL core concepts in focus—education, continuous improvement, and accountability.
- Develop tests to ensure each component of your application meets security requirements.
- Study the most common application vulnerabilities and develop programming standards to ensure you don't include the vulnerabilities in your application.
- Identify and store programs, files, and schema definitions in a centralized, secure repository.
- Control and audit changes to programs, files, and schema definitions.
- Organize versioned programs, files, and schema definitions into versioned components.
- Organize versioned components and subsystems into versioned subsystems.
- Create baselines at project milestones.
- Record and track requests for change.
- Organize and integrate consistent sets of versions using activities.
- Maintain stable and consistent workspaces.
- Ensure reproducibility of software builds.

Using these best practices as guidelines will help your organization develop more secure applications and be more responsive to your customers.

CHAPTER SUMMARY

Securing applications that someone else wrote is one thing. Writing your own applications and ensuring they are secure requires a different focus. Before starting any development activities, prepare to develop secure applications. Preparation includes establishing or adopting a framework and using it to develop standards and procedures. Writing secure applications requires that your developers start off by receiving proper training on secure development topics. Then, they'll work closely with your security personnel to incorporate security into any development project from the beginning.

In this chapter, you learned how useful models and frameworks can be. You learned about how to formalize the software development process and how some large organizations structure their secure development activities. You read about the importance of controlling the development process and how SCM can provide the structure to develop complex applications. Take what you've learned and start directing your organization's development activities toward writing secure application software.

KEY CONCEPTS AND TERMS

Agile development

Building Security in Maturity
Model (BSIMM)

Configuration Control
Board (CCB)

Decomposition

Deliverable

DevOps

Schema

Security Development
Lifecycle (SDL)

Software configuration
management (SCM)

Software Security
Framework (SSF)

Sprints

System Development Life
Cycle (SDLC)

CHAPTER 14 ASSESSMENT

1. A deliverable is an object created as a result of project activities.

   A. True
   B. False

2. Which of the following is the most important concept in SDLC?

   A. Initialization
   B. Writing code
   C. Decomposition
   D. Disposition

3. In which SDLC phase do you collect information about your current computing environment?

   A. Initialization
   B. System/Information Engineering and Modeling
   C. System Analysis and Design
   D. Implementation

4. Testing occurs only immediately after code generation.

   A. True
   B. False

5. Microsoft identifies the most important component of security by placing the _____ phase as the first phase of the SDL.

6. Which SDL phase corresponds to executing your incident response plan?

   A. Requirements
   B. Verification
   C. Response
   D. Release

7. The _____ framework is based on secure development practices of 120 larger organizations.

8. Which SSF domain most closely maps to SCM?

   A. Governance
   B. Intelligence
   C. SSDL Touchpoints
   D. Deployment

9. A common application vulnerability that can lead to several other vulnerabilities is a lack of input _____.

10. A(n) _____ is a description of the data stored in a database.

11. Which SCM activity verifies that all of the components that are supposed to be in a configuration are in the configuration?

    A. Configuration control
    B. Configuration auditing
    C. Configuration identification
    D. Configuration status accounting

12. The _____ authorizes all change to an application.

13. A structured collection, or collection of specific item versions, is called what?

  A. Release

  B. Work package

  C. Configuration item

  D. Baseline

14. When trying to strike a balance between continuous deployment (CD) of software and doing so in a safe manner, which method would you use?

  A. DevSecOps

  B. Scrum

  C. Configuration Management

  D. Waterfall

Best Practices for Microsoft Windows and Application Security

THIS CHAPTER LISTS EACH OF THE BEST PRACTICES for securing Microsoft Windows computers and software. Use this chapter as a single resource to organize what you know about Windows security and apply it to your environment. These best practices will help you sort through a lot of information and focus on the steps you can take to make the biggest impact for your organization.

Chapter 15 Topics

This chapter covers the following topics and concepts:

- What the basic rules are for Microsoft Windows operating system (OS) and application security
- What the best practices for audit and remediation cycles are
- What the best practices for security policy conformance checks are
- What the best practices for security baseline analysis are
- What the best practices for OS and application checks and upkeep are
- What the best practices for network management tools and policies are
- What the best practices for software testing, staging, and deployment are
- What the best practices for compliance/currency tests on network entry are
- What the trends are in the management of Microsoft Windows OS and application security

Chapter 15 Goals

When you complete this chapter, you will be able to:

- Describe basic rules of Microsoft Windows OS and application security
- Use best practices for securing Microsoft Windows OS and application software
- Explain trends in Microsoft Windows OS and application software security management

Basic Rules of Microsoft Windows OS and Application Security

The basic rules of the Microsoft Windows OS and application security cover a lot of ground. These best practices are here to remind you to address basic security first. After that, you can fine-tune your OS, applications, and network. If you don't cover the basics first, many advanced hardening efforts will not be as effective as possible. Here are some administrative and technical best practices to ensure your basic environmental components are secure:

Administrative Best Practices

- Develop and maintain policies to implement each of the best practices in this section.
- Educate users.
- Assign user permissions via role-based access control, avoid assigning user permissions individually.
- Establish incident response capabilities.
- Ensure that you know which business functions are critical to your organization. Then, take whatever steps necessary to protect these functions in case of interruptions or disasters.
- Develop a plan to continue all critical business functions in case of an interruption. This business continuity plan (BCP) should cover all aspects of your organization.
- Define recovery time objectives (RTO) as well as recovery point objectives (RPO) for each critical resource. Identify resources required for the recovery process. You'll need to identify which parts of your disaster recovery plan are sequential and which ones you can work on simultaneously.
- Develop a backup plan for each resource that minimizes the impact on performance while keeping secondary copies of data as up to date as possible. Explore various options, including alternate sites and virtualization.
- Document all backup and recovery procedures. Train all primary and backup personnel on all procedures.
- Test all recovery procedures rigorously. Conduct at least one full interruption recovery test each year.
- Review your complete recovery plan quarterly (or more frequently), and adjust for any infrastructure changes.
- Update old password policies. Consult current National Institute of Standards and Technology (NIST) guidelines (https://pages.nist.gov/800-63-3/) for recommendations.
- Do not write down passwords. Use passwords you can remember. When you write down passwords, they are easier for an attacker to find and use.
- Never encrypt individual files—always encrypt folders. This keeps any sensitive data from ever being written to the disk in plaintext.
- Designate two or more recovery agent accounts per organizational unit. Designate two or more computers for recovery, one for each designated recovery agent account.
- Avoid using print spool files in your print server architecture, or make sure that print spool files are generated in an encrypted folder. This keeps sensitive information from being stored in plaintext on a print server.

- Require strong passwords for all virtual private network (VPN) connections.
- Trust only certificates from certificate authorities (CAs) or trusted sites. Train users to reject certificates from unknown or untrusted sites.
- Require multifactor (MFA) or two-factor authentication (2FA) for access requests to sensitive information.

Technical Best Practices

- Install anti-malware software on all computers. Consider using Endpoint Detection and Response (EDR) software to help increase computer security.
- Enable all real-time scanning (shield) options.
- Update signature databases and software daily.
- Perform a complete scan of all hard drives and solid state drives (SSDs) at least weekly.
- Perform a quick scan after installing or updating any software.
- Enable boot-time virus checking, including boot sector and memory scan at startup options.
- Remove administrator rights from all normal users.
- Apply software and OS security patches.
- Block outbound network connections that are not required for your applications.
- Automate as many backup operations as possible. Create logs and reports that make problems with backup operations easy to recognize.
- Verify all backup operations. A secondary copy of data with errors may be no better than damaged primary copy data.
- Export all encryption recovery keys to removable media and store the media in a safe place. Physically store your Encrypting File System (EFS) or BitLocker recovery information in a separate, safe location.
- Encrypt the Documents folder for all users. Since most people use Documents for most document files, encrypting this folder will protect the most commonly used file folder.
- Use MFA when using BitLocker on OS volumes to increase volume security.
- Store recovery information for BitLocker in Active Directory Domain Services (AD DS) to provide a secure storage location.
- Disable standby mode for portable computers that use BitLocker. BitLocker protection is in effect only when computers are turned off or in hibernation.
- When BitLocker keys have been compromised, either format the volume or decrypt and encrypt the entire volume to remove the BitLocker metadata.
- Use the strongest level of encryption that your situation allows for VPNs. Remove weak cipher options whenever possible.
- Use Secure Socket Tunneling Protocol (SSTP) IKEv2 for VPNs when possible. IKEv2 is the newest VPN protocol from Microsoft.
- Disable Service Set Identifier (SSID) broadcasting for wireless networks.
- Never use Wired Equivalent Privacy (WEP) for wireless networks—use only Wi-Fi Protected Access (WPA/WPA2/WPA3).

15

Audit and Remediation Cycles

Once you've covered the basics, you can move on to start addressing more advanced concerns. Don't assume that covering the basics once is enough. Auditing the status of your security controls and planning to fix any problems you find is an ongoing, necessary process. The Deming cycle provides a simple model on which to base your security administration. Auditing is a critical part of the cycle. The Deming cycle is also known as the Plan-Do-Check-Act (PDCA) process. The name comes from each of the four steps in the process:

- **Plan**—Establish your objectives and processes to meet a stated goal. In the context of routine auditing, the goal should be to assess specific security controls.
- **Do**—Implement the process you planned in the previous step.
- **Check**—Measure the effectiveness of the new process and compare the results against the expected results from your plan. You'll compare the expected results of your auditing information with a baseline.
- **Act**—Analyze the differences between expected results and measured results. Determine the cause of any differences. Then, proceed to the Plan process to develop a plan to improve the performance.

Being able to routinely validate security settings depends on proper use of auditing. These auditing best practices will cover most general environments:

- Maintain current backups of all audit information so that you can recover historical audit information in the case of a disaster.
- Do not enable Read or List auditing on any object unless you really need the information. Read/List access auditing can create a tremendous amount of information.
- Do not enable Execute auditing on binary files except for administrative utilities that attackers commonly use. Do turn auditing on for these utilities to help monitor their use.
- Limit enabling all auditing actions to files, folders, programs, and other resources that are important to your business functions. Don't be afraid to enable auditing for any object—just ensure you need the information you'll be saving.
- Enable auditing for all change actions for your Windows install folder and any folders you use in normal business operation. It is also a good idea to audit changes to the Program Files folder.
- Audit all printer actions. You may need to know who printed a document that found its way into the wrong hands.
- Ignore Read and Write actions for temporary folders but audit Change Permissions, Write Attributes, and Write Extended Attributes actions. These actions can help identify attacker activities.
- Develop Windows policies and Group Policy Objects (GPOs) that are as simple as possible and still satisfy your security policy. Complex policies are difficult to verify.
- Develop clear guidelines to evaluate each element of your security policy. An audit should be a structured process to verify your security policy, not an unorganized hunt for problems. Know what you will be looking for before you search through lots of audit data.

Security Policy Conformance Checks

Group Policy is an important component of secure Windows environments. Windows Group Policy helps centralize settings that ensure conformance with your security policy. Once you take the time to develop a comprehensive Group Policy, use it to both apply settings and ensure settings are correct. Here are a few guidelines that should result in an effective Group Policy:

- Define organizational units (OUs) that reflect your organization's functional structure.
- Create OU GPOs for controls required in your security policy.
- Use meaningful names for GPOs to make maintenance and administration easier.
- Deploy GPOs in a test environment before deploying to your live environment.
- Use security filtering and Windows Management Instrumentation (WMI) filters to restrict settings when necessary.
- Back up your GPOs regularly.
- Do not modify the default policies—instead, create new GPOs.
- Use the Group Policy Settings Reference spreadsheets for more information on available GPO settings. You can find these spreadsheets by visiting the website https://www .microsoft.com/en-us/download, and searching for Group Policy Settings Reference. Microsoft provides several versions to cover different Windows releases.
- Acquire the Windows Server Security Compliance Management resource from Microsoft to help design, deploy, and monitor your server baselines.
- Acquire the Windows 11 Security Compliance Management resource from Microsoft to help design, deploy, and monitor your workstation baselines.
- Use the Local Policy Tool (LPT) to automatically deploy recommendations from the Security Compliance Management toolkits.

Security Baseline Analysis

Baselines help you collect and analyze the data required for auditing needs without collecting a lot of extra data. A baseline defines the settings and data you want to collect for later comparison and trend analysis. The following guidelines will help you identify and create baselines you can use to ensure compliance with your securityspolicy:

- Create initial baselines that represent a secure starting point for each computer. Develop security templates in Security Configuration and Analysis (SCA) that contain the security settings for each type of workstation and server. Change the templates as needed and use them when building new computers. You can apply up-to-date templates to new Windows installations to quickly configure a new computer to your security standards.
- Run SCA using command-line interface options to compare legacy computer settings and configurations with your standards. Schedule scans to run periodically (weekly or monthly), and review the resulting output files for any identified problems.

- Develop batch files to run scans and collect ongoing operational information. Collect information using a set daily, weekly, or monthly schedule, and archive collected data files.

OS and Application Checks and Upkeep

An effective security policy ensures that your organization has all the technical controls in place to support its security goals. It takes more than just technical controls to meet all security goals, but security administrators mainly focus on deploying and maintaining technical security controls.

This list of Windows security administration best practices will help you deploy and maintain controls to support your security policy. Change the list to suit your organization, but pay attention to these suggestions. They can help you avoid wasting time and resources:

- Clearly state security goals in your security policy.
- Include all compliance requirements for applicable legislation, regulation, and vendor standards in your security policy.
- Use the PDCA method for all security administration activities.
- Communicate with all stakeholders—share as much information as possible.
- Strive for simplicity in all controls and systems—complexity invites failures.
- Search for controls that have little impact on users. Users tend to bypass controls that they find intrusive or difficult.
- Coordinate acceptable use policies (AUPs) with technical controls.
- Automate as much as possible—use scheduled jobs whenever you can.
- Use AD GPOs for as many security settings as possible.
- Coordinate physical controls with technical controls.
- Never allow a computer or mobile device that doesn't have current anti-malware controls in place to connect to your network. This rule applies to all computers and mobile devices—even laptops or smartphones owned by distinguished guests. Enforce the rule or be prepared to put your malware removal plan into action.
- Develop a plan to monitor system and network performance and follow it.
- Ensure the OS and all software is up to date for all computers.
- Periodically examine log files for suspicious behavior.
- Stay current on emerging attacks and trends and update your controls appropriately.
- Fully test your recovery plans at least annually (more often if possible). You'll never really know how your recovery plan works until you actually execute each of the steps.
- Define discretionary access control lists (DACLs) when necessary and modify or remove them when user account roles change.

Hardening your Windows OS removes as many vulnerabilities as possible. The best practices to harden your Windows OS are as follows:

- Install only the Server Core option when you don't need extra functionality.
- Select the minimum number of roles when installing Windows Server.

- For Windows Server, run the Security Configuration Wizard (SCW) immediately after installing the OS.
- Update each computer with the latest OS patches.
- Configure each computer for automatic Windows updates.
- Install and run at least one other Windows security vulnerability scanner.
- Create one or more user accounts with administrator rights.
- Disable the default Administrator and Guest user accounts.
- Disable all unneeded services.
- Close all ports not required by services or applications.
- Create GPOs for all security settings, including firewall rules.
- Use AD to distribute all configuration changes using GPOs.
- Create a backup of each GPO.
- Scan all computers for open ports.
- Limit physical access to all critical servers.
- Create an initial baseline backup.
- Change the AD Directory Service Repair Mode (DSRM) password periodically, at least every 6 months.
- Install anti-malware software on each computer.
- Ensure all anti-malware software and data are current.
- Use network access control (NAC) software or devices to control remote computer connections. Use NAC to quarantine systems that to not meet policy requirements.
- Use remote authentication methods to authorize remote computers and users.
- Require secure VPNs to access internal network resources.
- Use Internet Protocol Security (IPsec) with digital certificates to authenticate computer-to-computer connections in the datacenter.
- Require security awareness training prior to issuing access credentials.
- Require periodic recurrent security awareness training to retain access credentials.
- Provide continuing security awareness through different means.

The process of hardening applications is just as important as hardening your OS. These best practices will help you establish a solid foundation for securing your applications:

- Harden the OS first.
- Install only necessary services.
- Use server roles when possible.
- Use Microsoft Security Compliance Toolkit (SCT) to apply the least privilege principle to applications.
- Remove or disable unneeded services.
- Remove or disable unused user accounts.
- Remove extra application components.
- Open only the minimum required ports at the firewall.
- Define unique user accounts.
- Use strong authentication.

- Use encrypted connections for all communication.
- Encrypt files, folders, or volumes that contain private data.
- Develop and maintain a BCP and disaster recovery plan (DRP).
- Disable any server features you don't need.
- Ensure every computer has up-to-date anti-malware software and data.
- Never open any content or files from untrusted sources.
- Validate all input received at the server.
- Audit failed logon and access attempts.
- Conduct penetration tests to discover vulnerabilities.

Network Management Tools and Policies

Computers communicate using networks. A secure networking environment is crucial to overall security. To start securing your network calls for some best practices. These practices will provide a good set of guidelines for ensuring your network stays secure:

- Identify sensitive data.
- Protect sensitive data at rest using encryption.
- Establish unique domain user accounts for each user.
- Enforce strong passwords for all user accounts.
- Create new user accounts with limited rights and permission for services:
    - Do not allow any services to run as a domain admin user.
- Use Kerberos for secure authentication.
- Install firewalls to create a demilitarized zone (DMZ):
    - Place all internet-facing servers in the DMZ, such as web servers and other publicly accessible servers.
    - Use encrypted communication for all traffic flowing between the DMZ and the trusted network.
- Use encryption for all communication involving sensitive data.
- Establish firewall rules:
    - Deny all traffic by default and only make exceptions for approved traffic (implicit deny)
    - Allow only approved traffic for servers.
    - Filter inbound and outbound traffic for servers and workstations for malicious messages.
    - If your firewall supports it, automatically terminate connections with sources generating denial of service (DoS) traffic to mitigate DoS attacks in process.
- Install anti-malware software on all computers and establish frequent update schedules and scans:
    - Update software and signature databases daily.
    - Perform quick scans daily.
    - Perform complete scans at least weekly.
- Use WPA, WPA2, or WPA3 for all secure wireless networks.

- Disable SSID broadcast for secure wireless networks.
- Disable Wi-Fi Protected Setup (WPS).
- Do not enable wireless or mobile broadband cards while connected to your organization's internal network. Always disable your wireless adapter before connecting a laptop to the wired network.
- Do not allow visitors to roam around your facilities that use wireless local area network (LANs). Many access points can be physically reset to insecure factory default settings by pressing a reset switch on the box.
- Avoid connecting to public networks. When you connect to an open wireless network, don't expect privacy or security. In the event that you must use a public network, always use a VPN.
- If you have to use an open wireless connection, don't visit websites that require usernames, passwords, or account numbers, such as online banking. Use an encrypted connection or a VPN.
- Install a separate wireless access point connected only to the internet for guests.
- Disable or uninstall any services that you don't need.
- Invest in Intrusion Detection Systems (IDS) and Intrusion Prevention Systems (IPS) for finding and stopping suspicious network traffic.
- Perform threat hunting activities regularly to detect any hidden intrusions on your network.

Software Testing, Staging, and Deployment

Developing secure software can be a challenge. Regardless of whether you develop or purchase software, you must deploy and maintain it as well. Some general best practices for developing, deploying, and maintaining secure Windows application software are the following:

- Adopt a software development model to help define your organization's development activities and flow.
- Define activities for each phase in your model.
- Ensure all developers are trained on developing secure applications.
- Validate your software product at the end of every phase.
- Create separate software projects for each related group of programs or program changes.
- Do not begin a software development project by writing code—plan and design first.
- Keep the three Security Development Lifecycle (SDL) core concepts in focus—education, continuous improvement, and accountability.
- Develop tests to ensure each component of your application meets security requirements.
- Study the most common application vulnerabilities and develop programming standards to ensure you don't include the vulnerabilities in your application.
- Identify and store programs, files, and schema definitions in a centralized, secure repository.
- Control and audit changes to programs, files, and schema definitions.

- Organize versioned programs, files, and schema definitions into versioned components.
- Organize versioned components and subsystems into versioned collections.
- Create baselines at project milestones.
- Record and track requests for change.
- Organize and integrate consistent sets of versions using activities.
- Maintain stable and consistent workspaces.
- Ensure reproducibility of software builds.
- Test your software against all types of inputs using software testing tools

Despite your best efforts to secure your applications and operating system, you still may encounter attacks. You have already learned how important it is to have a well-thought-out plan to handle incidents when they do occur. A general list of best practices for handling incidents and investigations includes these steps:

- Harden OS and software to avoid incidents.
- Assess computers periodically to expose vulnerabilities.
- Validate and test all BCPs and DRPs (i.e., carry out scheduled exercises to test and practice plans).
- Get full management support for a computer security incident response team (CSIRT).
- Create a CSIRT.
- Define and assign CSIRT roles.
- Conduct a risk assessment to identify potential incidents that require attention first.
- Develop an incident response plan around the six steps to handling incidents.
- Create an incident reporting form.
- Distribute and publicize the incident reporting form and procedure.
- Test the incident response plan.
- Identify and acquire incident management software.
- Identify and acquire incident investigation software.
- Train key SIRT members on proper evidence collection and handling.

Compliance/Currency Tests on Network Entry

Some of the most sensitive points in your IT infrastructure are the entry points from remote users and systems. It is important that you carefully consider how remote users connect to your network and how you ensure these connections do not compromise your security. One straightforward way to control access to your network and any resource on it is to employ an aggressive user-based set of access controls. Computer security experts use many models to manage user accounts over large networks, but one particular strategy provides clarity and security. The AGULP approach provides a method for managing any number of users predictably. AGULP is an acronym that stands for:

- **A**ccounts
- **G**lobal groups

- Universal groups
- Local groups
- Permissions

The idea behind AGULP is to systematically nest individual user accounts in groups to make securing objects more general. The first step is to create separate user accounts for each user. Creating separate user accounts for each user's role adds an extra step of security. In this case, a user may have more than one account. You then add user accounts to global groups, according to the users' shared attributes. These attributes can be geographical or functional, such as manufacturing or human resources. Next, add global groups to universal groups, or groups that are defined for users in any domain in Active Directory. After that, add global groups and universal groups to local groups on computers that contain resources you want to secure. This strategy avoids the need to add individual users to local groups. Finally, you define the permissions for secured resources, or objects, for local groups. The AGULP strategy allows you to reduce the number of access control lists (ACLs) for each resource. Use AGULP to decide how many users and groups you need of each type to reduce the administrative load.

Additionally, to maintain secure access for remote clients, check this list of best practices:

- Map your proposed remote access architecture, including redundant and backup connections. Use one of the several available network mapping software products to make the process easier.
  - Update the network map any time you make physical changes to your network.
- Install at least one firewall between your VPN endpoint and your internal network.
- Select a VPN provider that your clients can easily access. If you select a vendor-specific VPN solution, develop a method to distribute and maintain the VPN client software to your users.
- Use global user accounts whenever possible:
  - Use strong authentication for all user accounts.
- Create a limited number of administrative accounts with permissions for remote administration.
- Develop a backup and recovery plan for each component in the Remote Access Domain.
  - Do not ignore backing up and recovering configuration settings for network devices.
- Implement frequent update procedures for all OSs, applications, and network device software and firmware in the Remote Access Domain.
- Monitor VPN traffic for performance and suspicious content.
- Carefully control any configuration setting changes or physical changes to domain nodes.
  - Update your network map after any changes.
- Require encryption for all communication in the Remote Access Domain.
- Enforce anti-malware minimum standards for all remote computers as well as server computers in the Remote Access Domain. Ensure all anti-malware software and signature databases remain up to date.

Trends in Microsoft Windows OS and Application Security Management

The landscape of security is constantly changing. Attackers are becoming increasingly more sophisticated and, in some cases, more aggressive. You've had opportunities to learn about known issues and vulnerabilities. These topics are crucial to your environment's security, but you have more to learn. As new threats emerge, you'll be responsible for adapting your environment to face them. As long as you have established a solid security policy and are diligently protecting your environment from threats, you should be able to react to new threats.

Good security practices help you react to new threats as well as existing ones. Don't ever think that emerging threats are the only ones you should consider. Many attackers focus on older, well-known methods. Even so, numerous organizations still aren't proactive about security and are vulnerable to these older threats. Stay vigilant against all known threats as you build defenses against new ones.

These emerging threats are likely to shape the security landscape for the near future:

- One of the most commonly used and fastest growing attack methods is **social engineering**. Social engineering is the process of an attacker tricking or convincing an authorized user to carry out an action or provide valuable information for which the attacker does not have authorization. In other words, the attacker gets the authorized user to do the dirty work. Many types of attacks depend on this attack method, and the trend indicates even more growth. The best defense against social engineering attacks is educating your users to recognize and report any social engineering attempts.

- Mobile devices are rapidly becoming the most attractive targets for attackers. While device theft is a valid concern, many attackers attempt to compromise mobile devices to use as bots. The mobile nature of these devices attracts attackers to create mobile bots to launch attacks. Mobile devices also commonly store large amounts of personal information. The information that makes mobile devices so convenient for users also makes them valuable attack targets. Most mobile devices run iOS or Android operating systems. Microsoft released Windows 8 and Windows Phone OSs to compete in the mobile device marketplace. While these mobile Windows OSs running on mobile devices are different from legacy desktops and laptops, many of the security concerns are the same. Although Windows Phone devices are no longer sold or supported, you may find some still in use and should make sure they are secure or replaced.

- Expect to see more scams by questionable security consulting or software firms. These companies use fear tactics to get users to purchase their product to remove security problems. These programs may not work, may be rebranded versions of freely available software, or may be malware themselves. Train users to install software only from trusted sources.

- As attacks become more data-focused, focus your controls more on data than on the containers of those data. Explore access controls in your applications and database management systems.

- **Cloud computing** will continue to grow as the environment of choice for organizations of any size. Cloud computing is the practice of renting computer resources from a provider instead of owning the resources. Operating in the cloud environment opens your data to many more vulnerabilities because your data reside on servers accessible from the internet. Use secure access controls to keep your data safe.

• Malware will expand and use legitimate network traffic to send itself to other computers. Malware programs are getting more sophisticated to avoid detection. Be vigilant. Recognize suspicious traffic and filter it out.

These are just a few of the expected trends that will continue or emerge in the coming years. Stay secure by ensuring good basic security, training and engaging your users in secure practices, and keeping all software current. These steps will allow you to withstand today's attacks and those that will come in the near future.

CHAPTER SUMMARY

You should be comfortable with the Microsoft Windows OS environment on both server and workstation computers. You should also know what you need to do to make each component of your IT infrastructure more secure. Windows offers many features and capabilities to deploy a secure and functional environment. You learned in this chapter how to distill all of the concepts on securing your Windows environment into targeted best practices that work for many different types of organizations. You know how to secure today's Windows environment, and you learned about developing trends to keep you current for challenges yet to come. You are now ready to establish and maintain a secure Windows environment.

KEY CONCEPTS AND TERMS

Cloud computing
Social engineering

CHAPTER 15 ASSESSMENT

1. Anti-malware software applies mainly to workstation computers.

A. True
B. False

2. What is RTO?

A. Real-time objective
B. Recovery time objective
C. Recovery turn over
D. Real turn over

3. Test your backup only when you suspect media corruption.

A. True
B. False

4. Even if you use the same password for a long time, it will remain secure.

A. True
B. False

5. Which of the following is an encryption recovery key that you should physically store in a separate safe location?

   A. DES
   B. AES
   C. SSTP
   D. EFS

6. Which protocol is the newest VPN protocol from Microsoft?

   A. IKEv2
   B. L2TP
   C. SSTP
   D. TLS

7. The Plan, Do, Check, Act (PDCA) process is also called a(n) _____ cycle.

8. Which printer actions should you audit?

   A. Remote access
   B. Print nontext files
   C. Change printer destination
   D. All actions

9. Which of the following tools will compare computer settings with your standards? (Select two.)

   A. GPMC
   B. SCA
   C. MBSA
   D. PDCA

10. Change your _____ Directory Service Restore Mode (DSRM) password periodically, at least every 6 months.

11. What program should you run on Windows Server immediately after installing the operating system?

   A. Group Policy Object (GPO)
   B. Anti-malware shield
   C. Security Configuration Wizard (SCW)
   D. Network access control (NAC)

12. What is the first step to take when hardening applications?

   A. Remove or disable unneeded services.
   B. Define unique user accounts.
   C. Harden the operating system.
   D. Ensure every computer has up-to-date anti-malware software and data.

13. To isolate web server computers from your internal network, place them in a segregated network called a(n) _____.

14. Which of the following is the best choice for secure wireless communications?

   A. WPA
   B. WEP
   C. SSID
   D. TLS

15. Which of the following is *not* a core concept of Security Development Lifecycle (SDL)?

   A. Education
   B. Availability
   C. Continuous improvement
   D. Accountability

APPENDIX

A

Answer Key

CHAPTER 1	Microsoft Windows and the Threat Landscape

1. B 2. A 3. D 4. C 5. A 6. D 7. A 8. C 9. B 10. A 11. B
12. D 13. C 14. A 15. B

CHAPTER 2	Security in the Microsoft Windows Operating System

1. C 2. A 3. D 4. B 5. D 6. B 7. A 8. C 9. C 10. D 11. C
12. B 13. A 14. C 15. C

CHAPTER 3	Access Controls in Microsoft Windows

1. C 2. A 3. B 4. C 5. A 6. A 7. C 8. D 9. A 10. B 11. B
12. C 13. A 14. C 15. D

CHAPTER 4	Microsoft Windows Encryption Tools and Technologies

1. C 2. A 3. C 4. A 5. D 6. A 7. D 8. A 9. B 10. C 11. D
12. B 13. A 14. C 15. A

CHAPTER 5	Protecting Microsoft Windows against Malware

1. A 2. C 3. D 4. B 5. A 6. D 7. B 8. A 9. C 10. D
11. A 12. D 13. Buffer overflow 14. A 15. D

CHAPTER 6	Group Policy Control in Microsoft Windows

1. A 2. 90–120 3. C 4. B 5. A 6. B 7. Active Directory 8. B
9. GUID 10. A 11. B 12. B 13. D 14. RSOP 15. C

CHAPTER 7	Microsoft Windows Security Profile and Audit Tools

1. B 2. Snapshot 3. A 4. C 5. MMC 6. A 7. C 8. A 9. B
10. B 11. D 12. B 13. B 14. Minimum 15. C

CHAPTER 8	Microsoft Windows Backup and Recovery Tools

1. B 2. A and C 3. C 4. Increases 5. Decreases 6. B 7. A
8. B 9. A 10. B 11. D 12. B 13. Bare metal recovery 14. B

CHAPTER 9	Microsoft Windows Network Security

1. Metropolitan area network (MAN) 2. B 3. C 4. Coaxial 5. A
6. A 7. Demilitarized zone (DMZ) 8. B 9. D 10. C 11. A
12. A 13. B and C 14. B 15. C

CHAPTER 10	Microsoft Windows Security Administration

1. B   2. C   3. B   4. A   5. B and C   6. Business continuity plan (BCP) *and* disaster recovery plan (DRP)   7. A   8. A and C   9. MBDA 10. B   11. B   12. A   13. C   14. A

CHAPTER 11	Hardening the Microsoft Windows Operating System

1. A   2. B   3. Hardening   4. B   5. A   6. C   7. A   8. B 9. Administrator   10. B   11. Nmap   12. D   13. B   14. B   15. PKI

CHAPTER 12	Microsoft Application Security

1. B   2. C   3. B   4. Web browser   5. A   6. B   7. C   8. A   9. B 10. A   11. C   12. Query   13. Transparent Data Encryption (TDE) 14. B   15. B

CHAPTER 13	Microsoft Windows Incident Handling and Management

1. B   2. A   3. B   4. Preparation   5. C   6. Lessons learned   7. B 8. C   9. B   10. A   11. C   12. B   13. Chain of custody log   14. A   15. A

CHAPTER 14	Microsoft Windows and the Security Life Cycle

1. A   2. C   3. B   4. B   5. Training   6. C   7. Building Security in Maturity Model (BSIMM)   8. D   9. Validation   10. Schema   11. B 12. Configuration Control Board (CCB)   13. D   14. A

CHAPTER 15	Best Practices for Microsoft Windows and Application Security

1. B   2. B   3. B   4. B   5. D   6. A   7. Deming   8. D   9. B and C 10. Active Directory   11. C   12. C   13. Demilitarized zone (DMZ) 14. A   15. B

Standard Acronyms

3DES	triple data encryption standard
ACD	automatic call distributor
AES	Advanced Encryption Standard
ANSI	American National Standards Institute
AP	access point
API	application programming interface
BSD	Berkeley Software Distribution
B2B	business to business
B2C	business to consumer
BBB	Better Business Bureau
BCP	business continuity planning
C2C	consumer to consumer
CA	certificate authority
CAP	Certification and Accreditation Professional
CAUCE	Coalition Against Unsolicited Commercial Email
CCC	CERT Coordination Center
CCNA	Cisco Certified Network Associate
CCPA	California Consumer Privacy Act
CERT	Computer Emergency Response Team
CFE	Certified Fraud Examiner
CISA	Certified Information Systems Auditor
CISM	Certified Information Security Manager
CISSP	Certified Information System Security Professional
CMIP	Common Management Information Protocol

COPPA	Children's Online Privacy Protection Act
CRC	cyclic redundancy check
CSI	Computer Security Institute
CSIRT	computer security incident response team
CTI	Computer Telephony Integration
DBMS	database management system
DDoS	distributed denial of service
DES	Data Encryption Standard
DMZ	demilitarized zone
DoS	denial of service
DPI	deep packet inspection
DRP	disaster recovery plan
DSL	digital subscriber line
DSS	Digital Signature Standard
DSU	data service unit
EDI	Electronic Data Interchange
EIDE	Enhanced IDE
FACTA	Fair and Accurate Credit Transactions Act
FAR	false acceptance rate
FBI	Federal Bureau of Investigation
FDIC	Federal Deposit Insurance Corporation
FEP	front-end processor
FRCP	Federal Rules of Civil Procedure
FRR	false rejection rate
FTC	Federal Trade Commission
FTP	file transfer protocol

GDPR	General Data Protection Regulation	**ITRC**	Identity Theft Resource Center
GIAC	Global Information Assurance Certification	**ITU-T**	International Telecommunications Union
GLBA	Gramm-Leach-Bliley Act	**IVR**	interactive voice response
GRE	Generic Routing Encapsulation	**LAN**	local area network
GUI	graphical user interface	**MAN**	metropolitan area network
HIDS	host-based intrusion detection system	**MD5**	Message Digest 5
		MMC	Microsoft Management Console
HIPAA	Health Insurance Portability and Accountability Act	**modem**	modulator demodulator
		NAS	network attached storage
HIPS	host-based intrusion prevention system	**NFIC**	National Fraud Information Center
		NIDS	network intrusion detection system
HTML	hypertext markup language	**NIPS**	network intrusion prevention system
HTTP	hypertext transfer protocol		
HTTPS	HTTP over Secure Socket Layer	**NIST**	National Institute of Standards and Technology
HVAC	Heating, Ventilation, and Air Conditioning		
		NMS	network management system
IAB	Internet Activities Board	**NTFS**	New Technology File System
IDEA	International Data Encryption Algorithm	**OS**	operating system
		OSI	open system interconnection/ online software inspector
IDPS	intrusion detection and prevention system		
		PBX	private branch exchange
IDS	intrusion detection system	**PCI**	Payment Card Industry
IEEE	Institute of Electrical and Electronics Engineers	**PGP**	Pretty Good Privacy
		PKI	public key infrastructure
IETF	Internet Engineering Task Force	**RAID**	redundant array of independent disks
InfoSec	information security		
IP	Internet Protocol	**RFC**	Request for Comments
IR	Incident Response	**RSA**	Rivest, Shamir, and Adleman (algorithm)
IPS	intrusion prevention system		
IPSec	IP Security	**SAN**	storage area network
IPv4	Internet Protocol version 4	**SANCP**	Security Analyst Network Connection Profiler
IPv6	Internet Protocol version 6		
IRS	Internal Revenue Service	**SANS**	SysAdmin, Audit, Network, Security
(ISC)2	International Information System Security Certification Consortium		
		SAP	service access point
ISO	International Organization for Standardization	**SCSI**	small computer system interface
		SCT	Security Compliance Toolkit
ISP	internet service provider	**SEC**	Securities and Exchange Commission
ISS	internet security systems		

SET	Secure electronic transaction
SGC	server-gated cryptography
SHA	Secure Hash Algorithm
S-HTTP	secure HTTP
SLA	service level agreement
SMFA	specific management functional area
SNMP	Simple Network Management Protocol
SOAR	Security Orchestration and Automation Response
SOX	Sarbanes-Oxley Act of 2002 (also Sarbox)
SSA	Social Security Administration
SSCP	Systems Security Certified Practitioner
SSD	Solid State Drives
SSL	Secure Sockets Layer
SSO	single system sign-on
STP	shielded twisted cable
TCP/IP	Transmission Control Protocol/Internet Protocol
TCSEC	Trusted Computer System Evaluation Criteria
TFTP	Trivial File Transfer Protocol
TNI	Trusted Network Interpretation
UDP	User Datagram Protocol
UPS	uninterruptible power supply
UTP	unshielded twisted cable
VLAN	virtual local area network
VOIP	Voice over Internet Protocol
VPN	virtual private network
WAN	wide area network
WLAN	wireless local area network
WNIC	wireless network interface card
W3C	World Wide Web Consortium
WWW	World Wide Web

Glossary of Key Terms

Access control | The process of providing and denying access to objects.

Access control entry (ACE) | An individual entry in a DACL.

Access control list (ACL) | The list of access permissions for an object.

Active Directory (AD) | A shared database of domain users, groups, computers, resources, and other information, along with network functionality to centralize and standardize network management and interoperation.

Administrative control | A management action, written policy, procedure, guideline, regulation, law, or rule of any kind.

Advanced Encryption Standard (AES) | An encryption algorithm adopted by the U.S. government in 2002 as the standard for encryption operations.

Agile development | A method of developing software that is based on small project iterations, or sprints, instead of long project schedules.

AGULP | An acronym for Accounts, Global groups, Universal groups, domain Local groups, and permissions. AGULP is an access control approach that systematically nests individual user accounts in groups that make securing objects more general.

A-I-C triad | *See* C-I-A triad.

Anti-malware shield | Software that intercepts all incoming (and optionally outgoing) information, scanning each message or file for malware content.

Anti-spyware software | Software designed to detect and mitigate spyware.

Antivirus software | Software designed to detect and mitigate some types of malware, including mainly viruses, worms, and Trojan horses.

Application server | A computer that runs application programs on behalf of remote users.

Application software | Computer software designed to allow users to perform specific tasks.

Asymmetric algorithm | A cryptographic algorithm that uses two related keys—one key to encrypt data and another key to decrypt data.

Attack surface | The collection of all possible vulnerabilities that could provide unauthorized access to computer resources; all of the software a computer runs that is vulnerable to attack.

Attacker | Any person or program that attempts to interact with a computer information system in an unauthorized manner.

Auditing | The process of collecting performance information on what actions were taken and storing that information for later analysis.

Authentication | The process of proving that provided identity credentials are valid and correct.

Authorization | The process of granting and/or denying access to resources based on the authenticated user.

Authorized user | Any user (person or program) that possesses permission to access a resource.

Availability | The assurance that requested information is available to authorized users upon request.

Backup | A defined collection of copies of files created in case the primary copies of the files are damaged or destroyed.

Bare metal recovery | A restore that includes the operating system and all configuration settings.

Baseline | A collection of configuration settings often collected and saved for the purposes of comparing to other similar collections of configuration settings; a structured collection or collection of specific item versions.

BitLocker | A Windows feature that encrypts entire volumes and normally uses a computer's Trusted Platform Module (TPM) hardware to store encryption keys.

387

BitLocker To Go | A Windows feature that encrypts removable media devices.

Boot device | Any device, typically a CD, DVD, or USB key, from which a computer will boot and load an operating system.

Buffer overflow | A condition in which a running program stores data that are larger than the memory location set aside for the data. The extra data spills over into adjacent memory, causing other data and possibly instructions to be overwritten. An attacker can place specific data in the overflowed buffer to change the instructions a program executes.

Building Security in Maturity Model (BSIMM) | A newly published framework for software development that is the result of a study of large organizations that develop software with a specific focus on security.

Business continuity plan (BCP) | A plan that ensures an organization can survive any disruption and continue operating.

Business driver | Any one of the components, including people, information, and conditions, that support business objectives.

California Consumer Privacy Act (CCPA) | A California state law, passed in 2018, that protects consumer privacy by requiring any organization that collects or uses private data to adhere to controls restricting private data collection, storage, and use.

Certificate authority (CA) | A computer that stores digital certificates and issues them to authenticated subjects.

Chain of custody | Documentation that provides details of every move and access of evidence.

C-I-A triad | Confidentiality, integrity, and availability, which are the goals of information security.

Cipher | An algorithm for performing encryption and decryption.

Class Identifiers (CLSIDs) | GUIDs used in the Windows Registry to identify objects and record many of their attributes.

Classification | A level of sensitivity assigned to an object by its owner. An example object could be assigned as top secret, secret, confidential, restricted, or unclassified.

Clearance | A security level assigned to subjects, authorizing them to access objects with an equal or lower classification. Clearance levels include top secret, secret, and confidential.

Cloud computing | The practice of renting computer resources from a provider instead of owning the resources.

Coaxial cable | Network cabling that consists of a single copper conductor surrounded with a plastic sheath, then a braided copper shield, and then the external insulation.

Common Criteria for Information Technology Security Evaluation | An international set of standards for functionality and assurance of computer security. The Common Criteria superseded the Orange Book as well as other standards.

Compensating control | An alternate security control that fulfills an original goal without implementing the primary control.

Compliance | The process of ensuring that the items in each domain of the IT infrastructure meet or exceed security goals.

Computer environment | A collection of computer and network devices connected to one or more networks, generally for the purpose of fulfilling business functions. Also called IT Infrastructure.

Computer security incident response team (CSIRT) | A team of representatives from IT, management, legal, and public relations that is organized to respond to incidents.

Confidentiality | The assurance that information can be accessed and viewed only by authorized users.

Configuration Control Board (CCB) | A person or group of people responsible for making decisions about changes to the system definition during the course of the development life cycle.

Container | A site, a domain, or an organizational unit in Active Directory.

Control | Any mechanism or action that prevents, detects, or addresses an attack.

Corrective control | A control that repairs the effects of damage from an attack. Corrective controls include virus removal procedures, firewall table updates, and user authorization database updates.

Cryptojacking | A malware attack in which the malware uses the victim's computer or device to mine cryptocurrency for the attacker.

Data at rest | Data that are stored on a persistent storage device, such as a disk drive.

Data in transit | Data that are currently being transported from one location to another, as in a transfer across a network connection.

Decomposition | The process of breaking down a software development project into distinct phases.

Decryption key | A piece of information that an algorithm needs as input to decrypt or "unlock" a document to make it readable.

Defense in depth | A security strategy that relies on multiple layers of security that require attackers to defeat multiple controls to access any protected resource.

Deliverable | Any object created as a result of project activities.

Demilitarized zone (DMZ) | A space created by using one or more firewalls to separate an untrusted network from a trusted network.

Deming cycle | *See* Plan, Do, Check, Act.

Denial of service (DoS) attack | An attack that sends a large volume of network messages that end up flooding the network and making it unusable for legitimate traffic.

Detective control | A control that detects when an action has occurred. Detective controls include smoke detectors, log monitors, and system audits.

Digital certificate | Another term for security certificate.

Directory Service Restore Mode (DSRM) | A special mode that allows administrators to create an offline copy of Active Directory (AD).

Disaster recovery plan (DRP) | A plan that ensures the infrastructure is operational and ready to support primary business functions.

Discretionary access control (DAC) | An access control method based on an object's owner and permissions granted by the owner.

Discretionary access control list (DACL) | The list of access permissions for an object, based on access granted by the object's owner.

Distributed denial of service (DDoS) attack | A DoS attack in which the controller instructs one or more compromised computers to flood a network with packets.

Documentary evidence | Any written evidence, such as printed reports or data in log files.

Domain controller | A server computer designated to handle Active Directory requests.

Due diligence | The ongoing attention and care an organization places on security and compliance.

Dynamic Access Control (DAC) | A collection of features that describe user and data attributes; these attributes help Windows protect files using policies that provide more control over who can access data.

Effective Permissions | The page within the Advanced Security Settings dialog box of Windows that displays calculated permissions for any user or group.

Elliptic Curve Cryptography (ECC) | A public key cryptographic algorithm based on the structure of elliptic curves.

Encapsulating protocol | A rule that handles addressing and encryption issues.

Encrypting File System (EFS) | A Windows feature that provides transparent file and folder encryption. Encryption keys in EFS are based on a user's password.

Encryption | The process of transforming readable information into unreadable information in such a way that anyone with a proper key can reverse the process, making the information readable again.

End-User License Agreement (EULA) | An agreement between the software producer and the end user. The EULA addresses issues regarding approved use and liability. Also called a Software License Agreement.

Enterprise Resource Planning (ERP) | An integrated collection of software programs that are used to manage many aspects of a business, including financials, human resources, assets, and business processes.

Event | Any observable occurrence within a computer or network.

Exploit | To take advantage of a specific vulnerability

Fiber optic cable | Network cabling that consists of a glass core surrounded by several layers of protective materials.

File Classification Infrastructure (FCI) | A feature of Windows that provides the ability to define classification properties for files.

File History | A primary feature of Microsoft Windows that maintains multiple versions of files for the purpose of restoring files to any previous state on demand.

File server | A computer or hardware device that has one or more connected hard disk drives, a network interface, and software to provide network access to files and folders on the attached disks.

File Transfer Protocol (FTP) | A popular protocol used to transfer files from one computer to another.

Firewall | A device or software program to filter data passing through the device or program, limiting network traffic to authorized traffic only.

Full Disk Encryption (FDE) | A form of encryption in which the disk controller encrypts each block. FDE is faster than FVE, since it occurs at a lower level than the operating system.

Full Volume Encryption (FVE) | A method for encrypting a single partition, either physical or virtual, on a hard drive.

Gateway | A network device that connects two or more separate networks that use different protocols.

General Data Protection Regulation (GDPR) | A comprehensive regulation in European Union law that protects the privacy of all EU individuals, requiring all global organizations that handle personal data of any EU citizen to comply.

Globally unique identifier (GUID) | An identification value that is unique across all environments to keep track of an object across many computers.

Group | A set of named entities that define a group of users for the purpose of defining permissions that apply to multiple users.

Group Policy | A centralized set of rules that govern the way Windows operates.

Group Policy Inventory tool | A utility used to collect deployed GPO and computer information that is used to verify Group Policy implementations.

Group Policy Management Console (GPMC) | A utility used to create, edit, and manage AD GPOs.

Group Policy Object (GPO) | A named object that contains a collection of Group Policy settings.

Group Policy Update tool | A utility to immediately deploy and apply GPOs.

Hacktivist | A hacker who is, or claims to be, motivated by political or social justice concerns and uses hacking skills to reinforce his or her chosen position.

Hardening | The process of making configuration changes and deploying controls to reduce the attack surface.

Hardware Abstraction Layer (HAL) | Software layer in the operating system kernel that provides the actual access to physical hardware.

Heuristics | The practice of identifying malware based on previous experience.

Hub | A network device with several connectors, or ports, that allows multiple network cables to attach to it.

Hyper-V | A product that supports creating and running virtual machines in Windows Server 2008.

Hypertext Transfer Protocol (HTTP) | An application layer protocol used to transfer content between web browsers and web servers.

Hypertext Transfer Protocol Secure (HTTPS) | A secure application layer protocol used to transfer encrypted content between web browsers and web servers. HTTPS encrypts traffic by sending HTTP messages over SLS/TLS.

Identification | Providing credentials that claim a specific identity, such as a user name.

IEEE 802.11 | A set of standards for wireless local area network (WLAN) communication protocols.

Incident | An event that results in violating your security policy, or poses an imminent threat to your security policy.

Institute of Electrical and Electronics Engineers (IEEE) | An organization that defines standards for many aspects of computing and communications.

Integrity | The assurance that information can be modified only by authorized users.

International Telecommunications Union (ITU-T) | An agency that defines standards for coordinating global communications.

Internet gateway | A gateway that connects a LAN to the internet.

Internet Protocol Security (IPSec) | A framework of open standards for protecting communications over Internet Protocol (IP) networks.

Intrusion detection system (IDS) | A network device or software that can analyze traffic and detect a potential intrusion based on traffic patterns.

Intrusion prevention system (IPS) | A network device or software that can analyze traffic and detect a potential intrusion based on traffic patterns and can also change firewall rules in real time to prevent further damage from an attack.

Kerberos | A computer network authentication protocol that allows computers to communicate in a secure manner across an insecure network and the default authentication protocol for Windows.

Kernel | The core part of an operating system that provides the essential services of the operating system.

Kernel mode | The highest privilege at which programs can run, allowing access to the physical hardware and kernel resources. Also called supervisor mode.

Key distribution center (KDC) | A computer designated to authenticate users and, upon authentication, issue Kerberos keys that will allow subjects to access objects.

Layer 2 Tunneling Protocol (L2TP) | A tunneling protocol used to support VPNs.

Least privilege user accounts (LUAs) | User accounts that are defined using the principle of least privilege.

Local area network (LAN) | A network that covers a small physical area, such as an office or building.

Local Group Policy Editor | Editor for local Group Policy settings.

Local resource | Any resource attached to a local computer—the same computer to which the user has logged on.

Logical control | An alternate term for technical control.

Malicious software | Software that is designed to infiltrate a target computer and make it do something the attacker has instructed it to do.

Malware | A common term used to describe malicious software, including viruses, worms, and Trojan horses, especially in combinations.

Managed service accounts | Accounts that administrators can create as managed domain accounts to provide automatic password management.

Mandatory access control (MAC) | An access control method based on the subject's clearance and the object's classification. MAC implementations often also require demonstration of a subject's "need to know" to receive access.

Message digest | A shortened unique string of digits that represents a file or message.

Metropolitan area network (MAN) | A network that connects two or more LANs but does not span an area larger than a city or town.

Microkernel | The portion of an operating system's kernel that resides exclusively in memory.

Microsoft Baseline Security Analyzer (MBSA) | An easy-to-use tool that evaluates the current security state of computers in accordance with Microsoft security recommendations.

Microsoft Management Console (MMC) | A graphical user interface framework that provides a centralized method to manage software components on Windows computers.

Multifactor authentication | An authentication process that requires multiple types of authentication credentials.

NetChk Protect | A security scanner from Shavlik that scans and analyzes the patch status of products MBSA does not support. Shavlik also produces the scaled-down version of its scanner called NetChk Protect Limited.

Network | A collection of computers and devices connected by some connection media.

Network access control (NAC) | A solution that defines and implements a policy that describes the requirements to access your network.

Network address translation (NAT) | A technique used in many firewalls that translates internal IP addresses into an external IP address. This feature hides the true IP address of internal computers from outside nodes.

Network Attached Storage (NAS) | A standalone network device with internal storage that is connected to a LAN and accessible to other LAN nodes as a mapped folder or drive.

Network Translation LAN Manager (NTLM) | An authentication protocol used in legacy Windows systems to support secure communications across an insecure network.

Nmap | An open source utility used to scan one or more computers or network devices for open ports and other information.

Node | Any computer or device connected to a network.

Nonrepudiation | This allows a sender to verify the source of a message.

Object | A resource to which access is controlled.

Online Software Inspector (OSI) | A consumer-based vulnerability scanner from Secunia that searches for vulnerable or out-of-date programs and plug-ins. OSI runs in a web browser and does not need to be installed on the computer it is scanning.

Open Systems Interconnection (OSI) Reference Model | A generic description for how computers use multiple layers of protocol rules to communicate across a network. The OSI Reference Model defines seven different layers of communication.

Orange Book | U.S. Department of Defense Trusted Computer System Evaluation Criteria (DOD-5200.28-STD); it was one of the early formal standards for computer security.

Organizational unit (OU) | AD containers that group computers either logically or functionally.

Permission | This defines what a user can do to a specific object, such as read or delete the object.

Personal Software Inspector (PSI) | A consumer-based vulnerability scanner from Secunia that searches for vulnerable or out-of-date programs and plug-ins. PSI must be installed on the computer before you can use it to scan for vulnerabilities.

Physical control | A device that limits access or otherwise protects a resource, such as a fence, door, lock, or fire extinguisher.

Plaintext | Unencrypted data, also known as cleartext.

Plan-Do-Check-Act (PDCA) | A quality method indicating a continuous process consisting of four repeating steps: Plan, Do, Check, Act. PDCA is also known as a Deming cycle.

Point-to-Point Tunneling Protocol (PPTP) | A tunneling protocol used to support VPNs.

Port | In the context of network protocols, a numeric identifier that programs use to classify network messages.

Pre-shared key (PSK) | A shared secret used by cryptographic algorithms to perform symmetric encryption and decryption.

Preventive control | A control that stops an action before it occurs. Preventive controls include locked doors, firewall rules, and user passwords.

Primary copy | The copy of any piece of information that you use most frequently.

Principle of least privilege | The practice of providing a user or process with only the necessary access required to carry out a task.

Print server | A computer or network device that provides the interface between the network and one or more printers.

Privilege escalation | The process of adding more authority to the current session than the process should possess.

Profiling | The process of comparing real computer configurations with known baselines for the purpose of documenting the pertinent differences with secure settings and similarities to insecure settings.

Protocol | A set of rules that govern communication.

Public key | An encryption key that can be shared and does not need to be kept private.

Public key cryptography (PKC) | A cryptographic algorithm that uses two related keys—one key to encrypt data and another key to decrypt data.

Public key infrastructure (PKI) | A general approach to handling encryption keys using trusted entities and digital certificates; the hardware, software, policies, and procedures to manage all aspects of digital certificates.

Query | A statement that accesses data in a database.

Ransomware | A type of malware that attempts to generate funds directly from a computer user by attacking the computer's files and limiting the user's ability to access data until some money is paid.

Real evidence | Any physical object that you can bring into court that you can touch, hold, and directly observe.

Recovery key | A key that can be used to decrypt BitLocker-protected data if the primary key is lost or damaged.

Recovery point objective (RPO) | The amount of data loss an organization can withstand before getting back to normal operations.

Recovery time objective (RTO) | The amount of time it should take to recover a resource and bring it back to normal operation.

Redundant array of independent disks (RAID) | A collection of disks organized in a way that protects data by duplicating it or writing extra information to reconstruct any damaged data.

Registration authority (RA) | A computer that authenticates subjects and directs the CA to issue digital certificates to authenticated subjects.

Registry | A database for Windows configuration settings.

Registry Editor | An editor for Windows Registry contents.

Remote resource | Any resource attached to another computer on a network that is different from the computer to which the user is logged on.

Restore operation | The process of copying secondary copies of files back to their primary locations.

Resultant Set of Policy (RSOP) tool | A utility that shows the settings that result from existing or planned GPOs for a specific computer and user.

Right | User rights define tasks that a user is permitted to carry out, such as take ownership of objects or shut down the computer.

Rights Management Services (RMS) | A security feature of Windows that can encrypt files that contain tagged sensitive data without requiring user interaction.

Risk | Any exposure to a threat.

Role | A predefined set of services, programs, and configuration settings that enable a computer to fulfill a specific set of requirements.

Role-based access control (RBAC) | An access control method based on permissions defined by a role (e.g., manager, authorized user, or guest) as opposed to an individual user (e.g., Michael Solomon).

Rootkit | Software that modifies or replaces one or more existing programs, often part of the operating system, to hide the fact a computer has been compromised.

Router | A network device that examines the destination address and then forwards the packet to the correct outbound port.

Schema | A description of components stored in a database.

Secondary copy | A copy of information created to assist in the recovery of the information in the event the primary copy is damaged or destroyed.

Secure Hash Algorithm (SHA) | A set of hash functions adopted by the National Security Agency as a U.S. government information processing standard.

Secure Socket Tunneling Protocol (SSTP) | VPN protocol that creates an encrypted tunnel over SSL/TLS.

Secure Sockets Layer (SSL) | The predecessor to TLS, SSL is a cryptographic protocol that operates at the transport network layer and provides security for communications across the internet.

Security Access Token (SAT) | A document used by Windows to store all SIDs associated with a process.

Security administration | The process of implementing the security controls within the IT infrastructure.

Security certificate | A document that contains identity information and a public key, along with other descriptive information. Also called a digital certificate.

Security Configuration and Analysis (SCA) | A tool that helps administrators to analyze a computer and compare its configuration settings against a baseline.

Security Configuration Wizard (SCW) | A Microsoft utility that provides guidance to administrators and creates policies based on the least privilege principle for the server roles you have selected either during installation or afterward using the Server Manager Utility.

Security control | A mechanism used to protect information and related assets.

Security Development Lifecycle (SDL) | A security assurance process that is focused on software development.

Security filter | A GPO filter that limits a GPO's scope to specific computers or users.

Security identifier (SID) | A unique identifier for each user and group in a Windows environment.

Security Orchestration and Automation Response (SOAR) | Software tools that help CSIRT teams coordinate information from multiple sources, automate initial IR tasks, and organize the steps to effectively respond to incidents.

Security template | A text file that contains a list of configuration settings.

Server core/server core installation | A Windows Server 2008 R2 installation option that provides a minimal environment that includes only programs necessary for the roles you select.

Service Level Agreement (SLA) | A contract between an organization or individual and a cloud service provider that details the services provided, along with response time guarantees and associated costs.

Service Set Identifier (SSID) | A unique identifier for a wireless network.

Shielded twisted pair (STP) | Network cabling that generally consists of two or four pairs of wires with a foil shielding around each pair to reduce external electrical and radio interference. Pairs of wires are twisted around each other to reduce interference with other pairs.

Signature | The unique set of instructions that make up an instance of malware and distinguish it from other malware.

Signature database | An organized collection of malware signatures used by antivirus or anti-spyware (or other anti-malware) software to identify malware.

Smart card | A card or device that stores information used for authentication or encryption.

Snap-in | An administrative program designed to run in the MMC.

Social engineering | The process of an attacker tricking or convincing an authorized user to carry out an action or provide valuable information for which the attacker is unauthorized.

Software configuration management (SCM) | A collection of best practices for handling changes in software projects.

Software Security Framework (SSF) | A component of the BSIMM that organizes the 109 BSIMM activities into a framework consisting of 12 practices in four domains.

Spoofing | The act of masquerading as another identity.

Sprint | One of the small project iterations used in the "agile" method of developing software, in contrast with the usual long project schedules of other ways of developing software.

Spyware | Software that covertly monitors and records pieces of information, such as web surfing activities and all data processed by the browser.

SQL injection | An attack that adds SQL statements to input data for the purpose of sending commands to a database management system.

Storage Area Network (SAN) | A collection of one or more standalone network devices with internal storage, often connected to computers via fiber channel, used to provide remote storage. SAN devices appear to computers to be local storage devices but are actually network devices.

Structured Query Language (SQL) | A computer language for accessing data in a database.

Subject | An entity requesting access to an object.

Supervisor mode | The highest privilege at which programs can run, allowing access to the physical hardware and kernel resources. Also called kernel mode.

Switch | A network hardware device that forwards input it receives only to the appropriate output port.

Symmetric key algorithm | An encryption algorithm that uses a single key for both encryption and decryption.

System Development Life Cycle (SDLC) | A formal model for the process of creating and modifying software.

TCP/IP Reference Model | A generic description for how computers use multiple layers of protocol rules to communicate across a network. The TCP/IP Reference Model defines four different layers of communication rules.

Technical control | A device or process that limits access to a resource. Examples include user authentication, antivirus software, and firewalls.

Threat | Any action that could lead to damage or loss.

Transmission Control Protocol/Internet Protocol (TCP/IP) | A combination of two separate protocols commonly used in internet network communication.

Transparent Data Encryption (TDE) | An option in several database management systems that encrypts all data in the database without any user or application action required.

Transport Layer Security (TLS) | A cryptographic protocol that operates at the transport network layer and provides security for communications across the internet.

Trojan horse | Software that masquerades as an apparently harmless program or data file but contains malware instructions.

Trusted Platform Module (TPM) | A microchip designed to securely store cryptographic keys.

Trusted source | A computer from which digital certificates are accepted.

Tunneling | A technique that creates a virtual encrypted connection and allows applications to use any protocol to communicate with servers and services without having to worry about addressing or privacy concerns.

Two-factor authentication | Authentication process that requires two separate types of authentication credentials.

Type I authentication | Authentication based on information only a valid user knows, such as a password or PIN.

Type II authentication | Authentication based on a physical object that contains identity information, such as a token, card, or other device.

Type III authentication | Authentication based on a physical characteristic (biometric), such as a fingerprint, hand print, or retina characteristic.

Unauthorized user | Any user (person or program) that does not possess permission to access a resource.

Uniform resource locator (URL) | A character string used to identify the location and name of a resource on the Internet.

Universally unique identifier (UUID) | An identification value that is unique across all environments to keep track of an object across many computers.

Unshielded twisted pair (UTP) | Network cabling that generally consists of two or four pairs of wires. Pairs of wires are twisted around each other to reduce interference with other pairs.

User Account Control (UAC) | A Windows feature that prompts users for a confirmation before escalating to administrator privileges.

User mode | Limited privilege for running programs that does not allow direct access to the computer's physical hardware or certain kernel resources.

Virtual machine | A software implementation of a physical computer.

Virtual private network (VPN) | A computer network that is implemented over an existing network, often to provide an encrypted tunnel to exchange data securely.

Virtualization | The ability to run two or more virtual machines simultaneously on a single physical computer.

Virus | A software program that attaches itself to, or copies itself into, another program for the purpose of causing the computer to follow instructions that were not intended by the original program developer.

Volume Shadow Copy Service (VSS) | A Windows service that assists utilities and applications in creating snapshots of a running Windows system.

Vulnerability | Any weakness that could allow a threat to be realized.

Web proxy | A server that receives a web request, processes the request based on defined filters, and acts on the request based on defined rules. Rules can include actions such as forward, drop, deny, and translate.

Wide area network (WAN) | A network that connects multiple LANs and WANs and spans very large areas, including multiple country coverage.

Wi-Fi Protected Access (WPA) | An algorithm designed to replace WEP by providing secure wireless communications.

Windows Management Instrumentation (WMI) | The infrastructure Windows uses to maintain and exchange management and operations data.

Windows service | A long-running program that performs a specific set of functions, such as a firewall, database server, or a web server.

Wired Equivalent Privacy (WEP) | A legacy algorithm designed to secure wireless communications.

Wireless local area network (WLAN) | A LAN in which computers and devices communicate using radio frequency transmissions.

WMI filter | A GPO filter that limits a GPO's scope based on a WMI query's result.

WMI Query Language (WQL) | A subset of SQL used to query Windows machines for management and operations data.

Worm | A standalone malicious software program that actively transmits itself, generally over networks, to infect other computers.

X.509 | An ITU-T standard that defines the format of public key (digital) certificates.

Zero-day attack | Active malware that either exploits an unknown vulnerability or one for which no fix has yet been released.

Zombie | A computer that follows the instructions sent from another computer.

References

Allsopp, Wil. *Advanced Penetration Testing: Hacking the World's Most Secure Networks.* Hoboken, NJ: John Wiley & Sons, 2017.

Anson, Steve, Steve Bunting, Ryan Johnson, and Scott R. Pearson. *Mastering Windows Network Forensics and Investigation.* Hoboken, NJ: John Wiley & Sons, 2012.

Arya, Kapil, and Andrew Bettany. *Windows Group Policy Troubleshooting: A Best Practice Guide for Managing Users and PCs through Group Policy.* New York, NY: Apress, 2016.

Berghel, Hal. "A Quick Take on Windows Security Evolution." *Computer 50*, no. 5 (2017): 120–24.

Bettany, Andrew, and Andrew Warren. *Exam Ref 70-697 Configuring Windows Devices.* London, UK: Pearson/Microsoft Press, 2018.

Bettany, Andrew, and Mike Halsey. *Windows Virus and Malware Troubleshooting.* New York, NY: Apress, 2017.

Bramwell, Phil. *Hands-On Penetration Testing on Windows: Unleash Kali Linux, PowerShell, and Windows Debugging Tools for Security Testing and Analysis.* Birmingham, UK: Packt Publishing Limited, 2018.

Carvey, Harlan. *Windows Forensic Analysis DVD Toolkit.* Burlington, MA: Syngress, 2018.

Chapman, Chris, and Steve Furnell. *Network Performance and Security: Testing and Analyzing Using Open Source and Low-Cost Tools.* Burlington, MA: Elsevier Ltd./Syngress, 2016.

Durve, Rohan, and Ahmed Bouridane. "Windows 10 Security Hardening Using Device Guard Whitelisting and Applocker Blacklisting." 2017 *Seventh International Conference on Emerging Security Technologies (EST)*. Piscataway, NJ: IEEE, 2017.

Ford, Jerry Lee. *Microsoft Windows Powershell Programming for the Absolute Beginner.* Boston, MA: Cengage Learning PTR, 2015.

Francis, Dishan. *Mastering Active Directory: Automate Tasks by Leveraging PowerShell for Active Directory Domain Services 2016.* Birmingham, UK: Packt Publishing Limited, 2017.

Gambrel, Bryan. *Security Fundamentals: Exam 98-367.* Chichester, UK: John Wiley & Sons Ltd., 2012.

Gibson, Darril. *Microsoft Windows Security: Essentials.* Philadelphia, PA: John Wiley & Sons, 2011.

Graham, James, Ryan Olson, and Rick Howard. *Cyber Security Essentials.* Boca Rotan, FL: Auerbach Publications, 2016.

Grimes, Roger A. *Professional Windows Desktop and Server Hardening.* Hoboken, NJ: John Wiley & Sons, 2006.

Hassan, Nihad A., and Rami Hijazi. *Digital Privacy and Security Using Windows: A Practical Guide.* New York, NY: Apress, 2017.

Johansson, Jesper M., and Steve Riley. *Protect Your Windows Network: From Perimeter to Data.* Boston, MA: Addison-Wesley, 2005.

Kim, Peter. *The Hacker Playbook 3: Practical Guide to Penetration Testing.* Independently published, 2018.

Krause, Jordan. *Windows Server 2016 Administration Cookbook: Core Infrastructure, IIS, Remote Desktop Services, Monitoring, and Group Policy.* Birmingham, UK: Packt Publishing Limited, 2018.

Krause, Jordan. *Mastering Windows Server 2019.* Birmingham, UK: Packt Publishing Limited, 2019.

Luttgens, Jason T., Matthew Pepe, and Kevin Mandia. *Incident Response & Computer Forensics.* New York, NY: McGraw-Hill Education Group, 2014.

Marak, Victor. *Windows Malware Analysis Essentials.* Birmingham, UK: Packt Publishing Limited, 2015.

Matrosov, Alex, Eugene Rodionov, and Sergey Bratus. *Rootkits and Bootkits: Reversing Modern Malware and Next Generation Threats.* San Francisco, CA: No Starch Press, 2019.

Miroshnikov, Andrei. *Windows Security Monitoring.* Hoboken, NJ: John Wiley & Sons, 2018.

Moskowitz, Jeremy. *Group Policy: Fundamentals, Security, and the Managed Desktop.* 3rd ed. Hoboken, NJ: John Wiley & Sons, 2015.

Moskowitz, Jeremy. *MDM—Fundamentals, Security and the Modern Desktop: Using Intune, Autopilot and Azure to Manage, Deploy and Secure Windows 10.* Hoboken, NJ: Wiley-Sybex, 2019.

Parsons, June Jamrich. *Computer Concepts 2018: Comprehensive.* Boston, MA: Cengage Learning, 2018.

Scambray, Joel, and Stuart McClure. *Hacking Exposed Windows: Windows Security Secrets & Solutions.* New York, NY: McGraw-Hill, 2008.

Schulz, Michael S. *MCSA 70-741 Cert Guide: Networking with Windows Server 2016.* Hoboken, NJ: Pearson IT Certification, 2017.

Sequeira, Anthony. *MCSA 70-740 Cert Guide: Installation, Storage, and Compute with Windows Server 2016.* Hoboken, NJ: Pearson IT Certification, 2017.

Shostack, Adam. *Threat Modeling: Designing for Security.* Hoboken, NJ: John Wiley & Sons, 2014.

Silberschatz, Abraham, Peter B. Galvin, and Greg Gagne. *Operating System Concepts.* Philadelphia, PA: John Wiley & Sons, 2013.

Simpson, Michael T., and Nicholas Antill. *Hands-on Ethical Hacking and Network Defense.* Boston, MA: Cengage Learning, 2017.

Sivarajan, Santhosh. *Getting Started with Windows Server Security.* Birmingham, UK: Packt Publishing Limited, 2015.

Stanek, William R., and William R. Stanek, Jr. *Windows Server 2016: Essentials for Administration.* East Olympia, WA: Stanek & Associates, 2016.

Stefanovic, Vladimir, and Sasha Kranjac. *Identity with Windows Server 2016: Microsoft 70-742 MCSA Exam Guide.* Birmingham, UK: Packt Publishing Limited, 2019.

Stokes, Jeff, Manuel Singer, and Richard Diver. *Windows 10 for Enterprise Administrators: Modern Administrators Guide Based on Redstone 3 Version*. Birmingham, UK: Packt Publishing Limited, 2017.

Svidergol, Brian, Vladimir Meloski, Byron Wright, Santos Martinez, and Doug Bassett. *Mastering Windows Server 2016*. Hoboken, NJ: John Wiley & Sons, 2018.

Thomas, Orin. *Windows Server 2016 Inside Out (includes Current Book Service)*. London, UK: Pearson/Microsoft Press, 2017.

Yosifovich, Pavel, David A. Solomon, and Alex Ionescu. *Windows Internals, Part 1: System Architecture, Processes, Threads, Memory Management, and More*. London, UK: Pearson/Microsoft Press, 2017.

Zetter, Kim. *Countdown to Zero Day*. New York, NY: Crown Publishers, 2014.

Index